THE REEL CIVIL WAR

The

REEL CIVIL WAR

Mythmaking in American Film

Bruce Chadwick

ALFRED A. KNOPF   NEW YORK   2001

THIS IS A BORZOI BOOK
PUBLISHED BY ALFRED A. KNOPF

Copyright © 2001 by Bruce Chadwick
All rights reserved under International and Pan-American Copyright
Conventions. Published in the United States by Alfred A. Knopf,
a division of Random House, Inc., New York, and simultaneously in
Canada by Random House of Canada Limited, Toronto.
Distributed by Random House, Inc., New York.
www.aaknopf.com

Knopf, Borzoi Books, and the colophon are
registered trademarks of Random House, Inc.

The photographs on pages 241 and 271 are used courtesy of ABC, Inc., copyright
© 2000 by ABC, Inc. All other photographs are used courtesy
of the Museum of Modern Art/Film Stills Archive.

ISBN: 0-375-40918-1
LIBRARY OF CONGRESS CONTROL NO.: 2001091008

Manufactured in the United States of America
First Edition

For Marjorie and Rory

CONTENTS

ACKNOWLEDGMENTS

LIKE MOST AMERICANS, I started watching movies about the Civil War on television when I was a child—in my case, in the 1950s. I also grew up on television's weekly western series, which dominated the small screen in that decade, and, like so many others, I tuned in each week to follow the adventures of Confederate veteran Johnny Yuma in *The Rebel.* During that same period, I visited the Gettysburg battlefield with my father for the first time. I never connected the two circumstances until I began work on this book. My love of history and my fascination with the way it has been presented in movies and on television certainly stemmed from my childhood.

My research for this book on films about the Civil War carried me to numerous libraries, large and small. The bulk of my research on the movies themselves was done at the Performing Arts Branch of the New York Public Library at Lincoln Center, in New York, which, in addition to hundreds of books, maintains thousands of folders of newspaper and magazine clippings about movies and plays. These clippings, from the 1880s, made the war's depiction in popular culture come to life for me. The librarians there were most helpful.

Research on the war itself, and on the way the nation remembered the war, and its effect on race relations, was done at a number of excellent libraries. I spent considerable time at Alexander Library at Rutgers University, where I lecture on history and film. The staff there provided me with valuable assistance. The entire staff of the Guarini Library at New Jersey City University, where I teach full-time, aided me for four long years, never turning down a request to find "just one more book."

I received much aid from librarians at local libraries throughout

New Jersey, such as the Morris County Library, in Whippany, New Jersey, and libraries in Morristown, Rockaway, Randolph and Chester.

I traveled to Virginia to check records and old manuscripts and newspapers not available elsewhere, and must thank the librarians at the University of Virginia, in Charlottesville, and at the Museum of the Confederacy, in Richmond, for their guidance.

This book is as much the story of the American people as it is a work about film, and I was fortunate to receive much expert support from four professors in the History and American Studies departments at Rutgers University, who were kind enough to read through the manuscript several times and offer advice: Dr. Susan Schrepfer, Dr. Lloyd Gardner, Dr. Michael Rockland and Dr. Jackson Lears. Dr. Lears, perhaps the country's premier cultural historian, was especially helpful in broadening my understanding of the connections between history and entertainment.

I appreciate the help of Pat Hass, a gifted editor at Alfred A. Knopf, on this project. She kept a watchful eye over me as I reshaped the book. Pat was able to reorganize my approach to the basic story. I also received considerable advice from another fine editor, Nancy Nicholas. Roseanne Currarino did yeoman (or is that "yeowoman"?) work for me as a research assistant. Many thanks, too, to my literary agent, Carolyn Krupp, of IMG Literary, who gave me constant support and, with great patience, offered considerable and helpful suggestions.

Finally, warm thanks go to my wife, Margie, who graciously listened to my endless stories of movies about the Civil War and spent countless hours helping me to research this book and reading each chapter as I finished them. Thanks also to my son, Rory, who was a sounding board for many of my theories about film and movies.

And thanks, too, wherever they are, to the managers and ushers at the State Theater, in Boonton, New Jersey, where as a little boy I fell in love with movies.

THE REEL CIVIL WAR

Blue, Gray and Technicolor

Myth: ". . . a notion based more on tradition or convenience than fact."

—The American Heritage Dictionary of the English Language

FLORA CAMERON, the attractive daughter of a slaveholder whose cotton business has been ruined by the Civil War, pulls her bucket from the small, bubbling spring in the thick woods and sits back on an oversized log, playfully trying to coax a squirrel down from a tree. The squirrel, sensing danger somewhere, darts its eyes back and forth. A few yards away, Gus, an evil-looking black soldier stationed in the area, stares at her lustfully, his shirt open over his bare chest. Flora, the quintessential Southern belle, catches sight of him from the corner of her eye and becomes visibly scared. Trying to disregard his presence, she gets up and starts to walk slowly through the woods to home and safety. Gus follows. Flora fears Gus because during the past few weeks he and other blacks have constantly harassed her and her family. Gus catches her and grabs her arm, pulling her towards him, and tells her he isn't married. His eyes wander over her body. She slaps him, pushes him down, and runs away, terror in her eyes.

The camera follows Flora as she runs through the sun-drenched forest, a lithe, terrified nymph with a sex-crazed black soldier in hot pursuit. Flora loses her way and winds up on the top of a cliff as Gus climbs towards her over the rocks—obviously intent on raping her. She gestures for him to back up and looks down over the edge of the cliff. She must either submit to Gus's ravenous sexual advances or leap from the cliff. Her thin alabaster arms flail in indecision. She is gorgeous in the warm morning sunlight. Gus, heavy beads of sweat on his forehead, hands extended to grab her, is a sadistic creature coming

3

out of the rocks to seize carnal satisfaction. Unwilling to submit to a black man, with death the only option, Flora leaps.[1]

THE PORTRAYAL of Gus, the lustful black soldier, was just one of the historical distortions in *The Birth of a Nation,* a 1915 movie that combined many of the misinterpretations of history in films about the Civil War that Hollywood studios have produced over the years. Hollywood has often done rewrites of history quickly and with little or no regard for the actual story. Even in their wildest dreams, the 1930s gangster couple Clyde Barrow and Bonnie Parker never looked as handsome as Warren Beatty and Faye Dunaway. Probably none of history's crude and barbarous pirates had the dashing personality of Errol Flynn or Yul Brynner. The tough, grizzled miners who rushed to California in 1849, or to the gold and silver strikes that followed in other Western states in the following decades, rarely exuded the élan of Joel McCrea or Randolph Scott. Few World War II soldiers fought with the swagger of John Wayne.

Hollywood hopelessly romanticized Billy the Kid, who in real life was not charming at all. Robert Stroud, the idealized "birdman" of Alcatraz, in reality was, his guards said, a psychotic. There were few cowards in Hollywood's version of World War II; most screen prostitutes had hearts of gold; pioneers in westerns were courageous. Indians, of course, were portrayed as howling savages.

Film has always been casual in its presentation of history. Driven by commercial considerations, the need for wide audience appeal, producers consistently distorted and sanitized the past. This has almost always been true of war movies, such as *The Bridge on the River Kwai,* a heroic and very successful 1957 British film about World War II that not only paid little attention to the truth concerning the construction of the bridge, but even put it over the wrong river. And such mangling has occurred, among the countless instances that might be named, in the conspiracy-laden *JFK,* the heavily slanted character portrayals in *Nixon,* the inaccuracies concerning blacks in *Mississippi Burning,* the fabricated scenes in *Silkwood* and *George Wallace* and the invented characters and inaccurate events in *The Hurricane.*

Sometimes little of true history is left but the fact that the character once lived. In the Civil War western saga *Arizona Bushwhackers,* screenwriters placed Southern guerrilla leader William Quantrill in Arizona, where he never visited, a year after his death in 1865.

Hollywood has also loved the "composite character" in historical movies, a character that never existed as such but embodies a mix of people who might have done so, created in order to move the plot along. And of course historical movies need invented love stories, whether it is the heavy breathing between Daniel Day-Lewis and Madeleine Stowe in the French and Indian War in *The Last of the Mohicans* or the teenage lovers reaching their own high tide in *Titanic*.

Most screenwriters and directors respond to such criticism with a shrug and an insistence that the "spirit" of the times or characters is more important than fidelity to fact. Filmmakers dealing with contemporary life sometimes have the same attitude. For example, when the acclaimed 1999 film *Boys Don't Cry*—the story of a real person, a woman who passed herself off as a man—was criticized for its inaccuracies, the director, Kim Peirce, responded that she could not let the facts get in the way of her feelings. "You can change facts. You can change characters. You can change everything in search of the truth," she said.[2]

Historians, of course, are concerned about the way history is battered in film and fiction and how screenwriters and novelists make history fit their stories, not the other way around. "The past is up for grabs for creative people," said historian David McCullough (whose biography *Truman* was turned into an HBO movie), speaking of screenwriters' rather loose adherence to historical fact.[3] Simon Schama, writing about the movie version of a work by Sir Walter Scott, argued that the tragedy is not only that history is rewritten and transformed, but that a nation's people absorb and believe the history that is presented in novels and movies instead of the actual history.[4]

Fictional stories or legends can become accepted as history. Novels and films about history, whether *Ivanhoe* in the nineteenth century or *Gone With the Wind* in the twentieth, become history because people accept their plotlines and characterizations. Or, as historian Jill Lepore said about armed conflict, "how wars are remembered can be just as important as how they were fought and described."[5]

Few periods in American history have been as romanticized, eulogized and hopelessly distorted through film as the Civil War. From the early silent Civil War movies, which depicted slaves as "happy darkies" eager to help their owner save his plantation and defeat the Yankees, to silly television series like *The Secret Diary of Desmond Pfeiffer,* the UPN comedy series about Abraham Lincoln and his fictional black English butler, the real story of the greatest conflict in American history has been revised so many times that a great many Americans whose knowledge of the war comes mainly from movies or television necessarily know little of the truth. Worse, they have little understanding of how the conflict changed the course of American life. The movie view was tainted, even though it continually trumpeted the spirit of the American people, Northerners and Southerners alike. Although it significantly affected the way we saw ourselves for generations—as a brave and good people—it greatly exacerbated the tragic divisions between the races.

The foundation for Hollywood's unreal reel Civil War, a moonlight-and-magnolias saga that featured trees dripping with Spanish moss, gentlemen drinking mint juleps on the veranda, women prettifying themselves for the ball and countless soldiers becoming instant heroes, was laid in cinema's infancy, the silent-movie era, and carried on through the 1930s. Although there was little interest in such films following World War I, audiences again went to see them throughout the 1930s, a decade that culminated in the greatest Civil War film of all, *Gone With the Wind.* World War II temporarily dampened Civil War–film fervor in the 1940s, but the blue and the gray began to clash again regularly on screen in the mid-1950s. Civil War stories have been part of American film and television ever since.

Right after World War II, writers in film and television found a rich new field for Civil War stories, one that would last through the 1970s—the already long-established western. The very first feature film, *The Great Train Robbery,* in 1903, was a western, and Hollywood's hundreds of subsequent shoot-'em-ups had thrilled audiences for decades. Then, in the late 1940s, writers began to put blue and gray army veterans into western storylines that stretched from Dallas to Deadwood. Billy Yank and Johnny Reb now fought together to ward off a new foe of the American people, the Indians.

It was not until the post–Civil Rights era of the 1970s that there occurred a radical departure from the deeply entrenched myths concerning the American nineteenth century, the entire period extending from the antebellum South through the Civil War and into Reconstruction. That departure was signaled most notably by the 1977 television miniseries *Roots,* which led an assault on all the tried-and-true legends Hollywood had created and re-created over the years. *Roots* became the foundation for numerous fresh analyses of slavery, the war and the war's major figures. Then, in 1989, came *Glory,* the (mostly) true story of one of the many all-black regiments which fought gallantly for the Union. *Glory* was followed by *Gettysburg* and, in 1996, *Andersonville,* about the dreaded Confederate prison camp in Georgia. There were new interpretations of the Civil War era and a sharp change in the American cultural climate. Another change was the appearance of thousands of "reenactors." These were civilians who dressed in blue and gray and re-created Civil War battles each year, bringing back to life in breathtaking fashion bayonet charges, artillery barrages, and cavalry raids. Directors began using reenactors in movies because they already knew the material and had the uniforms. Unlike earlier films, these movies had dramatic battle scenes that gave them an air of realism.[6] In the same period, PBS aired Ken Burns's well-received, heavily researched, nine-part documentary on the war, which presented slavery and black soldiers in a more well-rounded way. Impressed by its success, several cable television networks soon presented similar, docudrama-style series that seemed to add balance to long-held interpretations of the war.

However, these revisionist films did not emerge until seven long decades after the very first, silent Civil War films. This was mainly because the distortions presented in the approximately five hundred silent films on the war, all from the moonlight-and-magnolias school, came to be accepted as fact by later filmmakers. For example:

1. Southerners, who started the war, were always portrayed as heroic underdogs. Yet until the last year of the war there remained a real prospect of Confederate victory. What ultimately proved decisive was the South's loss of three key battles in the summer and fall of 1864. In early August, U.S. naval commander David Farragut led fifteen ships into Alabama's Mobile Bay; the attack resulted in the destruction of four Confederate ships and the securing of the region for the Union. Atlanta fell in September, after Confederate president Jefferson Davis decided against sending reinforcements to aid the

army there, which was outmanned more than two to one. Also in September, Union General Philip Sheridan drove the Confederate army of Jubal Early out of Virginia's Shenandoah Valley. Earlier, at Antietam and Gettysburg, Southern conquests might have led to victory.

2. The films ignored the intricacies of the slavery issue and paid no attention to the heated political controversies that helped to bring on the war, such as the civil strife in Kansas; splits in Congress over slavery in the territories; the emergence of the Know-Nothings and Free-Soilers; the creation of the Republican Party; the breakup of a major political party, the Whigs; the splintering of the Democratic Party; the secession of Southern states from the Union; the attack on Fort Sumter; and a host of issues tied to political and cultural differences between North and South. The films always blamed the war on the abolitionists.[7]

3. Films about Lincoln always presented him as saintly "Father Abraham" and overlooked both the dramatic political revolution from 1856 to 1860 that brought about his election and his ongoing concern to preserve the Union as well as free the slaves. Nor were Lincoln's complex personality, his political shrewdness, his military leadership or the constant attacks on him by Democrats, Republicans and the press ever shown.

4. Slaves were typically shown as helpful mammies, obliging butlers, smiling carriage-drivers, joyful cotton-pickers and tap-dancing entertainers.

5. Southern white women tended to be presented as stereotypically frail and delicate creatures who sometimes fell openly in love with Union soldiers. In fact, there is ample evidence to show that the women were just as tough as their men as they endured occupying armies, sieges and the pillaging and burning of their homes and farms.

6. Most Southerners in Civil War sagas are shown as wealthy slaveholders. In reality, less than 25 percent of all Southerners owned any slaves at all. Most were middle-class or lower-class farmers without slaves who struggled for a living.[8] Yet it was these nonslaveholding farmers—who worked hard on the land—who did most of the fighting and dying on the battlefield, making it "a rich man's war and a poor man's fight." The homes of most people who did own slaves were so modest that when researchers for *Gone With the Wind* went looking for archival photos or descriptions of sprawling manor houses with

verandas and white columns in Georgia, they had to report that they could not find any.

7. Most Civil War movies in the silent era ended the same way: with soldiers and civilians from North and South reconciling and establishing a once-again united country. In reality, the Civil War caused political and cultural strife between North and South that lasted for generations and led to the rise of the Ku Klux Klan, a crippled Southern economy, Jim Crow laws and strident segregation.

These distortions were not simply invented by Hollywood screenwriters lounging around swimming pools in Santa Monica on hot Sunday afternoons. Producers, directors and writers built their false history of the Civil War upon a solid foundation of earlier, carefully crafted historical and cultural interpretations of the era written and rewritten from the moment Robert E. Lee, dressed regally as always, bearing himself with great dignity, rode to Appomattox Courthouse in April 1865 to surrender the Army of Northern Virginia to General Ulysses S. Grant.

By the time the first one-reel, fifteen-minute feature films about the Civil War were being shown, many Americans had come to accept a dramatically revised view of the events and people of the war. They got their information from school texts, newspapers, magazines, history books, novels, Broadway plays, songs and poems . . . and then movies.

This cultural cleansing and revising seemed necessary to many, North and South, in order to reunite a nation fractured by a four-year conflict that saw the deaths of more than 620,000 American soldiers. There was a hard bitterness between most Northerners and Southerners at the end of the war, a chasm of grief and hatred that few believed could ever be bridged. One half of the country emerged victorious and the other half emerged not only defeated, but having lost one out of every four adult white males and witnessed the destruction of dozens of their towns and cities. While triumphant Union soldiers paraded through New York, Boston and Washington at war's end, disheveled Confederates returned to the smoking, burned-out ruins of Richmond, Columbia and Atlanta, the only Americans to lose a war until Vietnam. Southerners—soldiers and families—were devastated not only by the physical damage the war caused but by the psychological damage of losing the war, and with it the slave system, as well as by a turbulent Reconstruction and a morbid fear that they would always be subjugated by the North.

The only way for the nation to move on was for the war to be seen in the rearview mirror of history as a war not started by anyone, a conflict that had no winners or losers—just a tragic war in which men on both sides fought gallantly.

It seemed that to realize reunification, the Civil War's political and cultural history almost had to be rewritten so that the Southerners would never again be seen as harsh slaveowners or as the people who started—and lost—the war. Most politicians on both sides extended olive branches in the hopes of consigning to oblivion the disputes of the 1860s. Some Northern businessmen invested heavily in the South, particularly in railroads that would eventually help the Southern economy. Novelists, playwrights and magazine writers reinvented Southern slaveowners as noble cavaliers, fighting not for slavery but for states' rights and the honor of their Southern women and families. Historians produced dozens of commercial works and school textbooks that blurred and obscured the sharp edges of the conflict.

Was this rewriting, which persisted for forty years until the beginning of the film age, morally and ethically honest? It may not have been, but surely it was necessary, as Abraham Lincoln said in his second inaugural address, to bind up the nation's wounds. All of these writers, politicians and civic leaders probably did a very wrong thing to bring about a very right thing. And thus the true story of the Civil War became lost in a tapestry of cultural history woven together over several generations, with the result that many Americans came to see themselves the way the weavers desired. That tidy legend, through the power of the media, had become accepted history to millions by the time the first feature-length movie was shown in 1903.

Filmmakers seemed genuinely to believe they were telling true stories and, in their flickering images, offering honest characterizations. Certainly everything in their schools, politics and culture in the second half of the nineteenth century was telling them their stereotypes were the truth.

That misinformation was disseminated further as film quickly became the most powerful force in American culture, not to be replaced until the advent of television a half century later. Nobody expressed this better than Thomas Dixon, upon whose book *The Clansman* D. W. Griffith's *The Birth of a Nation* was based. "The moving picture man," Dixon said, ". . . is not merely the purveyor of a form of entertainment. He is leading a revolution in the development of humanity—as profound a revolution as that which followed the first invention of print."[9]

Within a few years of the debut of film, just about every hamlet in the country had a theater. By 1910 most Americans saw at least one film a week, and by the 1930s they saw two a week. The medium's power to influence people was enormous—just as it is now. Even though audiences who see current films in theaters or old films on television understand that movies about contemporary life are fiction, stories churned out by screenwriters toiling in the sprawling film studios of Los Angeles, they believe historical films to be accurate depictions of the past. They believe it because film studio publicity machines from 1903 onward have assured them that painstaking research went into the production of each historical film. Screenwriters also understand the past as seen by the public and write their movies to fit that past, or, as screenwriter William Goldman has said, write movies that are not necessarily true, but are accepted as true. "People think whatever they see is basically true," says historian Eric Foner.[10] And they often believe things to be true even when they are told they are not. At the beginning of the award-winning film *Life Is Beautiful* (released in the United States in 1998), the narrator tells audiences that this Holocaust story is a fable; yet a survey showed that most people who had seen the film believed it was a true story. What audiences saw was not real history, but cinema history. Very few people read interpretative books about the causes of the Civil War, but millions have seen *Gone With the Wind*. Gore Vidal, whose novel *Lincoln* has often been mistaken for biography, argued that filmmakers, not historians, are Americans' source of truth. "He who screens the history makes the history," he wrote.[11]

Many of today's filmmakers would agree. Some make historical films based not on history they have read but on history as they understand it from movies. Actor Danny Glover, who starred in and was the executive producer of the 1997 Turner Network Television movie *Buf-*

falo Soldiers, said he never read anything in schoolbooks about the Buffalo Soldiers, all-black cavalry regiments, but learned all he knew from the 1960 movie *Sergeant Rutledge.*[12]

Movies are legitimate historical documents, to be studied and analyzed, just as diaries and letters were in the nineteenth century and e-mail, taped voice messages and cyberspace Web sites will be in this one. Books go out of print; they are consigned to dusty library shelves or to cartons for Saturday afternoon garage sales. Magazines wind up in stacks bundled up with thick brown cord and tossed in recycling bins. Films not only remain through the years but, in an American culture that consumes them, are aired again and again on television. Americans may be more inclined to watch than to read. Americans have always seen films as their nation's story.[13]

Old films not only tell us the story of how filmmakers portrayed the past on the screen, but they tell us how the audiences of different eras saw the past in relation to their present and their hopes for the future. Many movies made in the silent era portrayed American apprehensions over the industrial revolution and how it had changed life. *White Slave Trade* (1910) explored the kidnapping of women for sexual purposes. *The Usurer's Grip* (1912) condemned the sordid practices of urban slumlords. *Why?* (1913) told the story of workers and their bosses in shootouts over child labor laws. Films produced in the middle of the Depression—specifically films such as *The Grapes of Wrath*—not only reflected the country's desperation but suggested to the frightened people out there in the dim recesses of the movie house that they would survive the economic nightmare just as the characters on screen would. (As Ma Joad reminded them, "We're the people.")

The movies about the Civil War era, shown from the first years feature films were screened, make up the largest group of films (more than seven hundred—approximately five hundred silent and two hundred sound) concerning any war or historical event in American history (nearly three times the number of films about World War II). And more than any other group of films, they represent the way Americans have looked at themselves in the past and the present. Civil War films have been critically and commercially successful. *The Birth of a Nation* and *Gone With the Wind* are among the top five box-office films of all time (with revenue adjusted for inflation). They so represent America that in 1998, when the *New York Times* ran a story about foreign companies taking over American publishing houses, the American novel whose jacket was used to illustrate it was *Gone With the Wind*.[14]

Film producers such as David O. Selznick (in *Gone With the Wind*) and directors such as John Ford (in *Fort Apache*) created a story that they saw as historically useful, a story that explained a troubled time in American history by framing it in a positive way. Others, too, including historians, college professors and journalists, have tried to understand the cultural meaning of the lore that attached itself to the Civil War. Historian Arthur M. Schlesinger Sr. said this legend was created to soothe the wounds of Southerners, that they "won on the screen what they lost on the battlefield." The mythmakers did not let malodorous incidents, unscrupulous characters or tarnished heroes get in their way. Ray Gill, a modern Civil War reenactor, one of the thousands of men who give up weekends to stage simulated battles, told a journalist that it did not matter on which side the soldiers fought, but that they were all Americans, all brave, and in honoring either side they honor America, period.[15] Many of these men, discussing *Gone With the Wind,* said that the struggles of North and South in the movie are the struggles of the American people anywhere and anytime. Perhaps poet Robert Penn Warren put it best when he wrote that people really don't want to remember their actual past if it had defects, that they have to manufacture a new one, that they *need* a new one, that we need to believe we were good and righteous before, even if we were not, in order that we can be good and righteous today and tomorrow. "Inevitably, the past, so far as we know it, is an inference, a creation, and this, without being paradoxical, can be said to be its chief value to us. In creating the image of the past we create ourselves, and without that task of creating the past we might be said scarcely to exist," he wrote.[16]

The myth of the hard-fighting Yankees and Confederates defending the America they believed to be theirs served as the inspiration for Americans preparing to go into battle in the Spanish-American War, World War I, World War II, Korea and Vietnam. It was those gallant Civil War soldiers and their women and children struggling on the home front for the good of the Cause, no matter which Cause, and a magnanimous, martyred President Lincoln, somehow bringing both sides together, that defined America for the Americans trying to get through the Depression and many later troubles. People were always confident that their forebears from the 1860s, the Americans they saw on the screen, were the great patriotic oaks from which they all sprang. A strong national consensus was created about the past that served as a sturdy foundation for the future. There was a reason why actor John Wayne, the quintessential American screen hero, who played American heroes in numerous films about World War II and the Vietnam War, played Southerners as well as Northerners in Civil War films.

These efforts at mythmaking also had the goal of reunification and nationalism. The Civil War was a horrific and deeply unsettling event in the American past. How could Americans have gone to war against other Americans? How could a nation that by the middle of the nineteenth century celebrated itself so much have become involved in a terrible war in which so many young men died? How could people ever be friends again with those who were on the other side? Such seemingly irreconcilable differences the mythmakers did reconcile through novels and movies, with their legends and happy endings.

But the myth had a high price. The only way mythmakers could wash away the bitterness between North and South and bring about reunification was to erase the fundamental cause of the war and all its death and destruction—slavery. The historical writings and popular culture of the late nineteenth century began this erasure, but it was the all-powerful film medium that, in thousands of darkened movie houses across the Republic, most effectively absolved the South of any blame for slavery.

The inevitable corollary to this absolution for slavery extended to white Southerners was the movies' complete denial of dignity to African Americans, the former slaves—whether at the turn of the century in the crude "Rastus" and "Sambo" films about contemporary blacks or in the Civil War dramas showing slaves before, during and after the war. Stripped of humanity on the screen, they became stripped of it in real life. Until the 1970s, Americans who sat in movie theaters saw an endless string of Civil War films in which African Americans were mostly depicted as groveling simpletons or, as in *The Birth of a Nation,* murderers and rapists. Movies, with their overpowering ability to shape opinion, convinced many whites that the disgraceful way in which blacks had been treated in and out of slavery over the decades was perfectly justified. If slaves occupied the very lowest regions in the reel world, put there by the supposedly well-researched Hollywood films, it followed that they should occupy it in the real world, too. Films showed Americans that they could be reunited after the end of the Civil War—but reunited in their whiteness.

Men and women of letters, whether historians, poets or screenwriters, have often ruminated about the effect of the past on American life. George Santayana famously warned that those who ignore history are condemned to repeat it. Gore Vidal sees any journey into the past as an opportunity to make conditions better for those living in the present. Some don't see much difference between past and present; William Faulkner said: "The past is never dead. It's not even past."[17] A prime creator of the popular image of the sweetly nostalgic Jazz Age, F. Scott Fitzgerald, reminded readers in *The Great Gatsby* that no matter what they think of the past, they are borne back ceaselessly into it.[18]

Myths are hard to change. A recent revisionist historical series, *Tkuma*, which was aired on Israeli television, debunked the view long held by Israelis and Jews worldwide that Jews simply fought heroically to turn Israel into a nation-state. It suggested instead that the venerated heroes of the Israeli army illegally deported and murdered Arabs and that, perhaps, members of the Palestine Liberation Organization had as much claim to present-day Israel as Israelis. This new and abundantly documented view of Israel's history was savaged by the leading political figures in the country. An exasperated Gideon Drori, an editor of the series, realizing the force of tradition and carefully constructed myths, said: "There's still disagreement over what the past is, and perceptions of the past are constantly changing."[19]

The past the producers, writers and directors of the Civil War films created, or rather re-created, idealized both sides. It featured well-intentioned leaders such as Abraham Lincoln and Jefferson Davis; brave soldiers, both North and South; fearless generals, whether Ulysses S. Grant or Robert E. Lee and Stonewall Jackson; glamorous cavalry leaders such as George Custer and J. E. B. Stuart; heroic charges, Union and Confederate; and, North and South, many thousands of fearful wives and sweethearts, waiting for their loved ones to come home from the front lines. It was an America of honor and integrity, courage and responsibility; of long and loud parades and quiet funerals; a nation wrestling with itself so as—the mythmakers insisted—to make manifest the dreams of the Founding Fathers and to become, in that bloody civil war, the greatest nation on earth.

It is important to explore the reasons why an entire nation of people wanted to, and needed to, revise their history in order to come together in the awful wake of the Civil War. Americans need to have a better understanding of how they moved on, so badly scarred, trying to become whole as a country and to make that country a symbol of democracy around the world. They needed to know that in 1915, 1939, 1976, and they need to know today. Politicians often tell them that the price of freedom has always been high; they need to know that the price of reunification and nationalism has been so as well.

The Civil War films evolved over the years, although the goals of the mythmakers never changed. The mythmakers gave us a past that demeaned African Americans and ignored much of actual history, a glorious and honorable past that probably never was, but a past we would like to have had. Like the newspaper editor in *The Man Who Shot Liberty Valance,* they ignored the facts and published the legend because they knew people wanted the legend. A nation and its people need their history, but they need myths and legends, too. Hollywood provided one.

CHAPTER ONE

I Wish I Was in the Land of Cotton: America Rewrites Its History

MANY HISTORIANS, intellectuals and public figures campaigned to eradicate the idea that the war was fought over slavery, and to free the South of any blame for it. They worked hard, too, to underscore the idea that no one actually caused the war and no one actually lost it, permitting Southerners to feel that somehow as Americans they had won a war, not lost one. Most of all, these mythmakers' work, whether in textbooks, poems or novels, tried to erase the pure horror of a war in which so many young men were killed. By framing it as a romantic conflict they somehow managed to turn the thousands of bodies lying on top of one another in Bloody Lane, at Antietam, into thousands of gallant young men riding horses or charging across fields in collective memory. Their efforts may have been contrived, but their goal, a reunified country, was not. The people of the United States needed to come together after the Civil War. These scholars and public figures helped to make that reunification possible.

The first steps towards reunifying the United States were taken even before the conflict ended. President Lincoln, delicately working to keep his numerous political coalitions in Congress together, engineered a mild reconstruction program in Louisiana after that state was occupied by Union troops in 1862. The president, while barring most former Confederate officeholders from political activity, did permit some state politicians to hold office in the "new" Louisiana. Lincoln later attempted to get Congress to approve a rather soft general reconstruction plan for all of the Southern states; under the plan only 10 percent of the residents needed to "rejoin" the United States in order to create a new government and have their state readmitted to the Union. This attempt at creating a smooth transition failed when federal legislators refused to go along, but at the time of his murder Lincoln was actively trying to bring occupied Southern states back into the Union, using the Army instead of Congress through his powers as commander in chief.

President Andrew Johnson, who agreed with Lincoln's low-key approach to reconstruction, took another step towards conciliation when he refused to execute the former Confederate president, Jefferson Davis, despite virulent public outcries, and instead kept him in jail for two years and offered no protest when the Supreme Court dropped all charges against Davis.

Political efforts to bring about reunification between North and South ground to a halt, however, in 1867, when Radical Republicans forced passage of the Reconstruction Act. That legislation, in effect for ten years, divided the territory of the defunct Confederacy into five military districts, gave freedmen the vote and the right to hold public office and opened the door to "carpetbaggers," Northerners who arrived at the end of the conflict, and "scalawags," Southerners who became sudden Northern sympathizers and whose corrupt business practices offended many Southerners. There remained throughout the Southern states a deep despair over the loss of approximately 300,000 young men, nearly one quarter of the adult white male population, and the devastation of dozens of towns and cities in the war.[1] The Union army had ripped up hundreds of miles of Southern railroad tracks, more than 50 percent of farm machinery in the South had been ruined, more than 40 percent of the South's livestock killed or stolen. Southern wealth during the war decreased by 60 percent. Between 1860 and 1870, the South's share of national wealth dropped from 30 percent to just 12 percent. In 1860, Southerners' average income was 68 percent of Northerners', but by 1870 it had dropped to 39 percent and stayed there for forty years.[2]

Except for assaults on a few small cities in the North such as Chambersburg, Pennsylvania, there had been little destruction in the Union states. Although Reconstruction laws enabled freed slaves to take tremendous steps forward as citizens and laborers, Southern whites saw these same laws as unduly harsh. The bitter feelings made political progress towards reunification difficult until the mid-1870s.

Public figures on both sides realized that the end of Reconstruction, despite the tattered condition of the Southern states, was the time to begin the healing process with a view towards bringing about the consolidation of the United States so that the nation, whole again, could move forward.

Reconstruction was ended by politicians in order to guarantee the election of Rutherford B. Hayes, who was narrowly defeated by Samuel Tilden in the popular vote in the 1876 presidential election. Nevertheless, a congressional electoral commission decided that Hayes had been elected president. As recompense, Hayes then reputedly agreed to withdraw all U.S. troops from the Southern states, effectively ending Reconstruction. Then, in his first message to Congress, Hayes made a bold statement on behalf of reunion. He told the legislators, and the people, that "To complete and make permanent the pacification of the country continues to be . . . the most important of all our national interests."[3]

Throughout the 1870s reconciliation between North and South continued. The first official Memorial Day was established in 1868, and by 1891 most states celebrated the holiday, honoring the dead on both sides of the conflict. In 1872, President Grant and Congress offered amnesty to all former Confederate officeholders and military officers. In 1875, Southerners returned the captured regimental flag of the all-black Fifty-fourth Massachusetts Volunteers. The Centennial, held in Philadelphia in 1876, was a nonpartisan celebration for all Americans, North and South. Business journals, published in both Northern and Southern cities, promoted reunification. In 1878, dozens of highly regarded Southern orators made tours of Northern cities, preaching reconciliation. Also in 1878, Northern doctors and nurses rushed to the South, bringing with them hundreds of thousands of dollars in relief money, to fight the dreaded yellow fever that crippled Louisiana, taking the lives of thousands, including the son of Jefferson Davis. Southerners publicly and privately acknowledged the magnanimous gesture. Confederate veterans accepted an offer to march in a Boston commemorative parade in 1875, and Massachusetts veterans a similar offer to march in New Orleans in 1881.

The 1870s saw the glorification of Lee, who died in 1870 and whose passing was mourned throughout both North and South. Lee's dignified surrender at the end of the war—and his quick ascension to the presidency of Washington College—elevated him from a mere general to a figure of heroic proportions. He was seen in the postwar North and South as a great man who happened to have lost the war, and who forgave the enemy and immediately went to work in higher education to help the South rebuild.

In the 1870s and 1880s Lee and other Confederate generals, plus some slain generals such as Stonewall Jackson and J. E. B. Stuart, were the subjects of best-selling lithographs. These were produced in the North by printers who realized they could make huge profits in the new, nostalgic Southern market. Surprisingly, the prints sold well in the North, too, and helped position the Southern generals in the minds of Americans as good men who fought bravely but lost. Many of the lithographs and paintings had religious overtones, such as a lithograph in Tennessee that showed Lee, ready for battle, standing

Movie advertisements such as this were based on earlier lithographs and magazine illustrations of the late nineteenth century.

next to a crucified Christ.[4] They also projected the great courage and dignity of the vanquished, an important step towards reconciliation and the idea that no one truly lost the war. Currier & Ives had so much business in Southern prints that by the mid-1880s the firm was selling more Confederate prints than Northern ones. Lithographer John Buttre of New York had so much Southern business that by 1884 he was selling eight different Lee lithographs.[5]

Southerners were building their own myths throughout this period, such as the Lost Cause and the image of the gallant boys who fought for four long years. Several groups of Confederate Veterans were formed, along with the United Daughters of the Confederacy, to commemorate the war and the fallen soldiers. Confederate publications, such as *Confederate Veteran* magazine, were started. Virginians built monuments to Lee and to Stonewall Jackson (an entire street in Richmond would eventually be graced by Confederate monuments).

Southern remembrance of the war began to change as veterans and residents began to equate lithographs, anniversaries and nostalgic newspaper and magazine stories of the war with a kind of victory. They slowly came to believe that while they had not won technically, they might have won emotionally, and that at least the Southern boys were just as brave and heroic as the Northern boys. This belief became so popular that by the 1880s Georgia's U.S. Senator John Gordon, a former Confederate general, was often introduced at political rallies as "the hero of Appomattox" to sustained applause, as if the Confederates had won a battle at the town where they surrendered.[6]

The 1880s saw steps towards political consolidation through the economy. Large Northern corporations began to invest heavily in new Southern textile mills, and these gave desperately needed jobs to Southern men and women. Northern railroad leaders spent millions building new railroad lines throughout the South, dramatically aiding its commerce. In an internationally publicized event in 1882, the Grand Army of the Republic, the largest group of Union army veterans, marched together with thousands of Confederate veterans in a commemorative parade. The twenty-fifth anniversary of the battle of Gettysburg was similarly celebrated in 1888 with a gathering of thousands of Union and Confederate soldiers.

The assassination of President James A. Garfield (a Union army veteran) in 1881 brought Northerners and Southerners together in grief, just as had the death of Robert E. Lee, to a smaller degree, in 1870. Then the death of Ulysses S. Grant in 1885 did even more. Thousands of Confederate veterans attended various memorial services for Grant, and his widow infused real emotion into the reconciliation movement when she asked several Confederate generals to serve as pallbearers. Mrs. Jefferson Davis, who had by that time become a friend of Julia Grant's, wrote a touching eulogy to Grant that was reprinted in many Northern papers.

By the early 1890s, all of the major Southern political leaders in the war, including Jefferson Davis, were dead. This enabled many Southerners to move towards reconciliation unimpeded by their feelings for the leaders of the Lost Cause. New political leaders, intent on reconciliation, took office. These new leaders certainly did not represent all of the people; many Southerners continued to care little about a united America, and remained bitter and uninterested in reunions of any kind, despite the best efforts of public officials to woo them. Moreover, movement toward the restoration of national unity came all too often at the expense, and to the detriment, of African Americans. Thus, in 1891 Congress defeated a bill that was designed to curb efforts by the strong Democratic Party in the South to prevent African Americans from voting. Southern Democratic Party leaders, who were now, thanks to all-white elections, assuming important congressional committee roles, began to return the favor by working with Northern politicians on a variety of those committees.

The final stage in the consolidation of North and South was reached in 1898 with the Spanish-American War. In Cuba, Southern and Northern soldiers fought on the same side, for the United States. Most of the soldiers who went to Cuba were mobilized and trained in Florida and other Southern states. Northern soldiers were treated with great friendliness and respect, which helped cement North-South relations, and President William McKinley shrewdly named former Confederate army generals Joe Wheeler and Fitzhugh Lee, the nephew of Robert E. Lee, as two of the four generals leading American forces in the war.[7]

AT THE SAME TIME that political figures in Northern and Southern states were taking steps towards consolidation, a similar movement was going on in American culture. In the late 1870s and 1880s, national magazines and newspapers, their staffs swollen by hundreds of well-educated young Southern writers eager to live in New York, Boston, Chicago and other Northern cities with publishing houses, began to take a more lenient view towards the South. Unity was also a major theme in both theater and literature.

After twenty years, many former soldiers, North and South, published their memoirs in an avalanche of books. Some were good and most were awful, but they sold hundreds of thousands of copies. These books, written by men now in their forties, were often forgiving accounts of the war which recast soldiers on both sides more as actors in some four-year-long play than as men trying to kill each other. Most stressed reconciliation.

In 1890, the ten-volume life of Lincoln by John Nicolay and John Hay was published. A decidedly pro-Union book, it was accepted as a pro-Southern book, too, as critics observed how mighty Lincoln must have been to defeat the Southerners. It also reflected the growing view that Reconstruction in the South would not have been as bad if the forgiving Lincoln had lived and the power of the Radical Republican congressional leaders had been curbed.

Right after the last shot of the war was fired, novelists began to see endless possibilities in nostalgic works about the South, works in which the facts were altered slightly to avoid any controversy. The long line of plantation romances that followed was accurately foreseen by a man who would himself write some of the most popular novels, Civil War officer and writer John Esten Cooke, who had served on the staff of the flamboyant cavalry leader and Southern hero J. E. B. Stuart. (Cooke was such a romantic that he buried his silver spurs in the ground at Appomattox on the day of the South's surrender.) "Ah! Those romantics of the war!" Cooke wrote. "The trifling species will come first, in which the southern leaders will be made to talk an incredible gibberish and figure in the most tremendous adventures . . . but then will come the better order of things, when writers like Walter Scott will conscientiously collect the real facts, and make some new 'Waverly.' "[8] What Cooke was predicting was not only romantic novels about the Southern army and its heroes, but a Sir Walter Scott type of legend in which the characters become not just heroes of the war but romantic heroes of eternal fame. He was right.

The courting of Southern beauty Barbara Frietchie (played by Florence Vidor in this 1924 film of that name) by a Confederate soldier, with a huge mansion in the background, exemplifies key aspects of the Plantation Myth genre of nineteenth-century literature.

The turn of the century also saw a new movement by American historians, journalists and novelists to portray the South of the mid-nineteenth century as a harmonious world that revolved around agriculture and the plantation system, a world organized and run efficiently by white aristocrats. These were the same men who controlled county and state governments. These leaders used that control to enhance their own lot, but at the same time sought to make life better for others. The theme of these books was that the aristocrats, the beneficiaries of the slavery system, not only provided decent lives for the slaves but also organized trade in such a way that the small farmers who did not have slaves could profit, too. The books also emphasized that the Southern attitude towards blacks was different from the Northern one. They argued that slavery was therefore acceptable in the Southern states prior to the war, even if Northerners thought it was wrong.[9] Postwar writers labored to create a view of the South as a separate country that should have been permitted to live by separate rules. Journalist-historian Edward Pollard defined that view when he wrote that the Constitution's true value was to serve as "a treaty between two nations of opposite civilizations."[10] Two nations, of course, could have two sets of rules.

Novels by Cooke, John Pendleton Kennedy, William Alexander Carruthers, Thomas Nelson Page, Mary Johnston and others painted a bright picture of plantation life that recent historians have savaged as wholly inaccurate, but it was a picture readers of the era wanted to accept.[11] Southern writers and editors began to emerge as forces in the New York literary world.[12]

One of the most successful plantation novels was *Four Oaks,* a traditional romance about a set of families who lived on large plantations and were benevolent to their hundreds of slaves. The farm in *Four Oaks* was designed by writer Elizabeth Bellamy to be a prewar plantation world unto itself. Such novels—of which there were many—not only validated the Plantation Myth for Southerners but pretended in effect that the war had never happened, keeping the old lore alive amid the rubble.

Northern magazines began to publish literature embracing this point of view in 1873, when *Scribner's Monthly Magazine* published a short story by James McKay called "Captain Luce's Enemy."[13] That story opened the literary door to a spate of stories favorable to the South. Northern publishers found their readers eager to heal the wounds of the war and eager to read these stories about the antebellum South, unrealistic as they were. McKay's story was about a Union officer who falls in love with a Southern girl and comes to admire the South and the Confederacy despite the war, and decides that many Northerners are mistakenly scornful of the South. A few months later, *Scribner's* published a series of stories by George Washington Cable set in New Orleans during the 1850s and '60s that buttressed that view.[14] A series of travel articles called "The Great South" followed. A year later, editors heralded the Centennial of 1876 with a plea for North-South reunification: "We long for a complete restoration of the national feeling that existed when Northern and Southern blood mingled in common sacrifice on Mexican soil. This national feeling, this brotherly sympathy, must be restored . . . Men of the South, we want you. Men of the South, we long for the restoration of your peace and your prosperity . . . To bring about the reunion of the country in the old fellowship should be the leading object of the approaching centennial."[15]

In 1881, *Scribner's* was renamed the *Century Illustrated Magazine* and it ran nostalgic articles, fiction and nonfiction, with titles such as "An Old Virginian"[16] and "A Boy in Gray" and graceful stories about the South in the 1770s by John Williamson Palmer. Throughout the 1880s, *Century* ran its long "Battles and Leaders of the Civil War" series, which later became a book, giving both Northern and Southern generals and colonels a chance to tell their stories (rather chivalrous ones) and giving American readers, North and South, a heroic view of the Southern military.

Fiction carried the moonlight-and-magnolias theme to even greater heights, whether in novels by Ellen Glasgow and others, short stories, poems or the humorous Uncle Remus stories of Joel Chandler Harris. (Uncle Remus was a former slave who spun nostalgia-soaked tales of happy days on the prewar plantation.)

Thomas Nelson Page's series of magazine stories, beginning with "Marse Chan," became the prototype for many stories and novels in the 1880s and 1890s and the basis for over a dozen silent films about the Civil War. "Marse" (Master) Channing is a gallant Southern planter who goes off to war. He is killed leading a successful charge, carrying the Stars and Bars flag of the South. His faithful slave, who had accompanied him in the war, brings his body back to Virginia and helps bury him on the grounds of his plantation after a teary farewell eulogy by his fiancée, Miss Anne, who lives on the plantation next door. The crestfallen Anne then leaves the plantation and spends the rest of the war caring for the Confederate wounded wherever she finds them. The backbreaking work finally kills her and she is buried next to Marse Chan under the wide oaks.[17] The theme of the stories is summed up in a line from the black narrator: "de good ole days before de war . . . dem was good ole times, marster, de best Sam ever see."[18]

In magazines or books, Page became one of the great writers of Southern nostalgia. His novel *Red Rock,* about the battle of two wealthy postwar Southern families against ruthless carpetbaggers and scalawags (it included a fight against a black man trying to rape a white woman), was published in 1898 and climbed to number five on the best-seller list in 1899. Later he published *The Negro: The Southerner's Problem,* an unflattering book about postwar blacks, and *Mam Lyddy's Recognition,* a story of a prototypical Mammy who after the war scorns freed blacks—correctly, the author suggests.

Joseph Hergesheimer's *Swords and Roses* was typical of the genre. Hergesheimer called the war "the last romantic war, when army corps fought as individuals," and wrote: "The war created a heroism . . . that clad fact in the splendor of battle flags." He went on to describe warm breezes, fine houses, bay blossoms, moonflowers and honeysuckle. In the foreword he announced, "here is a book of swords . . . of old-fashioned dark roses . . . of the simpler loveliness of the past."[19] His description of Confederate cavalry leader J. E. B. Stuart reads: "He was different . . . he wore a brown felt hat . . . with . . . sweeping black plume . . . his boots in action were heavy . . . he changed them for immaculate boots of patent leather worked with gold thread; but he danced as well as he fought in his spurs."

The cavalier movement in Southern literature began long before the Civil War. Author Richard Harwell traces it back to the 1830s. In 1836, he writes, a somewhat prophetic novel called *The Partisan Leader,* by Judge Beverly Tucker, of Virginia, was published. It chronicled the fictional story of a group of Southern states that secedes from the United States.[20] Russell Merritt, writing in the *Cinema Journal,* says the birth of the magazine the *Southern Literary Messenger,* with its romantic stories about the South, in 1832 began the moonlight-and-magnolias school.[21] From 1832 until the shelling of Fort Sumter, romantic short stories and novels had a tremendous effect on how Southerners viewed themselves. Ritchie Devon Watson Jr. explains: "The old Southwest's writers [that is, writers of the Deep South states] helped to convince southerners that they were a gallant and genteel race that lived according to a Cavalier code of conduct, a code that made it impossible to abide in unity with the rapacious and ill bred Yankees living north of the Mason-Dixon Line and north of the Ohio River. The Southwest's road to rebellion would be a fictional as well as a political journey."[22]

Post–Civil War literature included poems as well as fiction and they, like the short stories and novels, supported the legend. Poems with titles such as "The Cavalier's Glee," "A Ballad for the Young South" and "You Can Never Win Them Back," published during and after the war, made the Southerners the winners, regardless of the actual outcome.

In "You Can Never Win Them Back," an anonymous poet wrote:

> *You have no such blood as theirs*
> *For the shedding!*
> *In the veins of Cavalier*
> *Was its heading:*
> *You have no such noble men*
> *In your abolition den,*
> *To march through foe and fen—*
> *Nothing dreading!*[23]

Poet Frank Ticknor neatly tied the Knights of the Round Table to the "new" knights of the Old South in one of his poems:

> *The Knightliest of the Knightly race*
> *That, since the days of old,*
> *Have kept the lamp of chivalry*
> *Alight in hearts of gold!*[24]

Ticknor seemed to see great similarities between Confederate president Jefferson Davis and King Arthur:

> *Lit moonlit mist on midnight snow,*
> *The sun of battle smoulders low!*
> *Alas! The King at Camelot!*[25]

At the turn of the century, the book business suddenly boomed. The first best-seller lists came out in the 1890s and by 1900 record numbers of books were being published. More books were published in 1914 than in any other year until 1953.[26] It was another window for Southern revisionists to use fiction to tell and retell the story of the Southern soldiers and their ladies, and they leaped at the chance.

Many of the novels were written by unknowns who disappeared after one book, or by good soldiers who were bad novelists. Some of the authors were accomplished, however, and some of the country's very best authors wrote Civil War novels, including Louisa May Alcott, Horatio Alger Jr. and Henry Ward Beecher. Even the French novelist Jules Verne wrote about the war, in *The Mysterious Island*.[27]

All of these novelists and poets, writing from the 1830s to 1915, presented the slavery system as acceptable for its time and believed that Southerners had to defend it then and did not have to be ashamed of it later. These stories were written for Northerners, to legitimize the slavery system and its cultural roots. If nice people perpetuated the slavery system, it couldn't be all bad, and if it was, well, these were well-intentioned people who didn't know any better.

PUBLIC FIGURES and historians also believed that the South was the victim of Northern aggression, whether it was through cannons or legislation. They complained bitterly that Congress was controlled by the North, and discriminated against the South. Southern writers viewed various prewar tariffs as bullets aimed at them. Edward A. Pollard, the editor of a Richmond newspaper during the war, argued that the unfair tariffs of 1820, 1824 and 1828 were pro-Northern and led to the war. He wrote: "Whenever on sectional questions the North chose to act in a mass, its power would be irresistible and . . . no resource would be left for the South than to remain helpless and at mercy in the Union or to essay a new political destiny."[28]

Even former president James Buchanan painted the North as the aggressor and blamed John Brown's 1859 raid on Harpers Ferry for the start of the war.[29] In a book published the year after the war ended Buchanan wrote: "But even admitting slavery to be a sin, have the adherents of John Brown never reflected that the attempt by one people to pass beyond their own jurisdiction, and to extirpate by force of arms whatever they may deem sinful among another people would involve the nations of the earth in perpetual hostilities?"[30]

Historian James Rhodes, a Northerner with Southern sympathies, published many of his books and articles during the years in which silent movies about the Civil War were being produced. In a series of lectures published in 1913, Rhodes argued that slaveholders were attacked by the Union for defending "property" that was rightfully theirs. Planters believed that their "property," slaves, was "sacred as the ownership of horses and mules." Rhodes then tied that to "lost cause" chivalry. "As slavery was out of tune with the nineteenth century, the States that held fast to it played a losing game." Rhodes was telling audiences almost fifty years later that slavery was not wrong, merely out of favor in the North. This meant the Southerners, in any dispute about it, would be fighting for an honorable cause, even though they were bound to lose.[31] Rhodes felt that the South was not responsible for the slave system. He argued that the highly profitable cotton and tobacco industries could succeed only with slaves. Rhodes put the blame for the war on Stephen Douglas, who he said stirred up antislavery feelings in the North when he introduced the Kansas-Nebraska Bill in the U.S. Senate. Rhodes's interpretation was seconded by another historian, James Burgess, who also saw the South as victim. He viewed John Brown's Harpers Ferry raid, in 1859, as the first "battle" of the war,[32] instead of the attack on Fort Sumter in 1861.

Perhaps the staunchest defender of slavery and the plantations at the beginning of the twentieth century was William Dunning, a professor of history at Columbia University, and a Southerner, who wrote *Reconstruction, Political and Economic, 1865–1877.* Dunning was eager to reunite North and South, but only in terms of a Southern, white-supremacist point of view, and at the expense of African Americans. In the 1907–1940 period, this historian's views influenced most Americans, including filmmakers and their audiences. According to his critics, Dunning had a single view that governed his entire Civil War–era thinking: black incapacity was responsible for the failure of Reconstruction. He also argued that blacks' irresponsible behavior, urged on by unscrupulous abolitionists, poisoned the life of the entire South, black and white, creating a need for the Jim Crow laws and segregation that came later.[33] He wrote that "the root of the trouble in the South had been not the institution of slavery but the co-existence in one society of two races so distinct in characteristics as to render coalescence impossible."[34]

He defended Jim Crow laws and the Black Codes on the grounds that "the freedmen were not on the same social, moral and intellectual plane with the whites," and that Jim Crow laws "recognized . . . them as a separate class in the civil order."[35]

Dunning argued that there could be no comingling of the races and that blacks could never live within white society. In fact, he considered the dominant white society to be imperiled by blacks. He wrote of the effort at integration that "it played a part in the demand for mixed schools, in the legislative prohibition of discrimination between the races in hotels and theaters and even in the hideous crime against white womanhood which now assumed new meaning in the annals of outrage." He insinuated that rape by a white man was not as savage as that by a black man.[36]

Dunning taught hundreds of the country's top history students. To a large extent, his views became their views. His students, many from the South, had those views constantly reinforced by visits home, where they discussed the war and politics with family friends who were veterans of the Confederate army. Dunning's opinions appeared again and again in history books and textbooks his students authored through the 1940s, and effected a racist interpretation of the Civil War. It was not difficult for filmmakers, who had themselves read the books of Dunning and his students in school, to make audiences accept on the screen what filmmakers and audiences alike had been taught to accept in the classroom for years.

There came to be a battalion of revisionist historians intent on absolving the Confederacy of all blame for the Civil War, a group of educators, lecturers and writers determined to somehow paint the Big Lie of slavery invisible. If enough people said slavery did not cause the war, then it did not.

Later, other historians debunked these views and lamented that theater and film extended them to mass audiences. Writing in 1923, historian Charles Beard argued that many nineteenth-century historians, North and South, distorted the reasons for the war and helped create the myths developed in silent films. (Beard also believed that economics, not slavery, had brought on the war.) "The tragedy and heroism of the contest furnished inspiration to patriots and romance to the maker of epics," he wrote, referring to silent movies.[37]

Historian Warren Susman, writing of his own search for the true past, said that from 1900 to 1920 historians paid more attention to myth than to fact. Intellectual historian Van Wyck Brooks added that

Americans sought the "usable past" to help solve problems of the present—yet did not want the truth when it came to the Civil War.

This view of the war lasted for decades. It was the major theme of history textbooks used in colleges. Southern universities taught Civil War–era history in a way that solidified Southerners' view of themselves as victims. By 1913 more than half the universities in the South offered courses on the Civil War, Reconstruction or state history to supplement United States history courses. Many Southern schools, such as the University of Texas, even raised money to pay for professors' research for studies that supported the Plantation Myth[38]—this despite the fact that Alabama, Mississippi, South Carolina, North Carolina and Arkansas had, by that year, established impressive state historical archives loaded with Southern records for historians' use. The Southern History Association was formed in 1896 to help historians obtain resources to write revisionist histories of the Civil War and the Reconstruction era. The Library of Southern Literature, established a few years later, did the same thing.

The Southern educational view of the war became so strident, and so closely tied to the views of Confederate veterans' organizations, that in 1902 the American Historical Association appointed a committee to study the teaching of history in the South. Its findings were highly critical.[39]

In Northern universities, there was no mass effort to defend the South, but the "no loss" theme—the idea that there were neither victors nor losers in the war—permeated classrooms there, too. Northern universities often had a large number of students from wealthy Southern families who sent their children north, where they believed they could get a better education. Professors such as Dunning said that they came to much of their view of the South as the victim from their discussions with these students. Many of these Southern students returned home to teach in Southern colleges, but others taught at Northern colleges, further promulgating their convictions.

Authors critical of the moonlight-and-magnolias lore were attacked whenever their books came out. In 1892, William Trent wrote a critical biography of Southern writer William Simms that was vilified in Southern newspapers and on Southern campuses. He and other authors pulled back from controversy in future books. Sour reaction was so swift and so influential that colleges sometimes even fired academics who dared attack the cotton-fields tradition. In 1905, Henry William Elson published his *History of the United States,* which called the Civil War a "slaveholders' rebellion" and charged slaveholders with having sexual liaisons with slave women. The book was promptly banned at many Southern colleges.

THE AMERICAN THEATER followed the publishing industry, but the requirements of the theater were different from those of book publishers. Publishers could sell books about military campaigns and battlefield heroism, but stage plays could not re-create battles and did not have the budget for large casts. They needed small-cast plays, and especially love stories. The love story was the heart of the American theater in the 1890s; any play about the Civil War needed at least one but sometimes two or three romantic plots, and often a love triangle. These plays, carefully crafted to bring in nostalgia and love affairs, were extremely popular. They became an important precursor to the plots of many movies. The combination of valor, romance and history in the first Civil War plays proved quite profitable at theater box offices and paved the way for more, as always happens in profit-driven entertainment media.

The first such success on stage was William Hookes Gillette's *Held by the Enemy,* in 1886. An even bigger success for Gillette was *Secret Service,* a drama about spies for the Confederacy, which toured the country for several years. It premiered in 1896, was revived in 1915, and was later made into a movie. Other resounding box office stage hits in the 1880s and 1890s were David Belasco's *The Heart of Maryland* and James Herne Griffith's *Davenport.*

Although a few of the plays offered some accurate depictions of history (the wealthy Warrens of *The Warrens of Virginia* wind up starving in Reconstruction), most did not, or were ludicrous. In *The Heart of Maryland* a father becomes a high-ranking Confederate general who captures a Union officer, only to discover that the officer is his own son. Perhaps the most successful Civil War play was Bronson Howard's *Shenandoah,* turned into a 1965 film and later a Broadway musical. It first opened in 1889 and was produced in various theaters for years. Howard's characters are introduced during the bombardment of Fort Sumter and then wander through Virginia, in and out of the war, until 1865. All are reunited in the end as a spirit of reconciliation sweeps the stage.[40]

Plays tended to focus on stories either of individual Southern officers in the war, such as the fictional character Colonel Carter, or of a region, such as Alabama. Critics as well as audiences loved these dramas. Writing in the *New York Herald Tribune,* critic William Winter had this to say about *Colonel Carter:* "It is suffused with romance . . . imparts a high ideal of character and conduct. . . . The old social order of the South was far more romantic and interesting than any social order of the North either is now or ever has been. [The playwright] chose wisely in choosing a Southern plantation for the scene of his play. . . . You could see the large stars hanging in the deep, dark sky, and the still streamers of the gray moss and the great fans of the palm, and you could smell the scent of magnolia on the faint evening breeze. . . ."[41]

Together, literature and theater created more than enough lore about the Civil War and the Old South to supply a hundred screenwriters with a thousand Civil War plots for the new silent movies, according to historian Rollin Osterweis: "By the turn of the century, the Lost Cause Myth had captured the Yankee demesne, and was holding it firmly in feudal fief. . . . Nostalgia for an earlier, agrarian, more gracious American way of life occasionally had manifested itself. And this nostalgia seized avidly upon the legends of the Old South and of the gray clad knights who rode for her glory."[42] This cultural transformation of the war came at a time, too, when Americans felt smothered by materialism, the growth of cities, consumerism, the growth of industrialization, assembly-line work lives, unfair labor practices and the new corporate world that sprawled about them. They longed for the simple, rural life of the mid-nineteenth century, a time, they believed, when the stress and anxiety that were crippling them did not exist.

American collective memory was creating myths, too. Men and women gathered at the hundreds of anniversary commemorations of the Civil War and traded thousands of battle stories, each growing whenever it was repeated. These exaggerated tales found their way into newspaper and movie newsreel accounts of the reunions (259 newsreels between 1907 and 1916). The accounts of reunions with soldiers of both sides, read or seen by millions, always ended in handshakes.

It was into this nostalgia-washed landscape that Hollywood screenwriters moved at the turn of the century. They did not have to create legends. The myth had existed so long, and had been built so carefully in so many places and in so many ways, that it seemed real to most Americans.

The early general cinema relied on successful stage plays. Filmmakers, thrashing about for scripts that would sell tickets in the early days, were uncertain what the public wanted. A successful play was likely to mean a successful movie, and it was already scripted. Film directors assumed people had either seen the play or knew about it and that that would make them want to see the film version.[43] Newspaper entertainment reporters who had written about the play were likely to write about the movie.

Until 1908, many silent film studios were located in New York or in nearby New Jersey, making it easy for theater stars to work as film actors during the day. Performers would reprise their stage roles for the film, substantially reducing rehearsal time and saving producers money. The critical and financial success of Civil War stage dramas came about at the same time the film industry was searching for commercially successful plays. However, after the first few stage-to-screen transfers, movie producers stopped using plays because of royalty problems. To save money they began to generate their own movie scripts using standard theater formulas.[44] The move of many studios to Hollywood during the 1908–1915 period, to take advantage of year-round good weather, ample outdoor locations and nonunion workers, made Civil War films—with their outdoor scenes—even more popular.[45]

Most of all, the revised version of the Confederate army story promulgated by the hundreds of histories, novels and plays had two elements Hollywood relied upon: a love story and an underdog. The growing image of Southern women as beautiful belles and men as good-looking officers gave filmmakers the chance to cast their handsomest actors and loveliest actresses in these roles. Producers discovered that audiences enjoyed comedies and westerns but also liked dramas about history and nostalgia. Filmmakers were serious about their art, but their first need was to make money. The Plantation Myth, by the time it moved west, was perfect for Hollywood.

Film directors naturally made the Confederates the hard-fighting, noble opposition in their movies. Film after film showed the Southern male as the chivalrous soldier, forced to fight dastardly Northern troops who were sent south by misguided abolitionists, in order to defend Southern honor. On film, the Southerners were usually the heroes, even though historically it had been the Southerners who championed slavery, Southerners who ran the worst prisons and Southerners who actually started the war. The Confederates did fight for the honor of their women, their families and their plantations. But most of all they fought for a states' rights system that permitted slavery. The screen's version of the war, then, was merely a revision based on revision, founded soundly upon myth, the myth of another land and another people, but the kind of people Americans wanted themselves to be.

CHAPTER TWO

———

Lights . . . Camera . . . Action:
Moonlight and Magnolias

THE SOLDIER shakes hands heartily with his father on the porch of his home as troops are being marshaled in the distance. He hugs his mother and then slowly moves towards his blonde sweetheart, in her very best dress, her downcast eyes rising slightly to meet his. He leans over, smiles awkwardly, and kisses her very briefly, chastely, on the lips. The din of noise in the distance draws his attention and he waves abruptly to his friends, gathered nearby. Then he runs to the crowd and through it, joining his regiment as it begins its parade through town and towards the war. As the men march, shoulders back, eyes straight ahead, rifles pointing up towards God, hundreds of towns-people cheer lustily. As the troops disappear around the last building, all the beautiful young girls who have said goodbye to their lovers turn away, cringing and wiping tearful eyes with handkerchiefs.[1] (The cheerful sweetheart who practically collapses with grief when her lover has gone was a standard and effective cinematic device in Civil War movies. It gave an immediate human quality to a war story and underlined the girl-he-left-behind theme that was featured in so many of the films.)

That opening scene from *The Battle* (1911) is typical of the early Civil War films and a fine example of the way in which Hollywood adopted existing literature, theater and media for its stories. It contains the elements of movies to arrive later: proud parents, eager soldier, girl left behind, cheering crowds and the fervent hope that no one will be hurt, countered by the sad knowledge that many soldiers will never return.

37

The Battle, *made in 1911, was one of the first Civil War combat films. D. W. Griffith managed to film fully engaged battle scenes with only a few dozen extras by photographing all of the action in narrow areas, as he did here.*

THE DEVELOPMENT of the film industry was so rapid that by 1910 there were over ten thousand movie theaters in the United States. There were twenty-two thousand by 1924. Admission was cheap, usually just a nickel; movies were less expensive than baseball or vaudeville.[2] And they were readily accessible to all classes, becoming especially popular with the wave of immigrants entering the country at the turn of the century.[3] Many women and children, particularly those in urban areas, sought out inexpensive leisure, and theaters were open in the afternoons as well as the evenings, attracting factory workers before and after work shifts. Films were popular with the middle class, too, and to capture that audience, by 1908 large theaters were built and films were extended from five or six minutes to full fifteen-minute features.[4]

These early films were stories of crime, violence and sex[5] that upset many middle-class families and civic leaders. By 1908, six states and several major cities had created censorship boards to screen objectionable films.[6] It was also a time when, liberated by jobs, the suffrage movement and increased schooling, women began to visit political rallies, department stores and entertainment centers. "The cinema was a place women could frequent on their own, as independent customers, where they could experience forms of collectivity different from those centering on the family," writes Miriam Hansen.[7]

The heads of the brand-new film companies were mostly Jewish immigrants from Europe, drawn to America by its opportunities. In most fields, opportunities were denied, but in the motion picture industry there was not yet an establishment, and the newcomers saw enormous promise. The most influential producers in the early years were the Warner brothers, from Poland; Samuel Goldwyn, from Poland; Carl Laemmle Sr., from Germany; Louis B. Mayer, from Russia; and William Fox and Adolph Zukor, both from Hungary. Two Englishmen, Albert E. Smith and J. Stuart Blackton, started the Vitagraph Company, and Biograph was founded by William K. L. Dickson, another Englishman. These men knew little and cared less about American history. They wanted their new country to have a wonderful history and were determined to deliver it. They wanted a past all Americans could be proud of, especially newly arrived immigrants like themselves. They wanted a past strong in family values, one that honored women and children, a past in which people's dreams came true, where no man's aspirations were too large. They wanted to repackage American history and improve on it.[8]

They and their fellow immigrants had to start at the bottom in American life in that era, so they rooted strongly for the underdog. There was no better underdog, they felt, than the courageous Southern soldier, malnourished but fighting on against incredible odds in the outmanned and outgunned Confederate army for hearth, home and loved ones. The Civil War and these pioneer movie moguls were made for each other.

All of these trends came together at the time America was getting ready to celebrate the fiftieth anniversary of the start of the war. All around them, producers saw civic leaders making fiftieth-anniversary speeches and committees organizing anniversary reunions. Parades were planned and veterans were taking their uniforms to be cleaned. Filmmakers were convinced that this would make Civil War movies a successful and very profitable genre.

The first Civil War–era film was the 1903 version of *Uncle Tom's Cabin,* but the first true Civil War battle film was *Days of '61,* a ten-minute-long feature produced by the Edison Company in January 1908. It was the first to combine narrative with psychological characterization, layered onto a story of the war and its aftermath with, of course, the reunification of North and South as its finale. In it, an old woman reflects on the spring of 1861, when her eager suitor left her to fight in the Union army—he was gone for four long years. The film covers his departure, frontline battles, an ambush, a powder mine, the taking of a hill, the capture of artillery, victories and the boy's wounding. Then the heroic boy returns to his lover's arms and they are married. At the very end of the ten-minute film, the aging soldier appears and kisses the storyteller to assure audiences that they lived happily ever after.

Screenwriters for *Days of '61* were the first to concoct a North-South love story that also involved friends betraying their army to save friends and a young woman getting a last-minute reprieve from execution for her love. In Thomas Edison's film, the wounded Union soldier is nursed by the Southerner's sister at the same time that the Southerner, a spy, is chased into a farmhouse by Northern soldiers. The Union friend saves the Southerner, but is court-martialed and ordered shot for aiding the enemy. The girl appeals not only to General Ulysses S. Grant but, for good measure, to Abraham Lincoln and talks them into sparing her true love.[9]

The formula worked. It would be stretched thin over the next ten years to yield new plots for Civil War films. Most involved some kind of prewar friendship between men divided by the war, a girl of the North or the South, perhaps a mother or father fearful of a son's battlefield death, and some sort of device whereby a former friend, now an enemy, helps an enemy, saves an enemy, or survives an enemy. The girl, usually quite young, always winds up being swept into somebody's arms, war or no war. Some critics, unaware that variations of this formula would be around for years, deplored the contrived love affairs. As early as 1910, a critic for *Moving Picture World* complained that "our Civil War has furnished the background for many stirring photodramas, but most of them are marred by the inevitable trio of young people."[10]

Days of '61 was also the first picture in which historical figures such as Grant and Lincoln appeared (Robert E. Lee would be a frequent visitor, too), as filmmakers tried to add authenticity and also pull in parents with children for an "educational" film.

There were thirteen Civil War movies made in 1908, twenty-three such features in 1909, thirty-four in 1910 and then nearly one hundred per year through 1916. Many of the movies were largely pro-Union through most of 1908 and early 1909, probably because of the success of the first version of *Uncle Tom's Cabin.* But Southern theater owners, regional distributors and moviegoers soon began to complain, particularly after the release of *Escape from Andersonville,* a one-reeler about the notorious Confederate prison camp in Georgia.[11] A reader wrote to *Moving Picture World* in 1909 asking, "Why do all the Civil War movies have the northern army come out ahead?"[12] His letter was not only a plea for more balanced films but an indication that the reader, who lived in Florida, believed that the South had won the war.

The demand in the South for Civil War movies with a Southern theme confused and delighted movie producers. Most had assumed Southerners did not want to be reminded of the war, and they were pleased that they could now show such movies below the Mason-Dixon Line. These movies, however, had to have a Southern point of view in order to draw customers. Southerners did not want to go to the local movie house to see their heroes vanquished yet again.

The Southern point of view began to be evident in mid-1909 with the release of *In Old Kentucky,* a D. W. Griffith film, and *The Old Soldier's Story,* filmed in the South by Kalem Studios of Jacksonville, Florida. The studio executives had moved there to take advantage of good weather and the availability of nonunion workers.[13] The Southern point of view was also apparent in *Nan, the Girl Spy,* the first in a long series of movies about Nan which continued through 1912, all filmed in Florida by Kalem.[14] The perky Nan was a "wholesome Dixie orphan whose patriotism led her to espionage."[15]

The Nan series kicked off a flood of pro-South movies. *Moving Picture World,* the premier movie magazine of the day, said the films "should be especially dear to the Southern area."[16] The magazine also noted that in *The Old Soldier's Story* the scenery had "atmosphere of that part of the [South] country throughout" and even had the title cards printed in a Southern drawl ("You all . . . etc.").[17]

Films with a Southern view—the cavalier as underdog—might work in the South. But would they succeed in the North? Several were issued and did well in the North, just as myth-based lithographs and plays had, and a new genre, the Southern Civil War film as underdog epic and reunification saga, was born.

A number of frequently used, and popular, plot devices with some variations sustained Civil War films for twelve years; even horses got into the act. The novel *Black Beauty*, originally set in the English countryside, was made into an American Civil War film set in Virginia. Audiences were also thrilled by the adventure of Don the Wonder Horse, a circus stallion, who starred in *The Equine Spy*. In it, Don the Wonder Horse not only led enemy troops away from rebel supply trains but, between bags of oats, managed to steal key federal battle plans.

These plots would later become staples of American cinema. Don the Wonder Horse was the predecessor of Lassie, Rin Tin Tin and Trigger. *The Coward* was the forerunner of *The Red Badge of Courage*. Black Beauty would ride across the screen several times in his own films and inspire numerous other horse sagas. In generation after generation and in country after country, women in the movies would find love in the middle of war. All of these plots, many fantastic, entertained silent-film audiences. They offered underdogs, battles, intrigue and romance. And they continued the established myth that the war was an accident, caused by no one, won by no one but fought bravely by both sides.

Brother Against Brother, a William Selig film, premiered in 1909, and its advertising in trade magazines indicated the growing trend towards production of Civil War movies. One ad heralded it as "a worthy successor to the stunning *Days of Old Virginia*," another war film, and promised that it was "the greatest war story ever produced in motion pictures," again indicating the growing number of such movies.[18]

There were so many Civil War films in 1909 that *Motion Picture World* noted in an editorial: "War dramas are becoming popular . . ."

In that same editorial, in a strangely touching paragraph in the otherwise hard-nosed publication, the writer commented that one of the best features of the Civil War movies was the presentation of women: "Perhaps the most striking feature of this film is the picture of the sorrow of the women when the men departed for war."[19]

The year 1909 was also the first in which large battle scenes were filmed. The first movie with battles was D. W. Griffith's *The Honor of His Family,* released in December 1909. Griffith had fifty actors deployed as soldiers so that they always seemed like part of a much bigger battle. He filmed them very tightly to give the appearance of hundreds of soldiers fighting at any one time.[20] Despite this effort to economize, however, studio executives criticized Griffith for the num-

D. W. Griffith was already the country's most successful director when he made The Birth of a Nation *in 1915. Here he watches the daily "rushes," or footage, from* Hearts of the World *on a small screen in his office.*

ber of actors used in these scenes. They also said that the outdoor filming (with countless takes) was expensive.

Civil War films with a moonlight-and-magnolias, pro-Southern view became as popular as they did in large part because of the two men who made so many of them—Griffith and Thomas H. Ince, the most talented and successful film directors in the business.

By 1909, young Griffith was the most prominent filmmaker at the booming Biograph Studios. The tall, lanky director was easily spotted at any of his sets, indoor or outdoor, by the broad-brimmed hat he loved to wear. And, unlike most film directors, Griffith was a Southerner. His father, "Roaring Jake" Griffith, had been a colonel in the Confederate army and regaled his children and neighbors for years with stories of their "lost cause." "They were burned right into my memory," the son later wrote.[21] Jake had been an active participant in many battles, including Shiloh, and was wounded in fighting in the Sesquatchie Valley, in Tennessee. Later he fought at Missionary Ridge, near Chattanooga, and was part of the regiment that helped Confederate president Jefferson Davis during his unsuccessful attempt to escape after the South fell in April 1865. The highlight of most evenings at the Griffith dinner table, where other Civil War veterans also spun tall tales, was the great charge led by "Roaring Jake" in a buggy after his horse had been shot out from under him (this story grew in dramatic effect the more Jake told it).[22]

Jake's memories would contribute to fourteen Civil War films (D.W. directed ten, supervised one and worked as a producer on three) including, in 1915, *The Birth of a Nation*. In all of them Jake's son portrayed the South as a land of easy harmony, shattered by a war brought on by the North. The men were heroes, the women tender and lovely belles, and the slaves trusted and honored workers devoted to their owners. Nonetheless, the director always rather naïvely denied that he was influenced by his father, whose family had owned slaves before the war, or by his father's family or Civil War veteran friends. D.W. claimed that his boyhood in Louisville in what had been a slave state did not influence him either, nor, apparently, did the Southern literature, history and theater he was brought up on.

There were Southern villains in some of his films, too, as his supporters over the years always pointed out. In *The Informer*, which stars screen golden girl Mary Pickford, Henry Walthall plays a Confederate soldier who sells military secrets to the Union, a betrayal that brings about the death of his brother. In *The Honor of His Family*, a Confederate officer kills his own coward son. The 1910 film *The House with Closed Shutters* again shows a Southern soldier who becomes a coward and hides in his home. Another film of that year, *In the Border States*, has a Southern belle who spurns Southern lovers and falls for a Union officer. A Southern father in *The Soul of Honor* accuses his son of cowardice and orders him to kill himself.[23]

But, as noted, most of Griffith's films favored Southerners, directly or indirectly. One of his first Civil War movies, *In Old Kentucky* (with Mary Pickford in a cameo), is about two brothers, one of whom fights for the North and the other for the South. In the finale, the Union soldier tries to ambush his Confederate brother. He is prevented by their mother, who puts a gun to her head, threatening suicide, and makes him drop his weapon. In *The Guerrilla*, Griffith shows a defenseless Northern family attacked by what appear to be Confederate troops. But the troops soon take off their look-alike uniforms and put on rather ragged civilian clothes to show that they are not regular army, but rogue guerrillas. Confederate regulars, the director hints, would never do such a thing.

Even his plots that denigrate Southerners, when examined carefully, don't suggest that the South had rapists or murders and the like. They imply that given individuals were traitors to the Cause, turncoats whose actions underlined the premise that the real Old South was not like that (no good Southern father, for example, would order his son to commit suicide unless he was indeed a coward).

In 1911, Griffith made two back-to-back films, *His Trust* and *His Trust Fulfilled*, originally planned as one long film. They were released within three days of each other and hyped as a continuous story. They nailed together the framework of the Old South that other directors adopted. In *His Trust*, a Southern planter goes off to war leaving his wife and daughter at home with his loyal slave, George. Union troops burn the mansion, but the slave (played by white actor Wilfred Lucas in blackface) saves the women by hiding them in his cabin. The sequel, *His Trust Fulfilled*, opens four years later. The master has been killed in the war. His wife dies. The daughter, penniless, has a chance to marry an Englishman but has no dowry. The loyal slave digs up the money he has saved throughout his life and gives all of it to the girl. The two films bring together all the essential elements of the Plantation Myth: heroic planter/soldier who gives his life for the cause, marauding Union soldiers who pillage and destroy, widow who works herself into the grave to save the plantation and raise her daughter as a virtuous Southern woman who can marry properly, and a slave who loves his owners and gives them his life's savings because if they are happy, he is happy.

All of the studio publicity releases hailed this double feature as a truthful representation of life in the South during the Civil War. According to one release: "*His Trust* is the first part of a life story, the second part being *His Trust Fulfilled,* and while the second is the sequel to the first, each is a complete story in itself. In every Southern home there is an old trusted body servant, whose faithful devotion to his master and his master's family was extreme to the extent of laying down his life if required."

The releases, often reprinted in the *Biograph Bulletin,* a newsletter sent to the press and theater owners and distributors, were written by Lee Dougherty, a former newspaperman who soon found himself hiring actors for different Griffith films. In that same release for the double feature Dougherty describes the slave's farewell to his master's daughter: "George at a distance views the festivities with tears of joy streaming down his black but honest cheeks, and after they [the newly wed couple] depart for their new home, he goes back to his cabin, takes down his master's sabre and fondles it, happy in the realization that he has fulfilled his trust."[24]

Critics have charged that only a Southerner would create and stick with such a distorted scenario. William Everson goes so far as to write that it is impossible to believe that a Southerner could be impartial about the Civil War.[25]

Griffith may have been using early one-reelers such as these to hone his skills for something up ahead. "All of his Biograph films," writes Griffith scholar Jay Leyda, "had future projects in mind, especially the two large projects that were to be made after he left Biograph—*The Birth of a Nation* and *The Mother and the Law* . . . the Civil War films were trial scenes for *The Birth of a Nation.*"[26]

By 1915, Griffith had decided that silent films could be expanded from one- or two-reel movies for nickelodeons to long, one-to-two-hour features. He was convinced that movies were about to change forever and that he would change them. In this, certainly, he was right.

Just as influential in creating the Plantation Myth in the silent era was flamboyant director Thomas Ince, a compact man with a round face, small mouth and jet-black curly hair who loved to dress fashionably almost as much as he loved to play golf. Ince grew up in New England and was exposed to the Northern point of view by relatives who had fought in the war or knew people who had fought in the war. Nevertheless, Ince's interpretation of the war, partially fueled by the novels and plays of the day, was distinctly pro-Southern.

Ince was one of Hollywood's most innovative directors. That was apparent in his first Civil War film, *Cinderella,* a movie that not only marked him as a new force in silent film but, like the works of Griffith, built a pro-Southern framework for the director's own later movies and the films of others. The wildly inventive *Cinderella* is the story of a kindhearted Southern girl abused by her stepmother and stepsister when her father goes off to fight for the Confederacy. They banish her to the slave quarters, where she lives with a jolly Mammy who plays her fairy godmother. Prince Charming is a Union officer who wins a battle nearby and commandeers the plantation. Cinderella falls in love with the officer over the stepmother's objections, wins her father's approval when he returns at the end of the war, and marries the man. All the elements of the standard story—women subjugated by men, women swooning for good-looking men in uniform, and a loving and happy and very overweight Mammy—were in place. There was also the idea that the Southern woman was dominated by the Northern man, as the South was dominated by the North—and all relationships were happily resolved.

Ince churned out more than twenty Civil War features, outperforming even Griffith. They included *When Lee Surrenders, The Toll of War, For the Cause, When Lincoln Paid* and *With Lee in Virginia.*[27]

He had hit on a formula. "A director," he once wrote, "must know life, but he must know, too, how to project life, not in narrative form but by selected dramatic moments, each of which builds towards a definite crisis or climax that will bring a burst of emotional response from every audience."[28]

The best Civil War movie Ince made, one of the best anyone made, was the 1913 *The Battle of Gettysburg,* which showed the defeated Southern army as a collection of true heroes who could have won had they not been outnumbered. (Eighty years later, TNT's *Gettysburg* would take that same view, offering viewers a mesmerizing six-hour production.) Using the new Bell and Howell cameras, Ince photographed one of the clearest, sharpest films of the silent era. The movie was five long reels, or nearly one hour. Ince was so eager to make the movie look authentic that he had scriptwriters write dialogue for all the actors in each scene, so that they could mouth the lines to create a "sound." (Critics have wondered for years if Ince did this because he foresaw sound films and wanted to rerelease *Gettysburg* later.) Directions were written into the script for each actor's facial expressions and for every single one of several hundred camera shots. The film was jammed with battle scenes but, like the work of Griffith, also loaded with emotional closeups.[29] Those who saw the film, which no longer exists, claimed it was a masterpiece. In his many advertisements for the film, some double pages that screamed GETTYSBURG at the reader, Ince promoted the bravery of men on both sides. In all of the promotional language, and in the film itself, gallant men fight other gallant men in a battle for America. There is no clear hero or villain, no winner or loser.

The movie is thought to have been written by one of the top screenwriters of the silent era, C. Gardner Sullivan, a former newspaper reporter from Minnesota who later worked in New York. To make extra money, he wrote a one-reel story for the Edison Company. The company bought it and told him to write more, so he began to spend his free time during the day banging out action and romantic scripts for the silents on a small Underwood typewriter in his New York apartment, while continuing to work as a reporter at night.[30] He and Ince soon crossed paths. The producer-director liked Gardner's work because it was fast-moving, just what the silents needed. He bought several stories from the productive young writer in 1910 and 1911 and then, in 1912, in an unusual move, hired Gardner as his full-time screenwriter and put him to work on the first of a dozen films. The idea of hiring full-time writers started with Ince and Sullivan and grew over the years until hundreds of top writers, many of them novelists or former newspapermen or newspaperwomen, joined Hollywood writer stables.[31] *The Battle of Gettysburg* was the biggest and the best of Sullivan's work, and it was superb.

There is no evidence that any actual veterans of the war, North or South, wrote scripts. Of course, screenwriters did not need to have been in the army to do their work. Novelist Stephen Crane, who wrote *The Red Badge of Courage,* was never in the army, although many thought he was, and he answered critics by stating that writers, not soldiers, made the best writers.[32]

Ince loved Civil War films. In *The Pride of the South,* directed by Burton King, John Singleton Mosby, the flamboyant head of a renowned Confederate guerrilla group, Mosby's Rangers, learns that his daughter has married a Union officer. The officer is killed and she is banished from her father's home and winds up living in poverty—a just reward for a traitorous Southern belle. In *The Soul of the South,* one rebel brother falls asleep on guard duty. The other brother takes the blame and is sentenced to die. Their beautiful sister drives a buggy to reach Confederate president Jefferson Davis himself and beg for her brother's life. (The plot was similar to those in which a Northern girl races to Abraham Lincoln or General Grant for a reprieve.) The brother is pardoned. Viewers left the theaters certain that Southern women always stood by their men and that Southern politicians always did the right thing in the end. They also left the theater with a little bit of Civil War history. Ince, a demon for authenticity, not only hired Colonel Mosby as a consultant, but had the colonel, then eighty years old, portray himself in the film.

In another film, *The Toll of War* (1913), Ince even managed with historical and cinematic acrobatics to have Abraham Lincoln die in the bed of a gracious Southern woman. A female Confederate spy (sometimes it seemed on film that half the women in the South were working as spies) is about to be shot. President Lincoln intervenes, sparing her life. She stays in Washington and, a few weeks later, is at Ford's Theatre when Lincoln is assassinated by John Wilkes Booth. She begs aides to carry the mortally wounded president to her house, just a few blocks away, where he dies in her bed as she kneels in prayer beside it. Thus, in Ince's movie, the entire Civil War ends with the beleaguered Southern girl offering comfort to the dying enemy president and, as always, pleading for North-South reconciliation.[33]

Ince's more than four hundred films were produced at his sprawling studios deep in the vast, rocky Santa Ynez canyon some twenty miles from Hollywood.[34] He was able to buy the canyon, over twenty thousand acres in size, cheap. The studio had its own town center, bungalows scattered along the canyon floor and on some ledges, vegetable gardens, dormitories, a general store, large wooden stables for horses and spacious garages for cars. There was an oversized warehouse just for Civil War props, including cannons, muskets, rifles, pistols, sabers, flags, guidons, drums and other relics, most purchased from a military surplus store.[35]

The studio, quickly dubbed Inceville by the show business press, wasn't built for his Civil War actors, his stable of young showgirls, Mary Pickford, his tap dancers, his roaring automobiles, or his hopelessly handsome but still unknown young star, Douglas Fairbanks. It was built for the wild and raucous cowboys and Indians of the 101 Ranch Wild West Show.

Early in 1912, just a few weeks after he quit NYMP Studios, Ince arrived in sunny California with his wife; his favorite cameraman, Ray Smallwood; actress Ethel Grandin; and property master Charles Weston to join the fledgling K & B Studios in Edendale. Ince felt he needed to do something splashy to get the attention of his new bosses and to open up new avenues for himself. He happened to meet people who took him to see the owners of the 101 Ranch Wild West Show, a touring show modeled on Buffalo Bill's Wild West Show. Usually the show would get a few weeks' work and then return to Venice, California, to wait for further bookings. What its owners wanted was a more permanent schedule, with guarantees. In 1912, with touring shows on the decline and movies on the upswing, that was nearly impossible. Ince, a man of long-range vision, saw in the show the foundation of an empire for himself. He immediately leased the 101 Ranch Show and moved his entire studio to Santa Ynez canyon, where he built a little universe to make western movies.

All of the interiors for the Civil War pictures were shot on a huge, open-air, muslin-covered soundstage that was used for up to five films at the same time. Art director Sir Henry Irving created a series of different sets up and down the canyon. There was a New York street for urban movies, a park for small-town movies, several individual houses to represent homes in different locales, a frontier fort and an entire

Old West town. As soon as the 101 Ranch Wild West Show arrived at Inceville, Ince put his vision to work and began producing what would be more than three hundred westerns, including some of the best silent westerns made. Many starred a rookie Wild West performer named William S. Hart who would go on to be a cowboy matinee idol in the 1920s.

INCE AND GRIFFITH were the most productive and successful filmmakers of the silent era. Griffith produced eighty-six feature films in 1910 and seventy in 1911, and the figures for other years were similar. Ince averaged over one hundred per year in that same period.[36] Most of their films made money and were considered among the best of the silents. Of Civil War movies in particular, their output was relatively small—only thirty-two between them out of a total of about five hundred silents in this category—but these thirty-two included some of the most famous and financially most successful silent films on the war. Both directors worked with important companies: Griffith at first was with Biograph; Ince was with K & B, then with Mutual, and then with Universal before his untimely death.[37] Griffith and Ince were also known as the most prominent filmmaking innovators of their time. Over the years 1908 to 1915, they invented various techniques, from wide-angle shots to facial closeups, that have served ever since as staples of the cinematographic art.

Racism thrived throughout the United States in that era, in the North and South, East and West. Blacks could not sit downstairs in Southern movie houses, but they could not sit downstairs in many Northern ones, either. Professional baseball was segregated. Black heavyweight boxing champion Jack Johnson was so despised by many because of his race that any Caucasian fighter who stepped into the ring with him was quickly dubbed "the great white hope" by the press. The films of Griffith and Ince encouraged this attitude; they were seen by millions of people who believed what was on the screen. These films had great power, and that power, although used for the greater good of national reconciliation as the country approached the fiftieth anniversary of the end of the Civil War, simultaneously helped reinforce the existing racist climate.

Their reunification themes were echoed in other filmmakers' works in that same era. In these movies, all sins were forgiven, sometimes even on deathbeds. An example was *According to the Code*, issued a year after the fiftieth anniversary but representative of the entire period. In the film, a wealthy Southern planter, forced into poverty by the war, is reunited with his daughter, whom he had banished from the plantation for marrying a Yankee. They embrace and pledge eternal love, and then he dies. Romance traveled down a different road in *The Colonel's Oath* (1913), in which a tough Confederate war veteran who banished his son for marrying a Northern girl meets his daughter-in-law and can no longer hate his son. All are reunited. In *The Copperhead* (1911), a Southern man disowns his son for fighting in the Northern army. They are reunited after the war in time for the son to help the father avoid financial ruin. In *A Daughter of Dixie* (1911), a lovely Southern belle falls in love with a Union officer, loves him throughout the war, and loses all her friends because of it. At war's end, however, when they are reunited, her friends embrace her once again, as all Americans embraced the nation. In *War Time Pals* (1910), Frank saves Al's life during the war. Years later, police arrest Frank for stealing food for his starving child. Al hears about it and not only gets Frank out of jail but finds him a job and takes him into his home.[38] In *Fifty Years Ago* (1911), two lifelong friends who met as enemies in the war reflect on the merits of reconciliation.[39]

Fathers were reunited with their children. In *A Dixie Mother* (1910), a man who banished his daughter for marrying a Yankee takes her—along with him—back in a heartwarming reunification scene.[40] In *The Coward* (1915), a father takes his Confederate son's place in the army when he thinks the boy has deserted. The son returns to save the regiment, but is shot by his own father. He somehow survives and the two are reunited at the end of the conflict. "It is only when [the father] is made to understand the day's victory is due to the great bravery of his son that reaction comes . . . the old man takes the son into his arms . . . [It is] a denouement that is to be remembered," wrote a critic for *Moving Picture World*.[41]

To achieve reconciliation, filmmakers stepped gingerly. Although death was plentiful, it was always death in war itself, not death specifically caused by someone. The dying on the battlefield was always blurred and always occurred on both sides, but at the end of battles viewers were never certain who won because filmmakers tried to amend the war into a conflict in which no one won or lost. By the fiftieth anniversary of the war's beginning in 1861, history was left with nothing but winners.

THE RECONCILIATION-AND-ASSIMILATION theme of the Civil War films in that era was not so different from a theme of films about immigrants. Producers of Jewish "ghetto films" often offered plots with intermarriage between Jews and Protestants. In the real world, such marriages were few, but the intermarriage theme helped bind the new Americans to the old to forge the new nation. Griffith moved on to *Intolerance* after his Civil War films and in it, with the Tower of Babel as his backdrop, told immigrants of all tongues in the United States that integration and cooperation were the keys to success in the New World. Later, in the 1924 silent epic *The Iron Horse*, the transcontinental railroad is completed only when immigrant workers patriotically finish the job without pay after they are asked to do so. Title cards in other movies constantly told immigrant audiences of "universal" truths in the Old Country and the New Country. To tie himself even closer to the "universal" language of all immigrants, German-born producer Carl Laemmle Sr. even named his new film studio Universal.

All of the film magazines of the era pushed immigrant assimilation, too. An editor for *Moving Picture World* wrote in 1910: "The motion picture brings its note of sympathy alike to the cultured and to the uncultured, to the children of opportunity and to the sons of toil. It is literature for the illiterate, for the man of limited opportunity, or alien tongue. It knows no boundary line of race or nation."[42]

A subtle theme of the movies about the new immigrants in the United States was that they needed to be assimilated into American society to strengthen it, that regardless of their origins the immigrants were now Americans. That is the same theme struck by the Civil War movies; that all Americans had to work together, regardless of their histories. Many of the "uncultured" in the audience, the millions of immigrants, were looking for a "culture"—a new American culture—they could call their own. They went to the movies often in order to understand their new country. These victims of prejudice, in and out of work, unable to earn or save much money, enjoyed the equality that the movie house gave all of its patrons, not just the wealthy. The plots onscreen told them again and again that they, too, could become rich in America through responsibility and hard work—they, too, could be like the wealthy people on the screen.

Audiences understood, too, as anyone watching these rather simplistic movies today understands, that the films were not only historical stories but history designed as fables—lessons and morals along with charges and cannon fire. The fables, in the form of these fifteen- and twenty-minute productions, became part of cultural history, as believable and effective as books and newspaper articles.

Americans in the silent-movie era wanted their country to be a united land that had long ago happened to stumble into a war about states' rights and survived it. Now, in hundreds of movies on its anniversary, they celebrated it. And in celebrating it they celebrated themselves.

CHAPTER THREE

Weeping Mothers, Southern Belles and Nan, the Girl Spy: The Civil War Film Family and the American Family

THE FATHER in a Northern family has enlisted in the Union army and gone off to war, as so many have, leaving his wife and children behind. While he is off with his regiment, just a few miles from his home, Confederate guerrillas attack the house and begin to ransack it, moving from room to room, tossing furniture about and ripping up bedspreads and clothing, threatening family members' lives. The man's terrified daughter, who knows where his regiment is camped, breaks free of the guerrillas and runs for help. A Union sentinel at the federal encampment, not knowing who she is, shoots her by mistake. She begins to fade into unconsciousness, but manages to tell the sentinel about her father and what is happening at home. Union soldiers, led by her father, ride at full gallop to the house and drive out the guerrillas. There is no celebration, however, because the father's little girl is still unconscious. Finally, under a surgeon's care, she recovers and the family and soldiers celebrate. The daughter is saved and the family kept intact.[1]

That story, the plot of the two-reeler *The Common Enemy*, released by William M. Selig's company in 1910,[2] established a common framework for the Civil War silent movie: the family on the screen as the family of the nation.

Families were torn apart by the war and, at the end of the final reel, reunited so that they could move into the future complete once again. Some families were divided during the movie as one brother rode off to fight for the South and the other for the North. In movies,

Dorothy West proudly shows off her newly sewn Confederate flag to her appreciative brother, Henry Walthall, in The House with Closed Shutters.

men in uniform left their posts when they heard the family at home was in trouble. Fighting stopped when someone heard that a soldier's son or daughter was injured and on the battlefield. Other movies centered on disputes between sons and parents that needed to be resolved through the war. The theme of so many Civil War silents was that the family onscreen was in trouble—just as the family of the nation was in trouble—and something had to be done to help.

In *Brother Against Brother* (1909), a Union colonel is ordered to execute his own brother, a Confederate. He can't do that, of course, because his brother and personal family must come ahead of the war and then the nation will still profit because the family is kept together. Instead, he helps his rebel brother escape.[3] In the Essanay studios' *He Fought for the U.S.A.* (1911), one brother joins the Union army and another the Confederate. The boy in the Union army winds up saving the life of his brother in a battle.[4] In Vitagraph's *A Southern Soldier's Sacrifice* (1911), a rebel dies helping his Union army brother escape from a Southern prison camp.[5] In *The Brothers' Feud,* two brothers in the Union army who are in love with the same girl end their dispute over the girl, and all their bitter divisiveness, beside the bed of their dying mother—in the old homestead.[6] In *A Brother's Redemption* (1911), a family's oldest son is told that because of his age, strength and experience, he is needed to run the homestead and cannot serve in the army. The family decides that someone must serve in the army, however, to uphold their honor as part of the nation's family. The younger brother takes the older brother's place in the army and is killed. As he lies dying, it is clear that he has sacrificed himself for his own family and, in uniform, for the family of the nation.[7]

In just about all of the brother-versus-brother movies, particularly ones that involved Southerners, the importance and honor of relatives came before the importance and honor of the army. In some movies, brothers hated each other and fought against each other. These were designed to show that only something as evil as war could turn brother against brother.

Another familiar theme was the soldier who sneaks home to see his loved ones in jeopardy, at the risk of being executed for desertion by a firing squad. He always gets into trouble and is absolved when superiors learn that he has put devotion to family ahead of personal safety. In *Silent Heroes* (1913), the boy who goes home to visit his dying mother is called a coward by his army buddies. He proves his valor by leading a victorious charge against the enemy.[8] In *A Child of War* (1913), a Union soldier on sentry duty shoots his own daughter by accident. He carries her in his arms to his nearby farmhouse so his wife can care for her. He is arrested and ordered to be shot for leaving his post, but the wounded daughter comes forward to explain what happened and he is not only pardoned but congratulated for his actions.[9] In *The Heart of Lincoln* (1915), Colonel Jason leaves his Confederate regiment without approval to visit his very ill wife and daughter on their plantation. He is captured en route by a Union officer, who lets him go when he hears of the colonel's mission. The Union officer is arrested and sentenced to death for allowing an enemy to go free. But the colonel's daughter then leaves her sickbed and travels to Washington to plead, successfully, with President Lincoln to pardon both her father and the officer.[10] In *Baby Betty* (1912), a man discovers his small daughter ill and lying still in the middle of a battlefield while both sides fight around her. He signals to both North and South that this is his little girl and the battle stops as he revives her and then lifts her in his arms and carries her out of danger.[11] In *The Home of a Soldier* (1913), a man leaves the middle of a battle when told his nearby farm is on fire—and that his wife is in danger. Officers place him under arrest for desertion, but the army frees him when it learns he deserted to help his family.[12]

In some screenplays, the idea of family was extended to embrace the community. In *The Guerrilla Menace* (1913), two young Confederate soldiers are told of a Northern guerrilla band threatening their nearby hometown. They leave their regiment and together drive the marauding Union guerrillas away, protecting their families and, by extension, their community.[13]

The honor of motherhood and fatherhood was sacred in the silents about the Civil War, and a man's devotion to the idea of family, even if someone else's, was part of his personal honor and the honor of the nation. In *Lieutenant Gray*, brave young Lieutenant Gray is about to be executed as a spy when members of a Southern family he saved from guerrillas plead his case to General Grant.[14] Here honor comes before war. Mothers thought of each other. In *His Mother's Boy*, a Southern woman has the chance to kill the Union spy who killed her son. She can't, she says in subtitles, because in her mind she can see that boy's mother. She cannot fulfill the biblical code of an eye for an eye, cannot hurt another mother.[15]

Many Civil War features focused on the bravery of small children who save their parents or home. In *The Little Confederate* (1910), a Southern boy befriends a Union officer and talks the soldier into releasing his father, held captive by the regiment. In *Daddy's Boy and Mammy* (1911), a tiny Southern lad disguises himself as a Union army drummer boy with a regiment at a federal prison where his father is being held. He becomes friendly with prison guards and, after deceiving them, helps his father escape and returns with him to home and family.[16] In *A Little Lad in Dixie* (1911), the son of a Confederate soldier takes his wounded father's rifle and defends the pass that leads to his family's farm. He dies in his mother's arms, just as those who take up arms to defend the nation would die in the arms of the nation.[17]

Just as brothers took the place of slain brothers in army ranks, children did the same. A young Southern girl in *The Drummer Girl of Vicksburg,* disguised as a boy, takes the place of her slain drummer boy brother. She is captured in battle and, in a perfect reconciliation ending, marries the soldier who captured her.[18]

The theme of children and young people having a duty to help the family preserve its honor was apparent in several films. In *Heart Throbs* (1913), a Vermont mother banishes her daughter after the girl marries a Southerner. The husband is killed in the war and their plantation is ruined. The mother still refuses to reconcile with her daughter and the young woman dies in poverty.[19] Children often saved not only their family but also the nation, or their side. Sometimes the family paid a terrible price to stay together and to preserve its honor. In *The Boomerang* (1913), a Confederate spy kills his own father, who refuses to acknowledge the son's role in the war.[20] In *According to the Code* (1916), a wealthy plantation owner banishes his daughter because she has married a Northerner. In one heartbreaking feature film, *The Great Sacrifice* (1913), a man returns from war, beaten and bloodied, to learn that his wife, assuming he had been killed, has married his brother. In a very touching scene, he finds them together and realizes that they have come to love each other. He is careful not to let them see him, so that they will continue to believe him dead, and he slowly fades away, another victim of the war.

Another theme, the disgrace of cowardice, underscored the penalties for those who abandon or betray loved ones. In *The Favorite Son* (1913), one brother, Bill, not only saves his cowardly brother's life on the battlefield but later helps him escape from prison.[21] His reward: the coward tries to steal his sweetheart. The ending: the coward is killed in combat. The moral: don't betray family; don't betray the nation.

Cowardice was a stain on honor for nation and family and brought tragic consequences. A father in *The Field of Honor* (1917) is shot in battle by his own men when he runs from a fight. He cannot bring himself to tell his son he was a coward and kills himself.[22] One of the most heartbreaking films about father-son relations in the face of cowardice was *The Honor of His Family* (1909).[23] A man in the Confederate army flees the battlefield and runs home. His disgusted father shoots and kills him. Then the father slings his son's dead body over his shoulder and carries him back to the middle of the battlefield so that his comrades will think he died a hero in the war, not a coward on the run; thus the father preserves his son's honor, and his own.

Sometimes, it is true, movie film plots redeemed cowards, often through some contrived twist of circumstance or coincidence. In a film already discussed in the previous chapter, *The Coward* (1915), a Confederate deserts his post and, by accident, overhears enemy plans for an assault on the rebel camp, where his father is a soldier. He races back to camp and is shot by his own father, who does not know who he is. With his father's help, the wounded boy limps to the general's tent to convey the enemy attack plan; he saves the army and regains his father's love.[24]

All of these silent movies about families added an important personal connection for audiences with the Civil War they saw on screen. The heavy concentration on families, whether on parents and soldiers or wives and lovers and soldiers, helped to depoliticize the war. The films showed love and honor in families North and South and tried to make the audience see that men fought first for their families, not political goals. These stories also helped to soften the impact of any battle scenes in the films and support the idea that the war was never political, just an event that unfortunately happened.

In reality, American families were devastated by the war. Tens of thousands of women welcomed home husbands who were badly maimed in the war and could not work again, or could find only menial work. A large percentage of an entire generation on both sides lost fathers in the war. It was the most family-wrenching war in American history.

The beginning of the Civil War coincided with a new era in American family life. The old rural society where families worked together on farms to make the family's living was being replaced by the family in which the man worked away from home, the woman sometimes did so, and more and more children worked, either in stores or in the factories of the growing industrial revolution. Americans were proud of the new family and, moving about outside the home, a new sense of public participation, which gave rise to the abolitionist movement in the North.[25] The fervor of the evangelical religious movement of the 1840s was dying out as more families tested the new variety of religious denominations beginning to flourish throughout the nation.

Despite waning formal religious affiliation, men and women felt a great spiritual need for stronger families and better lives. They saw the war as a chance to achieve "spiritual resolution" and made it the focus of their generation.[26]

Men who went off to war wrote continually of how they missed their loved ones back home. Almost every letter home asked for news of how family members were doing. This was a way for them to know that no matter what horror they lived through in war, the family was always there for them upon their return.[27] Filmmakers liked this detail because Civil War silents were usually Southern-oriented and scenes of Southern soldiers returning to run-down farms in counties ravaged by the Union army were especially poignant.

Soldiers in silent films, as in real life, tried to replicate family life in camp, too, creating small, family-sized units in tent arrangements, dinner parties and small social cliques such as sports organizations or literary clubs. The re-creation of the small, friendly, and very reliable family unit in war helped get soldiers through the conflict.

At the end of the war, soldiers from both North and South returned to relatives who had suffered greatly. To ease everyone's pain, many families tried to forget the conflict and focus on prewar times. Despite the harshness of postwar Reconstruction, in the decades following the war there was great sympathy from families in the North for families in the South. Southern veterans in particular made their wives an important part of the postwar commemorations. Many United Confederate Veterans chapters had women's auxiliaries, such as the United Daughters of the Confederacy. These women played an important role in fund-raising for monuments, annual gatherings, national conventions, parades and meetings. Together with the men, such women's groups carefully reconstructed the antebellum, family-oriented South. Their broad-based membership gave these organizations enormous public visibility and the authority to help perpetuate the idea of the Lost Cause.[28]

As soon as the war was over, both sides were eager for the reunified family as symbolized by the union of North and South in the nation. One of the first of many books to express that theme was *Miss Ravenel's Conversion from Secession to Loyalty*, by John William De Forest, a prodigious fiction writer of the postwar era. The novel tells the story of a Southern girl married to a Virginian who betrays the

South by fighting for the North. She soon realizes that he is being unfaithful to her just as he is unfaithful to the South. Naturally, the betrayer of family and nation is killed in the war. The widow, Lillie, then falls in love with and marries an unglamorous but hardworking and trustworthy Union captain, Colburne, with whom she lives happily ever after. This plot suggested, as so many postwar stories did, that honorable men and women of the two sections could trust each other and live in harmony the same way the sections themselves could.[29]

The role of the woman in the antebellum period, especially the single woman, was an important element of Civil War feature films about families. In the silents, Southern girls were always loyal to their beaux gone off to fight the Yankees, but those without beaux tended to fall in love with Union soldiers. In *The Blacksmith's Love* (1911), a Confederate soldier's wife believes he is dead and remarries, to a Yankee. When she learns her first husband has survived the war she leaves her new groom and goes back to him, unable to substitute a Northern family for a Southern one. Loyalty switches were a popular theme. In the Biograph movie *The Blue and the Gray* (1913), a Northern girl falls in love with a Confederate soldier who saves her from the abuse of her drunken Union soldier beau and his comrades. That shift was taken further in *A Daughter of Dixie* (1911). In that Champion Company film, a Southern girl protects her Union sweetheart from a band of Confederate soldiers led by her own brother, rejecting the rebel nation and family to follow her heart to her own family. Like so many Civil War features, it emphasized that in 1911 the important thing was that Northerners and Southerners were all Americans.

In the many films in which Southern girls fell in love with Union soldiers the mythmakers were telling audiences that that could happen rather easily because, after all, the Union soldier was not an enemy and not a foreigner; he was an American. It underlined the idea, too, that Southern women in the silent era should see Northern men not as the enemy in the war or in 1912, but as potential lovers, and that Northern men should see how exciting Southern women were. If these women could fall in love with honorable Union soldiers, then the Southern soldiers they fell in love with were honorable, too, and this made men and women on both sides good and worthy. Unfortunately, they had been pitted against each other in a senseless war started by neither, but by a nefarious third party, the radical abolitionists. (There are no movies in which Southern or Northern women are seen falling in love with abolitionists.)

THE WOMEN in Civil War films were divided into three types: the dutiful mother, the lover and the spy. The dutiful mother was a figure that has endured throughout war films. One of the most striking scenes in *All Quiet on the Western Front,* the somber 1930 film about World War I, was of an aging mother embracing her son one last time before he goes off to war. That figure was seen again and again in World War II movies, in which the dutiful mother was always a very separate woman from the lover.

The dutiful mother in Civil War silents was an amusing distortion, like so many Civil War film distortions, because in reality she wasn't very different from the lover figure. Several thousand soldiers on both sides in the Civil War were under the age of eighteen, some as young as ten or eleven. Women gave birth much earlier in life in the mid-nineteenth century, some at sixteen or seventeen. Many of the real-life mothers of North and South, therefore, were just thirty-two or thirty-three years old themselves, hardly the doughty old types portrayed on film. They were as much lovers as the lovers depicted onscreen, though they could never be portrayed that way. The mother always looked the same, whether North or South, and she was always pivotal in a family drama. She had to be sturdy because the nation was sturdy. The mothers on film, whether burying their husbands, crying for their sons away at war or praying by candlelight for peace, had to represent the motherhood of a nation praying for an end to the struggle of 1861–1865.

One of the most interesting movies about mothers was *Right or Wrong* (1911). A Southern soldier steals across enemy lines to visit his dying mother. A Union soldier follows him with the intention of killing him, but cannot raise his rifle when he sees the poor old woman lying in the arms of her loving son.[30] Mothers were unfailingly patriotic. In *A Spartan Mother* (1912), a young Southern boy whose father and brother have been killed in the war flees a battle and runs home to his mother. The mother gives him the family's Confederate flag (merging personal family and national family) and tells him to go back to his regiment. Revived by his mother's love and his nation's flag, the boy goes back and promptly leads a charge that wins the battle.[31] At no time were mothers portrayed as the love interests of fathers, or as women with any real romantic or sexual needs. Their only role in these movies was to tearfully say goodbye to their sons going to war and tearfully welcome them back upon their return.

The young women, the lovers, in Civil War silents were all the same, too. They were luscious young girls, the focus of every oversexed young soldier's dream. However, they were seen as delicate little porcelain dolls—very chaste porcelain dolls, the cinematic products of the Victorian Age, when young women were the unattainable objects of desire. The Victorian woman of the 1860s, in the 1903–1915 period, served as a reminder to women to keep their place in the domestic sphere and not attempt to invade the male sphere—the voting booth (this was at the height of the woman suffrage movement) or the workplace.

Much of this image was carved out by D. W. Griffith. In the 1908–1915 period he defined the woman of the Civil War as a Victorian princess: beautiful, cultivated, well-mannered, well-dressed and shortly to be a fine wife and wonderful mother. No director showcased women as lovely virgins and good people the way D. W. Griffith did. In Civil War movies, she was moving through a dimension just before all of that, the courtship dimension, and primed for deep romantic affairs with good-looking men who wandered into her life. These were all soldiers, almost always in uniform. The idea that no woman can resist a soldier in uniform became one of the enduring myths of American culture. But these romantic affairs were never consummated in bed—Victorians could not be seen that way. The affairs had to end in marriage. Griffith's view, in sum, was that of an archetypically nineteenth-century man. According to critic Marjorie Rosen, writing in *Popcorn Venus*: "His puritanism was usually reflected in the conservative manner in which he [Griffith] handled his female characters. Griffith, because of his genteel Southern upbringing and Victorian heritage, gravitated toward and was most comfortable with the same sexless doll women the Victorians extolled, the pure and purely ornamental children that excited Torvald Helmer in Henrik Ibsen's *A Doll's House*."[32]

Women in silent films, on through the late 1920s, were idealized as virgin-heroines. There was a double-edged interpretation of the screen virgin, however. The beautiful virgin from the 1850s represented chaste and perfect Victorian womanhood in the era and her unblemished perfection represented the nation. If the nation put its women on a pedestal, it put itself on a pedestal. Men who viewed women as virgin-heroines were elevating themselves. Their recognition of women as virgin-heroines made them honorable; honorable men made an honorable nation.[33]

Lillian Gish, the pure heroine in Griffith's *The Birth of a Nation*, was a perfect virgin-heroine. So was Mary Pickford, discovered by Griffith in 1909, who made a career out of chastity. Pickford's carefully groomed screen persona of a doll-like virgin, admired by all women and cherished and honored by all men, made her "America's Sweetheart."[34] Bad-girl vamps, such as Theda Bara, represented the fallen woman, and any men who continued to like fallen women were fallen men, and dishonored.

Southern white women were even more venerated in films during the reunification period of America, 1865–1900, because their men had clung to them as they tried to sort out new roles for themselves in an integrated region overrun with freed blacks who they feared would take their jobs and sleep with their women. As long as their women were pure, Southern white men were pure and their nation was pure. In sanctifying their women, they elevated themselves and held down black men.[35]

What Civil War movies did for women in the 1910–1920 period was to show that since the 1860s women had been virgin-heroines and admired by men. It reinforced the view that most women at the time had of themselves and the view men had of them. Those films kept them on a pedestal, convincing them that historically they were right.

Some film historians have seen 1910-era women as extensions of the Victorian women[36] who curtailed their sexual desires, convinced that sentiment and romance were more important than physical lust. Such Victorian women also used held-in sexuality as a way to rein in their husbands and help guide the marriage. Their right to determine the time and place of sexual relations also gave them power in their marriage that they did not have in the social milieu of the era.[37] Filmmakers of 1915 were mostly men and eager to remind the women who were so eager to vote, work in department stores and factories and become equal participants in the male social world that they should be more like the Victorian women of 1861. The women who ran families, and not offices, were idealized in 1915, even if they didn't buy as many theater tickets as women who worked outside the home.[38]

The women in the Civil War movies fell in love with Confederate soldiers and Union soldiers with equal ease, but always gave away only their hearts, not their bodies. They swooned from Florida to Maine, pledged eternal love to short men and tall men, heavy men and thin men, with the implicit understanding that sex could come only with marriage and marriage could come only with the end of the war. The valiant soldiers, then, were not only fighting for victory and the reunification of the nation; victory would also bring unification with their women in marriage and in bed.

Directors invited their actresses to be as feminine as possible, but the characters onscreen could never actually give in to male lust.[39] After they had teased their soldier boys unmercifully, they had to do just about anything to avoid sex. If there was a code of honor in the Old South, there was an even stronger one in movies about the Old South: no sex please, we're Southern.

Women characters who gave in to the sexual ardor of their lovers, or who were at the point of having to give in, suffered terrible consequences because they had sinned. Elsie Stoneman, in *The Birth of a Nation,* is lusted after by a mulatto, who at least proposes marriage as he reaches for her, and backs off far enough that she can faint to avoid the seduction. In that same film, as we have seen, Flora Cameron is confronted with an even worse fate at the hands of a black soldier.[40] The black, of course, is the ultimate sinner in film—he tries to rape a Victorian white woman.

In most movies, sex was veiled, spunk was showcased and women were used as a means to absolve everyone, North and South, of guilt about the war. In film after film, women, North and South, are uncertain which side is in the right and therefore feel no guilt if they fall in love with a soldier, no matter which side. Which side a man was fighting for didn't matter, directors intimated, because the woman knew— although no one else did—that when the war ended the nation, just like the family, would be reunited.

That theme runs through *The Little Yank* (1917), in which a woman in a border state, neither North nor South, falls in love with a Confederate officer, even though politically her sympathies are with the North. Here again, the theme is that it doesn't matter whom she falls in love with because no one is wrong. She then finds herself caught in the middle of a pitched battle between the two armies. The boys stop fighting when they see her, let her pass through both lines to get to her home, and then resume fighting. The war stops for the woman—object of everyone's desire—who at war's end reunites the warriors.[41]

Women were also used to show that even bad deeds in war could lead to good deeds and true love at the end of it. In *A Maid at War* (1912), Eva breaks up with her sweetheart when he enlists in the Union army. In his clothes she finds dispatches that he has stolen from her Confederate soldier brother. Eva, with love of South greater than love of man, turns him in and he is arrested. Then, at the end of the war, when all is forgiven, the sweetheart comes back to the South and marries her.[42] These were the safe women, the women who lived according to the Victorian code.

There were exceptions: the "wild" women, the girl spies. Historically, there were several female spies, such as Belle Boyd. But there were not many and they were not very successful. If old photos are reliable, they were not very good-looking either. In the silents, there were more beautiful girl spies than there were trees in the Vienna Woods. Besides Nan, the girl spy,[43] who spied for the South, there were others in different films and film series. There was Pauline Cushman, an actress who quit the Broadway stage to spy for the North. There was the female spy in *The Daughter of the Confederacy* (1913), not to be confused with the female spy in a different movie, produced that same year, also called *The Daughter of the Confederacy*, not to be confused with the girl spy in *A Daughter of Dixie* (1916). Other spies included Sally the spy, Norma the girl spy, Ethel the spy and Virginia Cary, girl spy. There were more than forty silents about girl spies, twelve starring Nan.

The "wild" woman, the adventurous opposite of the prim Victorian, had been established through the real-life Annie Oakley in Buffalo Bill's Wild West Show, and in various characters such as Calamity Jane in dime novels, so the girl spies were not outside the realm of acceptability. As spies, of course, they had plenty of opportunity to meet and fall in love with soldiers on both sides of the war as well as civilians, but not once did a girl spy ever give in to a soldier's sexual

One of the standard wrinkles in the silents was the teenage girl who dresses as a boy in order to get into the fight, such as young Vivian Martin in Her Father's Son.

lust—and never once did they dawdle with a man at the expense of their mission. Many in the audiences loved them because they not only represented a sense of great adventure but proved that women could be as effective as men in a national crisis. Women, like men, would rush to volunteer to work for the army as spies. The producers who made the spy movies, and their writers, presented them to the "new woman" who was emerging in America, the working woman who sought more independence from her husband and family.

However, in spite of the few spy films, most filmmakers preferred the more popular, chaste Civil War lover whom they used to combat the adventurous "new women," who had begun to move out of their homes into the consumer society of the early 1900s. Not only were there many women in the workforce (8 percent of all union workers were women by this time), but many lived alone outside the home. These women were seen by civic groups, educators and church leaders as adrift and certain to meet a terrible fate, particularly prostitution or kidnapping by men involved in the white slave trade. The new women were the first wave of the women's movement—working towards equality in the workplace and in the voting booth—but there was much resistance to their lifestyles. Civil War films assured audiences that it was the chaste women and comfortable mothers, and not machine press operators and salesgirls, whom men came home to.

IF FAMILIES could reunite, and if, onscreen, Northern boys could marry Southern girls and Southern mothers save the lives of Northern boys, then, the mythmakers would have had audiences believe, the nation—North and South—was solid during the 1860s. The United States might have been torn apart by the abolitionists, but it was reunited and stronger than ever after the war. That total reconciliation could not be achieved only by soldiers on the battlefield. Filmmakers believed the whole nation had to be shown, including the women and lovers back home, children and friends. So by 1915, the fiftieth anniversary of the end of the war, these family-themed movies showed audiences that women were just as important as men in bringing the two sections back together, gently helping to bind up the nation's wounds, heal it and make it whole once more. After all, neither side was the enemy. Neither side was a foreign power. These were all Americans in 1865. They were strong and brave then and strong and brave in 1915, too. And they always would be.

CHAPTER FOUR

South of the Mason-Dixon Line:
Political Distortions

THE MAJORITY of silent Civil War films' stories began after the shelling of Fort Sumter.[1] Historically, it was the South's attack on Sumter that began the war; it was then that President Lincoln called up seventy-five thousand troops. But filmmakers realized that the Confederates could not be presented as victims if they were shown to have started the war. Since Sumter could not be explained away, it was ignored. Lincoln's troop call-up was conveniently penciled into the scripts of most silents as the cause of the war.

This permitted the Confederates to appear perpetually on the defensive. The rebels, who always began Civil War films as the victims—the innocent, assaulted party—were then portrayed fighting for what was right and protecting home and hearth against Northern agitators. They were a gray-costumed David battling a federal Goliath. Too-close attention to the actual political history of the 1850s and 1860s would have ruined that portrayal of the Southerner as the aggrieved party, and spoiled the Plantation Myth. Probing would reveal among other things slavery, evangelical religion, miscegenation on plantations, ill-educated Southern children, disease, poor Southern economic planning, quarrels over the territories and the Southern split in the Democratic Party, rebel guerrilla raiders in Missouri and Kansas, the uproar over the *Dred Scott* decision, the Missouri Compromise and the fractured election of 1860. This was not a terrain filmmakers of the silent era wanted to explore. Instead, they continually suggested that meddling by radical abolitionists was the sole cause of the war. That not only made the Confederates the gallant victims, but neatly got around the entire slavery question.

A scene from The Raid *(1954), a film about a Confederate attack in 1864 on St. Alban's, Vermont, in which the raiders, to raise money for the faltering Southern government, robbed three banks, and then torched the town. Films about such attacks on Northern towns were few and far between, because they were at odds with Hollywood's traditional view of Northerners as the aggressors in the war.*

The political storms that brought on the war can be traced back to the signers of the Declaration of Independence, who refused to include anything about freedom for slaves for fear that Southern delegates, many of whom were slaveholders themselves, would refuse to sign. The slavery dispute continued unabated through the years.[2] In 1808, Congress outlawed the importing of slaves from Africa. The abolition movement began in earnest in the early 1830s and, with strong backing from the Quakers, Protestant churches and the evangelical Christian movement, its adherents pressed the slavery issue daily in both North and South.[3] Several Congresses refused to decide the question of slavery and politicians kept passing political compromises to please the demanding South. The Missouri Compromise, in

1820, was one and the Compromise of 1850 was another. The Kansas-Nebraska Act of 1854, championed by Stephen Douglas, the leading Democrat of the era, was a third. That bill permitted each territory to decide whether or not it wanted slavery. It caused a firestorm in both North and South because it was strongly supported in the South, and it opened the door to any other territories deciding for slavery, too.[4] The Democratic Party split over slavery. Democratic leaders from the Southern states voted down any legislation that might curtail slavery and eliminate opportunities for any Southerners who wanted to move to the vast new territories with slave labor. Many Northern Democrats were against slavery. The other major political organization prior to the Republicans was the Whig Party. Whigs, too, were split, North and South, on the slavery issue, and their party collapsed.[5] A brand-new group, the Republican Party, a coalition of different elements, emerged from the turmoil with opposition to slavery as its main issue.[6]

In the 1860 election, Southern Democrats refused to support their compromising champion, Stephen Douglas. Their convention, held in Charleston, was little more than an organized riot. Factions battled for days over every single word in the platform, debating slavery well into the night and arguing for hours over whether to give Douglas the nomination. The convention broke up in chaos with no nominee yet chosen when the Southerners stormed out, abandoning Douglas, who was finally renominated at a second convention. Southerners then supported independent presidential campaigns by John C. Breckinridge and John Bell. Between them the two polled 1,438,660 votes, which if added to Douglas's 1.37 million would have been far more than the votes for Lincoln, who received only 1.8 million (but carried enough large states to win in the electoral college).[7] It was the Southerners who wrecked the Democratic Party and brought about the election of Lincoln.

The president-elect begged the South to remain in the Union, but within two months of his election five of the Southern states seceded and formed the Confederate States of America. In his first inaugural address Lincoln told the seceding states that the Union would not be the bully in any dispute. "You can have no conflict without being yourselves the aggressors," he said.[8] One month later, Confederate forces opened fire on Fort Sumter to begin the war. That was when Lincoln called for seventy-five thousand volunteers and the war commenced in earnest.

It was the Southern politicians, who represented the wealthy and politically powerful planter elite, who ruined the Democratic Party, who continually blocked antislavery laws in Congress, and who forced compromises that expanded slavery. It was the Southern states that defiantly seceded from the Union and the Southern forces that bombarded Fort Sumter. The South, then, was the continual political troublemaker from 1776 to 1861. The silent movies' version—that Northern abolitionists and the Union army were the aggressors and the South the aggrieved victim—was a complete revision of history.

Worst of all, Hollywood producers and directors deliberately forgot slavery, the single, root cause of the war. Filmmakers produced hundreds of films that ignored its emotional and physical abuses, from the murder of slaves to the sale of family members, and instead showed Americans a soft and gentle land where slaves were content with their lot. This blatant omission in film, the most powerful medium of all, made any true understanding of real history nearly impossible and was one of the causes of the racial strife that exists in America to this day.

Since most movies' time frame began after the attack on Fort Sumter, the nation's oversized political characters, on both sides, almost never appear in any of them (although Stephen Douglas is portrayed in the few prewar Lincoln features and Jefferson Davis, the Confederate president, sometimes makes a cameo appearance to pardon a soldier or accept some plans from a spy). Strong political power brokers in the North, such as William Seward, William Lloyd Garrison, Edwin Stanton and Horace Greeley, who opposed slavery, and their counterparts in the South, such as Alexander Stephens and Robert Toombs, who favored it, are conveniently overlooked to avoid any controversy over the causes of the war.

Generals appeared infrequently in silents. Few of the important generals in either army were in uniform when Fort Sumter was bombarded. Grant was a hardware store clerk, Sherman was headmaster of a Southern military school, Robert Toombs was a United States senator, Nathaniel Banks was governor of Massachusetts and Stonewall Jackson was a college professor.[9] To tell their stories filmmakers would have to confront the reasons why they went into the army, and face the politics of the time, North and South, that brought on the war.

General Ulysses S. Grant was shown as a character in several silents, but only in a subsidiary role. Despite his legendary career in the army and the presidency, Grant was never the subject of his own movie and always wound up as a bit character in films about Lincoln, Custer and even Mark Twain. He was first shown in *The Bugle Call* (1909) and then in *Lieutenant Gray* (1911) and *Grant and Lincoln* (1911).[10] Donald Crisp, who went on to become one of filmdom's finest actors, played Grant in *The Birth of a Nation* (1915) and in the 1920s Walter Rogers played him in six other films. Grant would be shown in another dozen films in the 1940s and the early 1960s.[11] The former hardware store clerk who became the commander of the

General William Tecumseh Sherman (John Wayne, left) talks with General Ulysses S. Grant (Henry Morgan) in How the West Was Won. *Sherman appeared in a few silents, but there were no biographies of generals on either side in the sound era. Explaining their stories would have meant an exploration of the reasons for the war, which studios wanted to avoid.*

Union army and later president was always portrayed the same way—unkempt dirty blue uniform, hat tilted back, hair awry, cigar sticking defiantly out of the corner of his mouth. Except for his brief appearance in *The Birth of a Nation,* Grant was always shown pardoning a spy, reuniting two lovers separated by the war, commuting a death sentence or nodding his head in conversations with Lincoln.

Robert E. Lee began to be shown in bit parts in silents in *The Love Romance of the Girl Spy* (1910). He appeared as a character in *Service under Johnston and Lee* (1911), *A Man's Duty* (1912), *With Lee in Virginia* (1913), *Between Two Fires* (1914), *The Warrens of Virginia* (1924) and *The Heart of General Lee* (1928). He and George Meade were substantial characters in the silent epic *The Battle of Gettysburg* (1913), but Lee was not the central character in any other Civil War film until another *Gettysburg,* made in 1993. Any historically accurate movie about Lee would have shown him as a staunch Unionist (Mexican War hero and commandant of West Point) who joined the Confederate army after much soul-searching.[12] That soul-searching would have dragged in all the social, cultural and political issues of the day, particularly the slavery issue, and this would not do—even surrounding the South's most glorious hero. To maintain the myth, filmmakers producing one- and two-reelers made two American military legends mere ornaments in their films.

Surprisingly, the general most often shown was Philip Sheridan, the Union commander whose twenty-mile ride to rally his troops in full retreat at the battle of Winchester in 1864 became the subject of one of the country's best-remembered poems, "Sheridan's Ride," depicted in four different silents.[13] Sheridan reappeared as a character in dozens of 1940s and 1950s westerns about the Indian Wars of the 1870s and 1880s, in which he had participated. The reasons for all the movies about Sheridan had little to do with North or South. His twenty-mile gallop made for wonderful action footage and moviegoers loved that. It also brought in Sheridan's faithful and famous steed Rienzi to rival Don the Wonder Horse.[14] Other generals from the Union who turned up in small roles in silents were Joe Hooker and George Armstrong Custer. Southern Generals included Stonewall Jackson, James Longstreet and J. E. B. Stuart.[15]

Oddly, Hollywood's Southern bias did not carry over into depicting the life of Union general William Tecumseh Sherman, who on his

"March to the Sea" in the fall of 1864 and his swing up into South Carolina in the winter of 1865 destroyed nearly everything in his path. Sherman's pillaging army appears to have been portrayed only three times, in *Hearts and Flags* (1912), *When Sherman Marched to the Sea* (1913) and *The Birth of a Nation* (1915), but the general ("War is hell"), who should have been an obvious target for pro-Southern filmmakers because of his destruction of every small village in his way and the wholesale burning of Atlanta, for some reason appeared in only a handful of the five hundred silent films about the war.

A further distortion springing from the Civil War silents and magnified in the sound movies that followed was the idea that politically and militarily the South never had a chance to win the conflict. This was necessary to position the South as the underdog, and have its soldiers fighting on, risking their lives, in their magnificent "lost cause." In reality the South was an underdog only in numbers, and numbers don't tell the entire story. The Union army as a whole did outnumber the rebel army, three to two, throughout the war and at some key battles, such as Gettysburg (eighty-eight thousand to seventy-five thousand). But there were many battles in which the two sides were relatively even in troop numbers, and sometimes the South outnumbered the North, for example at Chattanooga, where the South had sixty-four thousand men and the North just fifty-six thousand. At Mechanicsville, in the 1862 Peninsular Campaign, the rebels outnumbered the federals sixteen thousand to fifteen thousand.[16] Even in battles in which they were outnumbered, the rebels often won or forced a draw.[17] At Gettysburg, the North's greatest victory and the South's greatest defeat, the rebels might have won if not for the ill-planned and disastrous "Pickett's Charge."

The North may have had the larger army, but the South certainly had the better generals. Lee, the United States' best prewar military officer, was offered command of the Union army by Lincoln, but, loyal to Virginia, he left to fight for the South. He was joined by James Longstreet and J. E. B. Stuart. Thomas "Stonewall" Jackson, another West Point graduate, had fought in the Mexican War and later, while teaching at the Virginia Military Institute, studied tactics and strategy and developed considerable skills in those critical areas of warfare. The North at first was led by the charismatic but inept General George McClellan, who refused to engage the enemy for months, giving the South time to train its growing army.[18] Lincoln fired McClellan and went through a string of bungling generals until he settled on Grant. Weak commanders, in sum, often eliminated the federals' numerical advantage.

The North had a navy and the South did not, but the North's navy was substandard, with only 45 ships ready for action when the war began.[19] Its modest size prevented it early on from seizing any major Southern ports besides New Orleans (1862) and made it ineffective on the high seas. Union ineptitude also hurt the Navy. The federals guarding naval yards at Norfolk and Pensacola were surprised by Confederate attacks in the spring of 1861 and lost both key bases. The Union Navy was finally reorganized and grew quickly. Eventually it had 641 ships and blockaded most Southern ports throughout the war, cutting down on food and ammunition imports.[20]

The South quickly outfitted commercial ships for military duty and put to sea a small navy that was reasonably effective until the end of the war. The Southern navy was augmented by privateers—blockade runners (the fictional Rhett Butler was one) who continually outwitted and outran federal ships to deliver goods to the South. Although these blockade runners were stopped entirely by 1864, as the U.S. Navy grew, they were effective for most of three years, providing enough supplies to allow the Southern army to fight.

According to Civil War historian James McPherson, the South had several opportunities to win the war.[21] The Rebels actually won the first major engagement at Bull Run, just outside Washington, D.C. But they failed to chase the Union army back into the capital— a move that might have ended the war right there. The South had another chance to win at Antietam, in Maryland, when they invaded the North, but could do no better than a draw. Gettysburg was a third opportunity, which was lost with Pickett's Charge. As late as 1864, General Jubal Early surprised the federals with an attack on Washington, D.C., that almost succeeded. Local units guarding the capital had to be supplemented with large volunteer forces to push the Rebels back.

There are a number of other explanations for why the South did not win the war. England was a factor, too. Southern diplomats were certain England would either enter the war on their side or supply them with enough arms and money to win. British politicians, wary of backing the wrong side, waited. Until the end of 1864, public opinion in the North wasn't fully committed to the war. (In the summer of 1863, when a new draft was called, Northerners, fed up, rioted in New York, lynching six blacks.)[22] Viewing the course of the war politically, historians have charged that the South might have won if Lee had never invaded the North. They believe that his defeats demoralized the Southern citizenry. The Rebels, some have argued, should have merely defended Southern ports and cities and kept the Union troops at bay, in the plausible hope that after several years of mounting casualties Northern public opinion would force the Lincoln administration to end the war. The South also missed a chance to bring about a negotiated peace by devoting only small efforts to defeating Lincoln in the presidential election of 1864.

The South did not really lose the war until the fall of 1864, when Sheridan chased all the Confederates out of Virginia's Shenandoah Valley, Grant began to march on Petersburg and Richmond, Sherman burned Atlanta and commenced his March to the Sea, and the federal navy captured Mobile Bay, in Alabama. By 1864, too, the naval blockade was finally effective. And in that year England finally officially told the South that it would not provide help (although leading British politicians had made that determination in late 1862). Southern troop strength dwindled in 1864, too, because the supply of men had just about run out. When the war began, there were only about one million men over eighteen in the South (although some boys under eighteen did fight). By 1864, nearly all of them were in the army or had been killed or wounded, and the Confederacy had difficulty recruiting fresh troops. Conversely, the year 1864 saw the Union army at full strength. The North not only had five times as many men over eighteen, but by 1864 had more than 300,000 black freedmen and former slaves in all-black regiments, with 178,895 in combat. The Union army was so strong in 1864 that soldiers wrote home bitterly that they had had no chance to fight and been put in reserve.[23]

But, for more than three years, North and South fought evenly and the South had several chances for victory. The Hollywood view that Southern soldiers were from the beginning fighting for a "lost cause" was historically inaccurate, but it fit perfectly with screenwriters' desire to show noble underdogs.

CHAPTER FIVE

Rastus Loves His Pork Chops: African Americans from Sambo to Mammy

IT WAS A TYPICAL brightly colored poster announcing the latest Pathé Frères movie about American blacks. It hung on the front, street-side wall of a small nickelodeon in Journal Square, in the teeming business district of Jersey City, New Jersey. One of the city's streetcar tracks ran directly in front of the theater. That location made the theater easily accessible to viewers who wanted to duck in to see the fifteen-minute film on their lunch hour or in the afternoon or evening. On the poster, three white men are pulling a huge U.S. mailbag towards the back of a post office. Sticking out of the top of the cinched bag is the woeful face of bearded black Rastus, eyebrows shooting upwards in his familiar pose. Fans of the Rastus movies knew that he was off on another adventure. This one, starring the "comical darky with a faculty for getting into scrapes," was titled *Rastus' Riotous Ride* and involved good old black Rastus being driven around the city in the back of a postal truck and unceremoniously dumped on street corners.[1] It was one of the tamer Rastus films. The best known was *Rastus in Zululand,* in which the publicity department at Pathé described Rastus in a release as "an odd jobs man, that is he did odd jobs when he has to, but when there are a few small coins in his pocket he prefers to sleep." In the thin plot, Rastus, a "darky who needs warmth," falls asleep and dreams he has been captured by cannibal Zulu warriors in Africa. The rather ugly daughter of a chief comes by the pot in which he is being cooked medium rare and offers to save him if he'll marry her. Rastus, eyeing her, prefers to boil. Crowds in the darkened theaters roared at his antics.[2]

Rastus was typical of the silent films' racist presentation of American blacks. A series of Rastus films showcased him as a silly, shiftless fool (*How Rastus Got His Pork Chops* was another title). He was not alone. Pathé also produced a long series of similar black films starring a character named Sambo. Then, in films such as *The King of the Cannibal Islands* (1908) and *Coon Town Suffragettes* (1914), came Mammy, the traditional Old South figure of the overweight, overwrought older black woman maid, hands on hips and white bandana around her hair.[3]

Rastus, Sambo and Mammy were three of many pathetic stereotypes brought to the screen by white producers in order to portray blacks in a way that pleased white audiences. They were just the screen version of more than seventy years of Sambo-type figures who had appeared in magazines and novels about the South.

But films did not merely reflect America's racist stereotypes; they intensified them and turned them into a new kind of black, the Hollywood black, who bore little resemblance to anybody's history, black or white. The overwhelming power of the new film medium dwarfed small-circulation magazines and hardcover books and visually entrenched the idea of Rastus, Sambo and Mammy in the American psyche.

Hollywood was able to do this, Thomas Cripps wrote in his *Slow Fade to Black*, because blacks had no "usable past," the history of an ethnic group that gave it identity.[4] Even immigrants who were discriminated against had an identity. Jews, Poles and Germans came from somewhere and had roots, a history and culture. Blacks had no history and no literature. They were cultural putty and Hollywood ignored their actual past, slavery, and re-created it—and them.

The cultural climate of the era and the lack of connection with blacks' past made distortions possible and even predictable. Demeaning roles quickly became stereotypical. As early as 1896 African Americans were seen gleefully devouring watermelons in the silent short *Watermelon Contest. Minstrels Battling in a Room* showed black minstrels beating up a white man with bottles. By the time the flood of Civil War features began in 1908, these racist clichés were set in stone. Film distributors and theater owners began to get catalogs describing newly released films. Of the blacks in one the catalog copy said: "These darkies are of the 'Old Virginny' type." *The Interrupted*

Crap Game was described as a film in which "darkies" break up a crap game (another stereotype of blacks—as shiftless gamblers) to chase a chicken. A studio catalog called *Prize Fight in Coon Town* a movie "about two bad coons." *A Night in Blackville* was hyped as "hot stuff" about "two old coons." One movie's plot was given as "the catching, tarring and feathering and burning of a negro for the assault of a white woman." Other films featured black ministers eating stolen chickens and being chased by a white posse. Several showed black thieves surviving explosions and bridge collapses, like later cartoon characters who were impervious to everything.[5] Typical titles were *Chicken Thieves* and *Nigger in the Woodpile*.[6] Films created a cinematic world that not only reflected the racist world in which blacks actually lived, in both Northern and Southern cities and towns, but reinforced it. Already existing racial attitudes were exacerbated by these movies.

There were some reasonably decent films about blacks made in the 1890s. In some, black men saved black children from danger. Black bands were featured, or an African American would be seen leading a parade of black marchers. The 1903 version of *Uncle Tom's Cabin,* a pro-black film, gained wide distribution (later Uncle Tom films were stereotyped and had substantial plot shifts from the original Harriet Beecher Stowe novel). As films were expanded into fifteen-minute melodramas, writers began to change the image of blacks on screen. Producers were apparently wary that films had become far too popular to permit anything but demeaning, false, exaggerated racial images, images, that is, which would not offend white audiences. They were nervous, too, about growing white-black friction across the country and the fear that friction put into the middle class. Race riots in Colorado in 1899, and in both Atlanta, Georgia, and Brownsville, Texas, frightened white America, as did the rise of powerful black spokesmen such as Booker T. Washington and W. E. B. Du Bois and the establishment of the National Association for the Advancement of Colored People (founded in 1909). An elaborate two-hour movie about the 1910 heavyweight championship fight in Reno, Nevada, in which black boxer Jack Johnson knocked out aging white champion Jim Jeffries, was banned in several states and shown with great caution in others for fear of riots following several minor black-white altercations around the country after the match. Two years later Congress banned all fight films, fearing that blacks would continue to win championships in the ring and that those victories might continue to inflame white audiences.[7]

At the same time, large motion picture studios were beginning to gobble up smaller ones. These new studios began to produce hundreds of films aimed at large, middle-class audiences. The development of fifteen-to-thirty-minute features, which were shown together as double or triple bills, gave producers from 1908 to 1915 a chance to distribute movies into middle-class neighborhoods as well as working districts, greatly increasing profits. Those middle-class audiences, in large and small cities, were white.[8]

Directors not predisposed to racism by their upbringing still reflected the racist tendencies of the day. William M. Selig, director, producer and studio owner, met black entertainer Bert Williams early in his career when he was promoting what he called "a genuine fast black show." Selig remembered Williams, who most who knew him said had an air of nobility about him, as a man with a "deep, wide, open watermelon expanse of a mouth."[9]

More demeaning films about blacks came out of Hollywood, such as Edison's *The Pickaninnies* (1905), Essanay's *Dancing Nig* (1907), Kalem's *Voodoo Vengeance* and *The Zulu King* (1913) and, of course, more of the Rastus movies. These characters of the 1910 film period were the predecessors of the Sambo- and Mammy-style faithful butlers and maids in the 1930s and 1940s.[10]

Cinema had picked up the distorted images of blacks from vaudeville, too. At the turn of the century vaudeville houses would be packed for a "coon show," a variety show starring black performers or white performers in blackface. Such shows all included bawdy comedy routines, cakewalk dances and demeaning sexual skits. Blacks were always portrayed as oversexed, lazy and shiftless men and women who had no skills except dancing and banjo-playing.

These shows, such as "Coon and the Chink," whose title showed Hollywood's equal disdain for Asian Americans, "Jes' Lak White Folks," "Bandanna Land" and "Dat Famous Chicken Debate," traveled the national vaudeville circuits along with the more famous minstrel shows, where the "coon" stereotype was developed in the 1840s.[11]

Sambo was the predecessor of Rastus and had been a figure in literature and the theater long before he made his debut in films. He had surfaced in the 1840s and 1850s and was a creation of slave-owners. Sambo was a simpleton, a child, a fool with little intelligence who, supervised properly, could be a docile, manageable and productive slave. If not handled well, he could become the much-feared rapist beast. He was a creature of the white imagination, and such a powerful one that he slowly crept into song and literature and came to be real in the minds of many Americans throughout the country in the decades before the war. He was such a compelling invention that many slaves deliberately behaved like Sambo in order to please their masters and avoid owners' prying into their private lives. Once Sambo arrived on the screen, which had such power with the masses, his image was soon planted firmly in the minds of Americans, North and South, and that image did considerable damage to African Americans.[12]

Movie producers and directors felt comfortable with promulgating a distorted racial image because the minstrel shows had created it and white Americans accepted it. The minstrel shows, whose popularity had waned after the Civil War, had a revival at the turn of the century, and in the 1908–1915 period, when most silents about the war were made, the shows were more popular than ever. In a March 1910 edition of the *New York Evening Telegraph* the page following a review of a new Civil War movie, *The Common Enemy,* carried a large ad for the most famous minstrel show of the day, Lew Dockstader's, with an illustration of Dockstader, in blackface, smiling at the reader. Just about any kind of racial slur, if presented in song and dance, was popular in white minstrel shows and on the vaudeville stage. One of the most successful song-and-dance numbers in the white minstrel shows was "You May Be a Hawaiian on Old Broadway but You're Just Another Nigger to Me."

The most successful of the 1900-era "coon shows" was "The Two Real Coons," starring the multitalented Williams, one of the premier entertainers in American history, who, in order to get jobs in the "coon shows," had to blackface his own black face. He and his black partner then entertained mostly white audiences who roared and applauded the "coon" portrayals of blacks by blacks in blackface in a grotesque carnival of caricature.[13]

This caricature was easily carried over to the movies. Daniel Leab, in *From Sambo to Superspade*, writes that blacks in plots were presented as "an uneasy menace, a dancing machine, a comic stooge, a faithful retainer, a cheerful flunky, a tainted unfortunate or an ignorant savage, a composite of qualities that were the opposite of the values treasured by white American society."[14] John Killens writes that movies of that kind were "the most anti-Negro influence in this nation."[15]

Two white gentlemen, Burt Wheeler (left) and Robert Woolsey, belittle a servant in Dixiana.

This was a time when millions of immigrants entered the United States, mostly from Europe, and moved into overcrowded tenement ghettos in the nation's big cities. There was immediate friction between the new white immigrants and blacks over jobs. Because

African Americans were willing to work so cheaply, immigrants had to lower their own wage expectations. This was the same time, too, that blacks began an exodus from the Old South to Northern cities in search of more cheap-labor jobs—jobs held by immigrants. Job competition would produce several race riots in 1919.

IN MOST MOVIES about history, however, blacks in slavery were seen differently from blacks of the 1903–1920 period, such as Rastus. To silent-movie audiences, the Civil War era's view of blacks served as an acceptable explanation for how blacks had become so foolish, so childlike and, eventually, so dangerous. Movies, as playwrights, novelists and magazine writers had already told the public for forty years, showed what happened when slaves were freed—they grew into Rastus.

One of the first Civil War features involving blacks was *The Confederate Spy,* from Kalem Studios, in 1910. In this fifteen-minute feature, a slave leaves the plantation to accompany his owner, who is working as a spy for the Confederacy. The owner is wounded on the way to complete his mission and cannot move. The slave, knowing how important the mission is to the South, leaves him and not only delivers the papers but rounds up a regiment of Confederate troops and leads them back to his owner, who is just about to be attacked by Yankee troops.[16]

Devotion, a Thomas Ince film shot at Ince's ranch, is more complicated. A slave somehow wanders onto a battlefield and finds his master badly wounded. Braving fire from all directions, he gets his master to a Union doctor, saving his life. The doctor (as in so many Civil War silents) is no mere doctor: he turns out to be the former suitor of the planter's daughter. He operates successfully and then the planter remembers where he hid the money he needs to pay the mortgage on his plantation. The slave rejoices.[17]

In *Her Little Slipper* (1911), a fifteen-minute feature, a slave referred to as "Uncle Jim" finds his master dying on a battlefield, another victim of Northern aggression, and carries him all the way home so he can die with his family on the old plantation. Years later, after emancipation, Uncle Jim returns to the plantation for a loving reunion with his owner's daughter.[18]

In *Swords and Hearts* (1911), a handsome Confederate officer returns from the war and finds his plantation bankrupt and in ruins. He
learns, though, that all is not lost. His faithful slave has joined with a
poor white girl who lives nearby, and who secretly loves the officer, to
pay the mortgage. All live happily ever after under the tall oaks.[19]

Slaves loved their owners so much on film that they came up with
ingenious ways to save their lives. Yankee troops arrive at a plantation
looking for the master in *Uncle Pete's Ruse* (1911). Faithful retainer
Uncle Pete tells the troops that they are too late, that his owner has
just died of smallpox. He even talks the Union troops into helping
him bury an empty, but weighted, coffin as his master, smiling thinly,
escapes.[20]

Slaves who did flee plantations in the silents never wavered in
their loyalty to their owner. In *None Can Do More* (1912), Arthur Malcolm's faithful and trusty retainer manages to escape the plantation
and makes it to a border state. He soon discovers that his former master has been captured and put in a hellhole Union prison. The slave
gives up his own life to help his master to escape.[21]

It is true that some owners and their slaves did have close bonds.
Owners went to slaves' funerals. They let some slaves run parts of
their business enterprises. Their wives gave presents to slave girls
about to be married. Slaves cared for their masters when they were
sick. Slave children played with white children. Silent movies, however, went well beyond acknowledging that and turned these relationships into ridiculous plotlines and clichéd characters.

One of the most powerful and traditional images of African Americans in slavery, promulgated in the silent films, was Mammy. The
stereotypical Mammy, developed in earlier films, appears in many
Civil War dramas. She spends most of her time washing clothes,
cooking meals, supervising kitchen staff, ordering field hands about,
taking care of the children or laughing at something silly a black man
has done. Perhaps her most important function in films, from early
silents to *Gone With the Wind*, was raising the master's white children, particularly the girls.

Mammy was just as protective of the owner and his family, and the
Confederate army, as any male slave in Civil War films. In *Old
Mammy's Secret Code* (1913), a Mammy working for a family in Peters-
burg, Virginia, uses pieces of wash she hangs out to dry as a secret

code to alert local Confederate forces to the movements of Union troops. The Union troops finally figure this out and execute Mammy, who gladly dies for the Southern cause.[22] In *Mammy's Rose* (1916), a Mammy sits in a rocking chair after the war and, looking back sadly, tells friends how rough life was for her and her owners during the conflict—a conflict brought about by Northern aggression.[23]

In almost all films not specifically about a Mammy, the Mammy figure still makes an appearance. Usually she is grossly overweight and ties up her hair in a white kerchief. She was often portrayed as temperamentally more white than black, and as siding with the whites in almost any dispute with black slaves. Her presence in the white home, films suggested, elevated her above the other slaves on the plantation, even above friends and members of her own family.

The real Mammy existed, and worked hard, but her true role is difficult to evaluate. Several historians, such as Eugene Genovese and Richard Hofstadter, suggest that any woman working in the owner's house had to behave like a subservient laborer, and love the owner's children—regardless of her true opinions—in order to guarantee some comfort in her own life and comfort for her family. Others, such as Deborah White, suggest that the role of Mammy was far less influential than portrayed in film and novels and that white women had more control over their families and homes than the traditional Mammy.[24]

The screen's Mammy was a solid, well-defined figure, admired North and South. She was a fixed character from 1903 through 1939, when Hattie McDaniel played her in *Gone With the Wind* and defined her for audiences once and for all. The real Mammy, like the real Sambo, shunted aside in literature and theater from 1865 to 1903, was buried for generations by the power of film.

Even if plots involving slaves were not absurd, they were turned about so they could show the South and its residents as victims. In *The Little Strategist* (1917), two white children convince their mother not to sell two slave children. The moral of the story is not that white women love little black slave girls, but that the only reason this white woman wanted to sell them was that the plantation was in ruins and she was in utter poverty—all caused by Union troops.[25] Here the message is that the deep impact of losing the war was felt not only by soldiers but by families.

Big Sam in *Gone With the Wind* is the prototypical faithful retainer, a man whose own emotional life is centered on his owner, Gerald O'Hara, and not other blacks. At the end of the movie, he happily marches out to dig trenches to help the Confederates in a vain effort to "save" the good people of Atlanta from the hated Union army.[26]

This idea of a demeaned minority whose members want to help their oppressors was perpetuated in various Griffith films. In *The Battle at Elderberry Gulch* a Mexican risks his life to save whites. In *The Massacre,* a Native American scout saves an army regiment at war with his own tribe.[27]

Real history, of course, doesn't record very many incidents of freed slaves giving their lives for their owners or any Mammies working directly for the Confederate army or as spies against the Union army. These inventions were created by filmmakers to complete the moonlight-and-magnolias montage of the Civil War.[28] The concept of

In this 1913 version of Uncle Tom's Cabin, *Henry Pollard as Uncle Tom prays that Little Eva's life be spared.*

a happy land full of gentlemen rudely attacked by Union troops could work only if the slaves who had caused all the uproar were content with their lot. If movies had projected a real picture of unhappy slaves eager to be free, slaves who showed thin cordiality to their owners only out of necessity, the scope of these movies would have changed. That view would have destroyed the Plantation Myth forever. Realistic Civil War and slavery movies simply could not be made if any rapprochement between North and South on the eve of the war's fiftieth anniversary was to be cemented. Such movies could not be made for another reason: they would have engendered sympathy for African Americans and ruined the political efforts of North and South in the 1900–1915 period to hold them down in the workplace and social world. Most of the silents depicted slaves as not only satisfied in slavery, but willing to give their lives to preserve it.

The only movies that diverged from this party line, if slightly, were the *Uncle Tom's Cabin* movies. There were nine different silent versions of Harriet Beecher Stowe's popular 1852 classic, the book that bolstered abolitionists' antislavery campaigns from its publication through the start of the war.[29] The first movie version was one of the first silent features made, in 1903, just a few months after the premier feature film, *The Great Train Robbery*. Edwin Porter, who directed *The Great Train Robbery*, was eager to direct *Uncle Tom* because he, like so many others, was convinced that any famous book or play would mean decent box office as a movie. He was right, and it was filmed with slight changes again and again by different directors. Lubin Pictures rushed its version out six months after Porter's. That wasn't the only time that the popular Uncle Tom appeared twice in the same year. Both Thanhouser and Vitagraph put out versions of it in 1910, and in 1913 both Kalem and Imperial released productions. Other versions appeared in 1914, 1918 and 1927. Most were badly directed and woefully acted and did not fare well at the box office. Those films maintained Stowe's abolitionist bent but solidified the frequent distortions of blacks in film, as Uncle Tom and the other characters, such as Topsy, were continually portrayed as brutes or fools and their owners as benign gentry.

Blacks had been unhappy with the many blackfaced white actors in the Uncle Tom movies.[30] In film, though, whites in blackface were appropriating an entire black culture and reinterpreting it. Whatever oral histories were passed down from generation to generation by slaves and freedmen never got to the screen. The few real blacks in Civil War silents played field hands or were merely part of the scenery. Very few had speaking roles and the only times blacks actually starred in movies were in *Uncle Tom* films, and then in only two of the nine productions. The two blacks who played Uncle Tom were Sam Lucas (1914) and James B. Lowe (1927).[31] Many actors playing Uncle Tom were old minstrel stars. The most famous was minstrel icon Lew Dockstader himself.[32] *Uncle Tom* and its many productions (it was even produced by a German film company in 1960) also provided jobs for white actresses, some of whom played Topsy in blackface. In a publicity coup, Marguerite Clark, a top actress of the day, portrayed both white Little Eva and black Topsy in the same 1918 production of *Uncle Tom's Cabin* and was hailed by critics for showing how well a white girl could play a black girl. The Duncan Sisters, a popular vaudeville team, reworked the story of Topsy and Eva, with Rosetta Duncan in blackface as Topsy. The sisters produced and starred in their version on Broadway, to dreadful reviews. Stephen Zito, writing in *The American Film Heritage,* deplored these portrayals of blacks, particularly those of Topsy: "Topsy is one of the most damning racist portraitures in American film: she is ignorant, thieving, superstitious, undisciplined and given over to swearing and biting; she eats bugs . . . and butts heads with a goat."[33]

There were even silent cartoons developed out of the *Uncle Tom* story. In 1926, a cartoon character named Dinkey Doodle, created by J. R. Bray, leaped into the Uncle Tom saga with a five-minute cartoon. Dinkey, tired of the old slave story, changes the ending and runs off with one of the heroines.[34] Then, in 1927, near the end of the silent era, even Felix the Cat adapted Uncle Tom. Felix was one of the most popular cartoon characters of the silent era, a persnickety cat who later crossed over to sound. His creators at the Pat Sullivan studios put together a five-minute animated parody of Stowe's story for him in which the aging stereotypes were trotted across the screen once again.[35]

Civil War movies accurately depicted slaves—but only those seen in the minstrel shows. They were all heavily blackfaced, wore kinky-hair wigs and shuffled about the plantations. When talking to owners, they were always half bent over in subservience. When standing

Blacks were often portrayed as servants in Civil War movies and were never given credits in the films or in publicity photos. Here, an anonymous black actor looks on as Lewis Stone, Marguerite Clayton (at left) and a second woman dine in the silent According to the Code.

behind the featured white player in a scene, blacks usually shifted from one foot to the other and nodded and smiled at each other, retainers ready to retain at the snap of an owner's fingers. African Americans who complained about the paucity of roles or about black-face were blacklisted. In 1927 Universal Pictures produced the first true big-screen, three-reel version of *Uncle Tom's Cabin* and gave the title role to James B. Lowe, a fine black actor. Lowe complained when filming was over that despite his work, there were still too few black actors working in Hollywood. Universal fired him, and he never worked in films again.[36]

Blacks who did find work in Civil War films, even playing stereotypical slaves, were not viewed favorably by mainstream newspaper critics, who were all white. A writer who reviewed the 1914 version of *Uncle Tom's Cabin* said that it was "well acted, considering that the cast is made up of genuine colored people."[37] The whites in blackface kept their distance from the few real blacks during filming.

When pressed by the National Association for the Advancement of Colored People and the Urban League to explain why African Americans were not used in films, producers always shrugged their shoulders and said that no experienced black actors were available. This was not true. Hundreds of talented black actors were traveling about the country in black minstrel shows and appearing in black theaters and black nightclubs, particularly in New York, where early movies were made. Later, when most studios moved to Hollywood, producers' excuse was that few blacks, much less black actors, lived in Los Angeles.[38] This was not true, either. By 1916, the year after *The Birth of a Nation* was released, there were enough blacks there to spur the first white homeowners' associations, created to implement restrictive clauses to keep blacks out of residential areas. There were also enough blacks there at that time to make the KKK in Los Angeles one of the most active in the country by the early 1920s.[39] There were enough for the successful publication of a weekly black newspaper.

Because blacks could make no inroads in the white film business, they began their own movie industry during that same 1903–1920 period. Companies such as Lincoln Films, the Frederick Douglass Film Company, the Colored and Indian Film Company, Ebony Films, Democracy Films, Foster, Photoplay and Acme produced all-black films for black audiences, which were considerable. The racial film market was so large that by 1913 there were 214 all-black movie houses in America.[40]

Mainstream films in which slaves did not know their place were met with protests from white audiences. In *A Southern Girl's Heroism* (1911), a black girl named Topsie kissed a Union soldier and then walked off the screen arm in arm with him. Theater owners received many complaints from whites who saw the film, all angry about the black-white friendship. Whites also complained bitterly to theater owners who showed *The Soldier's Ring* (1911), in which a slave would not pull out a chair for a white visitor.

African Americans offended by the way they were portrayed

onscreen had no recourse. They had low status in the film industry, with certainly no control over casting or the content of films. Because black people, just 10 percent of the population, were not a viable part of the market for films, white filmmakers did not have to worry about their feelings or reactions in portraying them on the screen—they had to present the black American as seen by the white American, who bought the tickets. Any African American who wanted to go to the movies for pleasure was barred from most theaters in the Southern states or was forced to sit in a segregated seating section, usually in the balcony. Discrimination was just as prevalent in theaters in the North. Blacks had to sit in the all-black seating sections in the balcony.[41] Theaters in many Northern cities, such as Newark, New Jersey, maintained segregated seating through the 1950s.

In the South by the 1890s, at the dawn of the silent Civil War film, discrimination against blacks was so complete that ministers routinely warned their congregations that blacks were intent on the rape and pillage of white society. One Georgia pastor told his congregation to fear African Americans, that they would bring "mongrelism and the destruction of the Saxon womanhood of our wives and daughters," once again tying racial prejudice to the cavalier culture of knights and ladies.[42]

Those fears of rape stung even harder when enunciated by women, and women of influence. One of the most prominent race-baiters of the 1890s was the journalist-politician Rebecca Felton, whose husband was a congressman and who would herself one day become a U.S. senator. During an 1897 speech in Georgia, she warned a large crowd about the black rape of white women, saying, "if it takes lynching to protect woman's dearest possession from drunk, ravening human beasts, then I say lynch a thousand a week if it becomes necessary."[43]

A few years earlier, a Southern college president, lamenting racial freedom, announced that white women had to lock their doors at night to ward off black men, who all had rape on their minds. "The black brute is lurking in the dark, a monstrous beast, crazed with lust," he warned.[44] "A bad Negro is the most horrible human creature upon the earth," author Charles Smith said in 1893.[45] Others, including the most powerful men in the country, such as U.S. senators John Morgan, of Alabama, and James Eustis, of Louisiana, told crowds that not only were African Americans worthless and dangerous but God had made them so.[46]

Persecution was not restricted to the South. The silent era saw discrimination against blacks in the North, even at the most cultured levels of society. No less than a dean at Columbia University in 1896 wrote that "a black skin means membership in a race of men which . . . has never created any civilization of any kind."[47] And in the West, a black delegate to a Farmers' Alliance convention in the 1890s begged the executive committee to include African Americans in the alliance to give them some power over their lives. "You must appoint us . . . and make us feel we are men," he said.[48]

The same frustration was felt throughout black America during that era, when the Civil War silent films were building their images of African Americans. Black Americans had to overcome not only unfair stigmas attached to them by actual society, writes black cultural historian bell hooks, but stigmas added by influential films, many of them Civil War epics, that validated unfair stereotypes, seen by that society.[49] Putting that Jim Crow society up on the screen for the millions who went to the movies gave it, and them, legitimacy.

The restriction of black power of any kind, through lynchings, Jim Crow laws, poll taxes, vote fraud and unfair labor practices was so strong by 1912, the height of the silent Civil War film era, that John Rayner, a longtime black activist in Texas, gave up his political career and went into the lumber business. He told friends that there was no longer any hope for racial equality in the country.[50] The Southern states were so successful at portraying blacks as ignorant and unfit to vote that Northern political historians of the era routinely wrote that they were right and that "the theory that every man has a natural right to vote no longer commands the support of students of political science."[51]

Many of these Civil War silent films, shown in the 1903–1915 period, were historical—or rather, purportedly historical—documents designed to let audiences know exactly what everyone's place still was. The hundreds of thousands of blacks moving from the rural South to the North must remember that although their surroundings were different, their third-rung status was still the same. All the people on the top two rungs, who were white, worked very hard to keep the blacks on the third.

Much of the immigrant population, so fearful of losing jobs to blacks who worked for less money, accepted the views about blacks shown in silent films, suggests historian David Nasaw, despite the demeaning of immigrants in numerous silent films (in which there might even be title cards that poked fun at the difficulty immigrants had with the language). Everybody in the movies needs an enemy, movie people thought, just as some in real life might. Whom better than the blacks? Given that, the only way for them to have any kind of life at all in American society, even in segregated American society, was to know their place and stay nailed in it.

As the Civil War film era proceeded towards national reunification in 1915, the fiftieth anniversary of the war's end, blacks were targets for violence, a huge punching bag for the basest elements of white society, North and South. They had been pushed into a cultural wasteland, somewhere out beyond the other side of the tracks, across shantytown, past the street where Mr. Charlie lived, beyond the fences of The Man. By the time the Civil War films began to flicker on screens in movie houses throughout the United States in 1903, African Americans had become not only an abandoned race, but an invisible race, with no political, social, legal or cultural power to fight back.

CHAPTER SIX

The Birth of a Nation: The Greatest Motion Picture Ever Made . . .

D. W. GRIFFITH arrived in sun-drenched California on February 14, 1914, with his wife, Linda; G. W. "Billy" Bitzer, one of the best cinematographers in the business; and his loyal stable of actors—Henry B. Walthall, Mae Marsh, Bobby Harron, Blanche Sweet, Donald Crisp, Spottiswoode Aitken, Jack Pickford and Lillian Gish. He also brought assistant Christy Cabanne and story editor Frank Woods. The tall, thin movie director, wearing his signature broad-brimmed hat, towered over all of them as they stepped off the train at the Los Angeles railroad station, with its lovely Spanish mission architecture. D. W. Griffith moved through a train car and across a platform with a regal air, an air befitting the country's most successful movie director. There was a rich, patrician aura about him. He had a profile that belonged on a coin, with a high forehead, receding hairline, swept-back hair and a large, sharp nose that chiseled his face into people's memory. The director squinted slightly under the strong California sun as he looked around at what was then a small but growing city of nearly five hundred thousand people—a city surrounded by steep hills and orange groves on one side and the broad blue Pacific on the other.

Griffith was in California to expand the West Coast studio for Mutual Pictures, whose executives had hired him away from Biograph Studios for an enormous amount of money,[1] and he had enough power within his new company to guarantee top salaries for his staff as well.[2] He was earning between $35,000 and $50,000 per year in the motion picture business, more by far than any director at the time,[3] and by 1916 those earnings would increase to over $100,000, not counting profits from *The Birth of a Nation.*[4] Griffith had already produced or directed more than 400 films for various companies and 150 for Biograph. His movies made money wherever they played and his loyal troupe of actors, who left Biograph without hesitation when he asked them to join him, had become stars under his guidance. He was at the absolute height of his fame and power in the exploding world of motion pictures, the brand-new, spectacular medium of the masses.[5]

As soon as he and his wife found rooms, he began working in the small building that housed the Mutual studios. He told the press he was in California to make a one-reel feature called *The Escape,* but secretly he began to assemble battalions of extras, hundreds of horses, rifles, revolvers, uniforms, flags, costumes, buggies, caissons, cannons and twenty-three thousand square yards of white sheeting. He was going to make the longest and greatest motion picture of all time, a picture that would make him famous—for all the wrong reasons.

The film was *The Birth of a Nation,* a twelve-reel, three-hour feature that Griffith was convinced would change the look of movies forever. It was the kind of grand, sprawling epic which would move films into large theaters and make motion pictures an industry for the middle class, not just the working class. It was the kind of movie which would show audiences how action scenes could be combined with long, lingering closeups and fine acting in lengthy scenes to weave a seamless tapestry on film.

He had selected a Civil War novel, *The Clansman,* by Thomas Dixon, to adapt for his movie, and from that book he produced a film that was to be shredded by intellectuals, picketed by thousands of African Americans and torn apart for generations by film scholars as an ugly racist epic that denigrated all blacks as thugs and rapists and glorified the terrorists of the Ku Klux Klan. It was at once the best and worst silent movie of all time, a film that would, indeed, live forever—in ignominy.

Frank Woods had shown the director a copy of *The Clansman,* a scathing novel of Reconstruction that portrayed blacks as savages and the night riders of the KKK as heroes.[6] The author was an evangelical minister who was ordained by the Baptist church, finished his studies at Wake Forest University and spent a year of graduate work at Johns Hopkins University (where he was a classmate of future president

Woodrow Wilson and historian Frederick Jackson Turner). A fiery lecturer and avowed Southern revisionist historian, Dixon was pastor of the influential Twenty-third Street Baptist Church in New York, where he became close personal friends with one of his parishioners, millionaire industrialist John D. Rockefeller.[7] Griffith saw possibilities in Dixon's book right away and told executives at his company that he could envision the whole epic in front of him as he read it. "I could just see these Klansmen in a movie with their white robes flying," he said.[8]

Dixon's uncle had fought in the war and become a leader of a local Ku Klux Klan organization during Reconstruction.[9] The book was the second in a trilogy about postwar Southern history. The first, *The Leopard's Spots: A Romance of the White Man's Burden,* became an instant best-seller when published by Doubleday in 1902. Inspired and sure he was on the right track, Dixon published *The Clansman: An Historical Romance of the Ku Klux Klan,* in 1905. It, too, sold well. The final book in the trilogy, *The Traitor: A Story of the Rise and Fall of the Invisible Empire,* made it to the best-seller list in 1907. Dixon turned *The Clansman* into a stage play in 1905, while the book was still being sold, and it was a huge hit, playing theaters from coast to coast.[10] As a play, *The Clansman* was even more successful in the North than it was in the South.

The Clansman, as book, play and film, was a complicated, two-part story. The first part is the story of two sets of brothers, one from the North and one from the South, who go off to war. The second is the postwar story of the two who have survived, one from each set. After the war the Southerner's hometown, Piedmont, in the Carolinas, is taken over by rampaging blacks intent on raping white women. Other blacks, drunk and disheveled, seize power in the state legislature and pass numerous antiwhite bills, including some that would force white women to marry black men. The U.S. army units that have occupied Piedmont are all-black, and the soldiers routinely shove white residents off sidewalks and point rifles with bayonets at them. Black U.S. soldiers stalk white women, obviously planning rape, through much of the second half of the book and film. In their spare time, they shoot and kill numerous townspeople. At the end, members of the Ku Klux Klan, out to avenge any and all sexual threats to their women, capture and execute a black man suspected of rape.

It was the first truly complicated movie, involving a number of subplots and deep characterizations. It would be a sweeping drama, with large outdoor battle scenes, a twenty-minute ride by Klansmen in their long, flowing white robes, nighttime fighting and fires, haunting scenes of Southerners starving and a pathetic view of the defeated Southern heroes returning home to their villages.

In 1914, few movie directors or producers were willing to make such a movie because of its length and expense. Harry Aitken was the exception. The new owner (with brother Roy) of Mutual Pictures wanted something big to kick off his career, something majestic to elevate his company above the dozen or so other studios scrambling to best each other with one- and two-reelers. Aitken heard the story of *The Clansman* from Griffith, who had a vision of filming an epic.[11]

Griffith was eager to direct the kind of movie no one else would tackle. He was tired of short features. In 1911 he had produced a film called *His Trust,* a Civil War saga, as a single, half-hour-long story, one of the longest films in history up to then, but the men who ran his studio did not believe anyone would sit through a movie that lengthy, and forced him to cut it into two separate films, which were released within a week of each other as *His Trust* and *His Trust Fulfilled.* In 1913, he convinced Biograph to let him make *Judith of Bethulia,* a biblical epic, which ran just over an hour. Studio heads put it on the shelf as soon as it was finished and did not release it for a year because they were convinced it was too long to be successful. Disgusted with Biograph's narrow view of film's future, a disgruntled Griffith moved to Mutual. In February of 1914, Griffith had the actors he wanted, the property he wanted and the company he wanted.[12]

By 1914 he had directed fourteen different Civil War pictures. He mastered combat scenes in *The Battle* and multiple-angle filming in *The Guerrilla.* He had done a successful love story in *The Fair Rebel,* a brothers-together story in *In Old Kentucky* and one about cowardice in *The House with Closed Shutters. The Birth of a Nation* would include everything that he had done in his career, as well as his treatment of the Civil War and the South, in one memorable epic. He and Harry Aitken realized, too, that 1915 was the fiftieth anniversary of the end of the Civil War. Not a day went by, in California or New York, when a newspaper did not carry a story about some local Civil War anniversary celebration. Aitken and Griffith were certain that despite its record projected cost of nearly $100,000, *The Clansman* would be a box office bonanza.

The pair did not worry that their film did something that no Civil War film had done—that it took a radical step in the portrayal of blacks. In the first half blacks were shown as contented workers; in the second half they were malevolent rapists and murderers. There had been only a few films set in Reconstruction, all of them short. Griffith was breaking new ground when he portrayed blacks as docile during the war but violent after it. He was confident audiences would accept this racial violence even though it departed from the Civil War sagas they had seen over the previous twelve years.

In all of Griffith's previous Civil War movies, the Southerners were portrayed as heroes and the slaves as satisfied field hands.[13] They were all full of romances, love triangles, dutiful mothers, proud fathers and brave soldiers,[14] the groundwork on which he would build *The Birth of a Nation.* Each previous film had some element that eventually would soar in *Birth.* Each had a start-of-the-war scene, for no historical reason. Each then contained the same elements which were so marvelously filmed in *Birth.*

In *The Battle,* as in most Griffith Civil War movies, young men hear of the war's start and rush off to the recruiting office. They are hugged by their loving mothers, embraced by their proud fathers and cried over by their sweethearts. The men, in shiny new uniforms, then march off to war in a grand parade through town as townspeople cheer and nubile young girls toss flowers.

Griffith's nostalgic films had their critics, who accused him and other writers and directors of misleading the public by ignoring history in favor of legend and myth in the name of reunification. Russell Merritt later argued in *Cinema* magazine that the cavaliers of 1865–1915 literature, theater and film were "modern musketeers who duel, hunt, ride and rescue young ladies"; he found little if any historical accuracy in the entire canon of books, stories, plays and movies. "*The Birth of a Nation* is not an historical document any more than are Walt Whitman's poems about the [Civil] war or Shakespeare's historical plays," he wrote.[15]

Audiences of the era, however, brought up on Civil War legends, had little interest in the historical accuracy of these films, as long as all the girls were pretty and all the boys were valiant.

Griffith, ever the showman, began principal photography on *The Birth of a Nation* on the Fourth of July, 1914, with much fanfare and hoopla as his stars arrived on the set. Griffith had handpicked Henry Walthall to play the "Little Colonel," Ben Cameron, who is the founder of the KKK in the film.[16] The talented Walthall, a Southerner, born in Shelby City, Alabama, was a Griffith favorite. Griffith put him into any film that needed a lover. "He's excellent in romantic roles," he said. Griffith's cinematographer, Bitzer, thought Walthall's face was hauntingly handsome and used it in as many closeups as he could. *Birth* would make Walthall a star.

Mae Marsh was selected to play Flora Cameron, the younger sister.[17] Marsh wandered into Griffith's life as a slender seventeen-year-old when she showed up on the set to watch her older sister,

Reconciliation was a major theme in The Birth of a Nation— *as shown, importantly, through the romance between Southern gentleman planter Ben Cameron (Henry Walthall) and Elsie Stoneman (Lillian Gish), the sister of Cameron's Northern friend.*

Marguerite, in a one-reeler Griffith was directing. Griffith was intrigued by Marsh, whose reckless hair dangled over her shoulders. He walked up to her, shook her hand, bent down slightly, looked into her almond eyes and asked her, "How would you like to be in pictures?" She said she would and he soon signed her to a contract. "Mae Marsh was born to be a film star. Destiny itself seemed to have been her coach in acting," said the director, who began to have many quiet lunches and dinners with the gorgeous teenager. Griffith had also signed Lillian Gish, who was nineteen. Gish was cast as Elsie, the beautiful daughter of Austin Stoneman. Later, during the filming of *Birth,* Gish and Marsh wound up jealously competing for Griffith's attentions. Marsh often sat next to an open slat in her second-floor dressing room, which overlooked one of the studio sets, so she could spy on Griffith as he flirted with Gish. Griffith's overly friendly relationships with the two teenagers were the talk of Hollywood.

Miriam Cooper played Margaret Cameron, Flora's older sister.[18] Cooper scoffed at the rumors swirling about concerning Griffith and Marsh and Griffith and Gish, but she changed her mind when one day the director grabbed her in the backseat of his car and tried to kiss her. She refused.

Josephine Crowell, another regular, played the sisters' mother, Mrs. Cameron. Spottiswoode Aitken was cast as Dr. Cameron. Regular Ralph Lewis played radical political leader Austin Stoneman, Joe Henaberry was Abraham Lincoln, Mary Alden played Stoneman's mulatto maid-lover, and George Siegmann was black leader Silas Lynch. Almost all of the black roles in *Birth* were played by whites in blackface.

Griffith, a Southerner from Kentucky, began to re-create the Old South of his youth, the Old South that had been described so lovingly by his father, Jake, in front of the fireplace on cold winter nights.[19] Griffith shot all of his interiors in his Hollywood studio, but moved the cast and crew about Los Angeles and Southern California for the exterior shots. Everything about *Birth* was oversized. Instead of doing what many directors did, framing a small field for his cotton fields on the Cameron Plantation, Griffith moved cast and crew to shoot huge re-created cotton fields in the sprawling Imperial Valley. The scene gave the impression of a Cameron cotton plantation extending over thousands of acres.[20] The director, unhappy with suggestions by assistants that he close-frame Lincoln in a small set box to film his assassination, re-created Ford's Theatre,[21] the same size as the actual theater, with the same size stage, seats and boxes. This enabled Griffith to shoot sensational footage of John Wilkes Booth leaping to the stage after murdering Lincoln. In real life, Booth broke his leg when he landed on the stage, some twelve feet below Lincoln's box, and had to limp away. When the scene was filmed in Hollywood, the actor playing Booth, Raoul Walsh, twisted his knee when he landed, and he, too, had to limp off the stage, adding authenticity to the scene.

Griffith also re-created in full detail the South Carolina State Legislature's ornate assembly hall, on the basis of photos of the hall dating from the 1870s, leaving just one side open for his cameras. He even put in a balcony because one had been there in 1877. He bragged about his devotion to authenticity in building this legislative chamber, although what he would film there would not be authentic at all. Still, it was the scene of one of the most gasp-inspiring shots in the film, a shot duplicated again and again thereafter, of the empty chamber suddenly filled with people in a camera's millisecond. It was stunning.

The greatest challenges were the grand finale ride of the Ku Klux Klan, the battle sequences and the burning of Atlanta. Griffith recruited about a hundred professional cowboys from the Southern California area to work as cavalrymen and Klansmen in these scenes. He also hired engineers off-duty from the U.S. Army to help him set up his battlefield and employees from local military ordnance stores and gun stores to help with his military needs.

He ran into problems every day with his battles and Klan rides. The cowboys were able to work their horses beautifully, but the extras hired as riders could not. The cowboys had to teach them how to ride better and—to prevent a general stampede—keep them in some kind of order when the scenes began. Walsh[22] was a professional wrangler and cowboy and thus was chosen to head up one of the large units and keep order. John Ford, another experienced rider and sometime cowboy,[23] was an extra with another unit. One of the stuntmen working as a Klan rider was the German-born Erich Von Stroheim. *Birth,* then, had, in Griffith, Von Stroheim, Ford and Walsh, four of the greatest directors in film history all working together.[24]

Just coordinating the battle scenes seemed like a task for a real military general. Griffith hired two West Point instructors to set up the battlefield and told them to arrange the locations so that his extras could sweep from one area to another in long, extended charges. He also told them to set up a long, narrow area for trenches where one army would attack the other. Griffith was determined to film the largest battles ever seen on film. He advertised later that he used thirteen thousand extras in his battle scenes, but the true number was closer to five hundred.[25] Even five hundred riders and soldiers, however, many of them amateurs, still made up a small army.

The director needed close coordination for the burning of Atlanta. Everybody had to move from one location to another on a given signal so that they would all be part of the scene at the same time he had bombs going off and large clouds of smoke moving through the Imperial Valley. The scene was the first in film history to be filmed at night. Initially he tried firing blank shots as a signal for the different regiments to move, but that didn't work. Then he had a flag system put in place, but that failed, too. Finally he brought in people from the local telephone company and hooked up a complex system of field telephones to permit his "captains," people like Walsh, to communicate with him and with each other. Griffith was positioned on a sixty-foot-high wooden tower, built just for the scene, where he could see for himself where everyone was moving. It worked for Griffith then and worked so well for the Army Corps of Engineers that, with minor adjustments, the U.S. Army adapted those field phones for use during World War I.

Griffith used the same system for his battle scenes. The result was sensational footage of a kind never seen before in American movies. The highlight of each such scene came when Bitzer positioned himself in a hole in the ground and shot up, catching dozens of soldiers' horses leaping over the ditch. "The scheme worked with clocklike precision. The sub-directors received their orders, marshaled their forces and attacked the camera at the exact moment when they needed the right effect in the plot," wrote a reporter who did an on-location story.[26]

Finally, on February 8, 1915, the film, then still named *The Clansman,* and at $110,000 the most expensive movie ever made, was ready to open at Clune's Auditorium in Los Angeles. Many thought it would fail. Film mogul William De Mille (older brother of director Cecil B. De Mille) wrote studio chief Sam Goldwyn about the cost: "This means that even if it's a hit, which it probably will be, it cannot possibly make any money. It would have to gross over a quarter of a million for Griffith to get his cost back and, as you know, that just isn't being done. *The Clansman* certainly establishes Griffith as a leader and it does seem too bad that such magnificent effort is doomed to financial failure."[27]

Griffith wasn't worried. He had the longest, most expensive, most extravagant film of all time. How could it miss?

The first inkling of the tidal wave of trouble that was to break came a day before the Los Angeles premiere, when the city's chapter of the NAACP, protesting that the film should not be shown because it was insulting to blacks, obtained a court order to prevent the first screening of the film. However, a judge allowed the movie's second planned screening, and Los Angeles's police chief ordered more than a hundred police to guard the theater in case of protests by blacks. It was the first in what would be an endless series of controversies tied to *The Birth of a Nation*.

The injunction, and the protest by blacks in front of the theater, stunned Griffith and made Harry Aitken exceedingly nervous. Bad publicity, they were convinced, meant bad box office (though in this they would prove to be mistaken). What really made the money-conscious Aitken worry was that Los Angeles in 1915 was a relatively small city with, as they kept telling people, "few" blacks. What if the film was picketed or sued in cities like New York, Boston and Detroit, with larger black populations? The uproar caused in Los Angeles and complaints by black groups in New York, where the next opening was scheduled, were worrisome. Would anybody buy tickets?

Griffith and Woods were determined to keep *Birth*'s script as it was, but decided to cut out a few scenes to appease the NAACP. They excised a scene where slavers chase blacks through jungles in Africa, eliminated a title card telling viewers that Lincoln wanted to send the slaves back to Africa, replaced what was originally the actual rape of Flora by the black man on the rock with her suicide, and cut out scenes showing blacks pulling dozens of white girls into cabins with them.[28]

The National Board of Censors later upheld *Birth*: "If the picture tends to aggravate serious social questions and should therefore be wholly forbidden, that is a matter for the action of those who act on similar tendencies when they are expressed in books, newspapers or on the stage. On what basis of reasoning should a film play be repressed whose subject matter has already been allowed the freest circulation both in a novel and a play?"[29]

All of the controversy and attacks confused Griffith, who truly never understood the impact of the film he had made.

CHAPTER SEVEN

The Whole Truth and Nothing but the Truth?

D. W. GRIFFITH'S Piedmont, South Carolina, is a fictional town deriving its name from the geographic Piedmont Plateau, which runs through the western half of the Carolinas and Virginia. The town is charming, with large and small homes, many with handsome oaks in yards surrounded by white picket fences, a town like any town, North or South. When viewers are introduced to the Cameron family, its members are portrayed as refined people with a long tradition of graciousness and wealth, different from their friends, the Northern Stonemans. The demure, black-haired Margaret Cameron, for example, is introduced as "a daughter of the South, trained in the manners of the Old School."

The Camerons, slaveholders, live in a grand house in town with huge white columns. Mrs. Cameron sits quietly in a rocking chair on the porch while her husband, referred to as "the kindly master of Cameron Hall," reads a newspaper. Cats and dogs play at their feet. How could people who are kind to pets be evil?

When the Stoneman brothers, sons of U.S. Speaker of the House Austin Stoneman, visit their friends the Cameron brothers at Cameron Hall, they are given a grand tour of the plantation. Thus everything is framed within the Plantation Myth school of history. The two sets of brothers walk through enormous fields of cotton, which seem to stretch for miles, together with the Camerons' sisters, Margaret and Flora. They are chatting, ignoring the hardworking slaves around them who pick the cotton that keeps the Camerons rich. Their leisurely walk takes them to the slave quarters, a street of small, badly constructed wooden cabins, where they are entertained by slaves doing burlesque cakewalks to "Oh! Susannah." When the music stops, one of the Camerons shakes hands warmly with the slaves, who nod knowingly at him as if they are all good friends.

Later, when war breaks out (title cards insinuate that the North starts it), hundreds of Southern gentlemen in uniform and their ladies dance the night away at a magnificently photographed grand ball,

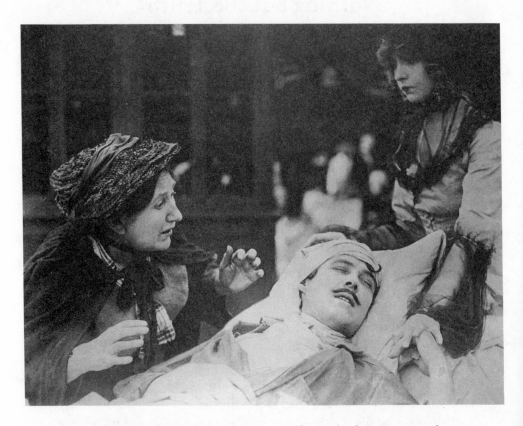

Audiences saw the southern Camerons in The Birth of a Nation *as a lovable family trying to get through hard times. Here an anxious Mother Cameron (Josephine Crowell) tends to her wounded son Ben (Henry Walthall) in a northern hospital. Ben's new love, northerner Elsie, looks on, holding his hand.*

held the evening before the local men are to leave for battle. Outside, a huge bonfire blazes and couples stroll together one last time through the haze. The next morning, the troops go off in a long parade through

One of the most moving scenes in The Birth of a Nation *is the parade of Confederate soldiers out of town on their way to meet the Northern enemy.*

town as their sweethearts and families cheer wildly. Flags fly, bugles sound, horses prance and hundreds of men march to war to "When Johnny Comes Marching Home" (played by theater orchestras).

In a rather oblique bending of history, Griffith has dozens of slaves trail the troops, firing guns and wishing that they, too, could be fighting to preserve slavery. As it rides out, the Piedmont regiment is cheered on by hundreds of other slaves, who wave their hands and hats, hoping for Southern victory over those who would give them their freedom. Upstairs in Cameron Hall, the younger daughter points to the state flag, whose motto is "Conquer we must . . . for our cause is just."

Ben Cameron gets on his flower-draped horse, salutes his family, and goes off to war. Upstairs, his sister clutches a Confederate flag to her chest. The Confederate soldiers are, as always, the heroes of this war, a war in which they fight for the Lost Cause of honor and family.

By now audiences are in love with the good-natured Camerons and fearful that something terrible will happen to the family. It does. Black soldiers from the North arrive in Piedmont. They burn down houses, shoot unarmed townspeople and ransack the buildings they do not torch. The black Yankees, dressed as savages and often bare-chested, are directed to look like gorillas from the jungle. They wear hats tilted at silly angles on their heads and their eyes are wide with excitement at their destruction of the town (the good people of Pied-mont are saved when a nearby Rebel regiment arrives and chases the marauders away). In the background, in scene after scene following the initial attack on Piedmont, women and children are clutching each other as Northern troops burn down their towns. But they can do nothing as the brave but hopelessly outnumbered rebels battle against overwhelming odds. Sherman burns down Atlanta as the inno-cent victims flee. The North wins at Petersburg despite Colonel Ben Cameron's gallant charge (one of the Stoneman boys saves his life at the end of it). Confederate soldiers must subsist on corn kernels. Women are down to their very last dresses. Children starve. Frame by frame, a gallant and peaceful people is destroyed in a war engineered by the Northern abolitionists.

While Ben Cameron is recovering from the war, physically and emotionally, blacks backed by the U.S. Army and congressional lead-ers of the Radical Republican Party begin to take over the Old South. Black politicians, led by sleazy Silas Lynch, Stoneman's protégé, get elected to legislatures (where audiences are shown—falsely—blacks outnumbering whites seven to one). Black soldiers push white South-erners off sidewalks. Laws are passed permitting blacks, but not whites, to vote and black soldiers shoo whites away from voting booths with rifles. Black legislators pass bills to approve black-white mar-riages and, as they vote, they gnaw on chicken legs, wiping their filthy hands on their pants, and get drunk. They leer at white women in the streets and stalk them through the woods for sex. They walk through towns telling now-freed slaves that they should stop working. These legislators are in charge, and they create chaos wherever they go.

What to do? Lincoln, "our best friend," according to the kindly old master of Cameron Hall, is gone (*Birth,* like so many Civil War silents, used Lincoln as a reunification bridge between sections). Congress won't help. The black army patrols the streets. The Confederate army has been beaten. To whom can white Southerners, the noble cavaliers who want only to be left alone, turn in their hour of need?

Enter the Ku Klux Klan.

It is kindly war hero Ben Cameron, seething at the way the freed slaves treat whites, who organizes the Klan. Throughout the remainder of the film that white-hooded vigilante group works hard to preserve justice for the whites in the New South. The climax of the film is their heroic charge to save the lives of white men and women trapped in a cabin and surrounded by black soldiers, a gallant and wonderfully filmed charge—with its own "Klan Call" orchestral music—that had moviegoers rising to their feet and cheering wildly.

Gus, a black U.S. soldier, is captured by the Ku Klux Klan and charged with the attempted rape of a Southern planter's sister, who leaped from a cliff and died rather than submit, in The Birth of a Nation. *He is given a speedy KKK trial and executed.*

The Birth of a Nation used and improved on every device of the Civil War silent film genre designed to reunify North and South and forge a new America. A Northern beauty (Elsie Stoneman) falls in love with a Southern gentleman (Ben Cameron). A Union friend (Stoneman) saves a Southern friend (Cameron) in battle. The dutiful mother successfully begs President Lincoln for a pardon. Lincoln, as always, is the saintly emancipator, just as the Southerners, as always, are portrayed as the gallant underdogs. The blame for the war is put squarely on the shoulders of the meddling abolitionists. Blacks, in the first half, are hardworking retainers who love their owners and cheer them on to victory in the war. The resident Mammy loves everybody and rebukes any other slaves who question the white family's behavior. At the end, everybody reunites with everybody else to show audiences that despite the Civil War, all Americans—except blacks—did, and should, live in harmony.

The Birth of a Nation was a blatantly racist film that egregiously slandered American blacks and helped to create a racial divide that would last for generations. In its adherence to Dixon's wholly fictional book, the movie took a huge step over the line and showed blacks during the war and in Reconstruction as rapists, thugs and murderers—all distortions presented as real history.

Worse than the idea that unchained blacks would take over the South (and the country) economically and politically, the film boldly suggested that they would take it over sexually, too. From political leaders to rough-hewn slaves throughout the film, blacks lusted after young white women. The first is Silas Lynch (George Siegmann in blackface), who is smitten by the beauty of Lillian Gish as young Elsie Stoneman.[1] Lynch's eyes devour young Elsie as she walks around the room. Unable to stand it any longer, he tells her near the end of the movie that he wants to marry her and moves menacingly toward her. She faints and saves herself. Her friend Flora Cameron meets a worse fate, of course, leaping to her death.

Earlier, when the black troops raid Piedmont, Griffith carefully crosscuts so we see the black troops move up the street and into the Cameron mansion at the same time the three women in the house move from room to room and finally to a hidden basement. There the girls pray for deliverance from the savage-looking blacks who are searching for them, intent on sexual gratification.

Rape and sex drift in the hot, lazy Southern air in *The Birth of a Nation*. Margaret Cameron, the older sister, whose beau has been killed in the war, sits next to a fence, sadly plucking the petals off a rose, the petals of her virginity her loved one will never have a chance to pluck. Black politicians carry posters with the slogan "Equal rights, equal politics, equal marriage." Lydia Brown, Austin Stoneman's mulatto servant and lover, is oversexed from the first time audiences meet her. She looks at men and rubs her breasts as her eyes roll lasciviously. A title explains that Stoneman's affair with her was "a great leader's weakness that was a blight to the nation."

Even apart from issues of race and rape, *The Birth of a Nation* was guilty of dreadful distortions and assumptions about history and people, and these made it a dangerous movie. The overriding theme of the movie is that blacks are surly people who can be controlled in bondage, but not when free. If given freedom, as they are in Griffith's version of Reconstruction, they will become black beasts, marauding from town to town, and destroy society. The Ku Klux Klan was necessary to rein in the blacks, to keep them in their place and save society. This was a dramatic switch from the accepted film presentation of African Americans merely as simple fools. Griffith had, with *Birth*, gone in a new and explosive direction.

In *Birth*, as in most silents, the North starts the war when Lincoln calls up seventy-five thousand troops to attack the South. On the title cards, a quote from President Woodrow Wilson's book *A History of the American People* tells audiences that "Congress wrought a veritable overthrow of civilization in the South" and "put the white South under the heel of the black South." (Wilson was born and raised in Virginia.)

It is a movie about an admirable high class (white) that is perpetually threatened by low classes (either Northerners or blacks). One of the most forceful scenes in the film is the burning of Atlanta by Sherman's army. From out of the columns of smoke billowing skyward, the Southerners flee Atlanta dressed in finely tailored suits and top hats. In reality, families tossed everything they could into wagons and got out of town before the fires started. No one bothered to dress up.

The Southland, as Griffith so quaintly called it, was a genteel place run by true aristocrats, and it functioned well. There were three levels of society—the planter aristocracy, the poor farmers and the slaves—and everybody knew his place. When one class threatens another, as happened when the freed slaves returned as black soldiers, any society would fall apart. The lesson, then, in 1915, when American audiences first saw the film, was that contemporary society could break apart just as easily then as it did in 1861 if one class—blacks—forgot its station and tried to replace a class above it—at that time, the poor whites and the immigrants.

In the film, the breakdown of law and order comes not because the blacks decided they could do whatever they wanted, but because the United States Army, with its all-black regiments, let them. The underlying reason for this breakdown is not the collapse of a race, but the breakdown of American politics: people can't function when a government can't function. And when a government can't function properly but needs to stay in power, that government, any government, turns to its army to keep order, which is exactly what the U.S. Army is doing in *Birth*. White Southerners, then, kept out of a political system that was breaking down, and without any kind of police help, had no resources to protect themselves and their families except through a body outside the government and established authority—the Ku Klux Klan. It is a perfectly reasoned argument but one whose basic assumption, that race caused the breakdown of the government, was completely fictitious.

Black leaders argued that *The Birth of a Nation* did more than mangle history; it completely fabricated it. The power of the movie, they feared, correctly, would make millions of Americans believe in events that had never taken place.

Blacks did not control the Republican legislatures of any of the eleven Southern states in Reconstruction. The only state in which black legislators outnumbered whites, with eighty-seven blacks and sixty-nine whites, was South Carolina, where Griffith's invented Piedmont was located. The blacks had a slender majority only in the lower house, though, not the upper, which controlled legislation.[2] Blacks usually represented no more than 25 percent of any legislative house, although they managed to get sixteen congressmen and one governor elected and were also represented by three lieutenant governors and several state cabinet members. South Carolina was also the only state in which black convention delegates outnumbered whites, seventy-six to forty-eight, but the South Carolina convention was one of the fairest and most visionary. It called for integrated schools; restored political power to interior regions that had long suffered at the hands of legislators from big cities; enlarged women's rights; voted for manhood suffrage for all men, black and white; abolished property qualifications for officeholders, black and white; called for the direct election of the governor; adopted the state's first divorce law; strengthened the state's fiscal power; reformed county governments; and

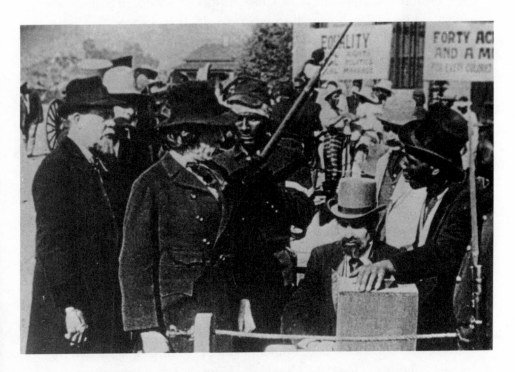

In The Birth of a Nation, *blacks are, quite inaccurately, depicted as preventing whites from voting.*

revised the tax system. This was hardly the work of the drunken, chicken-eating, barefoot rogues in *Birth*.[3] Although all of the Reconstruction legislatures called for equal voting and social rights for blacks and whites, not one of them ever passed or debated a bill for intermarriage.

Black legislators, aware of how important their every move was, were remarkably restrained. "The Negroes were seldom vindictive in their use of political power or in their attitude towards the native whites," said the editor of one Southern newspaper. "To be sure, there were plenty of cases of friction between Negroes and whites, and Negro militiamen were sometimes inordinately aggressive. But in no Southern state did any responsible Negro leader, or any substantial Negro group, attempt to get complete political control into the hands of freedmen."[4]

Surveys of states in the Reconstruction South show a pattern of responsible government by black legislators and, except in South Carolina, white majorities in all statehouses. John R. Lynch, of Mississippi, one of just two black congressmen from that state elected during Reconstruction, noted that black officeholders had minimal influence. "The State, district, county and municipal governments were," Lynch wrote, "not only in control of white men, but white men who were to the manor born, or who were known as old citizens of the State—those who had lived in the State many years before the War of Rebellion. There was, therefore, never a time when that class of white men known as Carpetbaggers had absolute control of the State government, or that of any district court or municipality. There was never, therefore, any ground for the alleged apprehension of negro domination as a result of a free, fair and honest election in any one of the South or reconstructed States."[5]

Many whites agreed with his contention. An editorial in the Jackson, Mississippi, *Clarion* in 1872 stated that its own coverage of the statehouse showed no black domination.[6]

Sensible government in Reconstruction legislatures was important for the overall political development of blacks in the South, and in the nation, and black legislators knew it. Historian Eric Foner notes that freed slaves in the Caribbean and other areas may have been given land by the government, but they were not given any political power. The U.S. government gave the ex-slaves some land, but the most important legislation was to give ex-slaves the vote. No black man elected to the legislature was about to jeopardize that opportunity.[7]

There was corruption in Reconstruction politics, but little by black legislators. The worst was by the white governor of South Carolina, Franklin Moses Jr., who, between 1872 and 1874, as legislator and governor, reportedly looted the state treasury and took bribes to use his influence to pass legislation.[8]

Congress gave African Americans citizenship and the right to vote via the Thirteenth, Fourteenth and Fifteenth Amendments to the U.S. Constitution. Black leaders marshaled local political groups into voting blocs and, like all political leaders, made an effort to get out the vote on election day. Black candidates took out ads in newspapers, stumped through their towns and counties and strung together coalitions to defeat strong white candidates. They organized and spoke at mass public rallies, held protests marches and demonstrations and started black newspapers when white publications would not aid them.

Blacks attempted to work with whites as sharecroppers, attempted to live with them in cities and towns and attempted to help them bring the industrial revolution to the Southern states, but failed at all these. White social and political leaders in the Southern states, given the opportunity for full integration, turned their backs on African Americans and tried, through open politics where possible and through vigilante groups, like the KKK, in secret, to crush them. At the same time, Southern whites angered Radical Republicans in Congress by treating Northern whites working or visiting in the South harshly.

In 1865 and 1866, efforts by the Andrew Johnson administration to achieve a modest reconstruction by utilizing federal agencies such as the Freedmen's Bureau, to aid former slaves, moved slowly, as did efforts to permit former Southern leaders to return to public office.

A series of race riots in the South in 1866 brought about the Reconstruction Act of 1867, seen as necessary to protect recently freed blacks and create democracy in the South. In one riot in Memphis—touched off by a dispute over a carriage accident—forty-six blacks were killed and three hundred injured. A New Orleans race riot a few months later resulted in the deaths of thirty-four blacks and injuries to more than two hundred.

Reconstruction turned the South into a colony occupied by the Union army. It was split up into five different military districts and run by military law. Former officials who had fought in the war were not permitted to hold office again and black officeholders were encouraged. The reaction of many in the South to the integrationist Reconstruction era was quick and violent. From 1867 to 1876, when Reconstruction ended, members of the KKK and other vigilante organizations managed to assault nearly 10 percent of all African Americans who attended any black political conventions held during that period. In 1867, one KKK group murdered sixty-one blacks marching in a parade and later, at night, swept through the area and murdered two hundred more. The KKK killed thirteen blacks following an election in 1871. Newspaper editors, black and white, were dragged from their homes and beaten, and their offices burned. And the savagery was often random and personal. One night a KKK group murdered and disemboweled a black man in front of his wife, who had just given birth to twins. Historically, the KKK were the villains in the South, not the heroes *Birth* made them out to be.[9]

Blacks in 1915 argued that it was not Radical Republicans who ruined the chances for integration in the South. They complained that the depiction of Austin Stoneman, clearly based on the political life of Radical Republican leader Thaddeus Stevens, was misleading and historically wrong. In the movie, Stoneman (Stevens) moves from Washington to South Carolina to oversee his "black empire." In reality, Stevens, seventy-three years old and quite ill when the war ended, never went south of the Potomac River bridge and spent most of his time in Washington and Pennsylvania. In the movie, Stoneman is a loving father to two fine sons (one was killed in the war) and a gorgeous daughter, Elsie. Stevens never married and had no children. He did have a black housekeeper, but there is no evidence that there was any relationship between them. There is no evidence that Stevens took more than a passing interest in the activities of any Southern legislatures, either, even though he was the primary sponsor of the Reconstruction Bill. The one radical policy that Stevens did push hard for, confiscation of all Southern plantations, was voted down by his own party in Congress.[10] Actually, the most hated Radical Republican in Congress was not Stevens but Senator Charles Sumner of Massachusetts, who had prodded Abraham Lincoln to emancipate the slaves since Lincoln's arrival in Washington, weeks before he was even inaugurated.

Finally, during or after the Civil War, there was never any recorded incident of black soldiers, whether in the Union army or in a militia during Reconstruction, shooting or killing civilians anywhere in the South, as they do frequently in the movie. When the war ended and the army shrank, eighty-three thousand blacks (36 percent of the remaining troops) were kept on by the federal government as a show of integrated strength, and most of them were based in the Southern states of Mississippi, Louisiana, Kentucky and Tennessee. The percentage was high because these men enlisted late in the war and were scheduled to serve three years. The presence of black regiments angered Southerners, who felt not only occupied, but occupied by the very men they had been forced to free.

What is true is that in 1865 several Mississippi planters complained to their legislators that black troops were secretly plotting with freed slave laborers to stage an insurrection and murder local white residents. In February 1866, Governor Charles Jenkins of Georgia forwarded a petition to army headquarters in Washington, D.C. The petition, signed by thirty-eight residents of Columbus, Georgia, describes black troop behavior there that was nearly identical to the scenes in *Birth*. Jenkins said that local residents claimed that black troops pushed and shoved white people off sidewalks and streets, abused and intimidated them, and that on one occasion a black soldier, shot by a white man, fired his weapon and wounded a white resident. And some Virginia residents charged that black troops destroyed their homes and used the wooden boards of the walls for firewood.

All of these charges were investigated exhaustively by the army or the government, and the investigations found that the black troops behaved in exemplary fashion; not one black soldier was prosecuted for criminal activity. Two white Virginia commanders backed up their black troops. General Godfrey Weitzel, after an investigation of alleged abuses, found black troops innocent and wrote General Grant that "the behavior of my entire corps during the last month has been most excellent." General E. O. C. Ord, in a separate report two days later, wrote Grant of troops in Richmond whose "conduct is spoken of [by residents] as very good."

The troops considered the least offensive to white residents during the early days of Reconstruction were, oddly enough, the very troops D. W. Griffith smeared in *Birth*—those in South Carolina. That state had the fewest black troops when the war ended and minimal complaints. The white commanders working there praised their black regiments. General George Meade, then commander of the entire Atlantic military district, wrote the secretary of war that after an investigation of white complaints the charges were found to be groundless. Colonel A. J. Willard, head of the military district in Charleston, South Carolina, agreed, finding, after his investigation, that troops were not guilty of any abuses and were, in fact, better soldiers than the white troops under his command and a symbol of hope to the freed people of the city.

Both army commanders and civilians in the occupied Southern states reported that black troops *were* instrumental in the founding and construction of numerous schools for black children, the development of local political parties and encouraging freed black laborers to work with white supervisors on cotton, tobacco and sugar plantations without confrontation.

In fact, black soldiers frequently complained of abuse by white residents. It is on record that a black sergeant in Columbia, South Carolina, reported that white residents broke into his home and looted it. One black soldier was badly beaten by two white police officers in Memphis, Tennessee. A black soldier in Kentucky who returned to his former plantation to remove his wife and children was arrested on charges of stealing the clothes that the children wore. White townspeople in Columbus, Georgia, in a heated dispute, shot a black soldier.[11]

Historically, the involvement of black troops in the Southern states, regardless of complaints, ended quickly because the federal government was under increasing pressure from white residents and politicians to remove them. Thousands of black soldiers were transferred to Texas and other Western posts and thousands more were honorably discharged, their places taken by white soldiers. By October 1866, the number of black troops in Southern states had been reduced from eighty-three thousand to twelve thousand and by 1867, the year the Reconstruction Act was passed—the time chronicled in *Birth*—there were no black U.S. Army troops in any of the Southern states.[12]

And most black troops did leave peacefully and without any animosity concerning their treatment. White officers commanding black regiments often reminded their men, as the regiments broke up, to live amicably with Southern whites. "Harbor no feelings of hatred toward your former masters . . . seek in the paths of honesty, virtue, sobriety and industry . . . to grow up to the full stature of American citizens," said one.[13]

There were only a handful of local black militias, usually found in small black communities, put together to fight off the Klan. In not a single instance did any of these units attack whites. To the contrary, in one notable incident in 1876, the local militia of Hamburg, South Carolina, a practically all-black rural community, was conducting a routine drill when two white men in a buggy began arguing with some of the militiamen. Later, the two angry white men brought back the Red Shirts, a KKK type of organization, which attacked the black militia and murdered a half dozen members.[14]

The protests in Los Angeles when *Birth* opened genuinely surprised Griffith, who believed he had directed a historically honest movie. And those were just the first wave. There was also talk of picket lines, injunctions and law suits in New York. Griffith and Harry Aitken arranged a private screening for seventy-five influential New Yorkers prior to the opening at Manhattan's Liberty Theatre. Those invitees included politicians, clergy, theater distributors and editors. Author Thomas Dixon was there, too. Attendees saw the just-edited version and loved it. Applause rocked the building. Dixon, who watched it from the balcony, ran downstairs, grabbed a jubilant Griffith by the arm and said, "Let's not call it *The Clansman* any more. It's too big for that. Let's call it *The Birth of a Nation*."[15]

Dixon's enthusiastic suggestion for a title change, and the unanimous agreement to go along with the idea, underscores the distorted view held by Dixon, Griffith and Aitken. Ignoring the true birth of the American nation in 1776 with the Declaration of Independence, which stated that *all* men were created equal (by implication, this meant both black and white), and the American Revolution, they believed that the United States was born in Reconstruction and white supremacy. The new patriotic title of the movie symbolized the racist view of its author and director, and, in the wild success of the film, of its national audience.

NAACP efforts to ban the film in New York by having the Liberty Theatre's license yanked started right after the Los Angeles premiere, but New York mayor John Purroy Mitchell seemed satisfied with Griffith's cuts, which eliminated the most racist scenes in the film. The NAACP then went to the National Board of Review, a 125-member group, in an effort to have the film banned. The national board found nothing wrong with it.

Thomas Dixon had a brainstorm. They had good reviews in the Los Angeles press, but what if they could get the president of the United States to promote the movie? Dixon had been a classmate of President Woodrow Wilson in graduate school at Johns Hopkins and the two had been friendly there. Dixon called the White House and within two days had an interview with Wilson. He asked Wilson to see the movie and if he liked it perhaps to say something they could use in advertisements. Wilson agreed to this favor because years before, at a low point in Wilson's life, Dixon had apparently arranged for his alma mater, Wake Forest, to award the then history professor an honorary doctorate.

The first-ever film screening for a president was held at the White House on February 18. Even though the movie had been running in Los Angeles for ten days and newspapers in many cities had run articles about the political storm it had started, President Wilson was willing to see it, and perhaps comment on it. Even more surprising was that his aides, who read many of the major newspapers in the country, let him be put in that position. According to Dixon, Wilson turned to him when the film ended and said: "It is like writing history with lightning. And my only regret is that it is all so terribly true."[16]

An elated Dixon called Griffith with the news and Griffith told him to come back to New York so he could get the story to their public relations man. Wilson, after he saw the quote in hundreds of newspaper ads, immediately issued a press release emphatically denying having made such a statement, but the damage was done.

Dixon continued to insist that the president had given him the quote at the end of the screening, and that Wilson had been pleased that quotes from his *History of the American People* were used in the film as historical sources to back up the plot. A careful reading of Wilson's book, though, shows that Griffith took huge liberties with the text. What Wilson wrote was that white politicians used the black vote to get into office and then ran corrupt state governments. Wilson never blamed blacks themselves for any of the corruption. He never wrote about the activities of blacks in any of the state legislatures, although one of *Birth*'s harshest and meanest scenes focuses on the South Carolina legislature.[17]

Griffith also in many cases quoted only parts of Wilson's sentences and used them wholly out of context. One title card describes black legislators as "men who could not so much as write their names and who knew none of the uses of authority except its insolence." Wilson used that line to describe the black voters who elected the carpetbaggers who ruined the Southern states. He was not referring to the black legislators themselves. At another point in the movie, a Griffith title card says before a picture of black legislators that the "white South" had come under "a black heel." Wilson's actual statement was that the black votes enabled white Northerners to control the white South.

Press releases for the movie stressed to reporters, editors and critics that the historical content of the movie was based largely on President Wilson's book. That was the foundation, Griffith said, for his portrayal of the Klan. What the president actually had written was that the Klan was founded because of the abuses of the white Northern carpetbaggers who took over the government. He said nothing about black violence. Wilson had nothing but disdain for the KKK; he considered them thugs and vigilantes and wrote in *A History of the American People* that Klan members "took the law into their own hands and began to attempt by intimidation what they were not allowed to attempt by the ballot or by any ordered course of public action."[18]

It is hard to believe that, even to help Thomas Dixon promote his movie, President Wilson said the film was a true depiction of an era he himself saw quite differently. That is particularly unlikely because during that very winter Wilson had come under heavy fire from immigrants about disparaging remarks he had allegedly made about them in that same book. Wilson must have read through his own book again to answer the immigrant groups' charges and at least leafed through his chapter on Reconstruction. If not, he surely must have reviewed it before he went to Dixon's screening to make certain he would not commit yet another gaffe. Presidents don't risk careers paying back small favors.

Dixon, for his part, inspired by his high-level personal diplomacy at the White House, decided to try it on the Supreme Court. The minister-author braved a chilly afternoon walk across the streets of Washington to see Chief Justice Edward White, a Louisianian, to try to get him and other justices to look at the movie. Some did. Intoxicated with his luck, Dixon then set up a third screening and persuaded several congressmen to see the movie. The important men who attended these screenings to see what the uproar was about unintentionally appeared to be giving the movie a high-level imprimatur, which Dixon hoped would quash the growing dissent that surrounded it.

There were no pickets at the March 3 New York opening, which was a huge financial and critical success. The mayor of New York and a local court turned down NAACP efforts to halt the screening. There were pickets in Boston for the movie's April 17 opening at the Tremont Theatre, however, and they threw the film, and all of Boston, into an uproar. When the NAACP failed to get an injunction, many blacks bought tickets to see the movie while hundreds protested outside. In the middle of the screening, a black member of the audience threw an egg at the screen. As if on cue, several other blacks in the audience set off stink bombs. This was at the end of the movie and people started shoving one another. At the final curtain the manager ordered everyone out of the theater. A blacks-against-whites melee began in the lobby and continued in the streets when hundreds of audience members surged into the crowd of protestors outside. Mayor James Michael Curley sent 260 police to quell the riot. The result was eleven arrests. The next day, Curley presided over a public hearing, attended by thousands of blacks, on whether to ban the film. Griffith defended the movie; an NAACP attorney attacked it. Curley, a clever politician, ruled that the movie would be banned for one day, that Sunday, but could reopen on Monday. He barred further protests.[19]

That was it. The NAACP sent thousands of brochures to its local chapters in every city where *Birth* played and dozens of chapters tried to get the theaters' and distributors' licenses revoked and the film banned, but without success. Several NAACP chapters went to court to get injunctions and failed. Newspapers, black and white, printed stories about the various efforts to shut down the movie, but the adverse publicity did not hurt the box office at all.

In fact, business seemed to be better in cities where protests over the film were reported in the newspapers. It thus appeared to demonstrate the truth of that old show-business adage, "All publicity is good publicity." Within the media, people raised their eyebrows every time a protest story about *Birth* appeared in a newspaper. "Cynical showmen have often wondered if Ted Mitchell [Griffith's public relations director] and company were entirely innocent of encouraging, for PR purposes, the spectacular opposition to the movie," observed one reporter.[20] But for every negative story in the papers, there were two stories about how good the movie was. Reporters who wrote about the film (in that era, there were no "critics" as we know them today), well aware of the protests and black complaints, thought it was the greatest film ever made and said so, believing Griffith's version of Reconstruction because everything that preceded it in literature, history and theater had programmed them to accept that view of the Old South.

Although Americans paid whatever was asked to see *The Birth of a Nation,* the attacks on the movie hurt D. W. Griffith deeply, and his pain was not eased by the record box office reports that flew over the telegraph lines from all over the nation. He went to the premiere of *Birth* in just about every major city, walked slowly to the middle of the theater stage—usually to deafening applause—and defended the movie in a speech.

It seemed that he believed that the story he presented of blacks as rapists and thugs, and of Klansmen as gallant heroes, was true. In 1915 he told critics that the story was based on fact and that his staff had researched it.[21] He said that he and his staff had read numerous books on the war. In advertisements, public relations wizard Mitchell emphasized all the research Griffith's staff reportedly had done. These ads claimed that for the single scene of Lincoln's assassination alone his researchers had consulted eighteen books.[22] The books they read, though, were not scholarly works or even commercial analyses of the conflict. They were superficial illustrated books, such as *Mathew Brady's Civil War Photographs: Confederate and Union Veterans, Eyewitnesses on Location, Harper's Pictorial History of the Civil War* and *The Soldier in Our Civil War: A Pictorial History of the Conflict, 1861–1865.* The staff relied on a biography of Lincoln written not by a historian or journalist, but by Lincoln's personal secretaries John Hay and John Nicolay. Another book was *Ku Klux Klan—Its Origin, Growth, and Disbandment,* by J. C. Lester and D. L. Wilson. If Griffith and his aides did read the same historians everyone else read during that era, they read James Rhodes and John Burgess, both Southern-biased, who argued that the South was not responsible for slavery or the war.[23]

The director never wavered from his defense and scoffed at suggestions that his Southern upbringing and his father's participation in the Confederate army gave him a distorted view of history. In a 1947 letter to *Sight & Sound* magazine, Griffith wrote: "In filming *The Birth of a Nation,* I gave to my best knowledge the proven facts and presented the known truth about the Reconstruction period in the American South. These facts are based on an overwhelming compilation of authentic evidence and testimony. My picturization of history as it happens requires, therefore, no apology, no defense, no 'explanations.' "[24]

Griffith was moved to write a pamphlet about freedom of speech to defend himself against constant attacks by the NAACP and the few whites who found the film offensive. He wrote: "The integrity of free speech and publication was not attacked seriously in this country until the arrival of the motion picture, when this new art was seized by the powers of intolerance as an excuse for an assault on our liberties . . . The motion picture is a medium of expression as clean and decent as any mankind has ever discovered. A people that would allow the suppression of this form of speech would unquestionably submit to the suppression of that which we all consider so highly, the printing press."[25]

Even if Griffith was so sure of his history, why did no one at Mutual Pictures expect the tidal wave of protest that came from black groups? How could such a big-budget movie, the longest film of its time, have been released without any thought of the reaction it might get? Recent scholars have suggested that Mutual did not anticipate any protest because the NAACP was only six years old when the movie debuted. But the NAACP already had some of the best lawyers in the country, already had a publicity office, already had printers churning out civil rights pamphlets, already had strong ties to black newspapers.

And the association had already carried out a relatively successful campaign against a movie called *The Nigger. The Nigger* was the story of a turn-of-the-century black man in the South who through a fluke in the voting system becomes the state's governor and is assaulted with trouble as soon as he takes office. The NAACP had no great problems with the script, although it was loaded with defamatory language, but they resented the title. They failed to get it changed in most places, but did get New England distributors to change it to *The New Governor*—a major accomplishment for an organization then just a year old. NAACP leaders had succeeded once and, when *Birth* premiered, were certain they could do it again.

The film business was a small community, and everybody in it knew what was happening to everybody else. Griffith and the Aitkens had to know the story of the NAACP and *The Nigger*. And Dixon, an avowed racist, had turned the Klan into heroes in not one, but three novels. He did it, he said, to "set the record straight" on Reconstruction.[26] In *The Clansman*, the novel, he presented Dr. Cameron as saying about blacks: that "for a thick lipped, flat nosed, spindle shanked Negro, exuding his nauseous animal odor, to shout in derision over the hearths and homes of white men and women is an atrocity too monstrous for belief." In Dixon's book there were numerous incidents of black soldiers bullying whites during Reconstruction, and long speeches by various characters denouncing the black race.

In the play *The Clansman*, the stage setting for the opening scene reads: "Negroes . . . all talking, shouting with noisy enthusiasm. Pocket flasks are passed from hand to hand. Negro troopers pass and are joyously saluted by crowd. Two to three white males come through, with dubious looks shake their heads . . . and exchange meaningful looks, exit to Cameron House . . ."[27]

In that very first scene, two blacks in a crowd are talking about their newly won right to vote, as new political leaders in Dixon's South restricted white voting rights.

DICK: How many times you vote, brudder?
GUS: E'vry chance I get—hain't keep no count.[28]

How could anyone reading such dialogue think *The Clansman* was an honest historical look at Reconstruction or African Americans of the era? Could it be that Griffith, through some convoluted thinking, decided that because he had considerably toned down Dixon's play he was telling an accurate story?

"The real story of Reconstruction has never been filmed," Griffith told Harry Aitken and his brother Roy at their first meeting. "It offers great possibilities for exciting drama and extensive camera techniques. Tom is a southerner. He knows how deeply the South was hurt and how long it took her to regain her strength. I, too, am a southerner. My father was a Confederate officer. I know the hardships southerners endured in defeat. . . . We must lay emphasis upon the revengeful congressmen and senators, and upon the unscrupulous white carpetbaggers. We must show them bent on revenge and plunder, stirring up the free Negroes, confusing them and creating misery and suffering among the southerners. Then we must have many Klan scenes."[29]

In 1965, fifty years after the film's premiere, Roy Aitken said that Griffith had complete confidence in Dixon's historical views and that both were fans of the Ku Klux Klan.

"Ah, the Klan," said Dixon to Aitken. "It was the Klan that saved the South."[30]

There was a reason Griffith admired the KKK. It wasn't until fifteen years after *Birth*'s first release, when it was reissued in 1930, that Griffith publicly let slip that his father was probably a member of the Klan. In a three-minute film segment that preceded the rereleased feature, Griffith (by his own arrangement) was interviewed by Walter Huston.

> HUSTON: Did you tell your father's story?
> GRIFFITH: Perhaps I did. I used to get under the table and listen to my father and friends talk about their struggle. Those things impress you deeply . . . I listened to him talk about fighting day after day, Mother staying up night after night sewing robes for the Klan. . . .[31]

Griffith always took full responsibility for the movie.[32] He was convinced his view was correct and was determined to impose it on everyone. Later historians, understanding the power of literature and film, have seen them as unbelievably powerful conveyors of legend and myth, such as those constructed by Griffith, and not of actual history. "Rhetoric *makes* history by shaping reality to the dictates of its political design: it makes history by convincing the people of the world that its description of the world is the true one," wrote Jane Tompkins in 1985.[33]

And that is what D. W. Griffith did. He did not make history with a vision; he made history fit his vision.

Film executives who screened the final cut saw nothing wrong with *Birth*. Neither did any members of the cast or crew. Chief cinematographer Billy Bitzer thought it was just another titillating, if rather long, sexual romp. Lillian Gish, there for most of the photography, said no one anticipated the firestorm of criticism.

"The first run-through of the complete film," Gish wrote later, "was to be shown to most of the cast that evening and we gathered in the small projection room. I was swept away with the others as the story unfolded . . . When the lights came on, we sat in stunned silence. As I glanced over my shoulder, I noticed that Mr. Griffith was still in his seat. When they could control their emotions, everyone gathered around him with praise and gratitude for having been part of it."[34]

The distributors who purchased the film, theater owners who screened it and most of the critics who reviewed it did not object to it, either. Audiences saw nothing wrong with *Birth,* its historical distortions and racial crucifixion, because between 1865 and 1915 the nation had moved to a point where blacks were hopelessly buried in the basement of American political and social culture, in the North as well as the South. To all those people out there in the dark, shifting in seats in theaters from Maine to Minnesota, the idea of Griffith's black rapists and murderers did not seem exaggerated at all.

CHAPTER EIGHT

Birth: Titanic Box Office and Tattered Legacy

THE BIRTH OF A NATION was the first heavily marketed movie, the beneficiary of a promotion drive that not only was unprecedented in the movie business of 1915 but would have impressed film companies today. Roy Aitken and D. W. Griffith were promotional geniuses themselves and had hired a great public relations director in Ted Mitchell. The trio seemed to think of everything. They printed thousands of programs and sold them at theaters. They not only used a quote supposedly from President Wilson, but even paid well-known writer Booth Tarkington to come up with a quote they could splash in ads across the country ("It will take the whole country by storm . . . ," Tarkington wrote for them).[1] In the towns on its national tour, they put up huge electric signs advertising the movie two weeks before it arrived. Griffith's publicity managers would send Mutual workers dressed as Klansmen to parade through a town as a publicity stunt the night before *Birth* was to open there. In New York, movie company administrators had horsemen in Klan costume restage the film's "ride of the Klan" through a city park.

Klan mania seemed to be everywhere. Josephine Crowell, who played Ma Cameron in the film, tried to make some money by designing a ladies' "ku klux hat," which was a dark blue conical affair made to look like a Klan hood.[2] Girls in several University of Chicago sororities staged a Halloween dance at which everybody arrived dressed as a Klansman.[3]

Besieged with requests for prints of the film from around the country, producer Harry Aitken decided to take the movie on the road, instead of merely mailing prints to theaters that requested them. Administrators, technicians and an entire forty-piece orchestra piled onto railroad cars on each of three separate trains and headed off to show *Birth* to the country. Also on each train were hundreds of extra folding chairs, at two dollars apiece, in case theaters ran out of seats and needed more. Each train also carried dozens of Civil War–era costumes for Mutual's workers to wear as ushers in the various theaters they toured.[4]

The real purpose of The Birth of a Nation *was the glorification of the Ku Klux Klan, seen here chasing black soldiers out of a small Southern town.*

Dozens of people were hired by Aitken in New York just to keep financial records for *Birth,* and an additional company, Epoch Productions, was formed by Griffith and Aitken to distribute the movie. Costs were high, of course, with the average road company piling up $150,000 a year in expenses,[5] but the grosses were record-breaking. Epoch's treasurer's report for the first six months of 1915 showed that

Birth's ticket sales just for the three traveling road companies were $1,802,792.[6]

Mitchell dreamed up the idea of *"Birth of a Nation* Specials," trains that Mutual Pictures leased throughout the country to bring people from outlying areas (particularly farm communities in the South and Midwest) to a nearby city where the film was showing. The cost was minuscule compared to the profits made on ticket sales.[7]

The movie's success was unprecedented. Some theaters showed the film for months, with the record being set by a New York theater that kept it for an entire year (today's blockbuster movie will usually run for just a few months in a single theater). Local theater managers quickly realized that *Birth* was so popular that they could charge just about whatever they wanted—with ticket prices averaging one dollar and in some places two dollars (about thirty-three dollars per ticket in today's money). Going to see *Birth* became a national obsession.

Many exhibitors assumed *Birth* would do better in the South than in the North, but in fact *Birth*'s biggest grosses came from Northern and Western cities, where audiences were just as accepting of the film's racial slant as those in the South. *Birth* was booked into Los Angeles for twenty-two weeks and Chicago for thirty-five weeks.[8] New York's Liberty Theatre, which had 1,246 seats, alone reported that in its forty-eight weeks it had 620 showings, which grossed $616,000.[9]

Harry Sherman, a film distributor who held rights to the Midwest and Southwest regional areas, said in 1949 that the accounting ledgers for his *Birth* tours showed that the movie earned $1.6 million over two years in Iowa alone, $8 million in two years over his nineteen-state territory and, when it was reissued for one year in 1921 in that same territory, earned another $4 million. Sherman's most impressive figures were from tiny Winslow, Arizona. "We rented," he said, "an empty hall and put up 1,100 wooden chairs. We charged $3 for the night shows and $2 for the matinees. We sold out two shows each day and left town after two days with $5,300."[10]

By 1921, at *Birth*'s first reissue, the movie was estimated to have grossed over $20 million, and by 1941, close to $45 million. By 1949, *Variety* estimated *Birth*'s total revenue at slightly over $50 million, close to $1 billion in contemporary revenue, making it one of the most successful movies of all time.[11]

The principals made a fortune. Thomas Dixon's share was $1.25 million. Griffith's was $1.11 million. Epoch Productions and the Aitken brothers netted some $3.5 million. Harry Sherman earned over $1 million, and Louis B. Mayer over $500,000 as New England distributor. Some of them invested the money wisely. Sherman moved to Los Angeles and became a film producer; he made considerable money as the man behind the long-running Hopalong Cassidy film series.[12] Mayer was more successful than anyone. He, too, moved to Hollywood and used all his money, plus whatever he could borrow, and, with partners, founded Metro-Goldwyn-Mayer (MGM).[13]

Others invested poorly. Dixon lost much of his money bankrolling his own films, five of them, over the next few years. Griffith sank the entire $1.1 million into his next picture, *Intolerance,* which was a disaster. It was said that Griffith made the picture to demonstrate that he was not a racist. He lost every penny. He soon found himself in raging battles with Harry Aitken over company policies and severed that connection to join others in a new company, Triangle Productions.[14] The Aitkens, who tried to expand too quickly, soon went out of business.

A large proportion of the press in 1915 loved *Birth.* A *New York Times* account was typical. "A great deal might be said concerning the spirit revealed in Mr. Dixon's review of the unhappy chapter of Reconstruction and concerning the sorry service rendered by its plucking of old wounds. But of the film as a film, it may be reported simply that it is an impressive new illustration of the scope of the motion picture camera," a reporter wrote.[15]

The *New York Journal* agreed. Dorothy Dix (syndicated by the Hearst chain) wrote in one of her many columns, "I believed that the silent drama could never touch emotions very deeply . . . *The Birth of a Nation* disproves this. Here is a war play the like of which has never been presented on any stage before . . . that worked the audience into a perfect frenzy."[16] In another story, Dix wrote that the film would make "better Americans" of those who saw it.

Writer Steve Talbot, of the *Lincolnian,* in Lincoln, Nebraska, scoffed at critics of the rape-suicide scene and said: "[Griffith's] masterpiece is the most thrilling exposition of the Reconstruction of the South and a half dozen of his colored characters are portrayed as possessing all the virtues of honesty, loyalty and devotion to their benefactors which history teachers say was a part of the Southern Negro's nature . . ."[17]

Life magazine agreed. "*The Birth of a Nation* is the biggest attraction of the season," according to writer James Metcalfe.[18] Novelist Rupert Hughes (who wrote the original program notes), reacting to efforts to have the film shut down, wrote: "It is hard to see how this drama could be composed without the struggle of evil against good. Furthermore, it is to the advantage of the Negro today to know how some of his ancestors misbehaved and why the prejudices in his path have grown here. Surely no friend of his is to be turned into an enemy by this film, and no enemy more deeply embittered . . . If authors are never to make use of plots which might offend certain sects, sections, professions, trades, races or political parties, then creative art is indeed in a sad plight. The suppression of such fictional pieces has always been one of the chief instruments of tyranny."[19]

Many critics and ministers who, like Hughes, believed *Birth* was a true story argued that it should be mandatory viewing in churches and schools. A critic for a Hearst paper wrote: "Children must be sent to see this masterpiece. Any parent who neglects this advice is committing an educational offense, for no film has ever produced more educational points than Griffith's latest achievement."[20]

The Reverend Lyman Rutledge, pastor of the Harvard Street Unitarian Church in Cambridge, Massachusetts, wrote that the film "presents . . . the glory of the Ku Klux Klan." He went on: "There is no possibility of ever effacing the vivid memory of those night riders. Their memory is to be forever associated with the thrill of joy. They stand here for that divine spirit which is above the law."[21]

Moviegoers, both North and South, seemed to love the film. "The awful restraint of the audience is thrown to the winds. Many rise from their seats. With the roar of thunder, a shout goes up. Justice is at hand. Retribution has arrived," wrote reporter Ned McIntosh of the opening in an Atlanta theater.[22]

There were some whites who disliked *Birth*. An editorial writer for the *New York Globe* wrote: "To make a few dirty dollars, men are willing to pander to depraved tastes and to foment race antipathy that is the most sinister and dangerous feature of American life."[23] Francis Hackett wrote a scathing commentary about it in the *New Republic*:

"Whatever happened during Reconstruction, this film is aggressively vicious and defamatory. It is spiritual assassination. It degrades the censors that passed it and the white race that endures it."[24]

There were influential white civic leaders who opposed it, too. The politically well connected Frederic Howe was the commissioner of immigration for New York and chairman of the National Board of Review. He found *Birth* abhorrent and urged members of the Board to bar the movie unless it was severely revised. He suggested cutting out the entire second half of the film. They ignored him.

Some of the country's leading intellectuals and social activists condemned it. The NAACP invited social workers Jane Addams and Lillian Wald, financier Jacob Schiff, and biochemist Jacques Loeb, all prominent whites, along with several influential white Southerners, to a screening of *Birth*. All attacked the film as untrue and unfair. It was "a pernicious caricature of the Negro race . . . unjust and untrue," Addams said in an interview with the *New York Post*. She added that the movie's version of history was slanted and that its depictions of blacks showed them to be "worse than childish and brutal and vicious—actually grotesque and primitive and despicable."[25]

Some members of state and city censorship boards objected to the inference that blacks in 1915 as well as in 1866 were murderous. The film was approved by the city of Chicago's censorship board, but with this proviso: "This court will have to assume that they who will witness the play [movie] will [not] be so stupid that they will be unable to comprehend that the people represented on the canvas were of two to three generations ago . . . in the succeeding time the Negro race has advanced immeasurably."[26]

Later, more and more Americans denounced the movie, their numbers growing as the years went by and Americans' view of black-white relations changed. Max Lerner, writing in the *New York Post* in 1950, deplored it, calling it "a classic of racist passions, rape and lynch-law." He added: "Having seen it, I want to tell you about it so that you may save your time for something better, and spare yourselves the ordeal. . . . The picture has been called an epic. It is just that—an epic of the rise of the Ku Klux Klan, with a justification of its birth and violence. I suppose the movie historians are enamored of its handling of big crowds, its battle and mob scenes, in the grandiose fashion which Cecil De Mille has dubiously carried on. But even on this score it has little that has not been done far better since in many Grade B westerns. . . ."[27]

Writing in 1976, Eric Rhode said: "*The Birth of a Nation* [was] to show the Negro as the greatest danger to the values he [Griffith] cherished. His racism [was] . . . a malevolence that suffuses the whole action and allied as it is with his gift for persuasion it results in a propaganda as noxious as the anti-Semitism of the Nazi Jew Suess."[28]

The heated opposition of the NAACP never cooled. In 1950, NAACP executive secretary Roy Wilkins blasted the film: "It glorifies the Ku Klux Klan, preaches hatred against Negroes and openly advocates mob violence against them."[29]

Film scholars have always wound up painfully fascinated and severely frustrated by *Birth*. Many of them view the film as a masterpiece flawed by racism that eliminates any chance for it to be appreciated. As silent-film historian William Everson put it:

> Inasmuch as *The Birth of a Nation* is quite possibly the single most important film of all time, and a film that is rarely regarded objectively because of its racial content, it is important to clarify Griffith's intent and to stress that, while difficult, it should be shown in an atmosphere that tries to separate form from content. Too many colleges and universities today pay only lip service to its innovations and present the film under a cloud of apologies. . . . It is no small tribute to the film's astonishing power that it can still sway audience emotions more than half a century after its production.[30]

Film historian Seymour Stern summed up *Birth*'s overall artistic and commercial impact best. He said that it: 1) established the director as the creative boss of the American film, 2) made motion pictures weapons of propaganda, 3) turned films into works of art, not just entertainment, 4) helped begin the science of film criticism, 5) made movies a mass medium and 6) made movies a topic of serious political, cultural and social dimensions. He added that *Birth* ushered in two-hour-and-longer features, dramatically expanded the size of the typical American movie house and showed all of Hollywood that complex plotlines and finely etched characterizations could be successful.[31]

Film critics writing much later, such as Molly Haskell in 1995, have agreed: "In Griffith's masterpiece, sublimity of expression was marred by melodramatic racism, yet *The Birth of a Nation*, warts and all, remains a milestone: the movie that catapulted the medium from its 19th century peep show origins into its status as the great new popular art form of the 20th century."[32]

The story of *The Birth of a Nation*—critical or historical—has never ended. Theaters that later tried to present *Birth* as part of a film festival or revival often encountered just as much difficulty with factions among the public as had Griffith.

The movie was reissued, with much hype, several times, beginning in 1921, as we have seen. Each time, publicists found themselves fighting for the Confederacy. Heath Cobb's publicity release for the 1931 reissue was typical: "The shrill rebel yell is once more being heard as the Confederate cavalrymen charge at the camera, the explo-

The combat scenes in The Birth of a Nation *were among the best of any Civil War movie, silent or sound. Here gallant Southerners have stormed a Union battlement, only to fail. The bravery of Southern soldiers was heralded in press releases whenever the movie was rereleased.*

sive commands of the officers shouted above the din, the cries of the wounded, the screams of shell and whine of bullets, are being authentically reproduced."[33]

That "historical" theme was picked up by local theater publicists. "The story itself will never lose its appeal and those marvelous scenes of love, romance . . . will always fire human hearts as long as American history holds its place in world regard," wrote another flack.[34]

The movie was shown in New York City after public protests in 1921, but banned in California following a heated campaign by the Colored Peoples' Protective League aimed at the Garrick Theatre in Los Angeles, where it was scheduled to be presented.[35]

In 1938 Otto Rettig, the manager of the Ormont Theatre, in East Orange, New Jersey, let theater patrons vote for the movies they wanted to see in a revival film series. *Birth* was on the list. The film lasted only three days (of a scheduled weekly run) before concerned black residents, led by Dr. Theodore Inge and Dr. Harry Mickey, convinced local police to shut it down. The two doctors, armed with a petition signed by 609 local residents, argued that the movie violated a 1935 New Jersey statute that forbade "the portrayal of things inciting of racial hatred," a law designed to curb the rising German Bund in the state.[36] "It [the movie] encourages hatred and mob violence," said Dr. Mickey, who added that dozens of teenagers in local schools engaged in racial disputes during the three days the movie was shown.[37] Local courts backed him up and *Birth* was closed. Rettig was arrested for violating a state law.

The movie was scheduled to be shown as a revival at the Riverside, California, City Museum in 1978 but the city council, under pressure from black groups, canceled it.[38] The local chapter of the Ku Klux Klan, however, obtained a print and showed the film in a park as part of its recruiting drive. More than two hundred local residents stormed the screening area with tire irons and baseball bats and beat up Klansmen. The local police were called in to quell what quickly became a riot. Police made twelve arrests. Dozens were injured during the five-hour melee and five policemen were admitted to a local hospital.[39]

Just two years later, the Richelieu Theatre, in San Francisco, announced a screening of the film in a revival series. A dozen protesters, calling themselves the International Committee Against Racism, burst into the theater in the middle of the showing, trashed the interior and destroyed the projection booth. The protesters chased more than a hundred patrons into the street.[40]

Over the years, in its many revivals, *The Birth of a Nation* was banned in a total of five states, nineteen cities and numerous small towns.[41] If it was presented at film festivals, the organizers themselves went to great lengths to denounce its content. It was shown at the Toronto Film Society on February 16, 1981, after the society president discredited it. "Racist remarks by characters in this film . . . do not represent the views of the Toronto Film Society," he stated.[42]

The opposition of black groups to showings of the film or discussions of it never ceased. In 1968, Dr. John Morsell, an aide to Roy Wilkins, said: "No one will ever know how much damage, how much poison, that one film injected into the attitude of the American film-going public. It is a vicious, rotten film."[43] *Birth* came under attack as recently as 1993, when a number of black ministers and columnists blasted the Library of Congress for adding the movie to its National Registry of Films. It was criticized again in 1999 when members of the American Film Institute voted it among the fifty best films of all time. Dr. William Gibson, chairman of the board of the NAACP, argued against the choice, saying: "*The Birth of a Nation* could never pass any test of historical significance."[44]

Birth's critics over the years were pleased that the film did not trigger more virulent racist films. That did not happen for several reasons. First, Griffith had no interest in a sequel to *Birth*. Second, other studios shied away from a *Birth* knock-off or sequel because of the cost and the controversy. But what really killed the commercial market for more Civil War movies was America's entrance into World War I. The European conflict was already taking place as *Birth* traveled from city to city. But American entry into the war in 1917 showed Americans an ugly war in their morning newspapers. Telegrams informed families of the deaths of their soldier sons, brothers and husbands. The Civil War, as portrayed in films, was a noble and chivalrous conflict. Real war, engaging America live in 1917–1918, without benefit of a screenwriter, was devastating. Trench fighting and mustard gas suppressed any interest in the American public for stories of cavaliers in the movies. It would be a generation before the memory of World War I receded far enough to permit another moonlit-and-magnolia-scented movie about the Civil War to succeed (the postwar market for Civil

War movies was so bad that the 1927 Civil War comedy *The General*, today considered a classic, was a box office disaster that almost ruined the career of its multigifted star, Buster Keaton).[45]

GRIFFITH GOT away with his inaccurate portrayal of blacks in 1915 because since the end of the Civil War blacks and whites in the American South had been suffering through a long and tortured relationship. According to historian Joel Williamson, the relationship went through three stages. The first was a "liberal" stage in which some influential whites and most blacks tried to live in harmony after the end of Reconstruction in 1876. The second, which began in the early 1890s, was a violent stage. The third, which began in the early 1920s, was a stage in which whites, firmly in power, simply ignored blacks.

In that first stage, some white civic leaders, including important politicians, educators and ministers, believed it was possible to integrate the South after the war ended. They saw genuine progress for blacks in many significant areas during Reconstruction and felt that some black politicians had become capable administrators. Liberals were confident that blacks could eventually succeed in raising crops on their own, although they knew that farming was difficult and not economically rewarding at first. They were particularly impressed by the progress of black children in schools for the first time, where it became evident that they were not slow in learning, as so many Southerners claimed during the two hundred years of slavery. These influential liberals were optimistic that, with assistance, the four million black Americans living in the South at the end of the Civil War could prosper and peacefully coexist with whites. These men and women, a minority but a powerful minority, worked towards integration in the Southern states during Reconstruction and until the early 1890s. Small towns and cities in South Carolina, the site of Griffith's fictional Piedmont, were filled with black and white families living adjacent to each other. Blacks and whites sat next to each other on railroad cars and in other public places in the state of Virginia, the heart of the Old Confederacy, and in other states below the Mason-Dixon Line. Wade Hampton, a Civil War hero, and former Confederate vice president Alexander Stephens advocated voting rights for blacks as early as 1878.[46]

Colonel Thomas Higginson, a white officer who had commanded black troops in South Carolina during the war, visited several towns in South Carolina, Virginia and Florida in 1878 and again in 1884 and reported generally harmonious relations between the races and mixed seating in public places.[47] McCants Stewart, a black magazine editor, wrote that in his trip through the South in 1885 he encountered no overt segregation; he was welcomed in parks, restaurants and taverns.

During the late 1880s, however, liberal efforts at integration slowed as a deep resentment towards blacks, and a fear of being over-whelmed by them, grew among many Southerners. (There were in toto about two hundred thousand more blacks than whites in the Deep South states of South Carolina, Georgia, Alabama, Mississippi and Louisiana after the war.)

White Southerners resented the appointment of many blacks to federal jobs, such as the position of postmaster, throughout the administrations of Democrat Grover Cleveland and Republican Ben-jamin Harrison (from 1885 to 1897); they had assumed these presi-dents would rid their lives of both blacks and the Radical Republicans who had ruled during Reconstruction. White Southerners were angry that Congress seriously considered a bill to send supervisors to moni-tor elections in the South, and saw it as a throwback to Reconstruc-tion. (They had somehow believed that the black race would die out, unable to function out of slavery, within a generation after the end of the war. They were wrong and did not know how to react.)

In the early 1890s, white Southerners had been hit hard by a depression in agriculture. Many white landowners went bankrupt as cotton prices tumbled by 33 percent. White farmers somehow blamed this on blacks and also accused the government of giving black tenant farmers land that was productive while leaving whites land that was not. Thousands of whites, in both farm and nonfarm jobs, wound up unemployed. These men felt they had been emasculated, profession-ally and socially. They were certain that they would not get their jobs back, or succeed if they were employed, because blacks would always work cheaper. They also imagined that these blacks had somehow become sexual beasts. They feared that their women, no longer feeling protected by their impoverished, emasculated, out-of-work men, would fall prey to black rapists.

This unfounded economic and sexual fear swept through the South,[48] and, with the 1890s depression, brought on Williamson's second stage of race relations: violence.

The violence began with lynchings. There had been some lynchings of blacks in the 1880s, but the pace quickened dramatically in the 1890s. During that decade, an average of more than 100 blacks were

Silas Lynch (played by George Siegmann), the black lieutenant-governor in The Birth of a Nation, *tries to seduce the lovely white woman Elsie Stoneman (Lillian Gish), who responds by fainting. This and other scenes in the film aroused the sexual fears of white men in 1915.*

lynched in the Southern states each year, with a peak of 156 lynchings in 1892.

Several blacks were lynched in Memphis, Tennessee, in 1892 following a confrontation in which a police officer was shot. White rage against blacks expanded as mobs roamed through the streets of some cities and started riots against black individuals and entire families. A black postmaster and his child were murdered and other members of his family shot in a riot in Lake City, South Carolina, in 1898. Later in that same year, following an election, white-supremacist mobs rioted in Wilmington, North Carolina. Several blacks were killed, dozens were wounded, and several hundred families were driven out of town. In New Orleans in 1893, white stevedores, fearing for their employment, beat up dozens of blacks they feared would take their jobs. A dozen blacks were killed and 60 badly beaten in another white-induced race riot in New Orleans in 1902. Similar violence took place in Atlanta in 1906 when whites rioted following inaccurate newspaper reports of black men raping white women. White mobs that roamed the streets killed 12 blacks and wounded 60; 10 whites were also injured in the riot.

White violence erupted in 1908 in Springfield, Illinois, where several blacks were lynched following a false report of the rape of a white woman by a black man. The white mob then turned on the black neighborhood in town and destroyed it. In East St. Louis in 1917, over 100 blacks were killed and the black section of town razed in a terrifying white-on-black riot in a dispute over jobs. Similar white-on-black riots over jobs occurred in 1919 in Longview, Texas; Washington, D.C.; Charleston, South Carolina; and Chicago. The shooting of a white deputy sheriff by an unknown assailant resulted in the deaths of nearly 200 black farmers near Elaine, Arkansas, that year.

What were perhaps the two most destructive riots occurred in the early 1920s. In 1921, a riot triggered by a rape rumor took place in Tulsa, Oklahoma. A rampaging white mob killed nearly 300 blacks and then burned down the entire black section of town. Two years later, in a similar incident, a white mob attacked the all-black town of Rosewood, Florida, killing 36 men and women and again burning the community to the ground.

One of the reasons violence was sustained was that the Ku Klux Klan, more or less dormant for forty years, was reborn in 1915, ironically because of *The Birth of a Nation*. A few months after the Los Angeles premiere of the film, William Simmons, an Alabama man, spurred by anti-Jewish sentiment in the South, began thinking about the reorganization of a "new" KKK in Georgia.

On Thanksgiving Day of 1915, following ten months of national publicity about *Birth* and its KKK heroes, and a week before *Birth*'s Atlanta premiere, Simmons and his followers rode down muddy roads ruined by a hard night rain to Stone Mountain, Georgia, and, in front of a huge burning cross stuck haphazardly into the wet ground, dedicated themselves to the hateful principles of the original KKK. On the morning that *Birth* opened in Atlanta, Simmons placed, directly opposite an ad for the movie in the *Atlanta Constitution,* an ad seeking new Klan members, thus marrying the movie and the KKK in the minds of readers. In the advertisement, the Klan announced that it was a "high class order looking for men of intelligence and character."[49] The newly organized Georgia Klan paraded in front of the Atlanta theater when *Birth* opened there and offered moviegoers a twenty-one-gun salute. After the movie's premiere in that city, Simmons and his cohorts, and subsequent Klan groups, redesigned their hoods and robes to look like those in *The Birth of a Nation.*[50] In its romantic glamorization of the Klan, *Birth* gave the KKK legitimacy among the millions of Americans who saw the film, a legitimacy no amount of parading, recruitment drives or advertisements could have bestowed.

The good will the Klan gained through the movie enabled it to mobilize thousands of followers, and by the early 1920s it had 3 million members (not just in the South, either; it had 236,000 members in Pennsylvania alone). The new Klan had become so powerful that in 1925 thousands of Klansmen paraded unopposed through the streets of Washington, D.C., in a show of force. One difference between this new Klan and its predecessor was that Catholics and Jews were added to blacks on its hate list. Some forty years later, William Peirce Randel, in *The Ku Klux Klan: A Century of Infamy,* wrote: "If any film has ever been a stimulus to intolerance, this one [*Birth*] certainly was. Its effect on the mass audience was to provide a kind of sanction for hate feelings and to glamorize secret societies devoted to preserving race distinctions and to resisting central government."[51]

The Klan's activities, whether private or public, kept white anger against blacks alive. This resentment had enabled the Democratic Party, crippled by Reconstruction, to return to power in the South and dominate politics for many years. Democrats saw radical white violence as an opportunity for political gain and capitalized on it. An example was a South Carolina farmer named Benjamin Tillman (known as "Pitchfork Ben") from the Piedmont area, where *Birth* was set. Tillman got into politics and at first was ambivalent about violence towards blacks. He began his career as a quasi-populist, intent only on trying to gain better lives for farmers, but quickly realized that the key to political success in his state was racism. He began espousing it in his campaign for governor in 1890. Once elected, he became in fact an ardent racist, preaching hatred in South Carolina during his term as governor and in Washington, D.C., where he served as a U.S. senator until 1918. He led Northerners to believe that the harsh race war he led against blacks in his home state for nearly thirty years was completely justified.[52]

Tillman was not unusual. Many Democratic politicians won election and stayed in office for several terms on a platform of racial hatred or at least tolerance for racists in their states or districts. Many reminded voters, too, that if they elected Democrats they would not have to fear what many whites had dubbed "bayonet rule": U.S. Army soldiers pushing Southerners aside with bayonets, as they were said to have done during Republican Reconstruction. The Democratic Party was able to hold political power with an iron fist. It carefully built a strong political machine, which operated efficiently throughout the Southern states. Much of the power was built on racism. Throughout the 1920s and into the 1930s, Democratic leaders solidified their grip on federal, state, county and city offices by defeating Republicans, but they also managed to quell splinter movements, such as the populists, within the party. In the 1890s and the early part of the twentieth century, the Democrats were so strong that they won elections throughout the Southern states easily, often earning as much as 75 percent of the vote.[53]

The Democrats were also convinced that another way to prevent the Republicans from gaining office was by suppressing the large numbers of black potential voters, and from the late 1890s until 1904 they passed a number of legislative bills that came to be known as "Jim Crow" laws. These bills required blacks to prove that they owned property, to pass difficult voting literacy tests and pay high poll taxes. These requirements made it practically impossible for most blacks (as well as many poor whites) to continue to vote. As an example, in 1904 the number of blacks registered to vote in Louisiana was just 1,342, down from 130,000 in 1896.[54]

Democrats also controlled state and county legislatures, and the courts dealt blacks a series of legal blows as judges upheld segregation in dozens of cases even before Reconstruction ended. In the slaughterhouse cases of 1873, *United States v. Reese* and *United States v. Cruikshank,* the court cut back previously approved legal rights for blacks. In the civil rights cases of 1883, the U.S. Supreme Court ruled that individuals might bar blacks from seemingly public places even if institutions could not. In 1877, the Supreme Court had already ruled, in *Hall v. de Cuir,* that states could impose segregation on public transit. Later, in 1890, in *Louisville, New Orleans & Texas Railroad v. Mississippi,* the court ruled again that states could mandate segregation on public transportation. In 1896, in the landmark decision that was to seal the fate of blacks in the South for generations, the High Court ruled in *Plessy v. Ferguson* that all segregation was legal as long as blacks had "separate but equal" opportunities or accommodations. Then, in 1898, in *Williams v. Mississippi,* the High Court ruled that states could take the vote away from blacks under certain circumstances.[55] These rulings not only permitted segregation in the South but encouraged it in the North, where public restaurants, trains, sports stadiums and entertainment halls began to be segregated, using the same court rulings that supported segregation in the South. In fact, many Northern states had had segregationist laws in place before the Civil War (many local Southern ordinances passed in the 1890s were based on long-standing laws in Northern cities), and abolitionists complained that segregation in the North was often as bad as it was in the South. Racial anger was so heated by the turn of the century that in 1903 Professor John Spencer, of Trinity College, wrote that there was more hatred between blacks and whites than at any other time in U.S. history.[56]

The animosity towards those who were different, and particularly the fear of racial intermingling, included others besides blacks. There was a genuine fear, both North and South, of a sexual tainting of the American-born white race by Irish, Germans and Italian immigrants on the East Coast. Southerners in particular feared immigrants, even though they advertised for Italian-American workers to replace the blacks who, fleeing persecution, began to move to the North after the turn of the century. Southerners feared any threat to white supremacy, whether it came from blacks, Japanese or Europeans. That same fear was duplicated on the West Coast, with the target being Japanese immigrants, whom whites dubbed "the yellow peril."[57] The apprehension, expressed in hundreds of "race suicide" speeches by Francis Walker, Edward Ross and others, was that immigrants would impregnate thousands of native-born white women. They argued that this would slowly bring about the end of the white race and usher in a dark-hued, ethnically mixed society. Between 1905 and 1909 more than thirty-five major magazine articles presented "race suicide" as a major national issue.[58] Those spokespeople were encouraged in the 1900–1920 period by the leaders of the far-flung eugenics movement, who believed that intermarriage between immigrants and native-born American whites was destroying the white race. In 1918, Madison Grant, one of the world's foremost eugenicists, published a best-selling book called *The Passing of the Great Race.*[59]

By 1902, when many of the Jim Crow laws were being passed (and Thomas Dixon was writing *The Leopard's Spots,* his first racist novel), Southern as well as Northern political leaders were supporting the efforts of Californians to curb the immigration of Japanese, even though few Japanese had immigrated to any Southern states. Southern senators voted sixteen to one in 1912 for a bill (which eventually failed) to require literacy tests for newly arrived immigrants in an effort to keep them out of the country.[60] Many Southern legislators lumped the new immigrants, men and women from Italy in particular, with the hated blacks at the bottom of the social ladder. (Vigilantes, unable to determine who was to blame in the theft of a goat in Alabama in 1910, chose five Italian workers and lynched them.)[61]

WHITE RIOTS against blacks in Tulsa, Oklahoma, in 1922 and Rosewood, Florida, in 1923 marked the end of widespread public violence against blacks. The third and final stage in black-white relations then began, a stage in which the white population of the South, easily able to control African Americans, simply ignored them.

By the 1920s, more than a million blacks who were unhappy with the white domination of the South had moved to the North and settled in New York, Pittsburgh, Detroit, Chicago and other major cities, creating large black enclaves. Chicago's black population jumped to more than 200,000 by the mid-1920s and New York's to more than

350,000. Those blacks who remained in the Southern states fully understood that their lives were completely controlled by the white majority and there was nothing they could do to change that.

Whites controlled educational funding in the South, as illustrated by the fact that in the 1920s Mississippi spent more than seven times as much money on white schools as on black ones. The average black student spent a total of just five years in school in his or her lifetime. Whites completely controlled Southern politics through the various Jim Crow laws, which continued to hold down dramatically the number of blacks eligible to vote. Consequently, whites constantly maintained power in all of the Southern state legislatures, held all of the congressional seats and dictated laws that protected the varied "whites only" establishments.

The criminal justice system was controlled by whites. There were no black judges in any of the Southern states in the 1920s, no black police chiefs and only a handful of black police patrolmen—and these were allowed to work only in all-black neighborhoods.[62] Blacks could be arrested and imprisoned on any number of minimal or entirely fabricated charges and placed in some of the worst prisons in America. Once in jail, they found it very difficult to get out because appeals had to be made to white judges and white parole boards. Most blacks served all of their time, and sentences were severe. A black man who merely helped another African American elude police pursuit in the 1920s, for example, was usually sentenced to five years in prison. Blacks deemed "troublemakers" by whites in Southern states were often jailed on flimsy charges of vagrancy or loitering. Blacks in the South were also sent to the notorious work farms, such as Parchman Farm, in Mississippi, where they served out prison terms at hard labor.[63] They often were placed in chain gangs and ordered to work for local farmers who "hired" them through the correctional system. Fear of the police and courts was everywhere in the black neighborhoods of the South and this fear made it easy for white Southerners to keep blacks on a tight leash.

Segregation remained firmly entrenched in the South in the 1920s. There were not only separate schools for blacks, but separate restaurants, bathrooms, drinking fountains, bars, train and bus station waiting rooms, parks and beaches. Major and minor league baseball stadiums were segregated, as were movie theaters.

Many factories throughout the region were segregated. In 1915, the year *The Birth of a Nation* debuted, the state of South Carolina, where the film's story was set, passed its sweeping "South Carolina Codes," which prohibited blacks and whites from working together in the same rooms in textile mills and from sharing the same entrances, exits, washrooms and bathrooms. This was typical of segregation in cities, towns and industrial plants throughout the South in the 1920s, 1930s and 1940s.

Since white domination of blacks was firmly established by the 1920s, there was no longer any need for public violence. The riots and killings that had extended from the late 1880s to the early 1920s had put blacks in their place and everybody, black and white, knew it. The black population of the South was by then completely under the thumb of the whites. White control was so total by this third stage that in 1928 Southern historian Ulrich Bonnell Phillips could write that "the central theme of southern history" was that the South "shall be and remain a white man's country."[64]

And, of course, if any blacks did get rambunctious, there were always the night riders of the KKK to kidnap them from their homes and lynch them in the nearest grove of trees as a reminder to all to mind their own business and keep out of the way of the white population.

White supremacists did fear white agitators, whether men and women living in the South or Northerners who had moved there permanently or temporarily. In their minds, these included liberals, labor organizers, communists, and Jews, such as Leo Frank, a factory manager charged with killing a white Southern girl under clouded circumstances and lynched by a white mob in 1915. They did not have to worry about blacks, though, who, completely ignored, became an invisible people.

Griffith's invented story of murderous, sex-crazed black troops in *Birth* was believable in a nation that had persecuted and then ignored blacks. Americans had always wondered just what the African Americans who lived in the South actually did long ago that made whites who lived there hate them so much. In 1915, D. W. Griffith finally seemed to show them exactly what blacks did—which was not at all what blacks did.

Film was no longer merely working as a mirror for the nation, showing Americans what they were like. It was working as a force, showing Americans what they should be like. And what they should be like was a country of, by and for white people, with little room for people of any other race.

Cinema also influenced the view of the Civil War espoused in the 1930s by people who had seen movies about the war as children. Perhaps the best example was an Atlanta schoolgirl who saw *The Birth of a Nation* and loved it so much that she asked her family to take her back to see it a dozen times. The girl organized her friends and staged a play based on *The Birth of a Nation,* with twelve-year-old boys and girls dressed as Klansmen chasing a classmate in blackface around her living room "stage."[65]

In 1936, this little girl, Margaret Mitchell, who grew up with *Birth*'s view of the Old South and of blacks, would publish *Gone With the Wind.*

CHAPTER NINE

Abe Lincoln in Hollywood

ACTOR RAYMOND MASSEY adjusted his slightly worn black stovepipe hat, straightened his neatly pressed frock coat, tugged on his shawl and sighed. The director motioned for him to step forward on the rear platform of the train car to give Abraham Lincoln's famous farewell speech. It was the speech the president-elect gave as he left his hometown of Springfield, Illinois, for Washington, D.C., and, within months, the outbreak of the Civil War. Massey had been going through this scene on the back of the train all week, through dozens of exhausting takes, and he was still not satisfied. Neither was the director, John Cromwell, who was exasperated but determined that the movie's final scene be perfect, even if it meant keeping on the set indefinitely six hundred bored and tired extras dressed as Springfield townspeople. So he had decided to film it at night to see if darkness would stimulate the laconic Massey.

Massey stepped forward. This time his voice seemed a bit different—haunting and evocative—and the faces of the extras changed. Feeling new tension, the extras moved forward as a group to get closer to the actor. Members of the crew, aware that something special was happening, approached the train car. As they listened, they knew that this was no longer just a scene in a movie—Massey had finally got Lincoln exactly right. As he spoke they were convinced, that warm night on a Hollywood studio lot, that they were face to face with Abraham Lincoln himself as he bade his dearest friends goodbye.

"No one not in my situation can appreciate my feeling of sadness at this parting. To this place, and the kindness of these people, I owe everything," Massey began in what would be the final take. "Here I have lived a quarter of a century, and have passed from a young to an

151

old man. Here my children have been born, and one is buried. I now leave, not knowing when, or whether ever, I may return, with a task before me greater than that which rested upon Washington. Without the assistance of that Divine Being . . . I cannot succeed. With that assistance, I cannot fail. Trusting in Him, who can go with me, and remain with you and be everywhere for good, let us confidently hope that all will yet be well. To His care commending you, as I hope in your prayers you will commend me, I bid you an affectionate farewell."[1]

As he finished, and looked out over the crowd and raised his hand slowly in farewell, the extras burst into wild and spontaneous

Perhaps the single most famous scene in all the Lincoln movies is the president-elect's farewell to his Springfield neighbors in Abe Lincoln in Illinois. *Here, as so often, he is presented as a tired, somber old man wrapped in a shawl.*

applause. It was applause for Raymond Massey, to be sure, but it was applause for Abraham Lincoln, too.

THE AMERICAN film industry's fascination with Abraham Lincoln, the tall, gaunt prairie lawyer who as a young man was said to be one of the strongest men in Illinois, has been as ardent as that of book publishers. Lincoln has appeared as at least a minor character in more than 150 films and another 50 made-for-television movies or television specials or series—more than any other American figure.

Producers churned out movies with Lincoln as either the main or a subsidiary character because he was such a gigantic and enduring American myth. When his assassination made him an instant martyr, his likeness began to appear all over the country on broadsides, handkerchiefs, dishes and money.

Lincoln ran for president just as the print business in the United States was starting to flourish. Political campaigns with their parades and outdoor rallies cried out for prints and the printmakers supplied them, producing dozens of different prints of famous Americans and making thousands of copies. The first one showing Lincoln appeared during the 1860 campaign. People bought prints and hung them in prominent places in their homes to show political partisanship at first and, if their candidate was elected president, to show patriotism. Lincoln's death kicked off a second boom in Lincoln prints because in 1861 Lincoln had grown his famous beard, making the previous images of him obsolete. All-new prints were needed, with beard.

Prints, prominent nineteenth-century visuals, had sanctified George Washington. Prints of the first president decorated homes throughout the land, the most famous one being the George Washington *Apotheosis,* a mythical scene in which angels carry Washington into heaven.[2] Within a few years of Lincoln's death, more than three dozen different prints were produced and sold across the country. One was a Lincoln family portrait, staged to look just like the popular Washington family portrait. This one connected Lincoln directly to the Father of His Country. Another was a remake of the *Apotheosis,* with angels bearing Lincoln into heaven, giving him the same sainted stature as Washington. In people's homes, and in people's minds, he had become a religious as well as political figure. By 1900, far more prints of Lincoln had been made and sold than of all other American figures combined, and by 1912, more prints of Lincoln had been made and sold than the 372 prints of England's Queen Victoria, the popular monarch whose venerators produced new works on her practically every month.

In the silents, Abraham Lincoln routinely became "Father Abraham," and frequently appeared as a doddering old man praying for the end of the Civil War. Joe Henabery as Lincoln does so in The Birth of a Nation.

Movies dealt in the visual image, and Lincoln's was monumental. Those prints of Lincoln impressed a visual image of him on the minds of all Americans, but they were especially popular with families. By 1903, the printmakers had established him as a singular American hero, the man who saved the Union and brought a divided people back together,[3] and this image of Lincoln was the link between the literature on the sixteenth president and film. Cinematographers took the static prints in everyone's living room and made them move on a screen. It was a natural progression. Also, the height of Lincoln's print popularity coincided directly with the height of the silent era's films about the Civil War—a perfect celluloid bridge.

In Lincoln, filmmakers found a single man who symbolized the desire of all Americans, whether in the nineteenth century or the twentieth, to live harmoniously together. "Any picture which has Lincoln in it appeals to a large number of people and this one is no exception. It exhibits his kindliness in the best light," wrote a reporter for *Moving Picture World* about *Lieutenant Gray*.[4] In film after film, from the early years of the silents through made-for-television films of the 1990s, Lincoln was routinely seen as a gentle giant, a towering emancipator in black suit, shawl and stovepipe hat: Father Abraham. In most, he was seen pardoning Northern and Southern soldiers, being kind to children, urging reconciliation in meetings in parlors, walking slowly towards some heavenly light up ahead and, quite often, being murdered in Ford's Theatre. America was spoon-fed a combination father–favorite uncle, beloved minister-schoolteacher, a loving, religious Lincoln, a political figure who embodied the best of humankind, a soothing figure somehow removed from both space and time, the universal President.

Actually, President Lincoln became, over the years, a cinematic doll, pasted together with clay and clothes. He was the single greatest catalyst in reunion movies, and the myths created about him on the screen were the strongest evidence and best examples of the power of the celluloid mythmakers. His character embodied whatever good qualities people saw in democracy, a silver screen compendium of the country's hopes and dreams. In movies he was a man always above politics, working for the good of all Americans, not just Northerners. These film images became embedded so deeply in people's minds that the real Lincoln may never emerge. Movies about President Lincoln were the locomotive for the films Hollywood produced about the Civil War, and these films, more than any others, symbolized the desire of producers, directors and writers to reunite Americans who saw them.

Who was the real Abraham Lincoln? There were three key elements to Hollywood's unrealistic portrait of the sixteenth president:

he was above politics, unambitious and interested in no other issue except slavery. But actually, Lincoln was an intensely ambitious man, a man who certainly needed no career prodding from his wife, as film-makers would have had audiences believe. He first ran for office at the age of twenty-three and continued to seek political office all of his life, often after colleagues had written his political obituary.

Lincoln was, in fact, a masterful politician who acted as his own campaign manager in the 1860 presidential election, a brilliantly planned race, and who during his four-plus years in the White House ran a split Republican Party as efficiently as a small company, often wooing dozens of Democrats to his side in key votes. Although the Civil War took up most of his time, Lincoln did more than serve as commander in chief. He signed the Homestead Act, which opened up the West for settlers. The states of Kansas, Nevada and West Virginia joined the Union during his terms of office. He authorized the nation's first paper currency, greenbacks; developed a system of national banks that gave the nation economic stability; pushed hard for the transcontinental railroad, which was finished in 1869 and united East and West; and established the Department of Agriculture to help farmers. And although his institution of the draft in 1863 was unpopular, it established a precedent that enabled the United States to succeed in two world wars and later conflicts.

Many realistic movies could have been made about Lincoln's life, including his relationship with archrival Stephen Douglas, his marriage, his career as a lawyer, the deaths of his sons, his disputes with the press, the four-way election of 1860 and his come-from-behind victory in the 1864 election, and the secession crisis. These stories might have given the moviegoing public a historically honest, more comprehensive and yet equally impressive view of him, but none was ever produced for fear of cracking the seventy-five-year-old statue American culture had erected of one of its greatest men.

IN THE SILENTS, moviegoers were given a lanky, shuffling Honest Abe, nodding away in his shawl, rubbing his thick beard and begging for peace. Writers and directors whitewashed Lincoln's personal life and ignored his frenetic political life, editing it out of his story. They turned him from a vibrant and brilliant political figure into a doddering old man. (He was the second-youngest man elected president to that time and a former wrestler.)

He was shown in familiar roles, debating with Stephen Douglas, giving the Gettysburg Address and meeting with generals. There were other formulas, though. One was the pardon scene.[5] The pardons were an accurate depiction of history and they were part of the Lincoln lore. The president, a compassionate and forgiving man, signed hundreds of pardons, particularly for soldiers under the age of eighteen, often going against pleas from army officials who saw executions as the only way to deter deserters (Carl Sandburg wrote that he was "both steel and velvet, hard as a rock and soft as the drifting fog").[6] Ann Rutledge provided another familiar plotline. Several films, such as *Lincoln the Lover* (1914), used flashbacks to tell the love story between Lincoln and the young girl.

Filmmakers anxious to slip Lincoln into their Civil War films often wrote in cabinet meetings so that Lincoln could discuss the war. Director Thomas Ince put the president into his 1913 epic *The Battle of Gettysburg* (1913) to report the Union victory.[7]

There *were* some films about Lincoln that showed his early years and his political life. David O. Selznick, who would later stamp the Plantation Myth on film with *Gone With the Wind,* did a one-reeler about Lincoln's 1840s law career in *The Land of Opportunity. Lincoln's Gettysburg Address* introduced a number of flashbacks to show political history from the American Revolution to Fort Sumter, even Lincoln's participation in the Black Hawk War in the 1830s, intercut with scenes of President Lincoln delivering the speech. Thomas Edison's *The Life of Lincoln* covered Lincoln's life from birth to death and depicted his campaign debates with Douglas in 1858, the 1860 presidential campaign and the Civil War in some twenty-five minutes.[8] But the only effort to show Lincoln's true political life, and through it the politics of the nation just before and during the war, was made by actor Ben Chapin.

Chapin began his career as a Shakespearean actor and portrayed Lincoln in one-man shows. By 1913 he was so immersed in these performances that he grew a beard, combed his hair the way Lincoln did and dressed and walked just like him. Chapin was able to break away from the Father Abraham–style movies only because he formed his own independent film company to make his dream films, together known as *The Lincoln Cycle*. Begun in 1917, *The Lincoln Cycle* was the forerunner of today's television miniseries. Chapin planned to write, direct and produce ten separate movies that were ten separate stories about Lincoln's life, all hinged together and released one after the other on a three-per-year basis. He received backing initially from Charter Features and later from Paramount Pictures.[9]

Chapin was convinced that only an independent film could break the string of syrupy Lincoln portrayals. "I had tempting offers," he said, "to lend myself to other Lincoln pictures and was promised as much as $1,200 a week, with no financial risk, no need to concern myself about the work of the rest of the company, no responsibility about the play. But that was just the thing I could not do . . . So long as I try to represent Lincoln I must be responsible for the manner in which it is done."[10]

The *Cycle* films were advertised as the most complex, and the ultimate, look at Lincoln. A publicity release promised a whole new view of the president: "No serial yet produced in motion pictures, bar none, can compare with the excitement, mystery, intrigue, love, villainy and heroics of the *Cycle*. From war to woods, from wooing to wedding, from wonder to wonders, the *Cycle* moves irresistibly along."[11]

The ambitious *Cycle*, the lone chance on film for a truly historical look at Lincoln and the Civil War in the silent era, unfortunately was never completed. Chapin died at the end of 1917, during the first year of production, and only parts of four of the ten films were shot. Without Chapin to pressure them, Paramount executives, unhappy with the footage they did have, lumped footage from the films into one long, eight-reel movie and distributed it as the unfortunately titled *Cycle of Photodrama Based on the Life of Abraham Lincoln (The Lincoln Cycle)*. It was a box office failure.

Full film biographies of Lincoln did not appear until the 1920s. Two brothers, Al and Ray Rockett, produced *Abraham Lincoln* in 1924 as the culmination of their theatrical hopes. The two young men were unable to interest any studio in the project and raised money on their own to produce their tribute to Lincoln independently. The Rocketts, unlike most producers, actually *did* research Lincoln's life in a fairly responsible way. They sent people to the Library of Congress, the Smithsonian and other depositories to unearth old newspaper and magazine clippings. They looked at hundreds of photographs of Lincoln, his cabinet, generals and the war itself and even interviewed old men, many of whom had been in politics in the middle of the nineteenth century and had known Lincoln. The very well done, scholarly film was over two hours long and contained the usual scenes about Abe and his early romance, his youth, the war and the assassination, but critics found it plodding. So did most audiences, and it was a box office bomb (readers of *Photoplay*, however, voted it the best film of 1924).[12]

Why weren't these movies successful if people had such a deep admiration for Lincoln? One reason was casting. Producers were convinced that audiences had such a vivid impression of Lincoln's appearance from the thousands of illustrations they had seen over the years that only an actor who bore a close resemblance to him could star in any movie about him. Instead of hiring good actors and trying to make them look like Lincoln, directors hired men who looked like Lincoln and tried to make them good actors.

The actor who played Lincoln the most in silent films was Ralph Ince, the brother of director Thomas Ince. Ralph had little acting experience and spent most of his life working as a bit player and handyman for Thomas. But he did have two qualities that made him Lincolnesque: he was over six feet tall and he was very thin. Ralph Ince, just twenty-four (Lincoln was fifty-two when he took office), was given a nice-looking beard, a brown wig, a few brief acting lessons and tickets to see Ben Chapin play Lincoln on the stage (he adapted Chapin's lanky stride), and was sent into the movies. He played Lincoln in nine films.[13] Critics enjoyed his work. A reviewer for *Moving Picture World* said about Ince in his first film, *Under One Flag* (1911): "The best thing in this picture is Mr. Ralph Ince's impersonation of President Lincoln. It is very good. The audience applauded warmly."[14]

Another actor who played Lincoln in numerous films was Frank McGlynn. Like Ince, he was an unknown bit player (oddly, he had been a lawyer, like Lincoln). McGlynn was six feet tall and his face bore a remarkable likeness to Lincoln's. The likeness was complete when McGlynn grew a beard. Like Chapin, he studied Lincoln to prepare for his role, and he did manage to convey onscreen Lincoln's ever-present sense of foreboding (although he was still basically a mediocre actor).[15]

People with no previous interest in acting, no connection to movies, the stage or Lincoln, wound up playing the president if they looked like him. Actor Lionel Barrymore often had dinner at Beefsteak Charlie's, a New York restaurant. One night in 1920 his waiter was Meyer F. Stroell. Barrymore was working in a Lincoln movie, *The Copperhead,* at the time. He was startled at Stroell's close resemblance to Lincoln. The actor returned a few nights later with the studio head, who was also amazed at the likeness. Stroell, who had never acted in his life, was signed to play Lincoln in *The Copperhead.*[16]

The man who starred in the Rocketts' film about Lincoln, George Billings, looked so much like the president that when old men who had known Lincoln met him they often burst into tears. Billings was not an actor, though, and eventually his clumsy reading of lines and awkward movement in front of a camera caused the Rocketts to fire him. But then they became uncertain that they could get anyone talented, and because Billings looked so much like Lincoln, the producers had a change of heart and brought Billings back, gave him a crash course in acting and sent him in front of the cameras (he later enjoyed a long career playing Lincoln on the vaudeville circuits).[17]

None of these impersonators could act very well, even after playing the president for years. The inability to make him come to life further ruined any chances for a true view of Lincoln and, through him, of the politics of the Civil War.

The other, and more serious, problem with putting Lincoln on the silent screen was his titanic historical stature. He was such a popular figure, shrouded in myth and legend, that writers had difficulty making him human, just as screenwriters have always had trouble with movies about George Washington and, in sports, Babe Ruth.

At the moment of Lincoln's death in 1865, Secretary of War Edwin Stanton, stunned and heartsick, muttered under his breath, "Now he belongs to the ages." By 1908, when the first silent films about the war were shown in neighborhood theaters, the slain president had been deified by the public. Anyone who attempted anything short of a uniformly glowing portrayal of Lincoln was criticized harshly. Few even tried. When Ben Chapin sought to put on his one-man show on Lincoln for the Lyceum Theatre circuit in the 1890s, he was turned down because exhibitors feared that deviation from the established Lincoln image would anger customers. Even Mark Twain (the "Lincoln of our literature," according to William Dean Howells) was against any stage portrayals of Lincoln. "I wanted to keep my memory and thoughts of Mr. Lincoln unmarred by any disappointment in seeing a made-up imitation," he said. Chapin finally got his show on stages twenty years later, in 1913, during the war's anniversary years.[18]

Thousands of veterans of the war who remembered Lincoln were still alive. They handed down Lincoln lore to their children, who handed it down to theirs. The Lincoln legend was amplified by many men who worked with him, notably his secretaries, John Nicolay and John Hay, who wrote a ten-volume biography that was published in 1890. Others followed. Legendary Lincoln even became the main figure in numerous novels, such as Hezekiah Butterworth's *In the Boyhood of Lincoln* (1892), Mary Hartwell Catherwood's *Spanish Peggy* (1899), L. Boyd's *The Sorrows of Nancy* (1899), Homer Greene's *A Lincoln Conscript* (1909) and Oliver Marble Gayle and Harriet Wheeler's *The Knight of the Wilderness* (1909). By 1915, there were hundreds of fiction and nonfiction books on Lincoln in libraries.

The Lincoln legend even crossed the Atlantic. In 1916, to the immense surprise of the British literary set, John Charnwood's 479-page biography, *Lincoln,* became a huge success in England. Two years later, John Drinkwater's play *Abraham Lincoln* was just as successful in British theaters. Movies and books positioned Lincoln as an emotional force to unite all of England—not to fight a civil war but to fight World War I (the play was presented successfully in New York, too, beginning in 1919).[19]

The Lincoln legend grew in the South, too. Lincoln's death in 1865 brought on Reconstruction, and with it a certain feeling in Dixie that if Lincoln had lived, his reconstruction plan, softer on the South, would have helped reunite the nation. In death, Lincoln, reviled in the South throughout the war, surprisingly became an acceptable Southern hero of sorts.

There was also a new force on the national scene. The Progressive Party was made up of middle-class activists who fretted about the industrial revolution and yearned for the simple times of the mid-nineteenth century. The aura of Lincoln as a venerated leader-above-politics president was so great that although the party was very influential during the period from 1912 to 1916, and eager to bring some order to an industrialized society they felt had gone mad, Progressives did not criticize or question it. They, too, saw Lincoln as Honest Abe and Father Abraham, and accepted the myth. The whitewashed Lincoln was a good counterbalance to corrupt politicians (individuals and big-city machines), who were as far as humanly possible, the Progressives believed, from being the Honest Abe of schoolbooks, lore and the screen. Filmmakers succeeded in their mission because to many Americans the Lincoln they read about and saw on screen was a perfect emblem of republican virtue.

This redesigned Lincoln was the next logical step in the reconstruction of Civil War history. And, again, because this Lincoln was on the screen and movies had so much influence, the movie version of the sixteenth president became firmly embedded in American lore. The myth was not manufactured simply to create an American saint, however. It was invented and used by novelists, poets and newspaper reporters, biographers and public figures, carefully and shrewdly, to give Americans a God-fearing president in office at the time of the Civil War who was completely above politics. The folklore that all Americans were gallant during the war, that there were no villains, only heroes, and that at the end all were forgiven, needed more than anything the idea that the most important and famous man associated with that war was not a politician but a saint. The wistful portrayals of him, and his murder, made him not only a beloved leader but a martyred one, a man who had died for his country—both sides of it.

ABE LINCOLN leans back on his chair on a farmhouse porch, stovepipe hat straight on his head, long legs—crossed at the ankles— resting on a table between General Ulysses S. Grant and General William T. Sherman. The men are having a nighttime meeting and Lincoln (played by Walter Huston) has just learned from the two generals that the South is certain to surrender within days. The long civil war will soon be over.

The two generals look like realistic army men. Sherman worries and moves his chair in and out. Grant, hat tugged down hard on his forehead, chomps on his ever-present cigar. Lincoln becomes starry-eyed at the generals' news. Looking heavenward and sounding like an aging preacher, completely removed from reality, he opens his mouth slowly and, as if speaking to God, says in a slow, hushed voice dripping with benevolence, "The Union! The Union! We'll have them all back again . . . We're going to take them back as if they'd never been away . . ."

Sound in films arrived with much fanfare in 1927 with Al Jolson starring in *The Jazz Singer,* and quickly gave America King Kong, the Busby Berkeley chorus girls—and Abe Lincoln. It wasn't long before the tall man in the high stovepipe hat, the historic stick figure of the silents, began to appear in sound films. By the late 1920s, filmmakers could present Lincoln not just in sound but in full, feature-length movies. Such movies would benefit enormously from sound. Sound would bring the battlefield to life. Sound would add an element to gunshots and make every depiction of the president's assassination a film highlight. Sound would not only enable producers to give theatergoers a rounded look at Lincoln, but permit them to hear in full resonance the Gettysburg Address. It was a wonderful opportunity finally to present Lincoln as the complicated and enthralling figure he was, but Hollywood already had the Father Abraham portrayal of him pressed as firmly into its vision as the footprints in the cement in front of Grauman's Chinese Theatre. Sound would allow longer views of Lincoln, better scripts and certainly better portrayals by actors (particularly by Henry Fonda in *Young Mr. Lincoln,* Raymond Massey in *Abe Lincoln in Illinois* and, on television, portrayals by Hal Holbrook and Sam Waterston). But no movie would stray beyond the accepted and beloved version.

The first sound film about Lincoln was *Two Americans,* a two-reeler produced by Paramount. It was a short, patriotic film that had a brief life in the theaters.[20] It quickly disappeared, to be followed in 1930 by the full-length, would-be masterpiece *Abraham Lincoln,* by none other than D. W. Griffith.

Griffith took on the story of Lincoln with the same energy he had given *Birth of a Nation.* He was determined to present Lincoln as the prototypical American leader. But an American leader, as others had learned, had to be presented in a special way. Griffith, the quintessential showman, wanted to do everything big, including getting the best screenwriter, the best actor and the best cinematographer.

His first move was an attempt to hire Carl Sandburg to write the script. Sandburg, of course, had already told people that his overall portrait of Lincoln was based on the Lincoln he had seen in *The Birth of a Nation* as a young man. Griffith, then, was hiring Sandburg to give him Griffith. The author wanted too much money, however—thirty thousand dollars, three times what Griffith offered—and the deal fell through. Griffith then hired poet Stephen Vincent Benét, another literary giant of the day (who did not get along with Griffith), and began preparations.

Benét's career as a screenwriter was short. Some of Griffith's assistant directors and aides hated his completed screenplay and Griffith himself tore it apart in a story conference. The poet promptly quit the project, and the final screenplay wound up being written neither by the distinguished author of the Lincoln trilogy nor by one of the world's finest poets, the author of *John Brown's Body*, but by Gerrit Lloyd, the movie studio's public relations director.[21]

Griffith chose Walter Huston, his close friend, to play Lincoln. But Huston was not nearly as tall as Lincoln. His five-foot-nine frame did not dwarf anyone, as the real Lincoln's always did. Griffith and his assistants did everything short of standing Huston on a box or making other actors stand in a ditch when they were with him. To make the actor appear much taller, Griffith photographed him with cameras at knee level and positioned other actors in scenes with him closer to the camera or farther away to make his Lincoln appear taller. Many of his scenes were shot with everyone sitting down so that no one would tower over him.

The movie covered President Lincoln's whole life, beginning with his birth in Kentucky and going on to his days in New Salem as a young man and his romance with Ann Rutledge. It then carried him to Springfield for his career in law and politics, and then to the Civil War. Until that point, the story was historically accurate. But once Huston's Lincoln gets to the White House, the characters the silents created creep into the script. Lincoln pardons a teenage soldier condemned to death for sleeping at his post. He signs the Emancipation Proclamation with great reverence. Mary Todd Lincoln is once again depicted as the same old whining shrew and irresponsible spendthrift as in every other Lincoln movie. Once again, as in all the silent movies, she becomes Lincoln's albatross, even though the real Mary

Lincoln was not only the love of Abe Lincoln's life but a good and loving mother and a finely calibrated political barometer for her husband. Few women in history have been savaged as badly as Mary Lincoln.

The film shows Lincoln naming dirt-tough Ulysses S. Grant as head of the Army. Sheridan's ride through the Shenandoah Valley to rally his retreating troops is a brilliant bit of cinematography that only Griffith could have accomplished. Lincoln is shown rejecting plans to punish Jefferson Davis, president of the Confederacy, and the generals and men of the Confederate army. And, as usual, he is murdered in Ford's Theatre at the end of the film.[22] Robert E. Lee, whose myth by 1930 was as large as Lincoln's, is shown pardoning a Northern spy and then falling to his knees in prayer when he learns the war will soon be over.

Some critics enjoyed aspects of the movie and found Huston's depiction of the president deeply moving. Robert Roman, looking back in 1961 in *Films in Review,* was impressed with the crowd scenes, the authentic look of the sets, Ian Keith's portrayal of John Wilkes Booth, Huston's saintly look as Lincoln, and the assassination scene. Overall, though, he did not think it was a good movie. "He attempted too much too quickly," he wrote of Griffith.

Others were more critical, particularly of Huston's work as Lincoln. A critic for the *New York World* felt that Huston did not look much like Lincoln, that his heavy makeup could have been improved and that his eyes did not look right: "[They] did not express the weariness which was Lincoln's. Youth, and a trace of Broadway, shone through Mr. Huston's paint and powder."[23]

The real problem with the movie was that while nearly all the characters in it, from Phil Sheridan to Mary Todd Lincoln to John Wilkes Booth, did bear a faint resemblance to the historical personalities on which they were based, Huston's Lincoln was the same tired old kitchen mop the silents presented on bended knee. The movie is filled with scenes of meetings, whether with officers or cabinet members, and in all of them, someone else is always in charge and Lincoln sits silently by until the end, when he stammers something about the Union and the Almighty. Huston's Lincoln walked through the movie as a saint among sinners, offering a kind word here, a gentle wave there, constantly muttering about these awful dreams he had in which he saw the ship of the Union sailing safely through the storm but himself dead.

Huston's demeanor in the movie, the logical result of all the silent-screen depictions of the president, is essentially religious. Lincoln always speaks with his head tilted towards heaven or, if bad news reaches his office in the White House, keeps his head tilted down towards hell. He always remains calm, no matter how panicky others around him become, the steady hand at the helm. He dresses like a walking wake, usually all in black. He talks with his eyes, widening them in joy and narrowing them in sadness. His speeches are delivered in a deep bass (unlike Lincoln's high, reedy voice) and are so soppy that no one in a real setting would have paid attention for more than a moment.

And, naturally, the movie was full of the historical inaccuracies typical of so many Civil War films. Lincoln never gave a combination "malice towards none / of the people, by the people, for the people" speech at Ford's Theatre the night he was murdered. Sherman and Grant never wanted to shoot Robert E. Lee. The army Sheridan defeated in the Shenandoah Valley in 1864 was led by General Jubal Early, not Lee. For these and other reasons, the film got negative reviews and did not do well at the box office. The Great Depression, just a year old, was hitting the film industry, and the Griffith film suffered from that as well.

Although this was the last full-length film about the president until 1939, Lincoln did not disappear from the screen in the 1930s. As noted, his character appeared again and again as a bit part in numerous Civil War films, and a familiar face greeted audiences beginning to return to the theaters in the mid-1930s as the Depression eased a bit—Frank McGlynn. The actor, who had had such success playing Lincoln in silents, returned first to lend Lincoln's stature to a silly Civil War movie called *The Littlest Rebel*, starring Shirley Temple; it was a huge hit, thanks to the child star's devoted fans. The plot carries Shirley to the White House to see Lincoln. But first she dances her way through several plantations with the fabled tap-dancer Bill "Bojangles" Robinson, who, naturally, plays a good-natured slave devoted to his owners and all their chipper little relatives, like Shirley. The girl's father in the film (played by John Boles) is a good-hearted

Confederate officer (and another Southern victim) who has broken out of a Union prison but has been recaptured and sentenced to death. Shirley brings all of her charms to the White House to plead for his life while sitting comfortably on the smiling president's lap.

McGlynn appeared as Lincoln twice in 1936. He played him in a vivid assassination scene in *The Prisoner of Shark Island,* a story about Dr. Samuel Mudd, the physician who was sent to a prison in the Dry Tortugas for setting John Wilkes Booth's leg after the assassination. (The morbid fascination with Lincoln's assassination was far-reaching. The silents constantly showed his murder and, beginning with *The Prisoner of Shark Island,* there would be three full-length features on the unfortunate Dr. Mudd.) Later that year, McGlynn was back again as Lincoln in *Hearts in Bondage,* directed by Lew Ayres. He was the centerpiece of a cabinet scene in which he and others planned war strategy; then, in a rather touching scene, he was filmed walking along the banks of the Potomac, deep in thought.

In 1937, McGlynn played Lincoln again in several films—all bit parts. In *Western Gold,* a Fox film, he sends an officer out west to recover gold that belongs to the Union army. He sends another officer (Joel McCrea) west to do the same thing in *Wells Fargo* (the film included a nice speech about reconciliation). He listens to yet another appeal for a condemned soldier's life in *Man Without a Country* and has a cameo in *The Plainsman.*

None of these films in which Lincoln appeared had much impact beyond their links to all the other Civil War films concerning the idea of national reunification. None of them was very good and none featured any of the country's top performers. But as the Depression of the 1930s continued and World War II loomed, and as Americans embraced another gifted national leader who had brought the country together—President Franklin Delano Roosevelt—Hollywood produced some good movies about Abraham Lincoln, directed by its top directors and starring its very best actors.

THE TWO most powerful of these appeared nearly back to back in 1939 and 1940—respectively, *Young Mr. Lincoln* and *Abe Lincoln in Illinois.* Eventually they would form the largest part of the foundation of the Lincoln myth in American film and culture because they were later seen by millions on television. Although, compared to earlier treatments, both were much longer, more intelligent looks at Lincoln's character development, and both offered a much more authentic view of the man who became the sixteenth president, that authenticity was largely superficial; both were firmly rooted in the Lincoln legend.

The films premiered after decades of literary interest in Lincoln. They were not merely the successors of the silent films, they were also an extension of the literary works. Through the 1920s, writers had continued to turn to the always saleable Abe Lincoln for dozens of novels. There was a revival of interest in Lincoln biographies beginning in 1926, with the publication of Sandburg's *Abraham Lincoln: The Prairie Years*. It continued through the end of the 1930s, making the sixteenth president a constant figure in bookstores and libraries. As the Great Depression gripped the nation in the 1930s, books on Lincoln were particularly popular, and this led Hollywood producers to believe that movies about Lincoln could be successful as well.

The year 1940 was the seventy-fifth anniversary of the end of the war and producers assumed that Americans would want to see Lincoln movies on that anniversary, just as they had in the 1910–1915 anniversary years. They knew, too, that newspapers and magazines would fill their pages with numerous stories about the upcoming celebrations, just as they had at the time of the fiftieth anniversary. All of these news stories would serve as free publicity for films about the war or Lincoln. Producers had seen the film industry prosper in the latter half of the 1930s as the Depression eased a bit and millions of Americans went to the movies to find escapist entertainment. And throughout the late 1930s producers had seen historical film dramas, usually biographies, do well at the box office. These factors led them to believe that they could make money with movies about Lincoln, and films, of course, are produced to make money. The Lincoln films, though, wound up achieving other goals.

The two Lincoln movies premiered on the eve of World War II, as Hitler's armies were marching through Europe and there was talk of U.S. involvement in the war. The screenwriters saw both *Young Mr. Lincoln* and *Abe Lincoln in Illinois* as opportunities for American propaganda, aimed at uniting all Americans, North and South, white and black, to stand up against Germany, like the reconciliations that always took place in Civil War movies. In the heyday of the silents, 1908 to 1917, the movies had asked Northerners and Southerners to reunite as one country to celebrate the fiftieth anniversary of the war. In 1939 and 1940, film writers and directors were asking everyone to celebrate the seventy-fifth anniversary of the war's ending and to unite against the Nazis.

The ideal of a united America to weather the Depression and perhaps war, if it came, was perpetuated throughout the 1930s in novels, magazines, newspapers and films. The novels of James Fenimore Cooper, which mourned the passing of a virginal America, trampled by foreign armies in the French and Indian War, enjoyed a renewed surge of popularity. Oliver La Farge's *Laughing Boy* (1929) urged readers to adopt cultural pluralism. Stuart Chase's 1931 best-seller, *Mexico: A Study of Two Americas,* convinced many readers that simple villagers in Mexico had a better life than Americans in industrialized society. Studies of neurotic behavior were being read widely by Americans who wanted somehow to comprehend the collapse of what they had thought of as a simple way of life underneath the weight not just of the Depression, but of factories, pollution, crime, and cold, unfeeling corporations.

The 1930s was an era, historian Warren Susman wrote, in which years of fear, anxiety and economic chaos came to a head. To combat it, many people felt that they had to understand their distinctive nationalism, and that to do that they had to define clearly their culture and way of life. If they didn't understand their nationalism, and embrace it, they could not defend it against Germany or any other foe—from without or within.[24] Films told Americans that they lived in a unique and wonderful country and had to unite against those who would destroy it, such as Nazis and Communists.[25] Filmmakers, like novelists, reassured audiences that they lived in a unified and completely classless society. America was a great country because its people had made it great before, and now, despite their troubles, would make it great again.

Who could be a better symbol of American nationalism in time of strife than Abe Lincoln, the man who had led the nation through one war and would, in spirit, surely get us through another?

The first of the two definitive films on Lincoln, *Young Mr. Lincoln,* starring Henry Fonda, opened in June 1939, three months before

The portrayals of Lincoln changed in the sound era. Here, in Young Mr. Lincoln, *Henry Fonda plays the future president as a very easygoing country lawyer with no ambition, talking to the mother (Alice Brady) of two brothers falsely accused of murder.*

Hitler's invasion of Poland triggered the real war in Europe, and it was as much a movie about Roosevelt and World War II as it was about Lincoln and the Civil War.

The story of *Young Mr. Lincoln* was fictional, but very loosely based on a real-life case in which the son of a Lincoln friend, William Armstrong, was charged with murder. Historically, Lincoln won an acquittal for Armstrong when he was able to prove to the jury that there was no moonlight on the night of the killing, making it impossible for the state's eyewitness to have seen the act committed. In the movie version, two brothers are arrested for murdering a local rowdy in Springfield during a Fourth of July celebration. Their mother, who arrives right after the murder and is thought to have seen one of the boys commit the crime, refuses to testify, jeopardizing both. There is an eyewitness who says he saw one of them commit the murder. Neither boy admits guilt. The case seems hopelessly stacked against the defendants until Lincoln, their lawyer, tugs out a *Farmers' Almanac* to study the brightness of the moon on the night of the murder to determine whether or not the prosecution's eyewitness is lying—and shows that he is. Audiences knew then that all they needed to get through 1939 were two standard reliables: Honest Abe Lincoln and their trusty *Farmers' Almanac.*

The "almanac" murder trial had become one of the pillars of the Lincoln lore, as important in the legend as the log cabin, the Lincoln-Douglas debates and the little girl who asked Lincoln to grow a beard. All of the critics wrote about the movie trial as if it had been an actual event, and not the fiction it was. Herb Cohn, for example, in the *Brooklyn Daily Eagle,* on June 3, 1939, referred to it as "the popular trial."

The trial is the centerpiece of a film that shows off Lincoln as a solemn, law-abiding, justice-seeking attorney whose great compassion will not let a mother choose the gallows for one of her two sons. It also underlines the Lincoln legend of the frontier orator who could regale any crowd with a funny story and a shrewd lawyer who could, at the last moment, wangle the truth out of the most careful hostile witness and win the case.

The trial, however, was merely a little drama within the larger message of the movie—that Abraham Lincoln was a good and decent young man, devoted to the truth, the law and the nation, who later became a great president because of those qualities. This message is telegraphed to the audience during the opening credits, when the background music is a full-march rendition of the Civil War song "The Battle Cry of Freedom."

Everybody knows before the movie even starts that they are going to be spoon-fed the making of a great man. Lincoln is introduced at age twenty-three in the middle of his first political campaign. He is portrayed as a hardworking general store clerk who will probably soon go out of business because he gives everyone credit or barters food and clothes for books. Within minutes, he is seen courting beautiful Ann Rutledge, who tries to get him to be ambitious ("Ambitious?" he asks, uncomprehending) and then visiting the grave of the girl whom he loved deeply. There, he makes up his mind to become a lawyer. He moves on to Springfield.

Director John Ford draped the movie in Americana and Lincoln lore, hitting all the familiar marks in the Lincoln legend, from riding the circuit to studying on his own to his rivalry with Stephen Douglas. The familiar image of Lincoln on horseback, dressed in black and wearing his tall stovepipe hat, comes early. Then there are several scenes of Lincoln alone, reading books. Soon after comes a Fourth of July parade which gives the film its patriotic backdrop. Lincoln solemnly doffs his hat to honor aged veterans of the American Revolution as they ride by in a carriage. He later helps a team of buddies win a tug-of-war and himself wins the local "rail-splitter" contest. The scene of the Fourth of July festivities is full of patriotic music, banners, political speeches and the traditional arrival of all the people from the outlying districts coming to mingle with the city folk as one nation. The celebration has everything except Mom and apple pie. They come next. Mom is Mrs. Abigail Clay, the mother who will not testify against her two sons in the murder case. The apple pie is one of several Lincoln is asked to taste as a judge in a pie-baking contest.

Throughout the film, Lincoln is often photographed alone, his eyes always lifted a bit, looking towards some future horizon. There always seems to be some lighting on his head, suggesting a halo. The background music is either heroic or religious to reinforce the portrait of him as, of course, the young version of Father Abraham.

The end of the film underscores the Lincoln lore and ties it to 1940 prewar politics. Lincoln wins the court case, and when he emerges from the courtroom meets Douglas. Douglas, portrayed as a well-dressed, rich, influential and very powerful politician throughout the movie, tells the young Lincoln that he will never underestimate him again. Lincoln responds in kind. The audience knows that they will clash again in the Lincoln-Douglas debates. Douglas and the people with him then withdraw. The front door to the courthouse blows open and a shaft of light enters the hallway, bathing Lincoln in its glow. Alone, in black, a mourner of some kind, Lincoln walks out of the building towards the light as an unseen crowd cheers wildly (as it will cheer him wildly when he is elected president).

A moment later, in the film's final scene, after saying goodbye to Mrs. Clay and her sons, Abe turns down the chance of a ride back to town and chooses instead to walk up to the top of a hill. He walks alone, one hand holding his stovepipe hat on his head as a storm brews. With his eyes, he follows the Clay wagon until it disappears over the horizon (the wagon is the movement of the people towards a new nation just over the hill in 1865 and the twentieth-century American nation going over the hill towards trouble). As he walks, thunderclaps, which sound like cannons, assault him from every side and bolts of lightning illuminate him and the landscape. He walks on towards the future (and the nation's future in 1940) and his solitary destiny, a lone man in a terrible storm, as heroic music plays in the background.

Young Mr. Lincoln won generally good reviews. "One of the most profoundly stirring biographies to have come out of Hollywood. Substance, stature and tempo far out of the ordinary," wrote entertainment columnist Bland Johaneson in the *New York Daily Mirror*.[26] Some liked it because history overcame romance—a rarity in Hollywood in the 1930s. "[It was good] because the hero kisses nobody," joked Archer Winston in the *New York Post*.[27] Some thought Fonda was a bad choice because he was so famous, but others believed Fonda's stature merely enlarged the stature of Lincoln and brought him to life for Americans. Robert Roman wrote: "Henry Fonda's performance . . . is still vividly remembered and its effectiveness was the result not only of Fonda's acting ability but of wonderful bits of Americana with which John Ford surrounded him . . . Fonda's makeup was very effective. His nose and forehead were built up; his cheek had Lincoln's mole; and his slow smile seemed to be Lincoln's own. So did his voice."[28]

Fonda himself was worried about portraying such a well-known figure. He turned down the role when it was first offered to him (there was talk that Tyrone Power would do it) but then changed his mind. "He is too big a man in everybody's heart and affection . . . I [tried] to make every gesture, every word significant of the sort of man I knew Lincoln was to become," he told an interviewer during a break in filming.[29]

These movies, *Young Mr. Lincoln* and *Abe Lincoln in Illinois*, give us a useful look not only at Abraham Lincoln in the 1840s, but at the United States in the 1930s. If the Americans of pre–Civil War America were looking for someone like Abraham Lincoln, then so were

Americans in the 1930s—for many of the same reasons. Historical movies unlock doors to their contemporary audiences, letting us look at history twice—on the screen and out there in the dark.

Like so many other Americans, Midwesterner Robert Sherwood, author of the play on which the movie *Abe Lincoln in Illinois* was based, grew up absorbing the myth that theater, movies and histories created about Abraham Lincoln. Asked to write his first school essay at thirteen, he chose the sixteenth president as his topic. Sherwood also saw as a boy the British writer John Drinkwater's play about Lincoln when it opened in America in 1920, read a few Civil War books[30] published in the 1920s and 1930s and sat through numerous silent movies about the Great Emancipator. He read several history books to research Lincoln's life, but in the end he said he used *Abraham Lincoln: The Prairie Years*, the first part of Carl Sandburg's popular biography of Lincoln, as the basis for his play *Abe Lincoln in Illinois*, which won the Pulitzer Prize in 1938.[31] His view of Lincoln, he said, was based on Sandburg's view, which as we have seen was based on Griffith's, which was based on the long line of Father Abraham myths. Sandburg, like so many others of the era, made Lincoln a deeply religious president, above politics, working for the good of all. And so, then, did Sherwood.[32]

Sherwood was an isolationist throughout the 1930s, but the more he read about Lincoln, the more his political views changed. He saw in Lincoln everything that democracy stood for and in Hitler everything that threatened it. By the time the play opened he was an outspoken interventionist and an ardent supporter of President Franklin Delano Roosevelt. The play *Abe Lincoln in Illinois* was in rehearsal the same week that the Munich Pact was signed by Germany and England in September 1938. The "peace" accords gave Europe false hope but solidified the feelings of many Americans that the Nazis had to be stopped. Sherwood was such an American. His diary entries for the summer and fall of 1938 are filled with political notes, and they chronicle his embrace of FDR. On August 18 he wrote: "Thrilled by President's two speeches in Canada, in which he came as close as he legally could (if not closer) to telling the world, and Hitler and the Japs in particular, that if it comes to war they can consider us a partner of the British Empire. Roosevelt has made a lot more than his share of history, and damned good history, too." On September 16 he thought of Lincoln: "We're certainly trembling on the brink now . . . If only I could look into some book to see what Abe would have to say. Jesus! It's dreadful!"[33]

Later, looking back at the buildup to World War II, Sherwood saw even more correspondences between Roosevelt and Lincoln. Sherwood compared Lincoln's attitude toward slavery in the years before the Civil War to the attitude of the American people as a whole toward Germany in the 1930s. "It was," Sherwood wrote, "the point of view of ordinary Americans—and Englishmen and Frenchmen, as well—in 1936 when they said [that] if the Germans want Naziism . . . that is their business, and not ours. It was when Lincoln saw that the spirit of acceptance of slavery was spreading—from Missouri into Kansas and Nebraska and on across the plains and mountains to Oregon and California—it was then that he turned from an appeaser into a fighter." Here was the parallel Sherwood drew between Lincoln's slow turn to war and Roosevelt's in his time.[34] Sherwood's theme for his 1930s audience was not that the South was the enemy—the enemy was Germany. North and South would now have to link arms to fight a common foe.

Abe Lincoln in Illinois picks up where the film *Young Mr. Lincoln* left off, and when that film version opened just a year later it seemed to be a sequel, even though it was made by a different film company and a different director. The casting of Canadian actor Raymond Massey in the film seemed wrong to the New York press, even though he had played the part on stage. "A Canadian playing Abraham Lincoln?" asked an editorial in the New York *Daily News*. The rest of the cast was controversial, too. Ruth Gordon earned solid reviews as the tempestuous Mary Todd Lincoln, but she was never the producers' first choice. They wanted Lillian Gish, but she turned them down, perhaps because the film suggests that Mary Todd Lincoln was not Abe Lincoln's true love.[35] That honor, in novels, plays and movies, always went to Ann Rutledge, his first sweetheart. Mary Howard played Ann as a perfect innocent, a simple and sweet young thing. Some critics chortled at this casting, since Howard was a former *Ziegfeld's Follies* girl.[36]

Massey himself was still not convinced of his ability to play Lincoln, whether on stage or in film. Though he recognized the connection all Americans felt to the sixteenth president, he had not grown up with the Lincoln legend, as American children did. So great were his qualms and uncertainty that after opening night of the play's preview in Washington, D.C., two weeks before the Broadway opening, Massey asked to be released from his contract. Sherwood sent a telegram saying, "If Abe could see you perform tonight he'd like it more than the Lincoln Memorial." Massey stayed and the play was a commercial as well as critical success.

Hollywood studios in the 1930s rarely went on location to film anything, and not one minute of footage of *Abe Lincoln in Illinois* was filmed in Illinois. A Hollywood sound stage served for all the interiors, and a back lot became Springfield. The producers did move outdoors to re-create the tiny frontier village of New Salem, but built it outside of Eugene, Oregon, near a river with a small waterfall. The village was constructed there in order to use the waterfall for the movie's fabled raft scene, in which the young Lincoln meets Rutledge.[37]

The film version opens in a log cabin in Kentucky with a scene that was standard fare in historical biographies of the era: Lincoln reading Shakespeare by the fireside. Lincoln's stepmother sends him off into the world after telling him in a hushed, sepulchral voice of the Bible's statement that "He that doeth the will of God abideth forever," thus giving the movie religious overtones in the first minutes. The real Lincoln story was far more complicated. As a boy, Lincoln despised his illiterate father and moved off the family farm as soon as he could, looking for adventure and a new life. He was definitely not the quasi-religious figure portrayed in the movie.

Lincoln soon arrives in New Salem, where he immediately establishes himself as a powerful man by outwrestling the local champion. The vanquished brawler had announced himself with "I'm the big buck of this lick," so Abe's victory symbolizes all later victories against great odds. When the defeated wrestler puts his arm around his tall adversary, he proclaims that "New Salem has a new champion." Ann Rutledge, nearby, tells the crowd that this is "the man we've been waiting for." Both, of course, are metaphors for the nation needing a new champion.

The film plays fast and loose with chronology. Lincoln first ran for the state legislature in 1832, but in the film it is 1835. Later, the film puts John Brown's raid on Harpers Ferry in 1857, instead of 1859. The movie also completely overlooks the political upheaval caused by the slavery question in the 1850s, the formation of the Republican Party and Lincoln's leadership role. In the film, Lincoln berates Mary in the telegraph office on election night in 1860, sending her home. Mary was actually sound asleep in their house on the other side of Springfield, certain, as her husband had warned her, that he had lost the election.[38] Sherwood knew, after four years of writing screenplays in Hollywood, that the movie business paid no attention to historical fact, so neither did he. "The picture is faithful to the play and contains almost all of the play's glaring historical inaccuracies," he admitted.[39]

As in most Lincoln sagas, Abe has his tragic romance with Rutledge and fails at several different businesses. He definitely does not want to get into politics, but, of course, local politicians prod him into running for the state legislature. He demurs at first, telling them in a frightened voice that politics would lead him to cities and he has had a dream that someone killed him in a city. But, of course, he does run and is elected and, on the day he leaves for the legislature, is shown as clearly unhappy about going. He nods knowingly to an old man who tells him that politics is corrupt and that he should stay out because he is "an honest man." All of his campaign banners announce him as "Honest Abe Lincoln."

Later he tells Steve Douglas that he hates politics and is getting out because "in politics ignorance is no obstacle to advancement and that in some cases an advantage." Then he becomes a lawyer and moves on to Springfield and destiny. Again, he's pushed to get into politics, and constantly begs off. His law clerk and later partner, Billy Herndon, keeps telling Lincoln that he has to get some ambition and fulfill his destiny. His wife, as usual portrayed as a relentless harpie, tells her friends, who are appalled that she married him, she is going to make him president of the United States whether he likes it or not. One woman calls him a lazy man who never gets anywhere because he stops along the way to tell jokes.

Lincoln clearly isn't ecstatic about his marriage; he cowers when his future comes up in any conversation with Mary. "I hate her for her infernal ambition," he says of his wife. In actual fact, as noted earlier, Lincoln was intensely ambitious, but managed to hide it behind his engaging personality. In the film, Lincoln has no great love for the men around him, who keep telling him he has to fulfill his destiny, which they indicate has something to do with freeing the slaves.

In Springfield, Lincoln begins his lifelong adversarial relationship with Douglas, played magnificently by Gene Lockhart, who portrays him just as he was—a great public speaker, marvelously gifted politician, brilliant thinker and genuine leader of men. In Lockhart's Douglas, audiences see a man who should have been president. His Douglas is also savvy, so when friends chortle over Lincoln's decision to run against him, Douglas remarks that although the country considers Lincoln a lightweight, he does not.

Critics loved *Abe Lincoln in Illinois*. "One of the season's finest pictures," wrote Eileen Creelman in the *New York Sun*.[40] "It has a power and beauty that never flags," wrote Mae Tinee in the *Chicago Daily Tribune*.[41] "It works because Sherwood has stressed simplicity of subject. [Lincoln says] 'I'm a plain common gentleman in a shirt tail so short I can't sit on it,'" wrote Herb Cohn, who had also admired *Young Mr. Lincoln*, in the *Brooklyn Daily Eagle*.[42]

The movie version of *Abe Lincoln in Illinois*, rewritten by Sherwood, drew even closer parallels between Franklin Roosevelt and Lincoln and between the fight against Nazism in 1940 and that against slavery in 1860. That connection was definitely in the original play, written as Hitler's power in Germany and Roosevelt's power in America grew, all carefully symbolized through the character of Lincoln. Everybody in the cast of the movie knew Sherwood was writing about the Nazis as slaveholders and Roosevelt as Lincoln. "If you substitute the word 'dictatorship' for the word 'slavery' throughout Sherwood's script, it becomes electric for our time," Raymond Massey said. The movie opened on the same day nineteen hundred Jews were slaughtered by the Nazis in Warsaw.[43]

RKO, which produced and distributed the movie, highlighted the timeliness of the film, as well as its ties to Americana, in press releases, quoting a pre–opening night review from the Daughters of the American Revolution: "A real treat. Raymond Massey makes of Abraham Lincoln someone we all know. Director Cromwell has preserved for us something priceless of the American tradition."[44]

Newspaper and magazine editors, columnists and critics, all saw the political message; they all tied the Lincoln message to the times. "[It is] full of truth of liberty and democracy which Lincoln held to be self evident and which are equally pertinent today as they were in his time. It is these modern parallels and Raymond Massey's fine and

sympathetic characterization of Lincoln . . . for many of the things
Lincoln said about the freedom of the human spirit are as applicable
to the world today as they were to his . . . for today . . . democracy is
in even greater danger than it was in his times," wrote William
Boehnel in the *New York World-Telegram*.[45] In an editorial published
after the play version opened, the *Washington Herald* wrote that the
film would be "opening the way for the movies really to make him live
again in a time when a nation needs him as much as it ever did."[46]

The subliminal message of the film was that Lincoln, and the horrific Civil War, *did* end the evil of slavery. Now, perhaps, in the late
1930s, another war was needed to stop a second evil, Nazism.

Roosevelt enjoyed the identification with Lincoln, particularly
since the opposition Republican Party had begun to strengthen itself
once again in the 1938 elections. He embraced Sherwood's Lincoln,
realizing that in so doing he was embracing himself. He had been promoting himself as a second Lincoln since 1932, when he asked Americans of all parties, just as Lincoln did in 1861, to unite behind him to
save the nation. Just before the play opened, he allied himself with
the spirit of Lincoln in a speech at Gettysburg. "Lincoln, too, was a
many-sided man. Pioneer of the wilderness, counselor for the under-
privileged, soldier in an Indian war, master of the English tongue, ral-
lying point for a torn nation, emancipator—not of slaves alone, but of
those of heavy heart everywhere—foe of malice and teacher of good
will," Roosevelt said of Lincoln (and himself) in 1938.[47]

The movie premiere in the capital was one of the highlights of the
1940 cultural season and made the front page of the *Washington Times
Herald,* complete with a photo of Raymond Massey shaking hands
with Eleanor Roosevelt. The Great Emancipator's emancipation was
not complete, however. Mrs. Roosevelt and first-night guests had to
walk past a picket line of African Americans protesting the fact that
the very theater in which the movie about Lincoln was being shown
refused to allow blacks admission for any of its films.[48]

Sherwood's friendship with Eleanor and Franklin Roosevelt had
blossomed since the play's opening two years earlier (Mrs. Roosevelt
wrote one of her syndicated newspaper columns about it) and by the
time the movie was released in 1940, Sherwood had become an ardent
FDR supporter.[49] He became such a fan that shortly after the start
of World War II he joined the White House staff as one of Presi-

dent Roosevelt's speechwriters. Roosevelt, looking to Sherwood for more Lincolnesque views, made the playwright one of his closest confidants.

Sherwood traveled all over the world with FDR so he could be with him whenever the President needed his skills. Many of the President's most important addresses to the nation, such as the fireside chats, the May 1941 speech declaring a state of national emergency and many of his 1944 campaign speeches bore the impress of the playwright's work. Sherwood took great pride in audience reaction to his work and FDR's words.[50] His best effort for FDR came in the president's last 1944 reelection campaign speech in Boston, in which Roosevelt reiterated his commitment to win the war and again denounced the Japanese and reminded voters whom they were fighting. Sherwood helped him declare: "I am sure that any real American would have chosen, as this government did, to fight when our own soil was made the object of a sneak attack. As for myself, under the same circumstances, I would choose to do the same thing—again and again and again."[51] Sherwood helped make the link between Abe Lincoln and Franklin Roosevelt complete.[52]

Carl Sandburg, a longtime Roosevelt supporter, whose first book on Lincoln gave Robert Sherwood many of his ideas for *Abe Lincoln in Illinois,* injected much of his view of FDR into the second part of his Lincoln biography, *Abraham Lincoln: The War Years.* The book was published in 1939, just before the seventy-fifth anniversary of the end of the Civil War, and on the eve of World War II. Sandburg's depiction of Lincoln as a war president of a people who, in 1860, did not believe they would soon be in a war was brilliant. He showed Lincoln as a man who, with little military background, could be an outstanding war president and a skilled commander in chief. He also underlined the premise of democracy at war: a civilian can and should be in charge of the military. The book, a great success critically and commercially, reassured many Americans that in Roosevelt they had that same kind of vastly capable man who could lead them into and through World War II. FDR embraced the book, as he had embraced Sandburg, perhaps because it tied him even closer to Lincoln. Roosevelt knew that in the coming years he needed that association to get elected a third time and—if there was war—to lead Americans into it.

Not only were *Young Mr. Lincoln* and *Abe Lincoln in Illinois* great propaganda, but both diverged significantly from the old Plantation Myth. Both avoided all plantation scenes and did not depict blacks as either thugs or Sambos and Mammies. They did not show Southern politicians or slaveholders as villains, but held up the slave system as the villain. No one was blamed for the war, either, because both films were carefully written so that they ended before the beginning of the war. Nearly twenty-five years after the heyday of the silent movies' cotton-fields lore, here was a sign that Hollywood was rethinking that simplistic view and building up the idea of reunification and national identity.

WORLD WAR I ended the first era of Civil War movies and World War II ended the second, and the Lincoln movies as well. The sixteenth president quickly disappeared from the nation's movie screens when World War II began. Whatever romantic notions about the Civil War and Lincoln film had conjured up prior to 1941 were immediately washed away by the grim reality of the latest war. Americans were too busy worrying about unknown places such as Guadalcanal and Bastogne to spend much time on Gettysburg and Shiloh.

It wasn't until 1951 that Lincoln again appeared as a character in a film. Leslie Kimmell played him in *The Tall Target,* about an assassination plot just before his inauguration. Stanley Hall played Lincoln in an assassination scene in *The Prince of Players,* a 1955 film biography about Edwin Booth, John Wilkes Booth's older brother. In a nice twist, Raymond Massey played the Booths' father in the film.

Not until the 1980s and 1990s would there be movies or made-for-television films and miniseries that would present a more truthful look at President Lincoln. Such greater realism was not possible in 1939, when parents took their children to see *Young Mr. Lincoln* in order to give them a civics lesson. The view of Lincoln as Honest Abe, the Railsplitter, the man on the penny, would pretty much remain intact for years—because the audiences wanted him that way.

Any true look at Lincoln, no matter how many files and papers were culled, would not show him as an underhanded politician, a duplicitous president, a roving husband, a tyrannical father or a man out of touch with the people. A true look at the prairie lawyer who became the sixteenth president would show him instead as a vibrant man, full of wit and good intentions, who was a genuine leader of men and women and a man who, regardless of whether or not he held office or power, was admired by all who knew him. Nobody can identify with the simple, religious, cardboard Lincoln Hollywood has given Americans, but everybody could identify with the real Abe Lincoln: a man who, like so many others, worked very, very hard (often failing) to become successful and never gave up on his personal dreams or his vision of the kind of nation he felt America ought to be, the kind it did become—thanks in part to him.

CHAPTER TEN

The War Comes to Tara

ATLANTA, GEORGIA, December 15, 1939: If the South had won the Civil War in a replay, Atlanta could not have been in a more celebratory mood than on this night, the night of the premiere of *Gone With the Wind*. Over seven hundred thousand visitors had booked hotel rooms throughout the city and in small towns as far as thirty miles away. Huge searchlights in front of the Grand Theatre, the site of the premiere, were so powerful that their beams scanning the sky in lazy circles could be seen as far as Macon, fifty miles away.

The excitement had been building for weeks. The governor of Georgia had proclaimed the day of the premiere a state holiday[1] and earlier in the week had waited at the airport, with other dignitaries, to meet planes carrying Clark Gable (who flew on the MGM plane, which had GONE WITH THE WIND painted in huge letters on its side), Vivien Leigh and producer David O. Selznick (Leigh's plane was kept circling Atlanta for forty-five minutes because the flowers the mayor of Atlanta was to present her were late). Thousands of citizens rented 1860s-style hoopskirts and suits for the occasion. Dozens of local department stores proudly displayed in their windows costumes from the movie, loaned by the studio. The governors of seven states were in attendance. Political notables such as W. Averell Harriman and Herbert Hoover mingled with celebrities Billy Rose, Carole Lombard, Laurence Olivier and a host of MGM stars.

At the Grand Theatre, there was chaos. The building's entire front had been remade into a replica of Scarlett O'Hara's plantation mansion, Tara, complete with white columns. The twenty-five hundred tickets, usually fifty cents but hiked to ten dollars for the premiere, had been sold out for months. On this, the climactic night, scalpers were getting more than two hundred dollars a ticket.[2]

The stars arrived in a long parade of convertibles as thousands of fans lining the streets cheered wildly. Everyone connected with the film in a major way was in Atlanta and in the parade except director Victor Fleming, who was feuding with Selznick. British actress Vivien Leigh, who played Scarlett, the everlasting symbol of Southern womanhood, in fact knew very little about Southern cultural traditions. As she rode along in her convertible, she kept hearing bands play "Dixie." She turned to the man next to her and gushingly told him that she thought it was a good omen for the success of *Gone With the Wind* that people were already playing its music.[3]

The night before the premiere, the stars had appeared at a Junior League ball. (Margaret Mitchell did not attend because the Junior League had snubbed her years before.) There were so many people who wanted to get in that a second ball was held down the street in a hotel. At the ball, Clark Gable danced with the daughter of the mayor of Atlanta and, one reveler reported, caused a local debutante to faint when he asked her to dance.

The jockeying for tickets to the premiere had gone on for months. Feuds erupted at Macmillan, publisher of the novel, when it was learned that the company was limited to six tickets. The head of the Atlanta chapter of the Daughters of the American Revolution became involved in a dispute with producers over complimentary tickets. After listening to her harangue at some length, an assistant producer snapped, "Wrong war!"

Studio moguls pulled out all the stops, sending a team of publicists to Atlanta to handle that opening and other publicists to other cities to prepare their premieres. Special programs were printed for the Atlanta opener. Selznick, always a stickler for detail, warned the printers not to make the program paper too crisp: he was afraid that as the pages were turned during the movie the crackling sound would drown out the dialogue. Also, knowing that huge crowds of spectators would be present, he was nervous about the publicity shots of the stars—the photos traditionally sent out by the studios; he was worried lest people in the crowds get into the background, and so he dispatched photographers to Atlanta well in advance to photograph the front of the theater, with its Tara façade, and had them send the photos back to Hollywood. The stars were then photographed alone, in Hollywood, and studio magicians superimposed these pictures over the Atlanta photos so they looked as though they had been shot at the premiere.

The audience in the Grand Theatre was hushed when Max Steiner's lush theme started to play and the film began, but the hush didn't last long. People wept at the scene in which thousands of Confederate soldiers lie wounded in an Atlanta square, roared their approval when Scarlett shoots a Yankee soldier and clapped their hands and sang whenever any ragtag band in the movie struck up "Dixie."[4]

A tense Scarlett, revolver in hand, just before she shoots and kills a Union soldier who seems intent on raping her. Audiences at the Atlanta premiere of Gone With the Wind *cheered when she killed the man.*

In retrospect, of course, it's clear that the movie could not miss: it was based on a number one best-selling book, it had a stellar cast and it was one of the first great technicolor extravaganzas. However, in the beginning Selznick had thought the movie a risky project. He had paid a record amount of money for the book rights, and he knew that production would be extremely expensive and that it would take a long time to shoot. The film would also be facing strong competition from the hundreds of other movies released in 1939. He did not know whom to sign on as chief screenwriter and was uncertain about his original choice for director, George Cukor.

To insure his investment he borrowed box office champion Clark Gable from MGM and agreed to pay his hefty salary of forty-three hundred dollars a week. Everyone told him Gable was perfect to play Rhett Butler and Hollywood columnists were so certain of the match that, writing about the casting of *Gone With the Wind,* some asked rhetorically in their columns, "Who will play Clark Gable?"

Gable, ironically, had no faith in the film's prospects, and did not want the part. "I didn't want [it] for money, chalk or marbles," he said later. He had to be talked into it. Then he had to be talked into crying on screen in the scene where he believes Scarlett is going to die. He had never cried before in a film, and he was certain it would ruin his masculine image. But his tears not only did not undermine his masculinity, they made him even more of a superstar.[5] One thing he was adamant about, however, was his refusal to take speech lessons in order to speak with a Southern accent. It turned out not to matter, and he came out of the movie as the matinee idol of all time.

The most sensual scene of the film, of course, is when Rhett picks up Scarlett against her will and carries her up the enormous, wide, darkened staircase towards the bedroom. It was considered one of the most erotic scenes of all time—although some women complained that what he did was rape. Actually, Gable and Leigh couldn't get the scene right and it had to be reshot twelve different times. Each time, Gable had to carry the actress in his arms up that long flight of stairs. After the final take, Gable was completely drained physically and had to rest. He could not have made it up the stairs one more time, much less raped anybody.[6]

The search to find an actress to play Scarlett (she was named Pansy O'Hara in the first draft of the book, but someone wisely persuaded the author to change the name), a public relations masterstroke, took two years. Just about every top star in Hollywood, as well as hundreds of unknowns from coast to coast, auditioned for the role. (A rumor started, never completely quieted, that when Selznick learned how much the production, plus Gable's salary, would cost, he decided to cast unknowns as Scarlett and Melanie just to save money.)[7] No one was signed. Selznick searched and his aides searched. They ran auditions in every major American city and sent scouts to small ones. They looked throughout the United States, Mexico and Canada. But always the women were too old or too young, too heavy or too thin.

Finally, having given up, and under enormous pressure to begin filming, Selznick decided to start shooting around the star. He climbed to the top of a high wooden tower one night in Hollywood to supervise the burning down of a studio set that on film would be the burning of Atlanta. Hundreds of people—cast, crew and firemen—stood around watching the enormous conflagration, which could be seen as far away as Santa Monica. At the very height of the blaze, as flames leaped into the Los Angeles sky and the heat became intense, Selznick heard the sound of feet climbing the ladder of the tower behind him. This was followed by the familiar voice of his brother Myron, an agent. The producer turned and, squinting because of the heat from the fire, looked directly across the platform at one of the most beautiful women he had ever seen—Vivien Leigh.

"David," said his brother, "I'd like you to meet Scarlett O'Hara."

GONE WITH THE WIND became one of the most successful movies of all time, earning over $60 million in box office receipts (close to $1 billion in today's money), and was seen by millions of Americans in its various television showings. It was estimated that between its first theater showing in 1939 and 1945 more than 120 million Americans, or just about every adult in the country, saw it. Many theaters ran it for a year; a number in the South had ushers dress as Confederate officers and Southern belles. There was such demand to see the movie that distributors gave up their restrictions and permitted more than one first-run movie theater in a city to show it. In New York City, the Empire, Ritz and Palace, all ornate first-run houses, showcased it for twelve months.[8] It ran for two years in Atlanta. A movie house in London showed it for four straight years. Demand for tickets was so great in some towns that theaters doubled prices and some added a second or third showing each day. In some markets, the movie was yanked from houses after six months to build demand from those who hadn't yet had a chance to see it, held in Hollywood for a time, and then rereleased to a second wave of ticket-buying madness. It was re-released several times over the years 1940–45. Each time it got new reviews that helped to stimulate new box office records.[9]

It also stirred up controversy with both Northern and Southern commemorative groups.

In the South, the search for Scarlett caused an uproar. Several chapters of the Daughters of the Confederacy threatened to boycott the film because an English actress landed the role. Indignation grew so intense that it spilled over onto the floor of the Daughters' national convention. Peace finally came when the group's president-general, Mrs. Walter LaMar, assured the ladies that as a world traveler she had met many British women and found them "most delightful."[10]

In the North, members of the Daughters of Union Veterans complained that the film wrecked the reputation of General Sherman, insinuated that all Union soldiers tried to rape Southern women and misrepresented the story of the war. "It is unfair that our boys and girls should be given such a distorted view of what actually took place," stated a resolution drafted by the group and read by a member at one of their meetings.[11]

GWTW broke other ground. Producer Selznick paid a then-record $50,000 for the rights to Margaret Mitchell's novel. It was the costliest movie made until that time, at $4.25 million, and also the most lavish. Selznick shot over 450,000 feet of film in order to edit it down to a final version of 19,980 feet. The producer had fifteen hundred scene sketches drawn, ordered two hundred sets designed and actually built ninety (including the old studio lot that he burned). He hired a cast of more than twenty-four hundred people; designers produced fifty-five hundred costumes.[12]

Along with *The Wizard of Oz, GWTW* was one of the handful of experimental color films of the later 1930s (only ten were made in 1939). One major reason that Selznick spent so lavishly on color was that Jock Whitney, one of moviedom's biggest investors, and one of *GWTW*'s largest financial backers, had invested in some of the early color movies of 1937 and 1938, such as *Nothing Sacred, Tom Sawyer* and *A Star Is Born.* Whitney was also a major investor in the company that produced Technicolor film and he pushed Selznick hard to make *GWTW* a guinea pig for the new process.[13] If *Gone With the Wind* had been filmed in black-and-white, its impact, then and later, would have been significantly less. It was a long movie, nearly four hours, in an era of ninety-minute to two-hour features, and, like *The Birth of a Nation,* it showed Hollywood that long movies could succeed at the box office. The film made Vivien Leigh a star, and Clark Gable a legend. (Twenty-eight years later, in 1967, when the movie was rereleased, many audiences broke into sustained applause at the point when he appears for the first time, at the foot of the staircase at the Wilkes party. A whole new generation of young women swooned as their mothers had years before at first sight of him.)[14]

Most critics enjoyed *Gone With the Wind.* But some, like Lincoln Kirstein, in *Film Magazine,* saw its historical flaws. He wrote: "History has rarely been told with even an approximation of truth in Hollywood because the few men in control there have no interest in the real forces behind historical movements and the new forces that every new epoch sets in motion. *Gone With the Wind* deserves our attention because it is an overinflated example of the usual false movie approach to history."[15]

GWTW, like other silent and sound films about the war, bolstered the four-pronged presentation of the Plantation Myth that the Old South was a special place ruined forever by history's lightning: 1) all white Southerners were rich plantation owners and, in their personal lives, well-educated, romantic cavaliers; 2) white Southerners loved their slaves and their slaves loved them and they all just wanted to be left alone; 3) the North started the war, forcing the gentlemen of the South to fight the Lost Cause for four long years, to lose in the end, but lose gallantly; 4) the South was devastated by Reconstruction— imposed by the federal government—and never recovered. *Gone With the Wind,* seen by just about every American in theaters and, later, on television, had the power to reinforce these myths and turn them into acceptable fact.

The first great distortion in the book and movie, carried over from the silent-film era, was that all Southerners were wealthy, lived on huge plantations and owned hundreds of slaves (the Tarleton Twins alone owned 106). When Selznick's people researched plantation homes in northern Georgia in order to design Tara, they had to report back to him that they could not find one that was as large as Selznick envisioned Tara and Twelve Oaks or one that had white-columned porches. Selznick shrugged and told them to design Tara as it appeared in the movie, anyway, and call it an authentic re-creation. Once his set designers gave him Tara (they painted the exterior of Twelve Oaks on a scrim), Selznick used it as the backdrop for a society in which everyone was rich and owned slaves. He was determined, like so many before him, to re-create a Southland of mansions and elegance, even if the one in *GWTW* never existed.

The massive and elegant Tara mansion—a designer's fantasy created on Selznick's orders in the absence of any real plantation house that was sufficiently large and impressive to serve as a model for it.

The fingerprints of *The Birth of a Nation* were all over *Gone With the Wind*. Just as *Birth* opened with scrolled wording telling viewers that the Southern states constituted a separate country ("the Southland") with separate cultural ways, living by its own rules, *GWTW* opened with similar scrolled wording—backed up by that gorgeous Steiner theme—informing viewers that there once was a "land of cavaliers and cotton fields called the Old South"; that there, "gallantry took its last bow"; that "here was the last ever to be seen of Knights and their ladies"; and that it was really "a civilization" that was now "gone with the wind."

In this separate country with its separate rules live two families, the Wilkeses and the O'Haras, who are presented in the first few frames of the film as wealthy but benevolent, good and decent people—very much like the lovable Cameron family in *Birth*. All the trappings of strong family life are shown: parents at home loving their children, respect for their institutions, friendship between siblings, family mealtime prayers and even pet dogs who romp on Scarlett O'Hara's front porch (just as the Camerons' dogs romp in *Birth*).[16] The Wilkeses and O'Haras, and the other slaveholders in the movie's Old South, are good to their slaves, who love them in return. The two families, like the Camerons, are so personable that they became very real to audiences. From the beginning of the film, viewers are cheering for them and resentful of anyone who tries to hurt them. (This opening scene of the likable family that engages in detestable practices was used with similar success in the opening wedding scene in *The Godfather.*) "You find you know these people as thoroughly as though you had lived with them for years," wrote Bosley Crowther in his rereview of *GWTW* in 1941.

Scene after scene shows reciprocal affection between slaves and masters—the film's second major distortion. "You must be gentle with darkies," Gerald O'Hara admonishes his daughters. Scarlett's mother is seen helping sick slave children. The irascible but likable Mammy sticks with the family through the war, spurning freedom, just to help them get through hard times. Big Sam is content. Even Prissy, who knows nothing about birthing babies, stays.

Many of the loving slaves are depicted as idiots or fools. Prissy's whining, witless character made any African American watching the movie cringe. Malcolm X said that of all the abuses of blacks in the film, the depiction of Prissy hurt him the most. A poll of women who watched the film showed approval for Scarlett's slapping of Prissy when the girl lies about her ability to deliver babies.[17] Although the liberal Selznick had the word "nigger" cut out of the film, in the book, characters repeatedly called each other "nigger" and the house servants sneered at the "field hands," whom they considered dumb. Southern city slaves referred to slaves on cotton plantations as "country niggers."

In the book, Melanie and Scarlett survive a kitchen fire at Tara set by Yankee soldiers (naturally). Both are covered in soot. Scarlett laughs at Melanie and tells her, "You look like a nigger." Melanie laughs back. "And you look like the end man in a minstrel show."[18]

In the movie's opening scenes contented slaves are picking cotton and driving wagons full of felled trees, and other such scenes abound. At the Southland's balls, parties and picnics, black servants lovingly prepare and serve food and are pleased to take the reins of their masters' guests' horses. Black girls gladly spend hours fanning the air to keep it cool while their owners' daughters take an afternoon beauty sleep. A servant braves pouring rain to chase and kill a chicken for the "white folks'" Christmas dinner. Mammy and another servant mourn, misty-eyed, that Yankee soldiers have stolen Tara's livestock. It is "a whole world that wants only to be graceful and beautiful," as Melanie Hamilton tells Ashley Wilkes, but meddling abolitionists from the North destroy it all by going to war against it.

That is the third distortion in the film. Mitchell, and then Selznick and his writers, quickly position the Northerners as the aggressors at the Wilkes barbecue early in the film, and the old formulation follows. Gerald O'Hara acknowledges that the South fired the first shot when it attacked Fort Sumter, but the movie immediately accuses President Lincoln of starting the war by calling for seventy-five thousand troops to put down the rebellion. Someone shouts that one Southerner can lick twenty Yankees. Someone else yells that gentlemen (South) can fight better than rabble (North). Another says that the Southerners can lick the Northerners in one, single battle. Rhett Butler then jumps into the conversation to warn the Southerners that the Yankees outnumber them and have a standing army and more supplies and factories to make weapons and ammunition. This immediately frames the Lost Cause for the audience, setting up the Confederates as underdogs who must fight gallantly even to stay on the field, much less win the war.[19]

That stated, *GWTW* then proceeds to show how the Lost Cause was defended for four long years in an unequal struggle against the

Union army. That is bitterly underlined by Ashley Wilkes, home on Christmas leave, when he says, "The Yankees keep coming and coming. There are always more."[20]

Scene after scene reminds viewers of the South's hardships: hundreds gather in an Atlanta street to get the lists of dead and wounded after Gettysburg. In one of filmdom's most vivid scenes, thousands of wounded troops lie moaning in a large Atlanta square, a tattered Confederate flag flying above as a stunned Scarlett walks among them. Atlanta hospitals are filled with the dead and dying, all put there by Yankees. Atlanta itself is burned to the ground by the Yankees and the good people there are forced to evacuate like rats. ("Yankees in Georgia!" wails Aunt Pittypat. "How did they ever get in?") Tara and Twelve Oaks are razed by the Yankees. Women like Melanie Wilkes have to turn over their gold wedding rings to the Confederate army so they can be used to buy supplies for the troops. Even Belle Watling, the notorious madam, supports the cause ("I'm a Confederate like everybody else").

Gentle Southern women like Scarlett must turn into murderers to prevent Yankee soldiers from raping them. The threatened rape of Scarlett by a Union soldier at Tara, symbolically the rape of the entire South by the U.S. Army, is averted when Scarlett shoots the soldier.[21] After killing him, Scarlett mutters that he was probably a deserter, suggesting that at heart all Yankees were cowards.[22]

Honest and law-abiding citizens in Atlanta are turned into looters when Atlanta is attacked, but they are not following their own instincts. They loot, Rhett Butler insinuates, because they must have a way to save themselves from the advancing Union army.

In the end, the South is devastated by the war. With vultures overhead, Scarlett and Melanie drag themselves back to Tara, driving their carriage past dead Southern soldiers, overturned wagons and burned-out Southern homes. Scarlett's mother dies of typhoid fever she has contracted while caring for the typhoid-ridden daughters of the Slattery family, the local "poor white trash," as the good plantation women always cared for those around them, black and white. Gerald O'Hara, practically mad, breaks his neck in a riding accident (in the novel he rides recklessly after being ordered to take a loyalty oath to the Yankees so that he could keep Tara, and in the film he rides after a carpetbagger Scarlett has just denounced as a "Yankee coward"). All of this has been caused by the Yankees. The movie conveniently over-looks the devastation wrought by Southern armies, such as the mas-sacre of black soldiers at Fort Pillow, in Tennessee; the torching of Chambersburg, Pennsylvania; and the deaths of thousands of prison-ers at Andersonville. (The death camp at Andersonville was such a touchy issue, seventy-five years after the war, that Ashley Wilkes's imprisonment at Rock Island, a Union prison in Illinois, mentioned in the novel, was snipped out of the movie to avoid raising the Anderson-ville issue on the Southern side.)

Southern reviewers grasped the many Plantation Myth meanings of the film immediately and hoisted it on their pens as Stonewall Jackson would have hoisted one of his Virginia cavalry flags. "The Lost Cause will never be lost," wrote a critic for the *Richmond News Leader,* "as long as there beats one heart which is pumped by one drop of southern blood . . . the real thing [history of the South] was painted for us. We wondered how the men and women of the South ever came out of that terrible tragedy alive or sane . . . [the film] was a truly great and moving experience."[23]

Of course, the true success of the movie lay not in the continued advancement of the myth but in the riveting character of Scarlett O'Hara, a fierce individualist who is the ultimate survivor of a destroyed civilization. She is an independent woman who survives everything to rebuild Tara and then her own life in Atlanta, symbolic of the rebuilding of the entire South and, for Depression audiences, the United States in the 1930s. Scarlett is also a far more complex character, and more believable, than any heroine of the silent era or other 1930s Plantation Myth films. She yearns for Ashley Wilkes until nearly the end of the movie, when she finally realizes, too late, that the man she should have loved is Rhett Butler, who desperately loved her. It was Scarlett's soap opera story, full of spectacular sets and scenes and vividly drawn characters, black and white, and Clark Gable's dynamic, roguish Rhett, that made *GWTW* succeed. Women loved it for Scarlett's independence and Rhett's charms, men loved it for Rhett's manliness and all loved it for its story of survival in a war-torn world and the taut melodrama of the death of what was pre-sented as a gracious world in simpler times.

That is why Selznick, the Hollywood producer, had loved the story, too, even if filming it meant taking a risk. He saw the book as two interwoven stories, both highly attractive—the survival of feisty Scarlett and her friends in a war, and a love story. But he quickly realized that what was a quintessentially Southern book could not be so unequivocally a Southern movie. All the basic elements of the run-away best-seller (it sold fifty thousand copies in its first day in stores and was the number one best-seller for nearly two years) were kept in the script, but much of the book's vitriolic portrayal of Northerners was deleted, and numerous anti-Northern references were cut out. The love story between Scarlett and Rhett was highlighted in the movie, and many of the nicely drawn but clearly Southern characters were eliminated. Numerous carpetbaggers were trimmed from the story, too. Although blacks were presented in stereotypical ways, the novel's worst depictions of them were removed from the film. One black calling another "nigger" was eliminated, as was a scene where Prissy eats watermelon with great glee.[24]

One of the biggest changes was the role of the Ku Klux Klan. In the book, Ashley Wilkes and Scarlett's husband, Frank Kennedy, are leaders of the KKK in Atlanta and lead a raid to murder blacks in retribution for an attack on Scarlett. Mitchell's most powerful defense of the Klan in the novel, and a telling scene, has Melanie Wilkes, the saintly Melanie, lying to federal officers to protect her husband and others in the KKK. In the scene, Melanie's sister India defines the role of Southern men and their women, and of the men in the Klan in particular. She tells a disbelieving Scarlett that her husband and Ashley are Klansmen and then adds, defensively: "They are men, aren't they? And white men and Southerners. You should have been proud of him."[25] In other words, men, Southern men, belong in the KKK.

Mitchell, and many other Southerners, saw the Klan as providing needed protection against blacks and white agitators in the 1870s— and in the 1930s, too.[26] "One of the earliest purposes of the Klan was to protect women and children," she wrote. "Later, it was used to keep the Negroes from voting eight or ten times at every election. But it was used equally against the Carpetbaggers who had the same bad habit where voting was concerned. Members of the Klan knew that if unscrupulous or ignorant people were permitted to hold office in the South their lives and property would not be safe. . . ."[27]

Selznick's fear, though, was that the Klan was undergoing a strong resurgence just as *GWTW* was about to open, and he despised the organization. The KKK had reportedly murdered or maimed dozens of people, black and white, throughout the country, North as well as South, in the spring and summer of 1939. Klansmen burned crosses in front of black homes and churches, as usual, but in the summer of 1939 they burned several as well in front of the homes of white Jews and Catholics and in front of synagogues and Catholic churches. Crosses were burned as far north as Jersey City, New Jersey. Deputy sheriffs and police officers in several Southern states publicly admitted to Klan membership; one was even a deputy sheriff in Fulton County, Georgia, where *GWTW* opened. According to Klan Imperial Wizard Hiram Evans in congressional testimony, the Klan even became involved in pressuring state transportation agencies in the awarding of contracts to pro-Klan contractors. By the time *GWTW* opened, KKK membership had soared to over three hundred thousand. Selznick did not want to help it increase further.[28]

The Klan set up its Georgia headquarters on Peachtree Street, where Mitchell lived and where she worked as a reporter for the *Atlanta Constitution,* so she drove past their offices just about every day (her black servant refused to go with her when she was going to be around KKK headquarters).[29] She had no qualms about the Klan and in a letter wrote: "I had not written anything about the Klan which is not common knowledge to every southerner."[30] The Klan was just as much a presence in Southern life when the movie came out as it was during Reconstruction.

Selznick did not want to romanticize the Klan, as Griffith had done twenty-five years earlier. He had just turned down an offer to remake *Birth* as a sprawling, four-hour-long color epic, and he also knew the KKK would have been box office poison in the North; so the Klan and all of its robes were conveniently left on the cutting room floor.[31] It is also probable that the Jewish Selznick remembered how *Birth* glamorized the old Klan, which harassed blacks. He did not want to glamorize the new Klan, which harassed Jews. "[I have] no desire to produce an anti-Negro film. We ought to be careful that the Negroes come out decidedly on the right side of the ledger," he told screenwriter Sidney Howard.[32] And he remarked to a friend that inclusion of the KKK might make the movie "come out as advertisements for society's intolerant groups. . . ."[33]

Selznick was careful not to talk publicly about leaving the Klan out of the film beyond that statement. If Ashley and Kennedy had stayed in the Klan, moreover, it would have completely undermined the movie's portrayal of them as harmless Southern victims.

That was just one of the several subtle but significant shifts in the Plantation Myth in the film version of *Gone With the Wind*. Eliminating the Klan removed vigilantism from Southern makeup and undercut any thoughts that Southerners, or anybody, should go outside the law for justice. (Mitchell told friends that she had little to do with the making of the movie, and there is no evidence that she protested Selznick's view of the Klan.)

Selznick also gave the movie a more progressive look at Reconstruction. At first, many historians agreed that Reconstruction was unfair and harsh, but later experts, such as Eric Foner, writing in the 1970s, suggested that it was helpful and necessary. In the book *Gone With the Wind*, there is only one view of Reconstruction: it was a deliberate and aggressive campaign by Northerners to destroy economically whatever Sherman and Grant's troops had not destroyed militarily.

In the movie, Selznick significantly toned down the book's harsh portrait of *all* Northerners in Reconstruction. It is not the federal government, soldiers, or Northerners in general who are the villains, but only the vile carpetbaggers, the overly eager businessmen who invade the South as the war ends. A pair of Northern carpetbaggers in a carriage refuse to give a lift to a dying Confederate soldier being carried home by his friend. The two bedraggled soldiers, covered in dirt and grime, are cursed out as "Southern scum." Gerald O'Hara wails that only Yankee carpetbaggers and scalawags (their Southern accomplices) now have money. Well-dressed carpetbaggers tell newly freed slaves that they'll be taken care of if they vote the way the carpetbaggers tell them to. Big Sam, a freedman after the end of the war, leaves Atlanta, disgusted with the behavior of these Northern invaders, who are clearly defined as *not* representing all Northerners.

There are numerous messages in the movie, some overt and some subtle, to suggest that Reconstruction was necessary and successful. One scene shows Atlanta being rebuilt so that its people can move forward. It lasts only a few seconds, a backdrop to Scarlett and Mammy walking down a street, but it is effective. The same scene shows dozens of U.S. Army soldiers, white and black, walking about, intimidating no one. There is a preponderance of unthreatening black soldiers. When, finally, Scarlett decides to work with the Northerners to make her new lumber business a success, Melanie argues that she is working with the same people who have ruined their world. Scarlett snaps that she will beat them at their own game. The inference is that Scarlett understands, as all should have understood, that cooperation between North and South would bring reconciliation, economic success and the rebirth of the South.

Selznick, although a prisoner of Hollywood's conventional depiction of blacks as retainers and fools, certainly gave them more character and presence than they had enjoyed in any other movie to that point. Mammy clearly runs Tara and the O'Haras feel genuine affection for her, and later, so does Rhett Butler. *GWTW* also clearly is not part of the "black beast" school of D. W. Griffith. Blacks are not marauding thugs, murderers, rapists or dancing fools here. Selznick took a huge step away from that idea in the scene where Scarlett rides through Shantytown and is accosted by two men, one white and one black. In the book, a freed black slave grabs Scarlett and runs his hand over her breasts while a white man grabs the horse. In the movie, a white man tries to grab her while a black grabs the horse.[34] It is a small scene, a swift moment in time, but it signifies a departure from the view of blacks promulgated in previous films.

Although the movie extols Southern manhood and female virtue and constantly shows the South as victim, the enemy—the North—is strangely missing. Somebody is clearly killing Confederate soldiers, somebody has won the battle of Gettysburg and somebody has fired all those shells into downtown Atlanta, but viewers never actually see the Union army doing anything. The only bluecoats who appear during the war are a few deserters, like the one Scarlett shoots. The army does not become a presence until Reconstruction, and even then its officers are portrayed as understanding. (Ward Bond, as the officer looking for Ashley, Rhett and the others one night when they stumble home pretending to be drunk, obviously knows that something is going on but chooses to do nothing.) The omission was a productive restructuring of the old lore and a new direction for Civil War films, towards an even fuller reunification.

Selznick was also determined not to star Southern actors in the movie. He went after Gable and deliberately cast British actor Leslie

Howard (who, like Gable, thought the movie would be a box office disaster) as Ashley Wilkes. Hattie McDaniel, who played Mammy, was from the Midwest (Margaret Mitchell lobbied hard, but unsuccessfully, to have Eleanor Roosevelt's White House maid play Mammy).[35] Howard and Leigh not only gave *GWTW* a more neutral look, but, as the crafty Selznick knew, guaranteed good box office for the film when it was released in England and then in Europe.

A NUMBER of films with Civil War–era themes had preceded *Gone With the Wind* in the 1930s: *Steamboat Round the Bend, Dixiana, Jezebel, So Red the Rose, Mississippi, The Texan, The Vanishing Virginian, The Little Colonel, The Littlest Rebel, Cotton Pickin' Days, My Old Kentucky Home, Dixie Days, Hearts in Dixie, Mississippi Gambler* and *Showboat*. Even the Three Stooges starred in their own Civil War film, *Uncivil Warriors*. Except for the highly successful Shirley Temple films *The Littlest Rebel* and *The Little Colonel,* however, most of these did only marginal business at the box office. Nonetheless, producers continued to believe that Civil War films had an audience.

These films developed an even more romantic and traditional view of the South than the Civil War silents. Southern plantation life is described nicely by Julie in *Jezebel* when she says to Pres, whom she wants to stay in the South: "Can you hear them? The night noises? The mockingbird and the magnolia? See the moss hanging in the moonlight. You can fairly taste the night, can't you? You're part of it, Pres, and it's part of you." The South is always positioned as a separate country in 1930s films.[36]

It was a country, too, that filmmakers defined as different from other parts of America. "Its [film] iconography includes mint juleps, stately mansions with white columned porticos, landscaped lawns and gardens, and fields of cotton in which contented darkies labor. This environment connotes an agrarian economy and patrician way of life. Additional associations are the cavalier and belle, genteel customs, the code of chivalry, leisure, hospitality and faithful slaves," wrote critic Ida Jeter about the 1930s Civil War films.[37] W. J. Cash, writing about all Civil War movies in that era, said that they were "stage pieces out of the nineteenth century."

By the 1930s, the role of blacks in films had become so familiar to audiences that blacks' demeaned and/or minimal status was as much a staple of American movies as the cavalry charge in the westerns, the hooker with the heart of gold, the pie-in-the-face routine of slapstick comedies and the Our Gang kids' clubhouse. After the black and white-liberal protests over the depiction of blacks in *The Birth of a Nation,* Hollywood producers were afraid to portray blacks in an unflattering light—or any light. None wanted controversy that might make the newspapers. To avoid any disputes over blacks they simply took their scissors and snipped them out of films, much as America snipped them out of daily life. Hollywood, burned badly by projecting its image of the "black beast" in 1915, would not touch the black man again in a substantial way for nearly fifty years. That retreat denied audiences a chance to view any meaningful interpretations of black life or realistic American life on the screen. After 1915, the only roles black actors could win were as butlers, servants, laborers, chauffeurs or waiters. The only way talented blacks could get into movies was to shuffle through films as Sambos or Mammies. Bill "Bojangles" Robinson got into some Shirley Temple movies and some tap-dancing duos, such as the Nicholas Brothers, and singers, such as Dorothy Dandridge, appeared in movies as nightclub acts. A few mainstream films about black life in the South, such as *Hallelujah!* in 1929, were made by Hollywood studios, but they were banned from many movie houses in the Southern states by local censorship boards.

Many of the actors portraying blacks in films continued to be whites working in blackface makeup, which demeaned blacks. As late as 1942, actors wore blackface in the Bing Crosby hit *Holiday Inn* (which introduced the classic song "White Christmas"). As one striking young blonde has her face blacked, she tells Crosby that she's always seen herself as pretty, and now look what she looks like (black). In effect, blacks were written out of movies.[38]

"Previously so recognizable in literature and light theater, the black character also came to be conveniently and repeatedly present in the new medium, film. And the more often the Negro persona was used, the more often the black's lowly status was confirmed. The South in its treatment of the Negro became not only more understandable but even forgivable," wrote Edward Campbell in 1980 in *The Celluloid South.*[39] A few years earlier, Daniel Leab had observed that "In the main, the black man on screen [in the 1930s] continued to be presented as emasculated, easily frightened, semiliterate, while the black women were shown as fat, excessively jolly menials."[40]

Advertising and publicity for 1930s films were degrading to blacks. Paramount, which produced *Mississippi,* starring Bing Crosby, urged theater owners to hire blacks to sit on bales of hay in the theater lobby and play Southern tunes on a banjo. Theaters all over America featured posters showcasing the grinning Five Cabin Kids, black children who performed in the movie. The studio referred to them alternately as "darkie" children, "those Ethiopian quintuplets" and "most entertaining bits of chocolate sweetness."[41]

Many of these films used the same plot device that was so effective in *The Birth of a Nation:* make the slaveholders lovable so that audiences embrace them and cheer for them. It worked. In *Jezebel,* Pres, played by Henry Fonda, spends much of the movie acting kindly towards the black slaves serving as butlers and maids in Jezebel's New Orleans mansion and on her country plantation, Halcyon. Finally, to show how much he loves them, he invites "Uncle Cato," the friendliest slave, to have a mint julep with him. Cato, who knows his place, tells him that it would not be proper for him to be seen drinking with a white man, but, since they are such great friends, he will have the drink—but down it inside a closet.

In *The Vanishing Virginian* (1941), Leigh Whipple plays a dying slave who asks to be returned to the old plantation, where he had spent most of his life with his beloved owner, so that he can be buried under the old magnolia trees near his familiar cotton fields.[42]

Journalists and critics were spoon-fed this theme in press releases. A PR blurb for one of the Civil War movies of the 1930s described it, typically, as ". . . the story of a proud plantation owner and his family when war clouds gather, precipitating a conflict that engulfs a peace loving people. . . ."[43]

The publicity easily influenced critics, who looked for the message and found it. Writing about a slaveholding family in a film, one critic concluded that they "treated their slaves humanely and deserved the affection portrayed in the film."[44]

Press agents for these films worked with the United Daughters of the Confederacy to stage world premieres in Southern cities. The movie company would send the director and stars to the premiere to garner local publicity, and the UDC worked to turn out a huge crowd for the premiere and the film's run in that city, building the box office with its mailing list of sixty thousand patriotic, dues-paying members and, incidentally, gilding the Plantation Myth image at the same time. One clever press agent came up with the idea of world premieres in the state capitals of each of the eleven original Confederate states.[45] Each premiere was hosted by that state's UDC leaders, all of whom got a chance to meet the movie's stars, get autographs and have a picture taken with them.

The studio publicity departments promoted these 1930s Civil War movies as historically accurate, and journalists and critics believed them. "Theatrical tradition, in its various manifestations in the past, via printed word, stage and screen, has popularized . . . Dixie gallantry," wrote a critic in *Variety* in 1935.[46]

One of the reasons the life presented in Civil War movies seemed authentic to so many was that by the late 1930s the Southern view and the general American view of slavery and contemporary blacks had changed. History books written in the 1920s ignored race as the most important factor in Southern history and instead said that factor was the economy. The rampaging black rapist had been ignored since the early 1920s and dismissed by historians, who were now arguing that blacks were pretty much invisible in the South, aimless children who did not have to be feared.

Black actors were seen as incompetent, as incapable of good performances—as illustrated by this studio press release: "The director [King Vidor] holds the opinion that the colored race is the most difficult of all people to handle as a group in the making of motion pictures. Fundamentally, living only for the joy they get out of life, they are inclined to laugh at serious things and this native comedy sometimes is difficult to overcome when sheer drama is necessary."[47]

Although few in number, filmmakers who did rely on historians then pushed any and all black characters in Civil War films deep into the background scenes of their films, as historians did in their texts.[48]

William Boehnel, a reviewer for the *Brooklyn Eagle,* notorious for his sharp-edged reviews, said about *So Red the Rose:* "It is a one sided picture, with the northern forces being made out as uncouth killers and the southerners—military and civilian alike—presented as the [essence] of self sacrifice and good breeding."

Beverly Hills, a pseudonymous critic for *Liberty* magazine, wrote about *So Red the Rose* and Civil War films in general in 1935. She realized how movies had influenced Americans' view of history. "The background—crooning plantation slaves, mint julep drinking gentlemen and elegant young ladies—is painted through the misty kindliness of time. Perhaps this isn't the South as it actually was, but it's a charming picture of how most of us imagine it."[49]

Slaves are portrayed as unruly in So Red the Rose. *Plantation mistress Vallette Bedford (Margaret Sullavan) uses her friendship with her workers to prevent an uprising when the Union army approaches.*

So Red the Rose, released in 1935, based on Southern writer Stark Young's best-selling book (Margaret Mitchell told Young she thought his book was "marvelous"),[50] was one of the most egregiously distorted films about the lives of slaves. One of the ways in which white writers and directors strove to make Civil War movies "authentic" was to insist on slave dialect in scripts. In *So Red the Rose*, the lines of dialect the black actors were given belittled them and made them seem a race of children. When a cannonball explodes on the plantation, a black kitchen slave shouts: "A message from Abraham Lincoln! Dat's what dat is! Abraham Lincoln done sent us a cannon ball to tell us he ain't far away!"

Later on in the film, the unruly blacks decide to revolt. Their leader, Cato, tells them to take all the livestock, and his plan is to eventually seize the plantation manor house itself. "It all belongs to us! We're the Kings! Marse Lincoln has given us de land. He has given us de houses. No more plowing . . . no more chopping wood. Just sittin' in the sun!"[51]

Newspaper critics quickly grasped, and accepted, the movie's presentation of a decent and controlled white South contrasted with its unstable black slaves. One critic wrote that the Negroes rioted in the movies only because the white man (the civilized race) was not around.[52]

Writing about *So Red the Rose,* Arthur Draper said that if it was successful, "it will be at the cost once again of provoking even sharper racial lines than exist in these states at the present time, of provoking an even greater hatred by the whites for the negroes, of breaking the solidarity between workers of all races that is today beginning to change the Old South."[53]

But Hollywood executives saw it another way: failure. *So Red the Rose,* despite being based on a best-seller and being given a cast of Hollywood stars and substantial publicity, did not do well at the box office. This sent a warning signal to the offices of David O. Selznick. He had paid Margaret Mitchell a large amount of money for the rights to *Gone With the Wind,* and he could not afford a similar box office flop. Perhaps because of Paramount's *So Red the Rose,* he dropped an initial idea to employ (at Mitchell's insistence) singing black field hands, and told writers to develop solid planter-slave relationships, cut out the word "nigger" and eliminate the KKK from the script. He was hopeful that Mitchell's book would turn out much better on the screen than Stark Young's.

IN HER NOVEL, Margaret Mitchell spent dozens of pages building up the idea of a gentle Old South populated by kind planters and slaves who loved them. She wrote about the shelling and burning of Atlanta, and its evacuation by the populace, at great length, drawing a heart-stopping picture of a great city turned into rubble by Sherman's army.[54] Again and again she showed the Union Army treating Southerners with disdain. In the book, Tara is raided twice by the Union Army and just about everything the O'Haras own is stolen.[55] Mitchell explained, through characters not used in the film, why the poor farmers wisely allied themselves with the rich plantation owners. They were certain that if they worked hard they, too, could own slaves, buy large plantations and become rich.[56]

She wrote scathing descriptions of Reconstruction, many of which seemed taken directly out of *The Birth of a Nation,* to show how the South was pillaged and ruined by carpetbaggers and recently freed slaves.[57] She dredged up every political, cultural and social argument she could think of to show how the Yankees had destroyed the South. She even charged that former mistresses of plantations had to wear rags while the wives of teachers from the North who were sent south to educate the former slaves wore the latest fashions.[58]

Into all of these scenes, Mitchell wrote the feelings that Selznick captured on camera—those of a defeated but noble people who with great dignity try to get on in a world wrecked by Northerners for no good reason except to free their friends the slaves, who then go about behaving badly. "They were crushed and hopeless, citizens of conquered provinces," Mitchell wrote of the Southerners. "They were looking on the state they loved, seeing it trampled by the enemy, rascals, making a mock of the law, their former slaves a menace, their men disenfranchised, their women insulted."[59]

No film script could capture all the drama and nuance of Mitchell's novel, but the writers for *GWTW* came close. They gave theatergoers a condensed yet forceful interpretation of the book and, in such a powerful medium, thus nailed down most of the legend.

It wasn't that Margaret Mitchell wanted to nostalgically glorify the Old South in *Gone With the Wind*—it was that she could not help doing so. Her entire background suggests that any book she would have written about the Civil War era would turn out to be based on the Southern view of the Old South, slavery, the war, Reconstruction and the KKK. Everything in her background, from stories she heard as a little girl to the books she chose to read, led her to write *Gone With the Wind* exactly the way she did—giving many Americans a distinctly Southern and distinctly mythologized view of the Civil War.

Margaret Mitchell was the daughter of a middle-class lawyer whose family had lived in Atlanta for nearly a hundred years. The Mitchell family refused to flee the city when it was bombarded by Sherman's army in 1864, and offered their home as a hospital for wounded Confederate troops. Her great-aunts were marvelous story-tellers who imbued Margaret with their own version of the Old South and slavery.

She grew up in a neighborhood many of whose residents had lived through the Civil War and Reconstruction (they were then in their late fifties and sixties) who filled her young ears with long, winding oral histories of their lives during that period. They complained about the deprivations of life in Atlanta during the war, the shelling by Sher-man's army and the torching of the city. They went over in great detail the strategies of the Southern armies. When she was five years old, the Confederate veterans who lived in the neighborhood took her horseback-riding and, along the way, continually built up the lore of the Old South, the South they wanted the next generation to remem-ber. That same year Mitchell, with others, hid under furniture in her home as an ugly race riot consumed Atlanta.[60]

As a child, Margaret was taken to parades commemorating At-lanta's Confederate dead and was taught Civil War poems and songs (her favorite was "I'm a Good Old Rebel and That's What I Am!"). Relatives told her all they knew about the Civil War, explaining in great detail how a perfectly successful world of agrarian farmers was wrecked by the reckless Yankee abolitionists with their wrong-headed view of slavery. She was regaled with long biographical accounts of Southern Civil War–era heroes such as Jefferson Davis, Robert E. Lee, Joe Johnston, Stonewall Jackson and Georgia's own Howell Cobb. She was told about Pickett's glorious charge at Gettysburg, the defense of Petersburg, Grant's inability to beat Lee at either Cold Harbor or Spotsylvania, the valor of the defenders of Vicksburg, the Confederate rout of the federals at Bull Run and Lee's gallant stand at Antietam. On Sunday afternoons, when she visited some relatives who were veterans, she thrilled in putting her thumbs into the bullet holes in the skull of a dead Confederate soldier.[61]

Mitchell often reminisced to friends about where the premise of

Gone With the Wind was born and explained how her mother took her towards Jonesboro—"the road to Tara"—and showed her the old ruins of houses where, she said, "fine and wealthy people had once lived." She told her that some of the ruins dated from Sherman's visit. "And she talked about the world these people had lived in, such a secure world, and how it had exploded beneath them," she wrote.[62] She joked to friends later that "I heard everything in the world except that the Confederates lost the war."[63]

As a child, she was also greatly influenced by the books of Southern writers, such as Thomas Nelson Page, whose syrupy Old South/cavalier novels sold so well throughout the South in the late nineteenth century. The works of Thomas Dixon had a particularly strong impact on her; she saw *The Birth of a Nation* when she was fifteen and read *The Clansman, The Leopard's Spots* and *The Traitor,* all anti-black, and enjoyed them.[64] "I was practically raised on your books," she told Dixon. "And love them very much."[65]

She and her childhood friends staged their own play based on *The Traitor,* playing Klansmen. In it they staged the lynching of a man, a role taken by little Margaret.

As a Southerner, Mitchell found it natural to turn to the past for heroes. She began writing *Gone With the Wind* in 1926, in the middle of another revival of the Lost Cause both North and South. In a conciliatory and surprising move, the American Bar Association published a heartwarming tribute to Robert E. Lee in 1924. That same year, with much pomp, Congress authorized a commemorative coin with Lee and Stonewall Jackson on it. One year later, Congress voted funds to fully restore Lee's Virginia mansion to its prewar splendor. In 1928, President Calvin Coolidge sent the U.S. Marine Corps band to entertain crowds gathered at several national reunions of Confederate veterans groups. In 1930, Congress voted funds to permit the placing of headstones on the graves of all Confederate veterans.[66] The commemorative trend showed up in publishing, too. In the late nineteenth and early twentieth centuries there were many historical novels about heroic Confederate figures. Major nonfiction works about Southern heroes appeared as well. The 1920s and early 1930s also saw dozens of flattering books about Jefferson Davis, Robert E. Lee and other luminaries of the Confederacy. Mitchell was certainly influenced by this resurgence of interest.

Southerners, of course, never fully recovered financially from the Civil War and struggled from generation to generation in a weak economy. They had been suffering economic woes for more than six decades when the Depression, following the stock market crash of 1929, hit the nation. What they wrote during that time about Southern leaders helped readers get through their troubles. "Heroic images can direct national action, overriding . . . negative circumstances and returning the people to its sense of wholeness and identity," writes literary critic Michael Kreyling.[67]

Margaret Mitchell saw herself as an Atlantan writing history about her beloved city and much-maligned South, with the mission of trying as hard as she could to defend the South against what she saw as historical inaccuracies about slavery in the nineteenth century and segregation in the twentieth.[68]

Mitchell used the personalities of people she knew, or composite personalities, for her characters and then started to sketch her story. (Fearful of libel suits, she always denied that the characters were based on real people.)[69] She then plunged into historical research in order to place her characters into the middle of the Civil War and Reconstruction in the Atlanta area. She read many different histories of Georgia, the Old South and the Civil War, including works on the siege of Vicksburg, the battle of Gettysburg, the fighting at Chickamauga and the assault on Atlanta. She clipped dozens of newspaper articles about the war and read old newspapers in libraries. Her research, she said, was voluminous.[70] Since she had checked all of these details, her novel had to be historically accurate, she told friends.

Mitchell, of course, made the same mistake as do so many novelists, screenwriters and directors: they accurately describe the thin tree in front of them and completely distort the forest around it. Director King Vidor made the same claim about his Civil War film *So Red the Rose*. He insisted on authentic detail throughout the film (the effort included an exasperating search for drawings or photos of silver mint julep cups). Yet he, like Victor Fleming in *Gone With the Wind*, would produce a hopelessly distorted historical drama that he assumed was accurate because the soldiers' rifles looked right.[71] This was a common practice in the making of westerns as well. Writers and directors would go to great lengths to make certain the guns and buggies they used were authentic re-creations, ignoring the way in which the film depicted Indians.

In all of the press releases, souvenir books and programs for *Gone With the Wind,* the producers stressed the historical accuracy of the book and the movie. The writer of the souvenir book assured viewers that Mitchell had checked "thousands of historical statements for accuracy."[72] But just about everything Mitchell had read had been written by a Southern author or reporter. There was little Northern influence in any of the books or magazine and newspaper articles she used as her references. Many of the works she accepted as accurate were, in fact, products of the moonlight-and-magnolias school of late-nineteenth-century history, the books of William Dunning, James Rhodes and others who trumpeted the virtues of the Old South.

In a 1942 letter, Mitchell recounted with great satisfaction her search for weather information related to Sherman's campaign from Tennessee into Georgia in 1864. Unable to find reliable information from history books, she used a turn-of-the-century novel, *Cease Firing,* by Mary Johnston, one of the pro-Southern writers she read as a child. There, in Johnston's novel, she found what she wanted and put it into *Gone With the Wind.* Fiction, for Mitchell, was fact.[73]

In relying on novels about the Civil War she was relying on writers with distinctly proslavery views (one of her heroes, Page, wrote of poor whites in the South that they "worked for less than the wage of the slave without any of his incidental compensation").[74] She was assuming that the novelists had found the factual data that eluded her and used it. Often, the data were not factual. Critics who have studied romantic sagas about the Civil War by late-nineteenth-century Southern novelists have said they often made up their data. For example, John Esten Cooke, who wrote *Surry of Eagle's Nest,* a novel Mitchell claimed was one of her favorites, was unable to find the romance and glamour he wanted in his research, so he made it up. "He constructed literary models of people as toy soldiers," according to literary critic J. V. Ridgely.[75]

At the time both of *Gone With the Wind's* publication and of the film's release, there was some public criticism of Mitchell's historical inaccuracy. But Mitchell discounted this criticism because it came mainly from the Communist *Daily Worker* and black newspapers, which she said had little credibility. There was very little criticism from the mainstream press. The movie, then, was seen by critics, journalists and the filmgoing public as an accurate historical version of events in Clayton County, Georgia, in the 1860s.

Years later, when Richard Harwell gained permission from the Mitchell family to publish a book of the author's letters, her private correspondence told a very different story. There were actually many complaints about Mitchell's accuracy in her depiction of the South, particularly of blacks, and from very reputable sources. These were never made public. One of the groups most critical of the history in *Gone With the Wind* was the Society for Correct Civil War Information, in Evanston, Illinois, run by writer and civil rights advocate Lucy Shelton Stewart.[76] Stewart was joined by an army of historical nit-pickers who found inaccuracies throughout the book: Mitchell had an opera staged in the wrong year, she had armies charging in the wrong directions, she stated, falsely, that federal soldiers looted Southern cemeteries, and so on.

Mitchell came under fire from a number of historians who wrote to inform her that she had made numerous historical errors in reporting the war, the most egregious of which was that General James Longstreet disobeyed orders from Robert E. Lee at Gettysburg.[77] Mitchell defended herself by sending critics a list of history books she had used for information, and in so doing actually exposed the weakness of her research—most of them were local history texts with a regional or political bias. Some were books by local historians, such as *Georgia: Land and People,* by Frances Letcher Mitchell; *History of the State of Georgia from 1850 to 1881,* by I. W. Avery; *Reconstruction in Georgia,* by Atlanta's C. Mildred Thompson; *Atlanta and Its Builders,* by Thomas Martin; and *The History of Georgia,* by Clark Howell. Some were heavily subjective memoirs by Southern generals, such as *Advance and Retreat,* by General John Bell Hood; *Narrative of Military Operations,* by General Joe Johnston; and *Reminiscences,* by General John Gordon. Others included Southern diaries, foremost among them *Life in Dixie During the War,* a tearjerker with a strongly partisan Georgian view by Mary A. H. Gay, of Atlanta.[78]

Mitchell argued that her information had to be right because, in addition to books, she had oral histories, eyewitness accounts from Confederate soldiers and even from survivors of the siege at Atlanta.[79] She chose, of course, to ignore the personal biases of these witnesses, their strong desire to enshrine the Stars and Bars in Southern memory. Her letters showed, too, that from the start she was determined to defend the South against seventy-five years of attack. In one letter, she sums up her view on the Civil War: "We wuz robbed."[80]

She was exceedingly defensive in the face of any criticism, particularly any accusations that she was a mouthpiece for segregation ("my book was not interested in propaganda"),[81] and became more defensive as the critical letters rolled in. She bristled at any attacks on her racism in the book or, later, the racism of the movie. She said these charges by African Americans were not true and were trumped up by people she referred to as "professional Negroes," or by Communists.[82]

Finally, she admitted that *Gone With the Wind* was the Southern response to *Uncle Tom's Cabin.* She told one correspondent: "It makes me very happy to know that *Gone With the Wind* is helping refute the impression of the South which people abroad gained from *Uncle Tom's Cabin.*"[83]

She never wavered in her defense of the historical research or outlook of *Gone With the Wind.* "The history in my tale was as waterproof and tight as ten years of study and a lifetime of listening to participants would make it," she argued.[84]

It was not.

CHAPTER ELEVEN

Absolution for the Old South

Literature in the end came to terms with these sentiments by yielding to the South in fantasy the victory it had been denied in fact.
—Arthur M. Schlesinger Sr.

WITH THREE HOURS and fifty-two minutes of celluloid, *Gone With the Wind* helped to quash seven decades of Northern attacks upon and ridicule of the South that had forced, and kept, Southerners on the defensive. Although the North itself still allowed blacks almost no rights, it was the South that was perceived as a citadel of severe segregation and racism. In the Northern states, the South was seen as stubbornly pushing its unfair voter residency and poll tax requirements, segregating its schools, bus stations and water fountains and upholding the KKK—considered a gang of thugs by the rest of the country—as heroic figures. Northern liberal editors, such as Oswald Villard of the *Nation,* conducted long campaigns against Southern lynchings. The *Crisis,* the magazine of the NAACP, slashed away at Southern racism in every issue. The zealous anti-Catholic campaign waged in the South against the presidential candidacy of New York governor Al Smith in 1928 was decried from coast to coast. And it seemed archaic that the blue laws forbidding liquor on Sunday in most Southern states remained in place after the end of Prohibition, long after they were abandoned in the North.

Except for the works of Thomas Wolfe, there were few best-selling intellectual works written in the South in the 1920s and early 1930s (the novels of William Faulkner, which sold well later, for the most part did not do well on publication in the early 1930s). Northern critics continually referred to the South as a cultural wasteland. One of the most notable of these critics was the *Baltimore Sun* columnist H. L. Mencken; in 1917 he published a long essay, "The Sahara of the Bozart," in which he charged that the South had no historians, novelists, scientists, critics or composers worthy of note. "Down there . . . a poet is now almost as rare as an oboe player, a drypoint etcher or a metaphysician."[1] Mencken (and others) also satirized the deeply fundamentalist religious beliefs of many Southern sects—he labeled the South the Bible Belt and then, mockingly, the Hookworm Belt, the Malaria Belt and the Chastity Belt. Southern traditionalists felt so beleaguered that in 1930 twelve writers banded together and produced a book of essays, *I'll Take My Stand: The South and the Agrarian Tradition,* which defended the history and way of life of the South.

The South was a frequent target of the national press, too, and five different journalists between 1923 and 1930 won Pulitzer Prizes for crusading articles and article series unmasking segregation and other Southern institutions. Northern writers and speakers and Hollywood screenwriters had combined to create a pathetic image of the Southern states. Many general-interest novels and movies depicted the Southerners of the 1930s as strikers and strikebreakers, moonshine producers and deliverers, cranky sharecroppers, illiterate tobacco farmers and ill-bred, ill-mannered blue-collar workers. Not only did Georgia novelist Erskine Caldwell's *Tobacco Road* become a runaway best-seller and successful play, but its title quickly came to symbolize the American view of the South.

Nothing held the South up to ridicule as much as the infamous Scopes evolution trial of 1925. The case against John Scopes, a part-time science teacher in a Tennessee school, was quickly dubbed "the monkey trial" by Mencken. Hundreds of journalists from all over the United States poured into tiny Dayton, Tennessee, to cover the trial, which featured fundamentalist champion William Jennings Bryan, arguing against the teaching of evolution in schools, and Clarence Darrow, defending it. Darrow called Bryan to the stand and made his defense of the Bible sound so silly and laughable even the Southern backers of Bryan and his cause joined in the laughter. The international coverage of the trial defined Southerners as stubborn, unthinking, Bible-thumping dolts, stuck forever in the past, living in small towns up in the hills and firing potshots at wandering tax collectors.[2]

Northern press attacks reached a zenith in the 1930s with the various trials of the "Scottsboro Boys." Nine young black men were charged with raping two white women on a train car in Scottsboro, Alabama, in 1931, found guilty by an all-white jury and sentenced to die. As the verdicts were announced, an all-white crowd outside the courthouse energetically sang "There'll Be a Hot Time in the Old Town Tonight." Northern lawyers defended the young men in a succession of trials after appeals courts repeatedly threw out the case on the grounds that the all-white jury had not been impartial. One of the two alleged victims recanted her story, and the young men, after long delays, were finally freed. The trials of the blacks, guilty only of their color, became a cause célèbre among Northern liberals, and for years the trial came to symbolize the backward, hateful segregationist views of all Southerners.[3]

A 1938 federal report said that the major problem facing the United States as the decade neared its end was the forlorn economy of the Southern states.

The South's defenders, unlike their ancestors, were no longer defending just the institution of slavery. The entire culture of the South was under fire and Southerners seemed to be racing from attack to attack, like people trying to put out hundreds of forest fires at the same time.

One of the first Southern defenders was Edwin Mims, a professor at Vanderbilt University, in Tennessee, who went on record immediately after the Scopes trial as a crusader for Southern progress. In many articles he insisted that the South was not as culturally depressed or segregationist as Northern writers had painted it during and after the Scopes trial. In articles such as "The South Pleads for Just Criticism" and "Intellectual Progress in the South," and a book, *The Advancing South*, Mims tried to show what he felt were the South's best faces.[4]

Another staunch champion was writer Donald Davidson, who saw the South as a distinctive region that could not be held to Northern standards and therefore was being assaulted unreasonably. "The northern press, with the southern press which takes its cue from New York . . . unanimously agreed that the South [was] guilty of numerous crimes against progress," he wrote in 1933. "Wherever they went with their missions of social justice . . . they carried with them a legend of the future, more dangerously abstract than the legend of the past."[5]

It was hard for these and other ardent cheerleaders, who included many newspaper editors, to cover up the genuine lack of modernization and cultural advancement in the region, even though their cause was helped by the fact that critics of the South, in the South, did not fare well. Several free-spirited, critical university professors were fired. (Deans too, such as Dr. Carl Taylor at North Carolina State, were dismissed.) One journalist, Clarence Cason, who wrote an indictment of the South, *90 Degrees in the Shade,* was fearful of how Southerners would treat him after publication of the book.[6]

The defenders of Southern culture always held their ground, despite attacks, and many felt they were treated badly over the years. "We went from history that celebrated the South, if in a defensive way, to the South as the citadel of the Devil, a place you couldn't say anything positive about without being denounced as a racist," said historian Eugene Genovese in the 1970s, in commenting on the way the South was described in the 1920s and 1930s. "The fact is that the South embodies much that's at the core of Western Christian civilization. If it has become at times the embodiment of the worst of that tradition, it has also embodied the best."[7]

Ordinary Southerners felt the same way. They saw themselves as residents of a struggling region constantly belittled by Northerners who did not understand the economic troubles they faced and their seemingly impossible problem with African Americans. Sociologist John Dollard lived in the South in the mid-1930s so that he could observe the region's culture and social system at firsthand. He reported his findings in his book *Caste and Class in a Southern Town.* The townspeople in his Southern community were racists and saw all who defended blacks as hopeless "nigger lovers." They told him that on visits to Northern cities they were disgusted when they saw blacks and whites riding the same trains and walking the same sides of the streets. The overwhelming majority complained that Northerners did not understand that Southern whites tried to be good to their blacks, but that no one appreciated their efforts.[8] Dollard also found that whites both North and South saw blacks as unmotivated, inhabitants of not only a lower class, but a useless lower class.[9] (This belief held firm despite studies in which employers at Northern factories said their black workers were not incompetent and, in fact, that their work was quite satisfactory.)[10] Southerners had lived through the 1920s and

1930s with certain problems and anxieties and wanted someone, somehow, to tell them that it was perfectly all right to feel the way they did, that they were good people whom history had treated unfairly and who were victims of unjust current criticism based on historically wrong assumptions.

Gone With the Wind finally did just that in the late 1930s. The ridiculous images of Southerners which so offended residents of the

An overriding theme in Gone With the Wind *is the close friendship between the O'Haras and their slaves. Here, Scarlett grasps the hand of Big Sam, her faithful field hand, who is on his way to dig ditches to help the Confederate army defend Atlanta against Union forces.*

Southern states were washed away in a minute by the publication of Mitchell's book. It transformed Southerners into considerate landed gentry who were kind to blacks, prayed at meals, read the great books and helped give America its rich agrarian way of life. The book and film changed Northerners' view of the South, replacing the moonshine-truckers-and-nymphomaniac-mountain-girls image of the 1930s with wonderful people like Scarlett O'Hara and Melanie Wilkes and heroic rogues like Rhett Butler from another generation. In *Gone With the Wind,* Margaret Mitchell influenced all Americans—especially as the film version appeared in theaters and, later, on television—and gave the South back its culture and its pride. In doing so, however, she reinforced the shackles that already gripped African Americans so tightly.

The book seemed to absolve whites in the 1930s of guilt for their insistence on white supremacy. It showed audiences that whites of all descriptions—low, middle and upper class—could get along, although this usually meant they were working together to hold black men and women down. Southern historian W. J. Cash wrote that the poor white attached himself to the wealthy white, whether in the plantation society of the 1850s or the textile mill society of the 1930s, because they were all white. By attaching himself politically, socially and culturally, a poor man became, in a sense, part of the rich white culture, leaving his own low, degraded state to the only people left to take it—the blacks. This system, in place from the 1870s on, enabled rich whites in the South to assume power and wealth as long as they somehow psychologically carried the rest of the whites along. They made the poorer ones feel that they were related somehow—distant cousins of a sort—and had to band together against the blacks to succeed.

Cash, who had his critics, also wrote that since farmers did not do slaves' work, they had nothing to fear from slaves unless slaves were suddenly free. Then poor farmers needed the protection of the politicians and the rich whites to defend them against black encroachment. Poor white people did not want blacks taking their jobs, joining their churches or, worst of all, sleeping with their women. Teaming up with rich, politically powerful whites seemed a way of maintaining racial barriers and keeping blacks in their "place."[11] That was the key to the growth of the monolithic, all-powerful Democratic Party in the South, which could guarantee white supremacy with its voting blocs in the House and Senate. Southern legislators agreed to approve various bills important to Northerners as long as no one touched the black-white division that had grown up in the South.

THE CRITICAL RESPONSE to the film *Gone With the Wind* from the press and leaders of civic groups was decidedly mixed—and divided by race. Mainstream white critics enjoyed the film. Some did find the portrayals of the slaves offensive and some still harped about two British actors as stars of the film. But overall, white critics appreciated the dramatic sweep of the film and the powerful characterizations. Reviewers for black publications did not enjoy it. While they felt that blacks were certainly better represented in the movie than in those that went before, they complained that white filmmakers still categorized them as Mammies, butlers and whining nannies.

The heads of black organizations were highly critical of *Gone With the Wind* when it opened. The film was picketed by more than one hundred blacks at its Chicago premiere[12] and later at its Washington, D.C., opening.[13] A group of blacks, led by several attorneys, tried unsuccessfully to have the movie banned from theaters in Canton, Ohio.[14] Reviewers for black newspapers condemned it. "[A] weapon of terror against black America," wrote a critic in the *Chicago Defender*. "Distorted and twisted history of an era." A reviewer for the *Pittsburgh Courier* wrote that the blacks in the film were "happy house servants and unthinking, hapless clods."[15]

African-American civic leaders saw the film undercutting the considerable and sometimes successful efforts they had made through the 1930s towards marshaling white support for integration. "Whatever sentiment there was for federal anti-lynching laws evaporated during the *Gone With the Wind* vogue," said Walter White, secretary of the NAACP.[16]

Most reporters and reviewers in the mainstream press, however, found little to fault; there was not even criticism of Hattie McDaniel as the prototypical Mammy who had appeared in so many Civil War silent films, magazine ads for cereals and syrups and cartoons (screenwriter Howard, in describing how she should look, was direct: she should be "aged and mountainous").[17]

The *New York Times* said it was simply "the greatest motion picture mural we have seen." The New Orleans *Times-Picayune* called it "deeply moving" and "tremendously effective."[18]

Critics accepted on good faith the publicity release assertions that the film was historically accurate and that it gave theatergoers an honest, authentic look at the entire South of the 1860s. One Richmond critic nodded knowingly and wrote that the treatment of blacks in the film was "in accord with all the stories and legends of slavery time Negroes."[19] Elderly Confederate veterans who saw it told reporters that it was all true.[20]

Surprisingly, although black newspapers criticized *Gone With the Wind*, their attacks were not as harsh as they had been about *Birth* and, after initial reviews, criticism abruptly stopped. Black critics and editors were then caught in the middle of the struggle to integrate movies. It was a racist movie and it portrayed blacks badly, but it did at least have some substantial black roles, particularly Mammy. It arrived at the end of a decade that had seen blacks make inroads into mainstream Hollywood films. African-American actors appeared in a number of movies and, while their roles were often small ones or stereotyped, they were at least getting work and opening studio doors. Some movies that used black actors were *The Prisoner of Shark Island*, *The Petrified Forest*, *Crooks*, *Of Mice and Men*, *Green Pastures*, *Fury* and *They Won't Forget*, plus a string of films with Bill "Bojangles" Robinson. The black press did not want to risk closing that avenue with a hard campaign against *GWTW*.

Sensing a chance both to push black equality in films and to mute any criticism of racism in *GWTW*, Selznick's public relations department waged a long and successful campaign to have Hattie McDaniel win an Oscar for her performance as Mammy. Some black critics urged McDaniel to turn down the award to protest the racism of the movie and the lack of work for blacks in Hollywood, but she accepted it, and did so in a gracious and well-received speech.[21] Who could protest a movie for which a likable black actress had won an Oscar?

McDaniel understood that progress toward racial equality in film and in the United States overall was likely to be slow. The actress, who participated in several marches for housing equality for blacks in the late 1940s, considered recognition for African-American actors important, regardless of the roles they had to take. When a black activist protested her portrayal of Mammy, she responded: "I'd rather play a maid than be one."[22]

There were some newspapers that denounced the movie, such as the *Daily Worker*, but as a Communist publication it was paid little attention at the time.[23] Some members of the New York Film Critics Association who believed it was a racist movie formed a bloc and, in their votes for Best Film of 1939, managed to defeat *Gone With the Wind* and steer the prize to *Wuthering Heights.*[24]

Criticism of the movie began to seep into the pages of newspapers, magazines and books by the late 1940s, but in a still basically segregated America it was not much heeded. "The most gigantic milestones to Hollywood's appeal to public patronage have been anti-Negro pictures like *The Birth of a Nation* and *Gone With the Wind*," said veteran screenwriter Dalton Trumbo in 1948.[25] "American filmmakers have concentrated on whitewashing the South . . . northern 'nigger lovers' were the villainous destroyers of the Old South and its glorious traditions," wrote film historian Peter Noble.[26]

It wasn't until much later, following the civil rights movement of the 1960s and 1970s, that critics in the mainstream press began to see

Hattie McDaniel—here in a scene with Vivien Leigh as Scarlett—won an Oscar for giving a bit of humanity to Mammy in Gone With the Wind.

the complete racial distortions and mythmaking in *Gone With the Wind*. Armed with hundreds of studies of slavery and race relations over the years, a number of them finally commented on the racism of the movie.

"The black roles are deplorable . . . falsifications. Not true to southern experience. The movie refuses to show the lives of black people away from the white people they worked for . . . it's a fairy tale, an ugly fairy tale," said historian Don Boyle in 1989.[27]

Some in the South saw *GWTW* and other 1930s Civil War films as creating unfair stereotypes of white Southerners, too. One was W. E. Debnam, a white radio broadcaster, who said they "painted the South as a backwards land peopled in the main by low-browed hoodlums smelling of lavender and old lace and sniffing away on magnolia blossoms and shuffling along a street with a mint julep in one hand and a bullwhip in the other going someplace to lynch a Negro."[28]

In the 1990s, critics of Mitchell's book zeroed in on the ways in which she compared slaves to animals. Jim Cullen, in *The Civil War in Popular Culture,* saw a "malignant resonance" in her descriptions of slaves, citing her sketch of Jeeves, of whom Mitchell wrote that he accompanied the Tarleton Twins everywhere, like their dog. Cullen also criticized Mitchell for giving Big Sam "huge black paws" for hands, describing a black living in postwar Shantytown as "a gorilla," writing that Mammy had a "monkey's" face and, late in the book, calling her an "ape."[29]

The same kind of demeaning portrayal was evident in the film. An example is the lines in which Prissy tells Scarlett that Tara might be under siege: "Dey's fightin' at Jonesboro. They say our gempmum's is gittin' beat. What'll happen ter maw and paw effen dey gits ter Tara?"[30]

Mitchell always defended her slave dialect. She said that slaves spoke that way in 1859 and should be depicted as speaking that way in 1939.[31] Her defenses of her dialect, though, showed the views she, like most Southerners, carried all her life. Fed up with criticism of black dialect, she shot back in a letter that underlined that view: "I scoured the back country of this section, routing out aged old darkies who were born in slavery days [for it]."[32]

She received complaints that the dialect set up her blacks as racial stereotypes just as badly as the "Uncle Remus" stories of Joel Chandler Harris. She blithely retorted that both the son and grandson of Joel Chandler Harris had read the book and told her they enjoyed the black dialect.[33]

Then, in one off-handed remark in a letter, she bragged that "the negroes have read it . . . in large herds."[34]

Critics of *GWTW*'s and other films' depiction of blacks feared that the effect of the celluloid racism would carry far beyond the last rows of the darkened theaters, and they were right. "What Hollywood thinks of the American Negro is best expressed by the roles given him in the motion pictures," wrote Arthur Draper, who added that filmdom's portrayals were "viciously antagonistic," and a "libelous presentation of southern negroes of the Civil War period."

GWTW SUCCEEDED because it appealed to audiences of the late 1930s and early 1940s who yearned for simpler times and a place of their own. The idea of the land as something very valuable and lost comes early in the film, when Gerald O'Hara, gesturing with his hand toward the vast expanses of his plantation at Tara, tells his daughter Scarlett that the land is "the only thing in the world that matters."[35] Viewers saw in *GWTW* a wonderful world that would never be again and yearned for it.[36] That desire to go back to a world of farms and country lanes appeared often in other successful films of the Depression era and in the works of John Ford and Frank Capra. MGM's *The Wizard of Oz*, which also debuted in 1939, offered a safe farm world in Kansas which Dorothy, tossed about by a tornado, and her audience, tossed about by the Depression, thought of as home ("There's no place like home").[37]

GWTW also succeeded because, first and foremost, it was a woman's book written by a woman, and it was a woman's film. From the very first scene to the final wail, it is the story of the whirlwind that is Scarlett O'Hara. It is her saga, her soap opera, her love story, her vanquished people, her rebirth, her individualism and her struggle. In Scarlett, women saw a little bit of themselves, whether it was a teenage girl teasing the boys as Scarlett teased the Tarleton Twins or an unhappy married woman churning inside about her inability to find love. Women who saw that movie identified with Scarlett and empathized with her misfortunes as they reveled in her triumphs.

Although about 25 percent of the women in America worked during the late 1930s and women had voted since 1920, they were still constrained, shackled by their role in the family and in society. Scarlett was the hellcat inside each of them. They dared not talk like Scarlett, dress like Scarlett, flirt like Scarlett or behave like Scarlett, and so they loved Scarlett for expressing their unspoken feelings.

Margaret Mitchell created Scarlett as an archetypical Southern belle. Then the character was revised by directors Victor Fleming and George Cukor and the screenwriters who worked on the movie. She fit the pattern of every belle out of Southern literature in that her charms, and not her looks, drew men to her. The first line of *Gone With the Wind,* the book, tells the reader that "Scarlett O'Hara was not beautiful, but men seldom realized it when caught by her charm." In novel after novel, Southern belles had been described just that way by different authors. It was thought that they needed to look plain so that all the plain-looking girls who bought the books could attach themselves to the belle and win their man, as their heroines did, without good looks.[38]

The masterstroke for Scarlett's portrayal on film came from Selznick himself. He made Scarlett beautiful, just as every woman wanted to be. She became the Old Southern belle turned independent woman turned beauty queen turned businesswoman. Scarlett had it all, except for one great flaw: she loved the wrong man and ignored the right man, which meant she lost happiness. That made her vulnerable and allowed the world to embrace her. Selznick then took that symbolic Southern beauty and made her a fierce, independent woman—even an opportunist—which then drew in a second audience that admired Scarlett—the postsuffrage, politically involved women who were buying books about successful women, voting for FDR because of Eleanor Roosevelt and flocking to films starring women such as Joan Crawford, Bette Davis and Katharine Hepburn.

HOLLYWOOD DID not know how to handle the Great Depression. Studios did not want to present the Depression as it was, in all of its spreading economic horror, to a people already reeling from its effects. People had to live hand-to-mouth every day, with more than a quarter of the population out of work and millions of others forced to work part-time or for severely reduced wages. They did not want to see their sad day all over again at night on a movie screen. If Hollywood felt it could not produce films that honestly depicted the Depression, what could it produce?

The motion picture industry certainly addressed the Depression in some films, such as *The Grapes of Wrath, Dead End* and a string of gangster movies, but it also produced a large number of escapist entertainment stories. If in the 1920s people went to the movies to be entertained, they went in the 1930s to escape the reality that was engulfing them. Studios began to produce escapist films that satisfied the public's need for fantasy. There were several successful genres: 1) gangster films, 2) shyster films, about society's corruption, 3) sex,

The key to the success of Gone With the Wind *was the romance between Rhett and Scarlett, here saying goodbye.*

4) cartoons, 5) westerns, 6) musicals, 7) screwball comedies and 8) Shirley Temple films.

Will H. Hays, head of Hollywood's censorship office, proudly proclaimed that Hollywood had done its job during the 1930s. "No medium has contributed more greatly than the film to the maintenance of the national morale during a period defined by revolution, riot and political turmoil in other countries," he said. "It has been the mission of the screen, without ignoring the serious social problems of the day, to reflect aspiration, optimism and kindly humor in its entertainment." No film did that like *Gone With the Wind*.

Gone With the Wind was an inspirational movie for theatergoers who watched Scarlett O'Hara go through a Civil War, almost losing her life and her home, and survive. Many unemployed men and women, some who stood on breadlines and others who stole bread to feed their families, felt their pulses race at the end of Part One when, before a blood-red sky, Scarlett stands outside her ruined Tara and, shaking a fist at God, shouts that she'll never be hungry again.

Gone with the Wind was escapist, a finely woven, wonderful soap opera and a rich love story, but it was most importantly a film about the survival of a tough woman trying to keep home and family together in the middle of turmoil. It tapped into the two most cherished beliefs of the American people: that hardworking individuals can succeed and that the family inevitably will triumph.

Audiences loved Scarlett's gritty determination not only to survive the war, using all of her wiles to do it, but also to rebuild Tara, the symbolic home for everyone in the audience, and to somehow establish the normal family life that eluded her. Scarlett's victory over financial hardship was the hoped-for victory of all economically wounded Americans who saw the film, but her inability to find sustenance and happiness in the love of a husband and a family was also a victory for those in the audience. The American people might be out of work, losing their homes and wearing shoes with holes in their soles, but at least they had loving families. Scarlett did not. So as long as they were rich in those things, and rich in spirit, they would make it. They would survive the Depression just as Scarlett survived the war.

Many men of that time saw in the woes of the movie's soldiers their own woes. They felt as wounded and helpless as the Confederate regiments.[39] The unemployed man, head of his household and the person relied on by all others to support the family, felt emasculated by the Depression. He could not work and take care of his family, just as the wounded soldiers could not take care of their family—the Old South.

The movie tied in to all the anxieties audiences felt in 1939. It was that anxiety, that fear, that held America in a vicious and deadly grip throughout the decade. (Roosevelt understood that as soon as he took office and warned the people that the only thing they had to fear was fear itself.) There was a bewilderment, too, in the movie, and it was somehow comforting.[40] Southerners did not understand what was happening to them. All they wanted to do was move along through the years in this peaceful life they had made for themselves, yet Northerners forced them into a war. The end of the war did not bring peace, but an economic war waged on the South by the North. In the 1930s Americans wondered: How could the Depression continue when so many wealthy people continued to prosper? How could little businesses fail on a daily basis when big businesses thrived? How could a noble and well-intentioned federal government and a visionary and experienced leader, Roosevelt, fail to bring them out of their economic nightmare?

There were dozens of grim labor strikes across the country that shook all Americans, not just the workers involved in them. Workers went on strike against their plant managers, angry that their wages were too low or had been slashed and irate, too, that many factories belonged to absentee owners who did not care about their employees. Striking workers were killed in picket lines and others were beaten by security guards. Many factories cut production from seven days a week to just three or two, and furloughed their workers. Wages were slashed as business revenues plunged and many factory workers saw their weekly pay drop from a paltry eight dollars a week to just three dollars. Real unemployment in some areas, particularly the Southern coal mine region of Tennessee and Kentucky, was much worse than public figures indicated. There, workers would be technically employed but in fact worked only a few days a month.[41] Because the mines, like the mills, tended to be the only business in a town, the towns and their people started to die because there was no other work. In April 1931, a newspaper estimated that nearly five thousand people in one coal community in the Cumberland Valley were starving.[42] The Depression hit the South harder than any other region in the country.

Northerners wondered how Margaret Mitchell had been able to anticipate the Depression of the mid-1930s with such insight. The novel included long conversations about the "depression" of Reconstruction and the anxiety people felt in the South in the 1860s and 1870s, and yet she wrote most of her book between 1926 and 1929, before the stock market crash (the author was unhappy with the book at first and let it sit in her home for several years before making some changes and finally handing it to a Macmillan editor in 1935).

The Southern states were wounded badly in the 1920s when the huge cotton market began to collapse. A boll weevil epidemic in the 1920s severely cut back cotton production. At the same time, foreign nations began to import cotton from other markets and opened their own cotton mills, cutting into the South's export business. In 1927, the South exported 11 million bales of cotton. By 1932 that number had been cut to just 8.7 million, by 1938 to 5 million, and in 1939, when *Gone With the Wind* premiered, to an all-time low of just 3.3 million bales.[43]

The drop in the cotton market meant that towns that had grown up around the textile mills in the South, in the heart of the Cotton Belt, suddenly turned into slums as many of their workers were laid off. This happened in the mid-1920s, before the stock market crash of 1929. Strikes began as early as 1929, before the autumn crash. In March and April of that year there were major strikes at mills in Greenville, South Carolina; Elizabethtown, Tennessee; and Marion, North Carolina.

Lawlessness increased all over the nation as the Depression settled in, but nowhere was it as problematic as in the South. In 1937, for example, the murder rate in New England was 1.3 murders per 100,000 residents, but in the South it was 23.7 murders per 100,000. Many Americans began to think that the United States was simply going to collapse upon itself. There was talk of revolution in many places. As the number of the unemployed grew, the prospect of a civil war in the streets, akin to the civil war in *Gone With the Wind,* escalated. This was particularly true in the South, where there was fear that an endless Depression would turn into a war between poor blacks and poor whites for whatever jobs existed.

But many who saw the movie considered it a sterling reminder that if people could retain their fierce individualism, just like Scarlett, they could conquer the Depression.

Readers' identification with the Depression was solid in 1936, but when the movie came out in the winter of 1939–1940, and was rereleased later in 1940 and in 1942, that identification was compounded by the anxiety over World War II. *Gone With the Wind* was a movie about the anxiety over the Civil War on the Southern homefront. Just three months before it opened in 1939, the German army invaded Poland. Polls showed that many Americans did not yet want to become involved in World War II,[44] but worried that the country would be dragged into it.

These fears of war connected perfectly with *GWTW*. Men watching the movie in 1939 and 1940 could envision themselves as the dead or wounded Confederate soldiers and women saw themselves in the scenes in which Melanie and Scarlett, wives of soldiers, waited for the lists of dead and wounded to be handed out.

Only some twenty years removed from World War I, which had devastated the European landscape, many Americans feared that World War II would result in the destruction of their country. In the summer of 1942, Atlanta's civil defense directors scheduled a simulated nighttime bombing raid on the city. They called for a 10 p.m. blackout and then had planes "bomb" the downtown area with bags of flour to show residents how widespread damage might be. As the bags of flour hit, civil defense workers set off a thousand firecracker-style explosions to create the sounds of an attack.[45] Apprehension grew after the war began, and fear of air attacks was so high that in 1943 the *Atlanta Journal,* the leading newspaper of Atlanta (the fictional setting of *Gone With the Wind*), ran several pages of pictures of destroyed European cities with headlines and captions that suggested that Atlanta might look just like that if it was bombed and that bombing was a very real possibility: DEATH, HORROR AND DESTRUCTION COULD SMITE ATLANTA ANY DAY: BOMBERS FROM HOSTILE CARRIERS MIGHT EASILY STRIKE AND ESCAPE, THIS MIGHT HAVE BEEN ON WEST PEACHTREE, THEY MIGHT HAVE DONE THIS TO GEORGIA TECH.[46]

The burning of Atlanta, in the 1940s just as in 1864, seemed a very real possibility. West Coast residents shared the fear. People in Los Angeles were afraid that the Japanese, who had been able to cross an ocean to bomb Pearl Harbor, would bomb California next.

Such destruction was already a reality for people in Britain, where *GWTW* was often shown from 1940 to 1944. The German Luftwaffe was raining nightly death and destruction on British cities as early as 1940. Residents witnessed scenes similar to the burning of Atlanta and looked out on charred and ruined cityscapes, just like those of Georgia as depicted in *GWTW*.

There were legends about the London bombing. The story of Mrs. E. M. Bloomfield, of Coventry, England, was typical. She and friends

A troubled Scarlett walks among hundreds of wounded Confederate soldiers lying in a makeshift hospital at an Atlanta railroad station. The graphic scene made an easy connection to World War II, already underway in Europe when Gone With the Wind *was released.*

had just arrived to see *GWTW* when a bomb hit the theater and blew it up. Bloomfield and her friends survived the collapse of the building by crawling under their seats. Elsie Kingdom managed to see the entire film at a London theater and was talking to a friend about the burning of Atlanta when the two women emerged from the lobby and saw the city and its docks on fire from another German air raid. Another woman, Doris Marston, had to scurry to the cellar of the theater where she was watching *GWTW* when bombs started to fall (she didn't see the last half of the movie until the late 1960s).

On the homefront, women readily identified with the women of *GWTW* whose men were off fighting in the Civil War. "In times fraught with danger and suffering with the shortage of all but the bare necessities it was easy to feel a kinship with the families in the South and it was not difficult to understand Scarlett's determination 'never to go hungry again,' " said Gila Wilding.[47]

But why did the film *Gone With the Wind* remain so popular after the 1930s and the end of World War II?

It succeeded for many of the same reasons as *The Grapes of Wrath, Citizen Kane* and *The Godfather*. When a nation has economic woes a film like *The Grapes of Wrath* or *GWTW* taps into human feelings about them. (Is there any fundamental difference between a bank taking over small farms in the 1930s and contemporary conglomerates downsizing and laying off workers?) Charles Foster Kane may be dead, but every generation has a rich and powerful person—think Bill Gates or Donald Trump—whose wealth and oversized personality intrigue people. Michael Corleone died (it took three movies, but he finally died), yet immigrants who come to America still find no true justice and often must turn to criminal organizations, such as Russian and Asian gangs, to obtain it.

GWTW was rereleased as a feature film in 1967 and did well. Why? It hit theaters on the heels of the Civil Rights movement and during a year when race riots exploded in many of America's largest cities, and so it touched off all the same controversies over race. The rerelease also came at a time when the Vietnam War was starting to divide America, and as a Civil War saga the film presented that same feeling of anxiety and trepidation. It was rereleased at a time when the United States was undergoing perhaps its greatest generational divisions, as battles over race relations and the Vietnam War drove a wedge between parents from the World War II era and their activist children, much as the Civil War divided families. *Gone With the Wind* was shown on television for the first time in 1976 and drew record ratings. Why? Americans were still angry about Vietnam. And by the mid-1970s soap operas dominated American television, and there was no greater soap opera than *Gone With the Wind*. Americans, battling high inflation, were again living through uneasy economic times. The government of the 1970s, having just weathered the Watergate scandal, seemed as divided as it was in the late 1850s. The 1976 rerelease also came at a time when the women's movement was picking up speed, and contemporary women embraced the emancipated Scarlett.

It remains a powerful movie because of its finely acted characters, sumptuous color, heroic music, soap opera plot and mythology about the American Way. Add the yearning it generated for simpler times and a bygone way of life, and the gargantuan story of troubled lovers caught in the greatest catastrophe of the nineteenth century. These are reasons enough to make any film powerful. Since its 1939 premiere, *Gone With the Wind* had earned much criticism for its muddled history and racism. Did Americans really care?

Frankly, my dear, they didn't give a damn.

CHAPTER TWELVE

Home on the Range: The Civil War Movie Goes West

THE PRODUCERS of the movie *Shenandoah* were certain that their sprawling 1965 epic about a loving Virginia farm family caught in the middle of the Civil War would appeal to the fans of Civil War movies and of the countless westerns that Hollywood was churning out every year. Also, they wanted to take advantage of the success of television, which had grown into America's number one form of entertainment. The most successful series on television by the early 1960s were westerns; *Gunsmoke,* beginning in 1955, had been the first, and it soon had a host of imitators. By 1959 seven of the ten highest-rated weekly series on television were westerns. From 1960 through 1965, at least three of the top ten television shows were westerns, and in 1965, when *Shenandoah* premiered, the number one show was *Bonanza,* another western.

Although *Shenandoah* was about the Civil War, its look was that of a standard western. The farmhouse owned by the main character, Charlie Anderson, played by James Stewart, sat in the middle of a sprawling five-hundred-acre farm. The farmers traveled through remote areas to and from a church and some stores. They rode horses, drove buggies, repaired fences and spread hay with pitchforks. As in many westerns, the farm was run by a good-natured widower assisted by his sons and daughters. A suitor courted Anderson's daughter. Therefore, given the western look and Civil War story, its producers were certain they had a vast audience for their film. Educators were already complaining about television's impact on their students, urging the nation's entertainment industry to produce educational stories for young people. If there had to be westerns, why not authentic westerns that told the *real* story of America, films that could be discussed in the classroom?

Shortly before the movie opened in theaters across the country, thousands of high school and elementary school teachers were mailed the "Classroom Study Guide to *Shenandoah*," a lavish black-and-white foldout guide that students could carry home between schoolbooks and teachers could hang on a classroom wall. The guide was designed to explain the plot and characters but, more important, to let teachers and students know that this film was actual history and not something stitched together by careless screenwriters.

After applauding the voluminous research that had gone into the making of the fictional *Shenandoah* (the studio claimed there had been six months of research into the history of Virginia, the Civil War and the Shenandoah Valley, none of which was apparent in the film), the guide proudly asserted: "In learning history, nothing beats a good Hollywood film." It argued, too, that *Shenandoah* was only the latest in a long line of Hollywood films that had portrayed history accurately and brought the authentic story of the world and its peoples to the public via the screen. These "authentic" historical movies included, the guide said, *Scarlet Empress,* with Marlene Dietrich as Catherine the Great; *The Private Lives of Elizabeth and Essex,* with Bette Davis; *Broken Arrow, Hudson's Bay* and *Custer's Last Stand* (which, of course, came about as close to historical accuracy as Laurel and Hardy in *Pardon Us*).[1]

Civil War movie historical interpretations may not have annoyed most people, but their film locations often did. Civil War Centennial Commissioner James Robertson Jr. may have called *Shenandoah* "the best Civil War drama ever put on film,"[2] but Virginians were furious with the producer for not making the movie in their state. Film scouts who toured the state apparently did not like the look of the actual Virginia and suggested the movie be filmed in Oregon. As a publicity writer explained: "The only place in the world that doesn't look like Virginia is Virginia."[3] Just a few months later, film director Andrew V. McLaglen again defended using Oregon as central Virginia's luscious Shenandoah Valley. "There is no place that looks more like Virginia than Oregon," he told an interviewer.[4]

Many of the Hollywood studios that produced movies about the West and the Civil War promoted their films as historically accurate, as films that finally, after all these years, told the "real" story of the United States. 20th Century-Fox blithely informed theater owners, the press and the public in a promotional flyer concerning its absurd 1969 movie *The Undefeated*—with an odd pairing of John Wayne and Rock Hudson as a Union and a Confederate officer who fight together against the Mexican Army in the 1870s, that "historical facts serve as the background for *The Undefeated,* a fictional account of the adventures which *probably* [author's emphasis] befell many people after the Civil War."[5]

Civil War films decreased in number in the 1940s, replaced by charges up Mount Suribachi, invasions of the Philippines and amphibious landings at Guadalcanal. Hollywood executives flooded the country with more than two hundred movies about World War II, creating a new subcategory within the war film genre.[6] In World War II films, good and evil were clearly defined, heroes believable and bigger than life (whether they lived or died), and the good guys, the Americans, almost always won. These films were wildly popular with the public and crushed whatever Civil War movie boom might have been rekindled by *Gone With the Wind.*

Executives at the Walt Disney studios discovered this in 1946, when they released *Song of the South,* which they believed to be a charming post–Civil War movie based on the Uncle Remus stories of Joel Chandler Harris. The film, which mixed live actors with animated characters, did not earn good reviews ("drab," said the *New York Times*)[7] and was immediately denounced by the NAACP and picketed by members of the National Negro Congress, whose officials charged that the film rehashed all of the old racist stereotypes that demeaned black people. (Eventually, after several rereleases, the film did earn a respectable $13 million.)[8]

So Hollywood writers found a whole new and majestic vista for their beloved Civil War heroes. The historic West of the 1865-to-1890 period had everything scenery-conscious movie producers and the moviegoing public could want—mountain ranges, canyons, raging rivers and arid deserts. It had bustling cities and towns such as Denver and Tombstone and a thousand small farms and ranches spread out across the landscape, and each valley had its own story.

Screenwriters had a dazzling array of real-life characters for their stories: Wild Bill Hickok, Wyatt Earp, Buffalo Bill, Calamity Jane, Billy the Kid. Best of all, they had a built-in enemy: Indians.

For plots, they had gold rushes in California, land rushes in Oklahoma, cattle drives, range wars, bank holdups, evil villains, heroic marshals, dance hall girls, fires, mines, duels in the sun, singing cowboys like Gene Autry and Roy Rogers . . . and Indians.

The West was a blank page for Hollywood. Few Americans knew anything about the real story of the West. They only knew what they had read in high school textbooks, which paid little more than superficial attention to the West and concentrated on events rather than social culture, and on legend. That made Hollywood's job easy.

To audiences in post–World War II America, the Old West was a land they learned about from dime novels, traveling Wild West shows and endless magazine and newspaper stories full of tales of good guys in white hats and bad guys in black hats. To Americans, the West was one long wagon train full of hearty frontiersmen and their loving wives and kids trying to make a new start in a vast new country, battling the elements and the Indians. The frontier folk always triumphed. It was, as historian Frederick Jackson Turner wrote in a line that Gary Cooper, John Wayne and John Ford would have loved, "the meeting point between savagery and civilization."[9]

The wide-open West, opened wider still by the movies, was a nation within a nation.[10]

John Wayne, greatest cowboy actor of them all, said he saw all westerns as Homeric epics, the stories of great journeys. The American western movies were popular not only in America, but all over the world, possessing, according to cinematic historian William Pilkington, "a universal appeal to a universal imagination." French film critic André Bazin called western movies "American odysseys" and felt their strength was in their morality and the recurrence of familiar and accepted legends.[11]

Best of all, from Hollywood's point of view, from about 1946 to 1975 the Old West was a marvelous emotional and cinematic safety valve from contemporary anxieties about the Cold War and reality, as the movies always had been. Here, though, in the dust-covered streets of Dodge City and the bars of Deadwood, screenwriters had a chance to create a kingdom for escapist entertainment. Film historian Phil

Hardy explains: "At a time when frustratingly complex issues like the bomb, the Cold War, the House Committee on Un-American Activities investigations and the Suez crisis were being raised, the West remained a simple, unchanging, clearcut world in which notions of good and evil could be balanced against each other in an easily recognizable fashion."[12]

The celluloid West was also the perfect place to move the homeless Civil War soldier. Even though the market for movies strictly about the Civil War had dried up, the new market for the western was the perfect place for the transport of Billy Yank and Johnny Reb, with all their historical and emotional baggage.

Hollywood's Western myths had some accurate historical grounding. Turner, whose papers and book on the American West became the bible of Western history in the 1910–1940 period, had dubbed the men and women who moved west members of "a new order of Americanism."[13] Screenwriters could easily adapt old characters and old adventures to that new order. The boys in blue and gray fit nicely. The movement of the real Americans of North and South right after the Civil War, and their celluloid counterparts, was a natural transfer, "the shifting of a battleground from the ravaged South to the still relatively empty West," according to Jenni Calder.[14] It was also a shift from the old plantation, with its dripping Spanish moss, wide verandas and rows of slave cabins to an open, arid West with plains, mountains and deserts. The Plantation Myth's setting had changed and the myth would as well.

There was a new breed of protagonists, men who had been hardened by the Civil War as people and as soldiers. The homesteader and rancher of the West, who never used his gun for more than hunting or, infrequently, to ward off Indians, was now joined by former soldiers who knew how to use guns quickly and efficiently. Some of them brought knapsacks of hatred to the plains of the West, too, and often wound up in arguments or fistfights. The introduction of these men into a brand-new society trying to build its own foundations created chaos and problems in the actual West and made for marvelous plotlines for the celluloid West.[15]

The post–World War II westerns were distinctly different from the silent westerns and the 1930s shoot-'em-ups. They were psychological studies in which characters were no longer all good or all evil. Dance hall girls were now complicated dance hall girls. Villains, especially, became multilayered, with deep psychological reasons for their behavior and, often, a shadow of justice or goodness to them that made audiences like them. Heroes now needed something beyond survival to fight for, whether it was their sense of honor, the law or the construction of a new empire. The new hero was also involved with families, whether his own family, others he defended or, in a string of films, families that traveled across the West in wagon trains. A new sense of family took over from the lonely rider who galloped over the horizon.

This psychological shift opened up the new, cinematic westerns even more for fictional Civil War characters, from Nathan Brittles to Johnny Yuma to Ethan Edwards, who trotted out of the War between the States and into the sunlit West with saddlebags full of emotional complications.[16]

The biggest reason why the Civil War characters slipped so seamlessly into the western movie was that westerns were already about myths—gargantuan ones. Americans might be weak in the history of the Old West, but that history had been mythologized to the point where reality and legend could not be divided. And everyone was familiar with the myths.

"If, as it is said, poetry is more real than history, the literary and iconographic poetry about the American west may rightfully share a place with historical chronicle in depicting the American western experience," said historian Rita Parks in explaining why audiences so readily accepted Hollywood's version of the West.

Even public officials were eager to embrace Hollywood's West, rather than the real West. Gale McGee, a U.S. senator from Wyoming, was one of them. He wrote: "There is no area of the country with a history more interesting and more distorted in the public mind than the American West. The struggles of the pioneer American to conquer the last frontier have caught and retained the imagination of the public to such an extent that a veritable mythology has developed around the Old West until dreams and reality have become all but indistinguishable."[17]

Hollywood's Civil War western characters fell into several distinct groups:

1. The embittered reb. He was once a hard-fighting Confederate

soldier who firmly believed in the cause of the South. He has moved west because his home was destroyed or his family killed by Yankees, or because he did not want to live in a town or county ruined and occupied by the Union army. The world and culture he cherished has been destroyed by the war, whether the physical world of his farm or the emotional world of his bygone society. In frustration, and with nowhere else to go, he has sought a new life on the plains, carrying all the old animosities with him.

2. The hard-fighting Union veteran who is pleased that the North won the war. The antithesis of the embittered reb, he has moved west not because of ruin at home but because of opportunity. He may have worked for the railroad in the West, become a marshal or purchased land and settled down. He is happy in his new life and, whenever he encounters former Confederates, tries to live harmoniously with them, which isn't always easy. The understanding Yank and forgiving reb, confronted with danger from either Indians or outlaws, team up to fight a common foe, forgetting their blue and gray differences.

3. The cavalryman. The men of the cavalry were drawn from both the Northern and Southern armies and were thrown together under the same flag, but a flag flown in a new country, the West. These men, usually officers, tried their best to live in a brand-new village—the isolated fort. They conducted minor skirmishes with each other but put their old feuds aside to fight together against the Indians.

In novels, many cavalry officers constantly referred back to the Civil War, and that formula was adopted by screenwriters. There were thousands of these references to explain the character through his war experience, whether it was a year or a generation before. A cavalry officer, O'Gara, in Michael Straight's *Carrington,* looks down at his dusty boots at a fort and remembers lying in the mud at Shiloh and watching a rebel soldier try to pull them off.[18] Howard Fast's novel *The Last Frontier* was a story about Dodge City, the wide-open and dangerous Kansas town that became the setting for so many novels, movies and television series. Explaining the trouble always caused by riders on cattle drives that went through Dodge, Fast wrote that "the Texas hands by the hundreds fought the Civil War over."[19]

In *Black Silver,* William Cox's transplanted rebel blames his woes on the war. "Ever since he'd come out of that Yankee prison he had been getting into one thing and another that didn't pan out," Cox wrote. "It was as though a curse had been put on him by the blue-jacketed devils who had beaten him and starved him in Maryland."[20]

Screenwriters often created brand-new Civil War characters and added them to westerns to make the films more interesting. They also believed that Civil War characters added genuine substance to western stories.[21] Another favorite trick was to identify a character simply as a former Confederate or former Yankee, tying the war into the story as part of his past, so that all of the moviegoer's already deeply ingrained feelings about the war could be utilized as emotional background. Making a character a Civil War veteran helped screenwriters, too, because that simple, immediately recognizable shorthand reference could save minutes of plot-building dialogue.[22]

It was not that the cotton-field lore had changed; writers just moved past it. The post–Civil War western presented the rebels as brave men who, now that the war was over, sought new lives and a clean slate in the West. Some were assimilated in the new West, and new nation, but some were not. They were bitter and angry men who did not accept the loss of the war or the alien world of the West where they found themselves, and rejected reconciliation. Whenever that happened, audiences understood that such men were wrong and those who accepted reconciliation were right.

The embittered rebel quickly became a recurring character in films about the Old West. He appeared in so many ways in so many movies and television series in the late 1940s, 1950s and 1960s that when producer Charles Wilson decided to adapt the Owen Wister novel *The Virginian* for television as an unprecedented ninety-minute weekly dramatic series in 1962, he changed the setting from the 1860s to the 1890s. "I want to avoid the embittered Civil War veteran heading west," he said.[23]

There were many such men on the move. Perhaps the most complex bitter Civil War soldier to move west and emerge in a western movie was Ethan Edwards of *The Searchers,* played by John Wayne. A hulking former Confederate army officer, the brooding Edwards arrives at his brother's Texas ranch, rich, in 1868, with no explanation of his whereabouts for the last three years. His brother and family are soon massacred by Indians. Edwards and a part white, part Indian nephew, Martin, decide to chase the Indians and retrieve the little girl they kidnapped, Debbie, who is Edwards's niece. Edwards hates all

Indians and is a complicated neurotic.[24] He is determined to find his niece, now a teenager, and kill her because she has probably had sex with Scar, the Indian chief who seized her. The two search for Debbie for five long years, throughout the West, in rain and snow, across deserts and mountains, before they find her.

Edwards, a mystery throughout the film, is bitter that the South lost the war and that he lost a country as well as his family. He is forced to wander in a new land, the West, which he does not like.[25] (Director John Ford believed: "He was just a plain loner who could never be part of a family.")[26] References to his life in the Confederate army are constant—at times overt and at times subtle. When audiences first see him he is still wearing his Confederate uniform pants and carrying his Confederate army jacket. When asked to take an oath to the U.S. government in order to join a posse to chase the Indians who butchered his family, he refuses, telling a Texas Ranger captain (Ward Bond) that "a man's only good for one oath at a time. I took mine to the Confederate States of America." Again, when asked why he didn't actually surrender at the end of the Civil War, he snaps: "I don't believe in surrenders. I've still got *my* saber, and I didn't turn it into no plowshare, either." He is as rebellious in the new nation, the West, as he was in the old, "carrying rebellion to the point of madness."[27] He is consumed by his hatred of Indians as his enemy in the war. "Edwards is the consummate loner, tortured by his own hatred," wrote one critic.[28]

His racial attitudes are a bundle of contradictions, too. He has racist feelings towards one group of color, Indians, but is kind and gentle to Old Mose, the childlike black cowboy who sometimes tags along with him. His contradictions come to a head at the end of the movie, when he finds Debbie, now clearly a wife and sexual partner of Chief Scar, yet cannot kill her, and instead embraces her.[29]

Abuses suffered in the war by Southerners constituted another theme used by writers of westerns. It was the prime motivation in the movies made about the James Gang and others who rode with guerrilla leader William Quantrill, or of those unfairly impoverished by the war. Quantrill, however, was never cast as a hero. The psychotic killer and horse thief was almost always shown as a social aberration, a demented man who dishonored the South every time he saddled up and rode out to burn down innocent farmers' barns or murder bystanders. That exclusion was underscored in *Dark Command,* when one of the victims in a Quantrill raid shouts as he rides by, "You're not the South." Still, though Quantrill himself fitted not at all into Hollywood's view of the Southerner as heroic underdog, his activities during the war made wonderful grist for scripts. Studios used him (or characters based upon him) in numerous movies over the years to show the seamy side of the Lost Cause, and he quickly became the exemplar of the bad reb who stained the honor of all the good and noble rebs.

Television westerns used many Civil War veterans in their plots. Nick Adams played an embittered reb transplanted to the West in the weekly ABC-TV series The Rebel.

Television, too, showed the embittered Southerner, with the hit weekly series *The Rebel,* starring a youthful Nick Adams. In the opening episode, young Confederate soldier Johnny Yuma (Adams) returns home after the Civil War, gray hat-brim raised slightly on his forehead to show his handsome face. He discovers that his father has been killed by Yankee soldiers and that the townspeople have now embraced the Union. He is heckled by crowds and finally, unable to endure their ridicule, throws a bomb at one group of people, killing several.

He then flees to the West, where he starts a new life, carrying his rebellious attitude into a new storyline each week.[30]

Johnny Yuma was perfect to symbolize on television the rebel of the war and the rebel gone west after it. The series, which started in 1959, coincided with the youth rebellion in the United States. Johnny Yuma, on his horse and with a Confederate jacket and cap, was a perfect 1860s match for Marlon Brando with his motorcycle and cap in *The Wild Ones* and James Dean with his hot rod and black leather jacket in *Rebel Without a Cause*.

Critics saw the ties immediately. "[It is] a study in the fundamental restlessness and rebellion of youth," wrote one critic about the series.[31] A reviewer from the *Los Angeles Times* compared the situation in the South to the aftermath of revolution of any kind and the character to everyman in a revolutionary journey. "The South was the side of rebellion against organized authority . . . [the series] is the romantic idea of the young man on the move, whether it is Candide or Johnny Yuma," he wrote.[32]

The television series about the rebel-moved-west was a natural outgrowth of the middle and late 1950s movies about teenage alienation and was aimed at young viewers. "Only young people had style and intelligence in a world where adults were characteristically awkward, dense or vicious," wrote Andrew Dowdy about *Rebel Without a Cause* in an essay that just as easily could have been about the appeal of the rebel (Yuma or Dean) to American teenagers.[33] The embittered rebel like Yuma was also an easily identifiable character who could and did anchor a television series or movie, just like the characters John Wayne had played.[34]

The Old West provided a landscape for such characters and a complex but very plausible social, cultural and political theater for violence that would never have been acceptable in movies about the East (despite the gangster films of the 1930s). But in western movies and television shows the Civil War soldier, born of violence in the conflict, was able to display that violent streak with an easy believability.[35] The West was a natural chronological and generational setting for the movement of the rebel from one generation (the war) to the next (the West). The natural clash of his iron-willed and cynical personality against a maturing new world on the frontier that had little room for him set up countless plotlines. "Since the time of the Civil

War, the traditional individual of the American character has come more and more into question. While the decline in the individual has frequently been deplored, it has even more frequently been regarded as inevitable," wrote Arthur Ekirch Jr. about rebellion in American youth from 1865 to 1955.[36] Hollywood gave Americans back the individual.

The great youth rebellion of the 1950s was more prominent on the screen and in music than in real life, but had a considerable cultural impact. These movies featured rebels of all kinds, whether Dean, Brando or the endless procession of actors riding motorcycles down highways or racing hot rods at midnight in any number of teenage films. Movies popular with young audiences at the time (teenagers and young adults have always made up the largest film audience) included *The Wild One, Rebel Without a Cause,* and *The Blackboard Jungle,* starring Glenn Ford. They were all released between 1955 and 1959 and starred young, independent heroes determined to rebel against whatever they believed held them down.

It was the movie persona of the Civil War Southern soldier. The motorcycle films and rebel movies of the 1950s were an adaptation of the Civil War rebel movie, and rebels in westerns were an adaptation of the 1950s rebel moved back in time. James Dean understood that and cultivated the cultural image of the rebel in society. "I'm doing it [the film] on my own . . . a rebel in my own way," he told a friend.[37]

Nicholas Ray, who directed the actor in *Rebel Without a Cause,* summed up James Dean and his 1955 rebel character in a way he might have described the rebels who moved west and were the antiheroes in so many western movies young audiences flocked to see: "He is jealously seeking an answer, an escape from the surrounding world."[38]

Part of the appeal of these "embittered rebel" films was that they gave adolescence a legitimacy. Young audiences for the rebel movies of Dean and Brando, and the westerns, cut across all sociopolitical/cultural boundaries, leaving adults in the 1950s to worry in real life as the older generation in the real West, and in the reel West, had about the young embittered rebs who moved among them.

A lengthy study of alienated teenagers of the 1950s conducted by Ken Keniston showed that alienation from contemporary society among the rich and well educated was just as strong as that among the poor and that the fascination with youthful rebellion in the 1950s was against more than economic conditions. Keniston concluded that, given the right conditions, alienation could touch an entire generation, regardless of the era. He wrote about the distance teenagers of the 1950s felt from their parents and society: "Personal fragmentation and a sense of homelessness result from social fragmentation and the shattering of the traditional community. The quest for positive values is made urgent and difficult by the absence of positive myth in society." He gave 1950s alienation historic overtones and said it was "the response to social stresses, historic loss and collective estrangement," adding that "a whole generation may share a similar history of personal development and therefore agree in finding the same stages hard and powerful."

Keniston concluded that people directly involved in historic loss, such as young soldiers in a war, suffer the loss most and find living in the new, different world the most difficult. That generation, whether it remains where it is or moves somewhere else, then finds itself in the position of the prehistoric nomad hunters. When they settled somewhere and were forced to live a quiet, nonviolent life in communities where civilization was trying to flourish, they could not adapt. In the mid-1950s, this description applied not only to teenagers who felt cut off from society, but to the generation of American men and women who had been involved in World War II, returned from the front.

Keniston's alienated young people in the 1950s, whether teens on motorcycles or war veterans trying to readjust, could have been versions of the Civil War's Southern soldiers, in history and on the screen, who lost a whole world and a whole generation, moved west to another region where civilization was trying to grow, and found themselves trapped, angry and alienated.[39]

THE OVERRIDING theme of many westerns with Civil War characters or plots was the building of American nationalism. This was important in the pre–World War II Civil War westerns, such as *Santa Fe Trail* and *They Died with Their Boots On*, in order to reconcile people's differences, whether regional, ethnic or political, to prepare for the possibility of the nation's involvement in the war tearing Europe

A scene from Santa Fe Trail, *with Ronald Reagan as George Armstrong Custer and Erroll Flynn as J. E. B. Stuart, serving together in a prewar U.S. Army regiment. Raymond Massey (on horseback at right) plays the abolitionist firebrand John Brown.*

apart. It was important during the war to bolster people's support for the fight and to define the enemy as truly evil. It was necessary after the war to remind audiences of the success and bravery of the army in any conflict and to remind them that America would always have enemies, such as the Soviet Union, and that the nation had to stay together in order to do battle with them and save democracy.

Santa Fe Trail (1940), a cavalry western, was the first of these nationalistic films. As a portrayal of history, it was a mess. The dashing Errol Flynn played Southerner J. E. B. Stuart and Ronald Reagan played George Armstrong Custer. For commemorative purposes they are put into the same class at West Point and the same regiment in the West. They are in love with the same girl. Their regiment is sent to

capture abolitionist firebrand John Brown, who, following the controversial Kansas-Nebraska Act of 1854, was burning and killing his way
across Kansas in an effort to keep the state free from the slaveholders.

The start of the war is clearly put on the shoulders of Northern
abolitionists, as always. Brown is portrayed by Raymond Massey not
only as a political fanatic who would rather kill than talk (the solution
to slavery, Brown says, is "armed conflict"), but as a religious madman
who wields "the sword of Jehovah." He is an out-and-out terrorist.
(Massey would play Brown again in the 1955 film *Seven Angry Men*,
again reinforcing Hollywood's view that the abolitionists started the
war.)

But *Santa Fe Trail*, directed by Michael Curtiz, has some of the
most poignant movie dialogue about the causes of the war ever heard
in a Civil War movie, dialogue missing from earlier Civil War films.
One of the best scenes is a conversation between Stuart and Custer,
on horseback, in which Southerner Stuart says that the South will
probably end slavery anyway, if given time, and war should be averted.
Both men agree that regardless of politics, it is not the job of the army,
or the abolitionists, to decide about slavery. The message hinted at is
that there certainly should have been an end to slavery, but it should
not have been necessary to go to war.

The ridiculous ending of *Santa Fe Trail* is yet the perfect nationalistic finale. Following the hanging of Brown, Custer and Stuart are
married to their sweethearts in a double wedding ceremony aboard a
train that is taking them west (the new nation). After the exchange of
vows, soldiers on the train break into patriotic songs, signifying the
need of soldiers from both North and South to remain together.

Film scholars have always seen *Santa Fe Trail* as a balanced film.
"This picture tried to straddle the fence, avoiding the taking of sides
as to who was responsible for the catastrophic Civil War," wrote one.[40]
Others thought the way the film deplored Northern violence was
a good counterbalance to films such as *Jesse James* about Southern
violence.[41]

The film's theme was not just subliminally telling people in the
audience in 1940 that Northerners and Southerners had to stick
together on the eve of the Civil War, but telling them that they had to
stick together in case the United States was pulled into the European
war. We battled and defeated fanatics in the past (John Brown), the

screenplay implied, and could defeat fanatics in the present (Adolf Hitler).

They Died with Their Boots On (1941) was a wildly inaccurate biography of Custer, played by Errol Flynn (ironically, the reckless Custer was the subject of a half dozen films, far more than Grant, Lee or any truly important general in the war). There is a smidgen of accuracy here and there, such as the correct year the Civil War started, but that's about all. At the beginning of the movie, Custer is seen during the Gettysburg engagement single-handedly winning a battle at Hanover, Pennsylvania. (He was there, but was certainly not responsible for the victory.) He moves west after the war and immediately captures Chief Crazy Horse, played by Anthony Quinn (who acts more like Zorba the Greek, perhaps his most memorable character, than the heroic chief).

They Died with Their Boots On, *released in 1941 and starring Errol Flynn, was yet another western about Custer, in which his Civil War years were (after a fashion) chronicled.*

In the world of *They Died with Their Boots On,* no one seems to have started the war and no one seems to have won it. A lovable Mammy waits on Custer's sweetheart. The men on both sides are valiant. Southern cadets who choose to fight for the South leave West Point with great honor and ride off to the strains of "Dixie."

Like *Santa Fe Trail,* the Custer film advocates nationalism. Except for a forty-four-second snippet, the Confederates, the historical enemy, are never seen actually fighting in the film. Custer leads charge after charge against an invisible enemy and wins them all, leading *American* forces to victory.

But the real point of the Custer story comes at the very end of the film. Custer tells another man that he knows that his troop will be wiped out by Indians at the Little Big Horn the next day (this is inaccurate; he had no way of knowing what would happen), but that the sacrifice is necessary to save other army troops in the area. The meaning was clear in the months before Pearl Harbor: Americans had to be prepared to sacrifice if war came to their doorstep.

Soon after the release of *They Died with Their Boots On,* America became immersed in World War II and Hollywood produced many gung ho war movies extolling the heroism of U.S. soldiers. One of the most chilling of all these films was not a story about the battles in Europe or the Pacific, but the Civil War–themed *The Ox-Bow Incident,* released in 1943. The film, directed by William Wellman, was one of the few in cinema history that did not show the Southern soldier as noble gentleman or innocent victim, but as harsh villain. It is the story of two men who ride into a Western town in the 1880s and become part of a posse to chase cattle rustlers. One of the leaders of the posse is a former Confederate major, Tetley, who insists that his weak, pacifist son, who has an aversion to violence, join them to become a man. The mob finds three men and hangs them, only to discover shortly afterward that they were innocent.

Major Tetley (played by Frank Conroy) was drawn by the screenwriter as one of the most vicious and authoritarian characters in all of film history. He is a psychopathic father who insists that only hanging people will make his son a man and that mob rule, not the rule of law, is the only law and order needed in society. For him, the success of the mob, under his leadership, brings back the glory days of the Confederacy.

The movie was based on a novel written by Walter Van Tilberg Clark. Published at the start of World War II in Europe, the book was an indictment of Nazi Germany, and its message was that uniforms (whether worn by a fictional Confederate major or the SS) should not give people authority and that the murder of innocent people is the inevitable result of mob rule. The book and movie are about the lynching of innocent men, but their reference was clearly the mob rule of the Nazis.[42] It was a lesson, too, that unruly mobs take over when good people stand by and do nothing. Good people, then, all over the world, had to rally in 1943 and stop the Nazis from overrunning Europe. The film used the Civil War to rally support for the current one.

Several reviewers commented on the film's message. "A strong-willed Confederate could convince weak men who could not rebel to do evil," wrote a critic in *The New Republic*.[43] Another, in program notes written in 1979, called the Tetley-led mob "American Nazism" and warned audiences that the film was a reminder that "it can happen here."[44]

The mob's leader, many writers and viewers agreed, was a torn and violent man who, deep inside, could never forgive the North for winning the war and could never truly put down his sword. A generation later, he is putting his uniform back on and taking out his frustrations and hate on three innocent people, a group of neighbors, and his own son. He was revenge personified, and he wore a Confederate uniform. He had become a symbol of everything hundreds of Civil War movies denied.

The Ox-Bow Incident was also an indictment of the South as it was in the late 1930s and early 1940s. The lynchings organized by the fictional Confederate major clearly stood for the lynchings of African Americans organized at the time by the Ku Klux Klan and other mobs at that time in the American South. Tetley was there on the screen to remind American filmgoers that the lynchings of innocent people were continuing and drive home the horror of it (one of the three lynch victims in the film was a Mexican, to make the racial point).[45]

Critics saw much merit in the film, but found it unsettling. One New York critic called it "the strangest western ever filmed . . . a grim, forbidding picture."[46] Another called it "a horrendous exhibition of sadism."[47] It was perceived as an anti-Nazi film, but also as a strong

A scene from The Ox-Bow Incident. *Ex-Major Tetley (Frank Conroy), wearing his old Confederate uniform, accuses three innocent men— Donald Martin (Dana Andrews, at left) and two of his friends—of murder.*

anti-Confederate and anti-Southern film, the only one of its kind until then. Coming just four years after *Gone With the Wind*, it was written about as a dramatic backward shift in Hollywood's portrayal of Confederates.

Yet critics of the day missed the most powerful dimension of the disaffected major's character: the bad reb. Tetley was so grotesque that audiences saw him as the Confederate aberration, not the norm. Honest rebel officers and soldiers would never have done what he did. Showcasing this man as a monster reaffirmed the idea that Confederates *were* noble cavaliers, not like him. Going a step further, the message was that Americans were noble and not like him. At the end of the film, upon discovering his mistake and being shamed by his son, Tetley kills himself, as people like him should.

Movies about the reconciliation of North and South in the West continued after the end of World War II. One of the best, in which the bitter reb makes peace with the Yankees, fights outlaws, saves the town and opens up the West for all Americans was *Dallas* (1950). Gary Cooper played an embittered Southern guerrilla fighter who is asked to impersonate Wild Bill Hickok after the war (Hickok fought for the North) and becomes a U.S. marshal in order to clean up the very Southern Dallas, Texas. Throughout the film, Cooper constantly mutters about Northerners who did not fight but paid someone else to take their place, about how much better soldiers the rebs were, about how all carpetbaggers are thieves, and says that the South should never have lost the war. The people of Dallas all seem to wear rebel army caps in crowd scenes, and another marshal, a reunification figure, bellows to Cooper that while the marshal fought for the South at Chickamauga, his brother fought for the North at Gettysburg. Cooper constantly rides faster, fights harder and shoots better than the Northerners, particularly former Union soldiers. At the end of the film, though, after he has cleaned up Dallas, driving the bad guys into the sunset, Cooper comes to realize that the only future for himself, the West, and the North and South is in a single, united nation. As his rival for a woman's heart leaves town to work for the railroad, Cooper, now a U.S. marshal, smiles at him, shakes his hand and tells friends: "That Yankee foreigner is starting to talk like an American!"

IN MOST Civil War westerns, it is the Indians who are seen as the evil enemy. The most bizarre movie to present North and South together against the Indians was *The Last Outpost* (1951). It begins simply enough: a Union cavalry unit in Texas is trying to transport gold and other supplies to Washington (a plot that surfaced in a half dozen westerns tied to the war) and must outfox a marauding Confederate cavalry regiment to do it. The Rebels learn that the Union cavalry is going to arm nearby Indians to attack the Confederates and, if need be, Southern-sympathizing Texas civilians. The Confederates sneak into an Indian camp to make peace and avert bloodshed, but are unable to keep their end of the bargain—freeing Geronimo from a nearby jail. The two key subplots, harking back to the days of the 1908 silents, are also firmly in place: the Union and Confederate cavalry leaders are brothers, and there is a romance with a gorgeous woman.

In the finale of *The Last Outpost,* the Indians go on the standard rampage and threaten to torch the local town and kill all the innocent men, women and children. They howl loudly, ride around in circles and wave their rifles in the air—as they do in all westerns.

The day is saved at the final moment, though, when the Confederate cavalry commander arms Union soldiers he captured earlier and leads a united attack to kill all the Indians and save the town. The strains of "Dixie" blast from the speakers as the soldiers in blue and gray, fighting together as white people against a common enemy—the Indians—charge across the prairie and drive off the foe. At the end of the movie, of course, the two brothers shake hands and predict a quick end to the war and the foundation of a new nation in which North and South will get along harmoniously. The Confederate brother then marries the girl. It is wonderfully ironic to watch *The Last Outpost* today. The suave Confederate commander is played by none other than Ronald Reagan, who, thirty years later, would be elected president by capturing an overwhelming majority of the South's electoral votes.

The idea of former rebs and Yanks teaming up to rid the new nation of enemies, whether Indians or outlaws, was the centerpiece of many westerns. One of the earliest, and most haunting, was *Shane.* In that 1953 film a former rebel soldier nicknamed "Stonewall," after Stonewall Jackson, is murdered by an outlaw who taunts him about the Civil War. At the end of the film Shane, a mysterious drifter, shoots the outlaw, in a fair gunfight, symbolizing the need of the new frontier to purge itself of rogues determined to carry on the war. These films usually included dialogue that restored good feelings. In *Showdown at Abilene* (1956), two neighbors who fought on opposite sides in the war, one now in his Union uniform and the other in street clothes, meet in a Western town. One eyes the other and says, "Take off that blue uniform and we can be friends again."

Major Dundee, a 1965 film, was another blue-and-gray frontier handshake. In the film, Charlton Heston played a tough Union officer who takes his Confederate prisoners of war and makes them part of the Union army so they can join in a raid to free several white children kidnapped by Apache Indians. The racism against Indians in the film was lamented by some critics. (By the mid-1960s, critics' view of the standard cowboys-and-Indians films was changing.) So was the casting of British actor Richard Harris to play a Confederate captain. "Ever since Vivien Leigh's Scarlett O'Hara, Hollywood has made a big thing out of British performers impersonating the aristocracy of the Old South," wrote one such critic.[48] Most reviewers enjoyed the film, however, and applauded the idea of North and South working together against a common foe, even if it was the Indian. This unity against a common enemy was ballyhooed for months by Columbia's publicity mill. The studio's writers put this headline into the ads that were mailed in press kits to newspaper editors from coast to coast: REBELS AND YANKS TOGETHER AGAINST THE DEADLY APACHE![49]

In *Arizona Bushwhackers* (1968), Howard Keel plays a rough Confederate officer released from a Union prison in the West so that he can clean up a frontier town. He is not cleaning it up for the South or the North, but for the United States. The movie was one of several that featured the patriotic redemption of outlaws.

A classic cavalry film was *The Undefeated,* released in 1969, in which another group of color, Mexicans, replaces the Indians as the enemy necessary to bring former Northerners and Southerners together. The film starred Rock Hudson as a Confederate officer who snapped after defeat in the war and burned down his plantation rather than sell it to carpetbaggers. As the mansion is consumed in flames, he rides off to gather up dozens of other farmers and ex-slaveholders and lead them to a new life in a new country, Mexico.[50] But once there, Hudson and his people are attacked by the forces of the Mexican nationalist leader Benito Juárez and must be saved by a U.S. Cavalry unit led by John Wayne. Once the Mexicans have been run off, the triumphant U.S. leader, Wayne, still in blue, and the defeated Confederate leader, Hudson, still in gray, take their joint army back over the border into the United States, where together they celebrate their victory—and new life in a postwar world—at, appropriately, a Fourth of July barbecue.[51]

There were dozens of cavalry movies in which veterans of the blue and gray joined regiments out west to fight the new foe, the Indian, to protect the ever-expanding postwar nation. The solid foundation for all of them was the late 1940s John Ford cavalry trilogy: *Rio Grande,*

Director John Ford (left) and actor John Wayne combined for a number of westerns involving Civil War characters, including the cavalry trilogy Rio Grande, She Wore a Yellow Ribbon *and* Fort Apache. *Here, Ford, Wayne and Maureen O'Hara take a break from filming on the set of* Rio Grande.

She Wore a Yellow Ribbon and *Fort Apache*. Each had powerful Civil War characters and each targeted the Indians. All three were directed by Ford, perhaps the screen's finest director, whose genius had turned a western shoot-'em-up into fine cinema in 1939 with *Stagecoach*, starring John Wayne.

Ford's father came to this country from Ireland in 1865 with the express purpose of fighting in the Civil War, but he arrived too late to join either army. Nevertheless, the senior Ford routinely regaled his family and friends with stories about his brothers in the Civil War. One brother fought for the South, two fought for the North and one fought for both sides. ("He got *two* pensions!" the elder Ford chortled.)[52] One member of the Ford family in South Carolina had his home burned to the ground by Sherman's advancing army.[53]

Ford smoothly integrated the backdrop of the war into his stories, while always trying to show that Southerners and Northerners were equally wise and, in battle, equally brave. He fully understood the all-American impact of Wayne as an actor and craftily cast him as, alternately, an ex-Confederate and an ex-Union officer in different westerns.

In *Fort Apache,* set in 1876, Ford has Wayne play a beloved and reliable U.S. Army officer, a former colonel in the Confederate forces.[54] Wayne saves the regiment and patriotically hides the negligence of his commander, a former Union colonel.[55] At the very end, Wayne takes command of the U.S. Army regiment and hangs on his wall a painting showing an exculpatory version of his predecessor's Indian attack. He then tells reporters that the Northern colonel was a genuine hero—unifying North and South with pride in the new cavalry.

In *Rio Grande,* Ford orchestrates a warm and wonderful reconciliation on two fronts. This time Wayne plays Kirby Yorke, a Union army officer. Yorke's wife, played by Maureen O'Hara, left him after his regiment, on orders, burned the family plantation. She took their son with her, but at sixteen he ran off to join the army. He has turned up in Wayne's cavalry regiment after the war, a regiment that fights Indians. The father proudly watches their boy become a hero—at the Indians' expense. O'Hara has moved to the fort to be near the son. Wayne and O'Hara are reunited at the end of the film and, clearly, so are North and South.[56] The son, a hero, symbolizes making the new, reunited nation heroic.[57]

She Wore a Yellow Ribbon also starred Wayne.[58] He plays a late-1860s Southwest cavalry commander about to retire. But when an Indian uprising begins he leads the cavalry on one last campaign. At the end of one battle, a trooper, identified as a former Confederate officer who joined the U.S. Cavalry at the end of the war, is killed in Indian territory. This man dying in alien territory symbolized, for Ford, the sacrificial death of the South to make way for the North-South army, now the army of the United States.[59]

By casting Wayne as a Yank, reb and, finally, U.S. Cavalry officer, Ford was telling audiences that all soldiers were, and are, good Americans. How could John Wayne play anyone but a good American?

Incidentally, the Civil War reunification ethic was also woven into dozens of later World War II combat films. The best example was *Operation Pacific* (1950), again starring Wayne, naturally, as a naval commander. He laments the death of a young sailor, killed in an enemy attack, and proudly tells fellow officers that the boy's father and grandfather had served in previous U.S. wars. He finishes with a flourish: "Why, his grandpappy served on the *Merrimack!*" The *Merrimack*, of course, was the Confederate ironclad involved in the famous Civil War battle against the federal ship the *Monitor*. In this scene Wayne was reminding his fellow officers, and the audience, that the Confederates were American heroes, too.

· · ·

What promised greater success for Hollywood than The Red Badge of Courage, *a 1951 Civil War movie based on the classic novel about combat cowardice by Stephen Crane and starring the most decorated hero of World War II, Audie Murphy (with bandanna). Audiences, however, did not want to see U.S. soldiers portrayed as cowards in any war, and the film was a box-office flop.*

ONE OF THE most heavily publicized Civil War movies of the early 1950s was *The Red Badge of Courage* (1951), faithfully based on Stephen Crane's novel. MGM announced that the film not only would be directed by John Huston, one of filmdom's true artists, but would star Audie Murphy, the most decorated soldier of World War II. The film was quite different from prior Civil War films. It tells the story of a scared teenager in the Union army who panics and flees in his first skirmish. He then returns and leads his regiment to victory. Full of nuances, the book and film are superb studies of human emotions not examined in previous Civil War stories.

American audiences hated it. In the era of lush color films, it was made in black-and-white and was criticized as visually unappealing. The real problem with the film, however, was that it was also released during the Korean War and just six years after the end of World War II. American soldiers had been brave in both those conflicts, saving the world from Nazism in the former and battling against Communism in the latter. Audiences were proud of America's role as defender of freedom around the world. They wanted to see their boys in uniform as leaders and heroes on the screen, defeating villains wherever they found them. In *The Red Badge of Courage*, a young American soldier was portrayed as a coward who turns and runs in the heat of battle. Americans did not do that. Despite the familiarity of the novel and considerable studio publicity, the film died at the box office.[60]

Although this movie failed, audience interest in the Civil War continued. The 1950s saw a string of heavily promoted, big-budget films with top stars—*Raintree County, Friendly Persuasion, Drums in the Deep South* and *The Raid,* among others. All had remnants of the Myth, but showed both sides in a more acceptable way.[61]

The Raid (1954) is the story of a little-known raid by former Confederate prisoners on the tiny village of St. Alban's, Vermont. It was directed by Leonard Goldstein, who once said, "I've loused up more history than any three directors in Hollywood." Sure enough, he turned the brutal attack, in which three raiders were wounded, one resident was killed and part of the town was burned, into a long and sappy romance between the rebel leader, played by Van Heflin, and a local woman, whose son adores him.[62]

In the 1950s and 1960s films tended to show a better North-South balance. In one of the finest films of the period the main characters refuse to take sides. In *Friendly Persuasion,* Gary Cooper and his law-abiding family are Quakers, opposed to war and violence. They find themselves trapped in the middle of the war when the oldest son, under intense peer pressure, leaves home and joins the Union army. Another picture that did not assign blame was *The Horse Soldiers.* One of the most balanced movies about the war, *The Horse Soldiers* was an account of the real raid into Mississippi by a Union cavalry regiment led by Colonel Ben Grierson. The army of the North is clearly the winner onscreen, and its colonel, played by John Wayne, is a fair and just commander. The Northerners fight nobly, but so do the Southerners. Their colonel, when captured, is proud and honorable. Southern schoolchildren, military cadets, try to fight the Yankees.

There were a number of antiwar films which used the Civil War as their vehicle. One of the earliest was Friendly Persuasion, *starring Gary Cooper (right) as a Quaker.*

Southern women risk their lives to spy on the Yankees. Both sides are gallant.[63] Critics noted that every time the Union army looked good, there was a scene in which the Confederate army looked good, even in defeat. A scene in which a Northern army doctor delivers a slave's baby is followed by a scene in which a Southern woman treats her slaves extremely well.[64] "North and South emerge heroically in the various encounters," wrote one critic.[65]

The 1960s, of course, brought the hundredth anniversary of the war. Hollywood producers, directors and screenwriters were certain, just as their predecessors had been certain fifty years before, that a big anniversary would generate many commemorative events— restaged battles, dinners, parades, festivals—and bring substantial media coverage. They were wrong. The fiftieth anniversary was celebrated as grandly as it was because many of the men who fought in the war were still alive and the war was fresh in the minds of many. The hundredth anniversary was little more than a circle on the calendar, although there were numerous restaged battles, and reenactors in large numbers simulated the fighting. The anniversary arrived at a time when the national calendar was already crowded. In the early to middle 1960s, Americans had to worry about Cold War strife, the space race with the Soviets, the Cuban missile crisis, the beginning of American involvement in Vietnam, the assassination of President John F. Kennedy, and the growing civil rights movement. There was only limited interest in the Civil War. Hollywood studios, ever attentive to the public pulse, produced only nine Civil War movies between 1960 and 1965.

By the 1970s Hollywood had made some films about race that were set in the Civil War era. *Band of Angels,* released in 1957, was one of those that were well ahead of their time. It starred Clark Gable as a wealthy Southerner (with a remarkable resemblance to one Rhett Butler) who falls in love with one of his slaves, played by Yvonne De Carlo, and is forced to flee the city because of the relationship. *The McMasters* (1969) is the story of a black freedman from Texas (Brock Peters) who has served in the Union army and returns home after the war to work for his former boss (Burl Ives). He is confronted with Southerners' postwar hostility.

Some of the hardest-working African Americans after the war were former black Union soldiers in Texas. They were among the most successful farmers, and some even became officials of the Farmers' Alliance, a large movement of disenfranchised farmers which developed into the American populist movement. Some of the best cowboys in the postwar West were black, but they were never shown on the screen. Nor were the black editors and writers who worked diligently on black newspapers or the African Americans who founded an all-black town in Oklahoma.

Occasionally black people were portrayed as settlers, cowboys and townspeople, but not often. John Ford gave black actor Woody Strode a daring role in the post–Civil War western *Sergeant Rutledge* (1960), in which he played a U.S. Army soldier. Jim Brown, the black former NFL football star turned actor, played a U.S. Army sergeant in the post–Civil War West in *Rio Conchos* (1964).

Dan Jackson landed a large role in *Mysterious Island,* the 1961 movie based on the Jules Verne novel about Union soldiers who escape from Richmond's Libby Prison via a hot-air balloon and are carried by a storm to a South Pacific island. There they battle giant crabs and an oversized octopus, tangle with pirates and bump into Captain Nemo himself.[66] Jackson was proud of his work in the film and bragged that the script did not call for him to be a black soldier, just a soldier, and he did not have to fit any of the old stereotypes. "I don't have to be comical or scared—just be a man," he said.[67] The film received good reviews and many newspapers did articles about its location filming in seven different countries and its striking special effects (including the way it showed the legendary submarine *Nautilus*). However, reviewers saw the movie as an action-adventure thriller and ignored the Civil War story and the new role for a black soldier. A headline from *Variety* summed it up best: CAPTAIN NEMO RIDES AGAIN![68]

Most of the Civil War films of the 1950s and 1960s that were not westerns were still pro-Southern; they followed the time-tested pattern of noble and scrappy underdogs versus monolithic federals. (There were some exceptions, such as *Journey to Shiloh,* in 1967.) But screenwriters were trying to show the North more favorably and pushing even harder for screen—and real—nationalism. They continually insisted that, regardless of uniform, all Americans were brave. And given the box office failure of *The Red Badge of Courage* earlier, it seemed that Americans agreed.

The 1970s saw three Civil War films featuring a genuine box office champion, actor Clint Eastwood. He starred in *The Good, the Bad, and the Ugly, The Outlaw Josey Wales* and *The Beguiled. The Beguiled* was perhaps the strangest Civil War film ever. Eastwood was cast as a wounded Union soldier who is hidden and given care at a girls' finishing school in the South. He seduces several of the girls, and a teacher, before they turn on him and kill him, prompting one amused critic to chirp: "Southern belles were much more dangerous than the Confederate army."[69]

Television shows of the day stressed reunification, too. In one early 1960s episode of the hit series *Bonanza,* a former Confederate colonel and medic turned postwar outlaw performs emergency surgery to save the life of Ben Cartwright's son Hoss. As he operates, he tells Ben that the only reason he became a criminal was that his farm was torched and his family murdered by marauding Yankees. He turned to crime only because of the acts of, here, bad Yanks. On an episode of *The Twilight Zone,* a Southern soldier who is hanged becomes—in a romantic dream sequence—the brave soldier of any nation.

In several other films, good rebs were distinguished from bad rebs to show that only good rebs were assimilated in the new nation of the West. A perfect example was *Love Me Tender* (1956). Elvis Presley plays the youngest of four brothers. The older three fought for the South while Elvis stayed home to help run the farm (and marry the sweetheart of the oldest brother when he was thought to be dead). The three soldier brothers and three of their friends wind up with cash taken from a Yankee train in what they feel was a legitimate act of war on the final day of the conflict. They divide the money and return home to become hardworking farmers (and listen to Elvis sing on the porch at night).

When they find out the money rightfully belongs to the government, the three brothers, who are *good* rebs, offer to return it. Their friends, however, want to keep their share. In an ensuing gun battle with U.S. troops, the bad rebs kill Elvis and are in turn gunned down by the cavalry. The three good rebs give back the money and return to the farm. At film's end, they are assimilated into the new nation. The bad rebs, of course, had to be killed.[70]

Love Me Tender had one of the most raucous premieres in the history of Civil War movies, or all movies. The film was Presley's first, and eager teenagers waited on long lines at movie houses to see their rock-and-roll hero. Once inside, they would chant, "We Want Elvis! We Want Elvis!" throughout the opening scenes until the singer appeared on the screen—to loud cheering and unrestrained screaming. There was applause every time Elvis uttered a line, especially a memorable classic such as "Yeah, what about it?" or the legendary "You ain't got no right to do this."[71]

Elvis's fame overwhelmed everything else about the movie, including its title and ending. The film was originally called *The Reno Brothers,* after the book on which it was based. But Elvis had just finished recording a new song, "Love Me Tender," as the movie was about to open. To cash in on what would surely be another Elvis hit, the producers made the song title the film title. Then, when sneak preview audiences harshly criticized the original script, in which Elvis is killed, and teen fans insisted that they would not see a movie in which Elvis dies, the producers listened. Writers added the always usable final scene that shows that the heroic dead never really die. In the new ending, which audiences loved, Elvis dies but his spirit lives on, singing from heaven to the mourners at his funeral.

As the United States moved through the 1960s and 1970s and the post-Vietnam, post-Watergate era, Civil War movies and westerns with Civil War veterans in them retained all of the mythology of the silents, but promulgated the notion that all Americans in the Civil War were gallant . . . and always would be.

Such films kept reminding audiences that errors were made by both sides in the Civil War and afterwards, but that then (and now) Americans put aside their differences for the good of the nation and its people. This was summed up best in a speech by a judge in an episode of the television series *How the West Was Won.* Speaking about the war, he said: "We did a lot of wrong things collectively and now we've got to get along collectively."

CHAPTER THIRTEEN

Kunta Kinte's Civil War

CIVIL WAR FILMS took a decisive turn in the mid-1970s. It was not a change brought about by improved cinematic technology, a brand-new film star or a historical discovery. A new age dawned because of one figure—Kunta Kinte.

Kunta Kinte was a character in Alex Haley's *Roots,* one of the best-selling books of all time. Kinte was born and raised in Africa, then captured by slavers and taken to South Carolina. *Roots,* published in 1976, was the story of more than one hundred years of American history as experienced by his family. It was a saga about black people, not white people, enduring pain and trauma. It was the story of fathers and sons, men and women, friendships, tragedy and triumph, all set against the backdrop of slavery. It was a departure from all past Civil War stories and a major revision of the Plantation Myth. Its unparalleled success as a book and then as a television miniseries surprised an entire nation.

The televised miniseries had its own historical roots in the expansion of black roles in American films and television throughout the 1950s, 1960s and 1970s. Black actors got more and better roles throughout that period. More important, American society had changed. There had been post–World War II developments such as the integration of sports and the public schools, and then the civil rights movement. These advances had changed American culture.

In the 1950s, talented black performers began to be cast in good parts. Actress Dorothy Dandridge starred in *Carmen Jones* in 1954 and *Porgy and Bess* in 1959. Sidney Poitier starred in *Edge of the City* in 1957 and *The Defiant Ones* in 1958. Harry Belafonte starred in several commercially successful films in the 1950s which were extensions of his enormously successful career as a singer and nightclub performer. A handful of other black performers, too, found that the door to Hollywood had opened a bit.

When in the 1960s the civil rights movement knocked down the Hollywood door that had barred them, black performers found themselves in demand for good roles in well-written films supervised by the medium's top directors. Audiences were treated to exceptional movies such as *In the Heat of the Night, Sounder* and *The Great White Hope*.

In 1967, Sidney Poitier, playing a doctor, very politely asked for the hand of a white girl in marriage in *Guess Who's Coming to Dinner*. Then, just two years later, Jim Brown had sex with Raquel Welch in *100 Rifles*, an event not probable just ten years earlier and unthinkable in the 1940s.[1]

Television producers, trying to attract black audiences as the medium exploded in the late 1960s, and eager to tap the talent bank of young black performers, accepted television integration and began to give substantial roles to black actors and actresses to see if their inclusion would help ratings. By the early 1970s, there were many top television series with black actors as costars, including *Mission Impossible* (Greg Morris), *I Spy* (Bill Cosby), *Star Trek* (Nichelle Nichols), *Rawhide* (Raymond St. Jacques), *Hogan's Heroes* (Ivan Dixon), *All in the Family* (Sherman Hemsley), *Mod Squad* (Clarence Williams III) and *Julia* (Diahann Carroll). The success of the first few led to the success of the rest. Then, in 1974, came the critically acclaimed ratings blockbuster black television film *The Autobiography of Miss Jane Pittman*, starring Cicely Tyson.

The success of television series with black costars led to mostly black comedy series, beginning in 1970 with *The Flip Wilson Show*. The likable Wilson's humor appealed to all audiences, black and white, and his show quickly became one of the most popular in the country. It was quickly followed by other highly rated comedy shows with mostly black casts, such as *Sanford and Son, Good Times, That's My Mama, The Jeffersons, What's Happening?* and *Get Christie Love!* These proved that shows starring black people could be just as successful at the box office and in television's crucial Nielsen ratings as their white counterparts.

But not all the movies and television shows were on as high a level.

The early successes led film executives to produce mostly black movies that became festivals of grotesque excess. They sought to cash in on the financial windfall caused by the sudden integration of movies. The thinking was that if Poitier could earn acclaim as a sophisticated black cop in *In the Heat of the Night,* then why not star Richard Roundtree as a supermacho, supersexy private detective in the *Shaft* films. The "blaxploitation" land rush in cinema was aided by hundreds of black actors and directors determined to grab their own piece of film's private-eye-and-cop kingdom, a longtime preserve of whites. In their eagerness, producers and writers went too far, creating stereotypical black characters that were just as fraudulent, and

A bare-chested black slave, Ken Norton, receives an impassioned hug from his owner's wife, Susan George, in Mandingo. *This was one of the early 1970s "blaxploitation" films that opened the door for the humanistic drama in* Roots.

just as distasteful, to audiences as the Sambo characters of the last generation. However, adolescents, a prime target audience for films, loved many of the blaxploitation movies, so those films lasted longer than they should have.

A progression of tasteless and badly written films that showcased black men as oversexed and black women as sex objects with no ties to family flooded America's theaters. They began with the *Shaft* films and included *Sweet Sweetback's Baadasssss Song, Superfly, Black Godfather, Black Caesar, Cleopatra Jones* and the Civil War–era films *Mandingo* and *Drum*.[2] So *Roots* was not only the successor to the finely made films starring some blacks, it was also the natural backlash against this pathetic cycle of exploitation films that filled theaters, particularly in urban areas. *Roots*, then, by arriving at one historical moment created another.

TELEVISION PRODUCER David Wolper realized that Haley's book was not only a tremendous story of men and women in slavery, but also a generational saga with vividly drawn and admirable characters that could sustain a long miniseries format. What attracted Wolper and the executives at ABC, who paid the author $250,000 for the rights to *Roots* and spent $6 million to produce it in 1977, was Haley's absorbing story of a writer in search of his past, and the story he found.

The story was full of the violence of slavery, but it was also full of love between the characters and, in chapter after chapter, generation after generation, their family's ability to bear all burdens, maintain their dignity and harbor an unshakable belief that one day they would be free. For the first time, it gave Americans, black and white, a more honest, if sentimental, view of life in slavery from the black point of view.

The miniseries cast some well-known performers, such as Ben Vereen, John Amos, and Leslie Uggams, and introduced two unknowns. Kunta Kinte as a young man was played by nineteen-year-old UCLA acting student LeVar Burton, who had never acted professionally before. Newcomer Lou Gossett Jr. was cast as Kunta's adult friend.[3]

Wolper and his producers, and ABC executives, were determined to employ as many black performers and workers as possible off-

screen to give integrity to the entire production.[4] The miniseries probably gave work to more black actors and technicians than any project
in entertainment history. The final working crew was 40 percent
black, the highest percentage or total number in all Hollywood history
up to that time. It did not have any black writers cobbling together the
mammoth script, but that was because Haley himself worked on the
script with a collection of white writers. Along the way they changed
some concepts of *Roots,* making it more romantic and more white:

• The storyline of the book was changed to include the character
Fanta, a love interest for Kunta Kinte, so that the opening episode
would have sex appeal.

• The old, crude slave ship captain was thrown overboard and a
new, liberal, guilt-ridden captain, played by Edward Asner, was put at
the helm.

• As many small roles that could be filled by Caucasians as possible were added to give the miniseries a whiter look.

Wolper did not envision *Roots* as a PBS special about slavery. He
saw a highly commercial miniseries that would succeed not because
it was instructional, or delivered any kind of racial message, but
because it was good television. "[Television] only has impact when it
reaches a mass audience . . . it ought to be entertaining," he said.[5]
Then, to make their $6 million miniseries succeed, ABC staged the
greatest promotional drive in television history. A thirty-minute video,
which included scenes from the episodes, the story of the production
and interviews with television executives who saw it as a huge hit was
played for hundreds of ABC-affiliate executives around the country in
an effort to get *Roots* aired everywhere. Heads of Southern television
stations, especially, were wined and dined.

The promos underlined ABC's biggest problem: How do you sell a
black series to a white audience? They did it with a prerelease publicity campaign featuring just about all the name white actors in the
show. "Our concern was to put a lot of white people in promos.
Otherwise, we thought the program would be a turnoff," said ABC
executive Larry Sullivan.

To ensure a large audience, ABC produced thousands of *Roots*
study guides, which were shipped free to teachers all over America.
The study guides went to kids who would go home and tell Mom and
Dad that the teacher wanted them to watch the miniseries so they

could learn about history.[6] The study guides, like all the press releases, stressed that theme—a universal story. "*Roots* speaks not just to black and white, but to all people and all races everywhere," trumpeted a blurb on page two of the press book.[7]

The huge campaign was to get America ready for a miniseries that was about black people but could be about any people, and that taught the lesson that dignity and triumph know no color. "Seeing on American commercial television slave beatings, slave rapes, slave family separations, constant daily humiliations and the basic inhumanity and corruption that have gone into making America the empire it has become, and witnessing the victorious spirit of those who survived it all, audiences have been affected in unanticipated ways," echoed the writer and anthologist Donald Bogle.[8]

The marketing campaign included a serialization of the book for newspapers.[9] There was, in easy-to-read, easy-to-publish form, a synopsis of each of the eight nights' episodes, which most major newspapers carried as a viewing guide for readers.[10]

Finally, ABC sent promotional videos to every major newspaper and radio and television station in America, held special screenings, delivered packaged videos of the eight episodes to newspaper entertainment editors and critics, and flew the lead actors, black and white, all over the United States to promote the miniseries. Some journalists said that even if it was only an average show, the "saturation bombing" by ABC's promotional and advertising departments would make it a hit.[11]

Despite all of their efforts, ABC executives were still worried as late as Sunday, January 23, when the first installment was ready to go. "We've never been concerned about reaching a black audience. They'll watch it no matter what happens. The question is, will we reach a white audience because there has *never, never* been a successful black drama series," said ABC executive Brandon Stoddard.[12]

He needn't have worried. Critics loved it, but not just because it was a finely made television series. They loved it because it told an unusual story that they thought might, just might, help bridge the racial divides that still kept so many Americans apart in the mid-1970s. These were chasms never completely bridged by the civil rights movement of the previous decade, that needed to be bridged for there to be any semblance of the reunited America that Civil War films always strove for. But this time the divisions were not just North and South, but North and South and black and white. *Roots* represented a successful counterattack on the tried-and-true Plantation Myth. The white owners in *Roots* were not all good to their slaves, the slaves were not all joyful cotton pickers, and there was not a cavalier to be seen. It offered a different view, a black view, of the boys riding off to fight for the Lost Cause, and added a new dimension in the 1970s to American understanding of the Civil War, a dimension many Americans believed was long needed. We would learn later that it was yet another myth.

Reviews were very good. The Associated Press called *Roots* "a riveting drama of black history."[13] The *Boston Herald Advertiser*'s critic said that it had the "concentration that is the very nature of the novel."[14]

There were complaints from some historians and writers, such as white novelist William Styron, the author of *The Confessions of Nat Turner,* who called the miniseries "dishonest tripe,"[15] but at the time few paid any attention to them.

Americans watching *Roots* were moved by the power of the generational story. The human drama that Haley and the other writers wove through the twelve hours made *Roots* the riveting history of a people. Now, 111 years after the end of the Civil War, that people, at long last, had their story told, and told in a week.

It was a disturbing and revealing story that dramatically affected all African Americans. Many felt the way Tony Brown, the host of a nationally syndicated television show, did: "Alex Haley told us who we are."[16] In the weeks that followed the airing of the miniseries, blacks told reporters and television commentators that television had finally given them their story in a powerful way, that through this Civil War–era series, television had finally shown that blacks had a strong and glorious heritage. It showed them, thousands said, that their ancestors may have been whipped and beaten and treated like dogs, but they survived and prevailed.

Much more important, *Roots* affected the racial views of millions of white Americans. These viewers could never look at blacks the same way again after watching in the comfort of their living room—

soda on the lamp table, bags of chips in their laps, their own kids leaning against a chair watching with them—what had happened to black people.

The emotional and psychological effect of *Roots* on both black and white audiences was considerable. Scriptwriters continually used the word "nigger" in dialogue in which white plantation owners discussed their slaves. At one point, an owner who buys a girl for breeding looks directly into her eyes and says, "I own you." The line went like a dart into the hearts of viewers. The effect was the same when Kunta Kinte has his foot chopped off as punishment for an attempted escape, and another slave looks down at it and says, "What kind of a man would do that to another man?" In the miniseries, families are separated. Slaves are sold by one plantation owner to another merely to pay off a debt.

What *Roots* really did, however, consciously and not consciously, was shatter all of the myths about slavery that had been delivered to the American public since 1865. The slaves in *Roots* were honorable family men and women, God-fearing and righteous people who lived good lives in bondage and made their way as best they could under difficult conditions. The slaves helped their owners to protect the slaves' families, but they did nothing to help their owners keep them enslaved. They did not cakewalk and tap-dance to "Dixie." They were not all Mammies and Sambos. *Roots* destroyed all of those myths and gave America an entirely different look at slavery.

Seeing the sheer horror of slavery had a profound effect on viewers, an effect no one in television anticipated. U.S. Representative Parren J. Mitchell of Maryland, chair of the congressional Black Caucus at the time, was so upset by the series that he had to stop watching after two episodes. The feeling was explained best by critic Mike Muncell: "The brutality and indignity the black men suffered at the hands of the white men are enough to provoke outrage in human beings of any color—and no doubt will."[17]

Before *Roots* was broadcast, ABC's Stoddard had, as noted above, told reporters that there had *never, never* been a successful black drama. Well, there was *never, never* an audience reaction like America's response to *Roots* during the last week of January 1977. On the night the first episode aired, *Roots* had a rating of 51.1 and was viewed in 36.3 million homes, making television history and breaking the record held by *Gone With the Wind* (1976), which reached 33.9 million homes. The entire country was hooked. After that first night people returned to the tale of Kunta Kinte and his family night after night for another seven long winter nights, giving the miniseries a record 35.5 rating overall.[18] It was seen in 85 percent of all American homes each night and had ratings a colossal 10 points higher than the

Actor LeVar Burton plays Kunta Kinte as a young man in Roots, *which set ratings records and had a profound impact on many Americans.*

second-most-viewed television show in 1977. Historically, all eight of its episodes were rated among the thirteen most watched television shows of all time (newly inaugurated President Jimmy Carter, who rarely watched television, had all the episodes sent to him for private viewing).[19] Business at restaurants, movie theaters and sporting events was way down during *Roots* as Americans dropped everything to follow the saga.

At first the effects of the series based on the book were far-reaching. Schoolteachers discussed *Roots* for months. It was debated in college fraternities and sororities, where students gathered to watch it each night, and in newspaper offices, loading docks, mail rooms and airport lounges. LeVar Burton became an overnight star and within days of the first airing was besieged for autographs wherever he went (many African Americans asked him to autograph family Bibles).[20] Magazine editors quickly tried to make characters from *Roots* icons of popular culture, and one headline on a story about the series read: IS KUNTA KINTE THE NEXT FONZIE?[21] Political columnists wondered if *Roots* would have an immediate effect on U.S. foreign policy towards Africa.[22] Thieves broke into bookstores and stole thousands of copies of the book and hawked them on street corners for five dollars.[23]

Alex Haley, who had assisted in writing *The Autobiography of Malcolm X*, became a literary superstar, and ABC went ahead with plans to produce not only a show about his life, but two more series based on *Roots*. The book sold another million copies after the debut of the miniseries. Haley told anyone who interviewed him at the time that the great achievement of *Roots* was that it dispelled many false assumptions about black contributions to American society[24] and that *Roots* "was meant to be."[25]

Haley also claimed to be pleased, though not surprised, that his depiction of the atrocious treatment of blacks in slavery did not trigger a black reaction against contemporary white society. He told an interviewer: "I've not heard one murmur of radicalization from blacks. I have heard ebullience and happiness that the story has been told. The blacks who are buying books are not buying them to go out and fight someone, but because they want to know who they are. *Roots* is all of our stories. It's the same for me or any black—which person, living in which village, going on what ship, across the same ocean, slavery, emancipation and the struggle for freedom."[26]

Others saw *Roots* as a mass cultural catharsis for both blacks and whites. Lance Morrow, writing in *Time* magazine, said: "Oddly, many whites seem to feel not guilt but an unexpected shock of identification with blacks, while blacks experience a larger shock of pride at glimpsing a complete vision of where they have been and what they have overcome. Neither race has ever seen it quite that way before."[27]

Academics hoped that the series would do for race relations and black self-esteem what hundreds of textbooks never had. "To see the spirit with which their much maligned ancestors survive slavery is a great corrective to any lingering inferiority that blacks feel," said Howard University sociologist Clifton Jones.[28]

Roots changed the face of television. It not only validated the miniseries as a new and successful format, but it rearranged Hollywood thinking about what audiences wanted when they walked into a movie theater or sat down in front of a television set. It exploded many of the old industry verities. It ended the belief that audiences will not sit through a long movie or television show, the conviction that period costume dramas as a genre were dead, and the notion that shows with social relevance cannot find an audience. "There is an audience out there waiting for excellence," wrote Dave Kaufman in *Variety.*[29]

BUT WHAT kind of excellence?

In the years since the first airing, some critics have charged that in *Roots* a brand-new set of mythmakers dismantled one set of stories only to create others, and that the new ones were just as historically inaccurate as the old. Philip Nobile, among others, accused Haley of inventing some sections of the purportedly nonfiction book, which he had claimed was based on his own family's story. A *New York Times* book reviewer said that the author should have assembled his factual data in some sort of formal statement to distinguish it from fiction.[30] Some historians similarly criticized Haley for mixing up fact and fiction and convincing an entire country that the work was a true account of his own personal family history, a marvelous past that, in some respects at least, never happened.[31] After the success of the book and miniseries, the novelist Harold Courlander charged in a suit that Haley had borrowed heavily from his 1967 book *The African.*

Haley consistently defended the authenticity of *Roots,* but did pay a $650,000 settlement to Courlander and told reporters that three passages in *The African* had found their way into *Roots.* In 1997, on the twentieth anniversary of the publication of *Roots*, Lisa Drew, an editor at Doubleday, its publisher, acknowledged the book's murky portrayal of history, but said that its positive influence on America was more important. "Its impact is emotional rather than factual," she said.[32]

Authentic or not, *Roots* had several long-term effects. It stimulated the interest of many Americans, black and white, in their family histories, and thousands began to trace their lineage. Family searching became so popular that computer software was developed for it, libraries began to acquire hundreds of books on genealogy, and many established genealogy sections. Colleges began to develop courses and entire programs on black studies and, later, ethnic studies. An already strong trend among black Americans to adopt African names and wear African-style clothing was reinforced.

Americans' fascination with the book *Roots* itself, however, soon fell off. High school courses built just around the book *Roots* disappeared quickly. Interest in *Roots* travel tours lasted no more than a year or two, and the anticipated great wave of black and ethnic historical rediscovery never occurred. According to writer James Sleeper, the reason for *Roots*'s limited long-term influence lay in the past that Haley tried to re-create. When, Sleeper wrote, African Americans were finally given the impetus to explore their past, with the complete support of white America, they found that they were not really Africans after all. They were Americans. They had lived in bondage for 250 years, had been treated badly after emancipation and in contemporary America were still beleaguered by problems, yet they saw themselves as Americans. Whatever success they were going to have, present or future, would be in a country that, even in the face of the remaining difficulties and injustices in its treatment of them, was still their country. The warm feelings gained from reading or seeing *Roots* extended only so far. The rest of the journey in race relations required a focus on the future, not the past.

Nonetheless, that past, as portrayed at any rate in *Roots,* has continued to trouble Sleeper and many others. They have charged Haley with creating a fantastic myth about the African-American experience, first in Africa and then in America. In Sleeper's words: "*Roots* represents an attempt to re-create, in Judeo-Christian idiom, a journey which millions of Africans did not undertake."[33]

But this mythological journey, perhaps never taken by African Americans, was similar to the mythological journey never taken by white people in hundreds of silent and sound movies about the Civil War era—a journey taken, and thoroughly enjoyed, only by the myth-makers.

CHAPTER FOURTEEN

The Modern Era

THE ACTORS portraying Confederate soldiers under the command of General George Edward Pickett waited anxiously, some standing and some kneeling, others gripping various state and Confederate flags. Ahead, on top of a hill, thousands of other actors dressed as Union troops waited for the attack. To the right, crew members moved a long row of cameras into place. A special effects coordinator finished lining up explosives for the beginning of the assault. At a signal, the men portraying Confederates stood up and began to walk out of the woods and onto the open field. Obeying directions shouted from the right and following prearranged paths across the field, they moved towards the enemy in "Pickett's Charge" on the third and final day of the battle of Gettysburg.

Thousands of "reenactors" were used to play the soldiers of the Union and Confederate armies that day in the filming of Turner Network Television's production of *Gettysburg*. Reenactors—men and women history buffs who dress in period costumes to help reenact historical events—began to appear in the early 1960s. They helped museum and battlefield curators stage Civil War battles during the hundredth-anniversary celebrations. By 1989, when *Glory* was released, reenactors had become as well trained as many professional soldiers. The soldier reenactors had spent approximately six hundred dollars each on their uniforms, two hundred dollars or more on their rifles—all authentic. And as they refought the battles of the war for days at a time, the men often lived like soldiers in tents they had purchased.

Film and television producers sent camera crews to the various restaged battles and filmed them to use in their Civil War movies.

The Civil War received a whole new look when the courageous exploits of an all-black regiment, the Fifty-fourth Massachusetts, were highlighted in Glory, *in 1989.*

They also began hiring reenactors to spend several weeks on location for additional filming. The reenactors served two purposes: they were Civil War military buffs who fought just as the federals and rebels fought and gave films a marvelously authentic look, and they brought their own tents, uniforms and weapons, saving the filmmakers money. The footage, whether in Pickett's Charge in *Gettysburg,* or the Fort Wagner assault in *Glory,* was dazzling, and it gave audiences a riveting look at the brutal war never previously seen in simulated and hackneyed Hollywood battle scenes.

Reenactors also knew a great deal about the battles they were refighting, and they served as on-the-spot historical advisors. They told directors where troops moved in certain battles, how they would have fought and exactly how far away they would have been when musket firing commenced. Many had become experts in the weaponry of the period (Civil War reenactment companies often have their own artillery batteries) and advised filmmakers on how and where to fire cannons—and even brought their own cannons.

Dale Fetzer, of Historic Impressions, a company which supplied the weekend soldiers to films, said his reenactors gave films authen-

Reenactors, seen here in a battle scene from Gettysburg, *added excitement and authenticity to the Civil War films of the 1980s and '90s.*

ticity: "Our biggest accomplishment was that the staff of the 54th created a regiment under the same or similar circumstances that faced a Civil War colonel. He had volunteers, draftees, a mishmash of competence, people who wanted to be there and people who didn't. There were long periods of intense excitement and danger as men charged up hills with fixed bayonets as explosives blew up around them. It all comes across in the film. This was a very realistic army taking the field."[1]

Said Robert Lee Hodge, who worked on *Gettysburg:* "One of the greatest things that filming offered the re-enactors was the opportunity to film on the actual battlefield. To see over 40 full-scale Civil

War period cannons firing and over 4,000 re-enactors marching across the very field where Pickett's Charge actually took place was breathtaking! The officers yelling commands, fife and drum music playing in the air and ground charges exploding—it was truly emotional."[2]

In the years since reenactors began to work, Hollywood had undergone dramatic advances in technology and stunt work. This was clear in films such as *Gettysburg,* released in 1993. As long lines of Confederate soldiers moved towards Cemetery Ridge during Pickett's Charge, dozens of stuntmen dressed as Confederates trotted with them and then, on cue, following a carefully planned explosion nearby, leaped off springboards buried in the field. Soldiers' bodies appeared to be blown up and into the air.

The reenactors sat around campfires and played Civil War–era musical instruments, like dulcimers; and played Civil War card games, like whist; and talked endlessly about battles and personalities. "It didn't take long to develop a camaraderie among the reenactors, just like it didn't take long for soldiers," said Rick Faulcon, of Washington, D.C.[3]

Glory was the first major Civil War movie to use hundreds of reenactors, employing some six thousand white amateur soldiers and more than two hundred blacks. *Glory*'s crew also spent much time, effort and money re-creating Fort Wagner, the centerpiece of the film's finale.[4] The realistic sets impressed many residents of Savannah, where the battle was filmed. The producers built a huge, three-sided beachfront fort (the fourth side was open for the cameras and directors) to serve as their Fort Wagner. Workers under the guidance of the Georgia Department of Natural Resources labored for three months to erect the thirty-foot-high fort, reenforcing it with sand walls, plywood, ten truckloads of timber, steel beams and wood cornices. People from the area watched the construction of the fort day by day. When it was finished, one resident of Jekyll Island, where the fort was erected, gazed admiringly at it, shook his head and said, "With forts like that, I don't know how we lost the war!"[5]

Critics applauded the authenticity of the Civil War films made in the 1980s and 1990s, particularly the work of the reenactors. "The battle scenes are some of the best ever filmed. These are not the soldiers of Griffith or Huston, swarming over hills and ducking behind trees, but nakedly vulnerable opposing flanks, armed chiefly with one-shot rifles, and backed by mortars . . . ," Gary Giddins wrote of *Glory* in the *Village Voice*.[6]

Glory was doubly daring for filmmakers because it was not only a film with vivid and frightening battle scenes and finely etched dramatic characters, but a film that shattered the great Civil War movie taboo—it told a story of African Americans. The movie opened at the same time as interest in the war overall was growing. James M. McPherson's Civil War book *Battle Cry of Freedom* won the Pulitzer Prize in 1988 and sparked a whole new wave of nonfiction books about the war. As the war's 125th anniversary approached, the books were followed by a collection of cable television documentaries about the conflict. Reenactor regiments grew in size as the restaging of key battles loomed.

Blacks had never appeared as combat soldiers in Civil War films except as part of the background. But now, in *Glory,* Hollywood was not only putting hundreds of blacks on screen, but at long last showing them as the heroes. The story of black soldiers in the Civil War had rarely been told and the tale of the Fifty-fourth Massachusetts Volunteers was not chronicled in books until the 1960s and the publication of Lincoln Kirstein's *Lay This Laurel* and Peter Burchard's *One Gallant Rush*. The role of blacks in the Civil War was in fact so obscure that neither Freddie Fields, the film's producer; Ed Zwick, the director; nor Denzel Washington, the star, knew the story.

Fields, a veteran Hollywood producer, happened to be in Boston one day in 1986 and, unable to hail a cab, decided to cut across Boston Common to his hotel. On the way, he walked past the monument to the black Fifty-fourth Massachusetts regiment there. "I had the same view of the Civil War as everyone else—Lincoln and the North beat the South and freed the slaves. I never knew blacks actually fought in it," said Fields, who produced or was involved with the production of such hits as *Crimes of the Heart, Looking for Mr. Goodbar, Poltergeist II* and *Rocky II*. "I knew the 125th anniversary of the war was coming up and thought right away that this would make a great movie, the unknown story finally told," he said.[7]

Ed Zwick, who had directed the hit 1980s television series *thirtysomething,* knew less about the war than Fields and nothing about black soldiers. "I never heard of the 54th and when I was a student at Harvard I must have walked past their monument in the Common a thousand times," he said.[8] Denzel Washington saw his character as a role model, but admitted he had had no knowledge of blacks fighting for the Union army. "I was a good student in school, read everything, and I never read that," he said. "We had a black and white view of history. I was eager to do the role to show people how brave these men were, that they were willing to die for their freedom."[9]

It was not easy for Fields to raise the needed $20 million for the film because, since *Gone With the Wind,* few Civil War movies had turned much of a profit. All period movies were expensive because producers needed outdoor locations and, most costly of all, thousands of extras wearing thousands of uniforms and carrying thousands of rifles. Now a Hollywood producer not only was trying to find investors for an expensive costume drama involving many extras and historic locations, but wanted to make the blacks the good guys.[10] Few period films did well at the box office, either. "Everybody told me I was crazy to do this," said Fields. "I told all of them the same thing. *Gone With the Wind* was a period film. *Gandhi* was a period film. *Lawrence of Arabia* was a period film. They were all great movies. It doesn't matter if a film is period. A great movie is a great movie."[11]

Neither Fields nor Zwick wanted to follow the traditional formula. The two were making a movie about black soldiers and from the very first screen treatment they wanted to make the unknown foot soldiers in the regiment, the men who did all the fighting and dying, the heroes.[12] The commander, Colonel Robert Shaw, played by Matthew Broderick, became the character with the most lines, but was not the focus of the story.[13]

In 1989, many black leaders were angry with the direction in which black historical films were going; they targeted *Mississippi Burning* (1988) more than any other because whites, not blacks, wound up as the focus of the story.[14] But *Glory* was different. The story of the black regiment, told through the men in it, was one of the most accurate Civil War films ever made. Scriptwriter Kevin Jarre (who wrote one of the *Rambo* movies with Sylvester Stallone) and Zwick did voluminous research to ensure they had the true story of the Fifty-fourth, and the other black regiments of the war. Shelby Foote, who later gained prominence as a commentator on Ken Burns's series on the Civil War on PBS, was hired as head historian.[15]

The fact is that many blacks wanted to fight in the Union army as soon as the war began. In May 1861, a month after Fort Sumter, Frederick Douglass wrote in his newspaper, "Let the slaves and free colored people be called into service and formed into a liberating army," and told Lincoln that he could enlist ten thousand blacks in a week.[16]

Blacks in the U.S. Army were certainly not new. Five thousand blacks fought in the Continental Army during the American Revolution (eight hundred fought on the British side, hoping a British victory would bring an end to slavery).[17] Hundreds more fought in the U.S. Navy during the War of 1812.[18] Lincoln, however, was at first fearful of having blacks in the Union army because of lingering Northern resentment[19] over slavery as the cause of the war.[20] (A dozen blacks were killed in the New York City draft riots of 1863.)[21] In 1863, however, as the war continued to go badly for the Union, he decided to enroll as many black soldiers as possible. Northern recruiters were soon overwhelmed with black volunteers and in the summer of 1863 began to form them into regiments. The Fifty-fourth lost half its men in its valiant charge on Fort Wagner, outside of Charleston, South Carolina, but the heroism of those men gave blacks a whole new image within the army. "But for three companies of the 54th (colored), our whole regiment would have been captured. They fought like heroes . . . ," wrote one white soldier.[22] (The first black to ever win the Congressional Medal of Honor, William Carney, earned it for bravery at Fort Wagner. All in all, a dozen black soldiers won the Medal of Honor during the war.)[23] Their participation helped turn the course of the conflict. By the time the war ended, more than 300,000 blacks had served in the Union army, 180,000 of them in combat, and 30,000 had died.

Black soldiers were always segregated in their own regiments, were always commanded by white officers and were routinely discriminated against, but they fought on, bravely, until the end. Zwick wanted to show their bravery. In an interview he explained: "After the Emancipation Proclamation, the easiest thing in the world would have been for these freed slaves to go away and start new lives. Real history shows us that these men did not want Abraham Lincoln to simply hand them their freedom—they wanted to fight for it. The whole idea of this movie is to tell people today that the blacks got nothing, that they put their lives on the line for themselves and families just like everybody else did."[24]

Glory was made to commemorate (and cash in on) the 125th anniversary of the war, to give Americans a realistic look at black soldiers and the psychological complexities of their lives in the Civil War. It widened the scope of cinematic investigation to include a look at *all* the soldiers for the first time and it also offered struggling young black men an inspirational movie.

It was a movie that explained not only the black soldiers' fight for freedom in 1863, but the fight within themselves for their manhood. The need to attain manhood was a subtle undercurrent running throughout the film. In slavery, black men had none; they were mere property. In freedom, they had it but were seen by a white society only as former slaves. In the movie, on the night before the battle one of the soldiers tells the regiment they have to "prove that we're men" and the soldiers nod knowingly. The black soldiers had to prove it twice— once to America and once to themselves. They saw the war as a chance not only to gain some equality with whites, but to show the next generation of blacks that the chains were gone.

In *Glory* there is a poignant scene, bathed in marvelous Dvorak music, in which the troops of the Fifty-fourth trudge past the huge white colonial mansion of a recently liberated slave plantation in South Carolina. A dozen small black children line the fence along the road to watch wide-eyed as the first black troops they have ever seen march by. A sergeant, played by Morgan Freeman, turns to one little boy, bends over slightly and says, "You ain't dreamin' . . . ," then marches off, the boy's eyes following him in admiration. This scene symbolizes the success of the Fifty-fourth.

While several television series portraying African Americans as traditional, hardworking middle-class families opened the door to films like *Glory,* many blacks still complained bitterly that shows like *Cosby* were a charade, that real black life was a struggle.

The statistics were that in the late 1980s over 55 percent of all black children lived hopelessly mangled family lives, with one parent, usually the mother. Other surveys showed that young black men were the most likely to go to jail, most likely to be murdered and least likely to earn a college degree. In short, despite the sanitized view of African Americans on television, the average young black male in the late 1980s was suffering from extremely low self-esteem and was unable to relate to positive male role models. Many drifted into urban gangs, dropped out of school and fell prey to drug dealers. In the interview quoted earlier, *Glory* director Zwick suggested as role models the men of the Fifty-fourth: " 'Black teenagers today want role models? They want some real-life, working-class men to look up to and complain they can't find any?' he said, his voice rising to an angry pitch. 'Here are 180,000 of them!' he said, tossing a *Glory* press book on the table."[25]

Glory's accurate presentation of the courageous blacks fighting for freedom in the Union army was a far cry from the scandalous portrayal of black soldiers in *The Birth of a Nation* seventy-five years before. After three quarters of a century, it helped correct Hollywood's view of history.[26] It also redefined the villain of the war. Except for a single, one-minute battle scene and a single moment at the end of the film, the Confederate army, while discussed, is never seen. The enemy is not that army. The enemy, wherever it is found, is racism. The movie shows that there was racism within the Union army almost equal to the racism of the South.

Glory won strong critical reviews. "Maybe one's good response to *Glory* derives from the sheer novelty of the thing and from admiration for the producer's gumption in flinging it in the face of the movie audience's indifference to the pre-televised past," wrote Richard Schickel in *Time*.[27] The *Los Angeles Times*'s Kevin Thomas thought it was one of the finest films of the year. "*Glory* is an eloquent, heart-tugging Civil War epic about the first black infantry regiment to march off to battle for the Union. And epic is the word," wrote Thomas, who singled out the work of Morgan Freeman and Denzel Washington.[28]

Glory won even stronger praise from historians, ordinarily critical of any historical movie. Analyzing the film in the *American Historical Review*, Gerald Horne wrote: "Hollywood finally gets this chapter of history right. Though not without flaws, this gripping drama underscores the decisive role of African-Americans in a war whose reverberations are still felt in the Constitution and does so in a manner that should inspire the viewer to pick up a history book and learn more about it."[29]

Writing of *Glory* in *The New Republic*, McPherson said: "It is not only the first feature film to treat the role of black soldiers in the Civil War, it is also the most powerful and historically accurate movie about the war ever made. If it wins the popularity it deserves, it will go far to correct the distortions and romanticizations of such earlier block-busters as *The Birth of a Nation* and *Gone With the Wind*. It may also help to restore the courageous image of the black soldiers and their white officers that prevailed in the North after the war, before the process of romanticizing the Old South obscured that image."[30]

Glory also allowed the development of projects for television about blacks in the military. One was *Buffalo Soldiers,* a Turner Network Television movie aired in December 1997, which starred actor Danny Glover, who also served as executive producer. The film was the story of the all-black cavalry regiments in the West in the 1880s, but Glover, who called the project "one of history's untold stories," said it was grounded in the Civil War. "He was a veteran of the Civil War," Glover said of his character. "He honed his skills in battle. He's the kind of soldier who follows orders and has strong beliefs in his own cap-abilities."[31]

The next major Civil War film after *Glory* was Turner's *Gettysburg,* based on Michael Shaara's Pulitzer Prize–winning novel *The Killer Angels.* The novel was written from the Southern point of view, with Robert E. Lee and James Longstreet as its main characters. Colonel Joshua Chamberlain, head of the Twentieth Maine Volunteers, who saved the battle for the North with their defense of Little Round Top, is the main Northern figure in the novel and a much more substantial figure in the film.

Ted Turner, head of Turner Entertainment (CNN, TBS, TNT), and a Southerner, who had a cameo role as a Southern colonel in the movie, quickly became committed to the project and spared no expense. Martin Sheen was signed to play Lee, Tom Berenger to play Longstreet and Jeff Daniels to star as Chamberlain. The producers hired nationally recognized Civil War historians such as Gabor Boritt, a professor at Gettysburg College, to assure authenticity. The film's luscious music was written by Randy Edelman, who wrote the music for *The Last of the Mohicans.* Filming took place at Gettysburg itself, on parts of the national battlefield, and the production company con-tributed fifty thousand dollars to the Association for the Preservation of Civil War Sites and another fifty thousand dollars to the Friends of the Gettysburg National Park. After difficult negotiations, the pro-duction company paid each reenactor group it used one thousand dollars plus ten dollars per man, and it had no problems attracting five thousand volunteers from forty-seven states.[32]

Gettysburg, a three-hour movie and later a six-hour miniseries (in which footage edited out of the feature was used), was hailed by many Civil War students, especially because at six hours it was able to investigate all of the complex subplots involved in the battle and develop deep characterizations of the key soldiers. Also, it had the best-staged Civil War battle scenes in motion picture history.

The reenactors in the film came to see the actors as the characters they were playing. Martin Sheen was startled one morning when he rode by a group of reenactors preparing for the Pickett's Charge scene. The reenactors were so immersed in the production that when Sheen appeared on horseback dressed as Lee they began yelling "Lee! Lee!" evidently taking the actor as truly the commander of the Army of Northern Virginia. Director Ron Maxwell had his cameramen begin filming and it became one of the most powerful scenes in the movie.

According to Maxwell: "One of the ironies of *The Killer Angels* [Shaara's novel] is that we understand and identify with each one of the characters. We have great sympathy for them; we care about them. We're attracted to them, we admire their zeal, their compassion, their commitment. Every character is quite exemplary, quite likable. At the same time, every one of them is ready to kill for what he believes in."[33]

Although the novel is pro-South, the movie attempts to offer a balanced look at the hopes and aspirations of men on both sides. They are all portrayed as heroes, from the men undergoing amputations in Confederate field hospitals to the young boys on Union lines, shot through the head. Long conversations that underline the devotion of men on both sides to their cause, which they clearly believe right, are included in the first half of the movie. Lee is clearly the hero of the piece, the valiant underdog trying to win against all odds, but he is portrayed as dead wrong on his decision to order Pickett's famous charge. Longstreet is seen as a courageous Confederate general with strong doubts about Lee's tactics. It is not just the big people but the little people who come to represent the bravery of all Confederates in the film. The best example is a scene in which a civilian scout, although told the charge will be a disaster, insists on getting a rifle and putting his life in jeopardy.

Courage on the Northern side is exemplified by Colonel Joshua Chamberlain, a schoolteacher from Maine, who keeps cool in the hot battle over Little Round Top, a key location, and orders a bold bayonet charge into rebel lines that gives the North a startling victory. Through Chamberlain, the quiet civilian-turned-soldier, the movie implies that all Northerners are brave. Here, too, there are little people who underline the theme. A group of detained deserters, who do not have to fight, take up arms anyway when they see the battle might be lost.

Again and again in *Gettysburg,* it is hinted that either side might have won if its luck had changed. The film is not about North and South, but about Americans fighting bravely for their country. In a telling scene, as Pickett's Charge is about to begin, General Lewis Armistead, who will soon die, stands with a British visitor. Pointing out a number of men in his command, the Confederate general reminds the Englishman that they are all related to Virginians who were among the founding fathers of America. Here, today, he proudly tells the visitor, they are fighting for Virginia, for their ancestors, for freedom. The very best elements in American history are conjured up in the touching speech, and the very worst elements, slavery and racism, ignored.

THE SORDID STORY of the Confederate prison camp Andersonville, in Georgia, had been one of the great taboos of Civil War cinema. Andersonville was a stockade prison built in the winter of 1864 on twenty-six acres and intended for ten thousand men, but its population quickly swelled to nearly thirty-three thousand.[34] Terrible conditions and the polluted stream running through its center resulted in the deaths of as many as one hundred prisoners a day; thirteen thousand died there in its one year of existence. The atrocities were so bad that at the end of the war its commandant, Henry Wirz, became the only Confederate executed for war crimes.

The horror of Andersonville in Union minds was compounded by the remarks of an editor for the *Atlanta Intelligencer,* who wrote at the time about the misery and deaths there: "we thank heaven for such blessings."[35] Many Southerners reading that cringed; they warned their political leaders that there would be dire retribution when the war ended.[36]

Andersonville did not fit into the Plantation Myth at all. Hollywood stayed away from it. The beginning of renewed interest in Andersonville began with publishers and the Broadway stage as the centennial of the war's outbreak approached. In 1960, MacKinlay Kantor won the Pulitzer Prize for his scathing novel *Andersonville,* about the atrocities at the prison camp. In 1959, Saul Levitt's *Andersonville,* a three-act court-martial drama that pitted Wirz against a determined prosecutor, was produced.

World events swiftly brought Levitt's indictment of Andersonville back into the public sphere. In late 1971, several U.S. Army officers were court-martialed for the brutal slaughter of civilians at My Lai in 1968, during the Vietnam War. The massacre and the officers' defense—that they were only following orders—drew worldwide attention, and comparisons to Wirz and the Andersonville story were inevitable.

Just after the My Lai massacre, Hollywood producer Lewis Freedman signed a deal to produce a series of dramas for CBS, which was battling NBC and ABC for television supremacy. His first selection was Levitt's play, and he decided—brilliantly—to hire actor George C. Scott, who had just won an Oscar portraying gung ho World War II leader George Patton, to direct. William Shatner played the prosecutor and Richard Basehart the weak and hapless Wirz. *The Andersonville Trial* was aired in 1970.

It was a finely crafted and emotionally devastating drama. Television's small screen created a narrow focus for the courtroom story, and riveting performances by Shatner and Basehart, and Scott's taut direction, earned the show good ratings and strong reviews. It was called "the finest video drama of the season,"[37] "a blessing to be counted,"[38] and "an embarrassment of acting riches."[39]

All the critics zeroed in on the issue of an officer's loyalty to his superiors versus his loyalty to mankind. "There's a scene in the story where a general refuses to postpone the Andersonville trial and bellows, 'The trial cannot be postponed into the next century,' but, with My Lai, it was," Freedman said, linking the Vietnam incident to his own drama about the Civil War.[40]

Scott concurred, and said that what made Wirz so culpable was that he had plenty of time to organize and plan the running of Andersonville, heard hundreds of complaints, saw thousands of men die and yet did nothing. My Lai, Scott told interviewers, at least occurred in a hot war zone, in the middle of combat, when the men charged were making decisions with little time to think about them.[41]

Diana Loercher, writing in the *Christian Science Monitor,* likened the trial of Wirz in America to the 1960 trial of Adolf Eichmann in Israel.[42] Tom Mackin of the *Newark Evening News* compared it to the Nuremberg trials.[43] Gail Rock, in *Women's Wear Daily,* suggested that the story paralleled the trial of the Chicago Seven—demonstrators arrested in connection with the riots outside the 1968 Democratic National Convention in Chicago.[44]

"It was a play for the times, echoing Dachau, Auschwitz and more recently My Lai, as well as moral issues raised by students dissenting from the war in Indochina while facing the barrels and bayonets of rifles in the hands of National Guardsmen 'obeying orders,' " said one critic.[45] Kay Gardella, in the New York *Daily News* saw the play as a message that cut across centuries. "It's a case of universal guilt, the guilt of one man becomes the guilt of all men," she said.[46]

A quarter century later, in 1996, the Southern prison was thrust into the spotlight once again in the richly produced television mini-series *Andersonville,* by Turner Network Television.

Andersonville, directed by John Frankenheimer, showed all the barbarity of the Andersonville prison camp. In a throwaway line of dialogue a character says, truthfully, that Northern prisons such as Elmira were just as bad. Actually, there were more than one hundred prison camps, North and South, and all were run poorly.[47] The film apportions blame for the exceedingly high death rate at Andersonville among Wirz, the cold, murderous guards, and the Confederate government, which, according to the filmmakers, knew all about conditions there and did nothing.

In Turner's miniseries, Wirz is not seen very often and the guards are little more than background figures. The real story is the prisoners' fight to stay alive under grim conditions and, within that story, how prisoners beat and murdered other prisoners. "Raiders," Union prisoners who beat up and killed others for food and possessions, are put on trial by their fellow prisoners and hanged. The scene was intended to show that Northerners in war were just as heinous as Southerners.

The viewers' first impression watching TNT's *Andersonville* is that the South was barbaric, particularly at Andersonville. But the real message of the film was that there were severe atrocities on both sides during the war. During the trial of the "raiders," their self-appointed attorney tells the crowd of prisoners that they turned into animals because they were in a prison where they were treated like animals. Clearly, war makes ordinary men commit terrible acts they would never consider in peacetime. In the end, it is not North or South but war itself that is the villain.

It was not just events of the war that received new analysis in films of the 1980s and 1990s. Reconstruction received a new interpretation,

Richard Gere works amid waist-high tobacco plants in a field, with his mansion in the background, in Sommersby, *a 1990s film about Reconstruction.*

too. In *Sommersby,* a 1993 film starring Richard Gere and Jodie Foster, and based on the French film *The Return of Martin Guerre,* townspeople speculate about the transformed personality of a Confederate soldier. Sommersby, played by Gere, returns to Tennessee after the war and attempts to run a mill with whites and blacks working side by side.[48] He is now an open-minded man, not the crude redneck who went off to fight.[49] Instead of beating his wife, as he did before, he now has a loving relationship with her, and together with their workers they drive off the KKK. (In a trial, Sommersby appears before a black judge.)

The aim of the film, of course, was to redefine the Southern soldier for a 1993 audience, giving him all new and politically correct views on race, class and women. It worked. "Master Jack has become populist Jack!" said one critic.[50] The relationship between the characters portrayed by Gere and Foster, too, gave a revisionist spin to the tried-and-true man-woman relationships in Civil War films. That's what enticed Foster to take the role. "In a time when women couldn't even sign their name to property . . . this [co-op farm] is a way for an unconventional woman to be an authentic person," she said, adding that the movie portrayed the real love that must have existed between Southern men and women during Reconstruction.[51] (The film was made in Virginia. The production used Warwickton, an old slave plantation built in 1851, and built a village of thirty buildings nearby as the town.)[52]

The movie was quite successful, grossing over $140 million. Its real success, though, was in once again rewriting Civil War history to show Gere's rebel as a well-intentioned, loving man whom anyone, North or South, could admire.

A different kind of look at history came from independent filmmaker Ken Burns, who convinced PBS that the best way to see the Civil War was through a comprehensive documentary television series. His acclaimed miniseries, which aired in 1990, was used as a teaching tool in many elementary and secondary schools (much the way *Shenandoah* had been thirty years before). It combined lingering looks at actual war photographs with views of those same battlefields today. The miniseries, like other Civil War productions from the 1980s to 1990, is aimed at tearing down many of the old myths about the conflict and, according to Burns, giving Americans a new and more realistic look at the causes of the war and the way in which it was fought:

> We labor under pernicious myths of the Civil War—from *Birth of a Nation* to *Gone With the Wind*. After the war, we smothered it with this gallant, bloodless myth that basically said it was a bunch of

white guys nobly fighting one another for these principles that didn't really have to do with anything. This is a country that holds as its favorite general a man who was, in fact, a traitor to the United States of America, responsible for more American deaths than Hitler or Tojo. And yet, we have the bigheartedness, the compassion to embrace the contradiction of Robert E. Lee. He is our greatest general. And that's where the Civil War speaks to us. Unfortunately, we perpetuated a lot of myths.[53]

Burns's most powerful new look at the war concerned slavery. Few films or television dramas had discussed slavery as the primary cause of the war because any such discussion made reunification difficult. Burns, however, spent an entire episode in his series discussing slavery, showing stark, vivid photographs of slaves with dozens of deep lash marks on their backs from beatings. He was intent on portraying powerful Southerners as men fighting a war that killed many thousands of people to defend what Burns saw as the indefensible slave system.

Using photographs and diaries, the series did make the fight of the ordinary soldiers admirable. Both sides became gallant and, by the end of the series, as in so many movies in the past, the viewer is left with the feeling that all the men fought for what they sincerely believed to be right.

These cultural works came at a time when, following the Vietnam War and the Watergate political scandal, Americans began to yearn for nobler national leadership, providing opportunity for more realistic productions about Abraham Lincoln. This had begun in 1964, when Jason Robards starred in a television revival of *Abe Lincoln in Illinois*. He played Sherwood Anderson's sainted President Lincoln in a more believable way. This continued in 1970 when ABC produced a musical about Lincoln, *Flatboat Man*. *Mr. Lincoln*, starring Roy Dotrice, which aired on PBS in 1981, portrayed Lincoln as a more ordinary politician, not a knighted savior. There were several dramas about the assassination, such as *They've Killed President Lincoln*, which aired on NBC in 1971. Hal Holbrook was a believable Lincoln in *Sandburg's Lincoln*, a series of specials during the 1974, 1975 and 1976 TV seasons, and played him forcefully in the sprawling and finely written 1985 miniseries *North and South*, based on John Jakes's nov-

els. (The *North and South* miniseries also portrayed sexual relationships between black men and white women.) Lincoln was written
into several movies, such as *Ironclads,* and miniseries as a minor character. In these films he was seen as a hardworking and conscientious
leader. Later, in *Tad,* a story about Lincoln and his son, he was seen as
a devoted father.

Among the best Lincoln films and television shows were those
centered on Mary Lincoln. The first lady's commitment to a mental
institution by her son Robert was the subject of an opera, *The Trial of
Mary Lincoln,* aired on PBS in 1971. She was brilliantly portrayed by
Julie Harris in *The Last of Mrs. Lincoln,* a televised play shown on
WNET in 1976, and by Mary Tyler Moore in *Lincoln.* These new
looks at Mary did not present her as a neurotic but as a woman ravaged by numerous tragedies in her life: the deaths of three of her four
sons and the murder of her husband.

In *Lincoln,* the President was portrayed by Sam Waterston as a
shrewd politician and deeply emotional man who worked hard to
steer his country through the horrific war, all the time worried about
his troubled wife and grieving for his dead son. It was one of the best
portrayals of any president. Later, in 1998, Turner Entertainment premiered *The Day Lincoln Was Shot,* based on Jim Bishop's book.
Although the movie followed the standard storyline of Lincoln's assassination by actor John Wilkes Booth, it gave audiences a very realistic
Abraham Lincoln, played by Lance Henriksen. His Lincoln was not
the old Father Abraham but a complex and vibrant political leader
determined to win the war but win it without a postwar bloodbath of
war crimes trials or executions. "I became determined to make Lincoln human. He was anything but a monolithic human being. It's not
just about the famous speeches; it's how he lived with all those things
going on around him. He never gave up," said Henriksen."[54]

Some movies of the 1990s started controversy over their interpretations of history. The release in 1997 of Steven Spielberg's well-made
film *Amistad,* the true story of a pre–Civil War mutiny of blacks on a
slave ship and their subsequent trial, triggered such a debate. The
movie won high praise from critics and most scholars, but others
attacked it as a seriously distorted account (*Amistad* expert Clifton
Johnson gave it a five on a scale of one to ten for authenticity)[55] or as a
classic example of a white director telling the story of African Ameri-

cans. "African-American stories always get changed to attract the cross-over, suburban audience," said Ishmael Reed. "I mean, when you make *Spartacus,* Spartacus is the hero, right? But I'm worried that a story about an African slave revolt is going to end up having John Quincy Adams as its hero."[56]

Others who saw *Amistad,* either as a film or as the 1998 opera, felt just the opposite; one critic of the opera charged that its composer

Matthew McConaughey, as white lawyer Roger Baldwin, talks to one of his black clients in a crowded courtroom in Amistad.

and director turned the story about whites helping blacks into little more than an African folktale.[57]

Some historians felt that everyone connected to the *Amistad* story, no matter which version, became ensnared in the legend. "Spielberg . . . passed up history for mythology. Yet most historians have, understandably (if mistakenly) kept mum. We know the score: We are supposed to be grateful that someone has finally put the horrors of slavery on the big screen," wrote historian Warren Goldstein, who added that he thought the film was "downright slanderous" of everybody involved.[58]

A moderately successful 1999 movie about guerrilla warfare in Missouri, *Ride with the Devil,* pleased critics and viewers looking for a new interpretation of the story of the usually reviled border state guerrillas but annoyed some who saw any understanding of them as wrong. Disputes erupted in theater, too. Another stage version of *Uncle Tom's Cabin* was produced in 1997, with the addition to the script of heated dialogue by actors about the criticism of the Uncle Tom story over the years.[59]

Other cultural works, such as the 1999 Broadway musical *The Civil War,* continued the time-honored theme of reunification. Reportedly based on a compendium of true stories, *The Civil War* simply merges legend with myth and labels it history. The sentimental songs salute the stories that have existed since the days of Thomas Nelson Page and have been faithfully re-created in so many Civil War movies: brother fighting against brother, the wife at home pining for her soldier boy gone to war, terrified Yanks, and rebs singing about their fearlessness and love of old Virginia. These scenes and stories use the cherished myths about the war to bring people in the audience together again, as they must have come together after the war, and remind them that out of the bloodshed came a great nation. Program notes describe the Union soldiers as men who "fight the battle of hardship in a war far from home" and the Confederates as "romantic, swashbuckling cavaliers to whom the war is a gleaming adventure."[60] These descriptions at the end of the twentieth century are not far removed from similar descriptions used by Hollywood and the stage at the century's beginning. However much the Plantation Myth has changed over the years, its basic foundation seems to have remained intact.

LARGE-SCREEN action-adventure military movies of any kind are not only difficult to produce, they are very costly. *Glory,* made for about $20 million, did wind up as one of the top thirty films of 1990 in terms of gross,[61] but did not earn as much net profit as producers hoped. *Gettysburg,* too, was a financial failure in its theatrical release. These two movies do have a longer shelf life than the old blue-and-gray stories, however, through video rentals and rebroadcasts on television. Television is a rich supplement to the cinema for Civil War stories. Television production companies can produce films for far less than it costs to make a feature film. Networks that purchase a film from a production company usually sign an agreement that gives them the right to air the film several times during its first year and repeat it frequently in subsequent years. A television movie seen by only 6 or 7 million people in one showing can eventually reach an audience of 20 or 30 million over several years. TNT has used *Gettysburg* brilliantly, usually showing the miniseries several times during the year and then showing it as a single six-hour saga as a holiday special on the Fourth of July. *Gone With the Wind* is shown repeatedly on TNT.

The advantage television has over theaters is that although television is driven by ratings, it does not require immediate results at the box office (this is especially true of public television). Movies for theaters about wars or historical epics must make money and make it right away: their costs are much higher because of specially constructed sets, thousands of costumes and large casts. (*Titanic* cost $220 million.)

The advent of cable television has meant numerous outlets for movies about history and the Civil War. Networks are positioned to produce their own new programming or buy independent productions. All of these seem to seek more sophisticated, educational programming produced in an entertaining way, which makes them potential venues for well-staged Civil War dramas. With repeated showings of Civil War–era films, these networks offer the opportunity for Americans to learn more about the most divisive and important chapter in their history through television, and not through theaters.[62]

Television producers have also discovered that audiences will enjoy well-done historical documentaries that use still photographs (such as Ken Burns's series) just as much as biographies of recent figures that use film footage. The producers have also found that shows using a combination of still photographs, paintings and dramatic scenes in which actors reenact history, such as the 1997 PBS miniseries *LIBERTY! The American Revolution,* succeed. And of course the History Channel has become an outlet for documentaries and films about historical events.

The tried-and-true nationalistic themes continue to appear in made-for-television films about the Civil War and films that allude to it. One of the most poignant was *Rough Riders,* a 1997 TNT film about Theodore Roosevelt and his regiment in the Spanish-American War. In one early scene, a small boy stands with his elderly grandfather, whose snow-white hair is tucked under his Confederate army cap. The boy and the Confederate veteran watch hundreds of U.S. Army troops who are training for combat walk past them in a Florida town. The boy, excited to see the troops who will be fighting for his country, tugs at his grandfather's sleeve and says in disbelief as he sees their blue uniforms, "They're Yankees!" The grandfather, an oversized reunification figure, nods knowingly, tugs on his rebel cap and tells his grandson, "No, son, they're Americans."

That idea of nationhood was underscored again in 1999, when Turner Network Television presented a stirring feature film, *The Hunley,* about the Confederate navy's submarine. The promotional ads that aired for weeks on TNT did not tell viewers that the *Hunley* was built to overthrow the government of the United States but rather that it was built "to save a nation," melding together, after 134 years, the notion that bravery in the Civil War, regardless of the army, was for the nation, the American nation.

MOVIES AND television dramas about the Civil War era have changed as the political, social and cultural views of Americans have changed. Following the Civil Rights movement of the 1960s, all audiences, black and white, were able to enjoy *Roots* and later *Glory* and add African Americans to the honor roll of the country, not exclude them. From the 1970s on, historians and filmmakers were able to offer new interpretations and information concerning the Civil War, to build a new, strong cultural nationalism that embraced all regions, races and ethnic groups. Americans were able to go to the movies or watch television and appreciate that new historical identity. Most important, Americans learned that they could appreciate diverse looks at their history because they had grown so much as a people.

Two events in the first year of the new millennium underlined that notion. The first Civil War–era movie of 2000 was *A House Divided,* a drama on the Showtime cable network which was set in the 1850s in the South. It told the story of a white slaveholder who rapes one of his teenage slaves and then brings up their white-skinned daughter as his own. This daring story of miscegenation and a mulatto child could never have been told a few decades before. But in 2000, the provocative story did not cause even a wisp of controversy for an American audience that had grown beyond those old taboos.

Earlier that year, in another symbolic event, the Confederate flag was lowered from the top of the statehouse in Columbia, South Carolina, the last statehouse to fly it. Over the years, many Americans had come to see rebel flags as symbols that celebrated slavery, not history. There were several weeks of heated political debate and protest marches, but little controversy after the flag finally came down. The Confederate flag was no longer needed as a symbol of Southern heritage. Southerners had another flag, the American flag.

NOTES

INTRODUCTION

1 Scene from *The Birth of a Nation,* Mutual Pictures, 1915.

2 Kimberly Peirce, quoted in *(Newark) Star-Ledger,* March 8, 2000.

3 David McCullough, quoted in James Kaplan, "Truth or Consequences," *TV Guide,* August 23, 1997, p. 29.

4 Simon Schama, "Onward and Upward with the Arts: Clio at the Multi-Plex," *New Yorker,* January 19, 1998, p. 40.

5 Jill Lepore, quoted in Scott Heller, "Studying War 'As a Contest of Words,' " *Chronicle of Higher Education,* March 27, 1998, p. A16.

6 Robert Seidenberg, "*Thirtysomething*'s Ed Zwick Goes to War—the Civil War," *American Film,* January 1990, p. 58.

7 James L. Sundquist, *Dynamics of the Party System: Alignment and Realignment of Political Parties in the United States* (Washington, D.C.: Brookings Institution, 1983), pp. 50–73.

8 Joseph Ingraham, *The Southwest, by a Yankee* (New York: Harper & Brothers, 1835), vol. 1, pp. 115–116; A. B. Meek, *Romantic Passages in Southwestern History: Including Orations, Sketches, and Essays* (New York: S. H. Goetzel, 1857), pp. 51, 52, 57–58. Daniel R. Hundley, in *Social Relations in Our Southern States* (New York: H. B. Price, 1860), reiterated their findings.

9 Thomas Dixon, quoted in Gary Crowdus, ed., *A Political Companion to American Film* (Chicago: Press, 1994), p. 117.

10 Eric Foner, in "A Conversation Between Eric Foner and John Sayles," *Past Imperfect,* ed. Mark Carnes (Chicago: Lakeview Press, 1994), p. 23.

11 Gore Vidal, *Screening History* (Cambridge: Harvard University Press, 1992), p. 81.

12 Danny Glover, quoted in Fletcher Roberts, "In the Black and White World of the Army," *New York Times,* television guide, December 7, 1997, p. 3.

13 Molly Haskell, *From Reverence to Rape: The Treatment of Women in the Movies* (New York: Holt, Rinehart & Winston, 1974), p. xii.

14 *New York Times,* March 8, 1998.

15 Ray Gill, quoted in Tony Horwitz, "Battle Acts: The Civil War Mania That Has Made Weekend War Games a National Pastime," *New Yorker,* February 8, 1998, p. 65.

16 Robert Penn Warren, *New and Selected Essays* (New York: Random House, 1989), p. 51.

17 William Faulkner, quoted in David Galef, "The South Has Risen Again, Everywhere," *New York Times,* October 18, 1997, Arts & Entertainment section, p. 39.

18 F. Scott Fitzgerald, *The Great Gatsby* (New York: Charles Scribner's Sons, 1925), p. 182.

19 Gideon Drori, quoted in Joel Greenberg, "Israel's History, Viewed Candidly, Starts a Storm," *New York Times,* April 10, 1998.

CHAPTER 1

1 James M. McPherson, *Abraham Lincoln and the Second American Revolution* (New York: Oxford University Press, 1990), p. 38.

2 See Donald Dodd and Wynelle Dodd, *Historical Statistics of the South, 1790–1970* (University: University of Alabama Press, 1973).

3 Rutherford B. Hayes, quoted in Paul Buck, *The Road to Reunion, 1865–1900* (Boston: Little, Brown, 1937), p. 102.

4 Thomas Connelly, *The Marble Man: Robert E. Lee and His Image in the American South* (New York: Alfred Knopf, 1977), p. 41.

5 Mark Neely Jr., Harold Holzer, and Gabor Boritt, *The Confederate Image: Prints of the Lost Cause* (Chapel Hill: University of North Carolina Press, 1987), pp. 68–90, 159.

6 C. Vann Woodward, *Tom Watson: Agrarian Rebel* (New York: Macmillan, 1938), p. 120.

7 See Buck, *Road to Reunion,* for a chronology of reconciliation initiatives.

8 John Esten Cooke, *Wearing of the Gray* (New York: E. B. Treat; Baltimore: J. S. Morrow, 1867), p. 204.

9 John Osborne and Editors of Time-Life Books, *The Old South* (New York: Time-Life Books, 1968), p. 57.

10 Edward A. Pollard, *The Lost Cause Regained* (New York: G. W. Carleton, 1866), pp. 45–62.

11 Fred Silva, ed., *Focus on "The Birth of a Nation"* (Englewood Cliffs, N.J.: Prentice-Hall, 1971), p. 136.

12 Thomas Cripps, *Slow Fade to Black: The Negro in American Film, 1900–1942* (New York: Oxford University Press, 1977), pp. 10–11.

13 *Scribner's Monthly Magazine,* July 1873.

14 *Scribner's Monthly Magazine,* October 1873.

15 *Scribner's Monthly Magazine,* August 1875, pp. 509–510.

16 John Williamson Palmer's story "An Old Virginian" appeared in the August 1881 issue.

17 Thomas Nelson Page, "Marse Chan: A Tale of Ole Virginia," *Century Illustrated Magazine,* April 1884, pp. 932–942.

18 Ibid., p. 942.

19 Quoted in James Randall, "The Blundering Generation," *Mississippi Valley Historical Review,* December 1940, pp. 3–28.

20 Richard Harwell, comp. and ed., *"Gone with the Wind" as Book and Film* (Columbia: University of South Carolina Press, 1983), p. 5.

21 Russell Merritt, "Dixon, Griffith, and the Southern Legend," *Cinema Journal,* fall 1972, p. 29.

22 Ritchie Devon Watson Jr., *Yeoman versus Cavalier* (Baton Rouge: Louisiana State University Press, 1993), p. 44.

23 In Albert Pike, *Lyrics and Love Songs* (Little Rock, Ark.: W. Allsopp, 1916), pp. 37–38.

24 Frank Ticknor, "The Virginian of the Valley," in *The Poems of Frank Ticknor,* ed. K. M. Rowland (Philadelphia, 1879), p. 22.

25 Ticknor, *Poems,* p. 53.

26 Fritz Machlup, *The Production and Distribution of Knowledge in the United States* (Princeton: Princeton University Press, 1962), pp. 208–210.

27 Harwell, *"Gone with the Wind" as Book and Film,* p. 7.

28 Pollard, *Lost Cause Regained,* p. 62.

29 For other works on the era, see C. Vann Woodward, *The Strange Career of Jim Crow,* and William A. Dunning, *Reconstruction, Political and Economic, 1865–1877* (New York: Harper & Brothers, 1907). For other books on the concept of Southern history in the cavalier tradition, see William R. Taylor, *Cavalier and Yankee: The Old South and American National Character* (New York: G. Braziller, 1961); Francis Pendleton Gaines, *The Southern Plantation* (New York: Columbia University Press, 1925); and Rollin G. Osterweis, *Romanticism and Nationalism in the Old South* (New Haven: Yale University Press, 1949).

30 James Buchanan, *Mr. Buchanan's Administration on the Eve of Rebellion* (New York: D. Appleton, 1866), pp. 57–66.

31 James Ford Rhodes, *Lectures on the American Civil War* (New York: Macmillan, 1913), pp. 1–6, 10–29, 41–66.

32 See Larry Easley, "The Santa Fe Trail, John Brown, and the Coming of the Civil War," in *Film & History,* May 1983, p. 30.

33 Allan Harper, "William A. Dunning: The Historian as Nemesis," *Civil War History,* March 1964.

34 William A. Dunning, *Essays on the Civil War and Reconstruction and Related Topics* (New York: Macmillan, 1931), p. 384.

35 Dunning, *Reconstruction,* p. 86.

36 Ibid., pp. 213–214.

37 Charles A. Beard and Mary Beard, *The Rise of American Civilization* (New York: Macmillan, 1927), vol. 2, pp. 28–54.

38 Gaines M. Foster, *Ghosts of the Confederacy: Defeat, the Lost Cause, and the New South, 1865 to 1913* (New York: Oxford University Press, 1987), pp. 188–190.

39 See Foster, *Ghosts of the Confederacy,* p. 182.

40 See William Henry Wegner, *The Representation of the American Civil War on the New York Stage, 1860–1900* (Ph.D. dissertation, New York University, 1966), p. 285.

41 See William Winter, *Shadows of the Stage* (New York: Macmillan, 1892), for history of these plays.

42 Rollin Osterweis, *The Myth of the Lost Cause* (Hamden, Conn.: Archon Books), p. 107.

43 Miriam Hansen, *Babel and Babylon: Spectatorship in American Silent Films* (Cambridge: Harvard University Press, 1991), p. 94.

44 Playwrights charged costly royalties of 5 to 10 percent for any presentation of their work. Studios began to hire their own screenwriters and frequently made them double as publicists, often churning out releases on their own films. It was less expensive to have a stable of writers altering stage plots than it was to pay royalties. That practice ended abruptly in 1907, when the publishers of Lew Wallace's novel *Ben Hur* sued Kalem Studios for stealing the book's plot for a film which Kalem claimed to be original. The publishers won a $25,000 judgment, a huge sum in that era, and the purloining of books stopped. Studios then turned to screenwriters for original stories.

45 Paul C. Spehr, comp., *The Civil War in Motion Pictures: A Bibliography of Films Produced in the United States since 1897* (Washington, D.C.: Library of Congress Publications, 1961), p. 3. Spehr's survey of silent films is a sturdy compendium of the war movies and their plots.

CHAPTER 2

1 Opening scene, *The Battle,* 1911.

2 Robert Sklar, *Movie-Made America: A Social History of American Movies* (New York: Random House, 1975), p. 4.

3 David Nasaw, *Going Out: The Rise and Fall of Public Amusements* (New York: Basic Books, 1993), p. 161.

4 *Moving Picture World,* January 11, 1908. Copy located in the Billy Rose Collection of the New York Public Library for the Performing Arts. Unless otherwise noted, all newspaper reviews and stories cited are from the New York Public Library's collections.

5 Kevin Brownlow, *Behind the Mask of Innocence: Sex, Violence, Prejudice, Crime; Films of Social Conscience in the Silent Era* (New York: Alfred A. Knopf, 1990), pp. 1–7, 188–219.

6 Sklar, *Movie-Made America,* p. 32.

7 Hansen, *Babel and Babylon,* p. 88.

8 Neal Gabler, *An Empire of Their Own: How the Jews Invented Hollywood* (New York: Crown Publishers, 1988), pp. 2–8.

9 *Moving Picture World,* May 17, 1914.

10 *Moving Picture World,* February 10, 1910.

11 Charles Harpole and Eileen Bowser, eds., *History of the American Cinema* (Berkeley: University of California Press, 1990), vol. 2, p. 178.

12 *Moving Picture World,* April 17, 1909.

13 *Moving Picture World,* February 27, 1909.

14 Gene Gauntier, who portrayed Nan, became one of the hardest-working actresses in Hollywood, appearing in nearly five hundred films. Gauntier, who got her start in pictures as a stuntwoman (she was an expert horsewoman), turned to screenwriting after she began the Nan series and wrote all of the remaining Nan spy thrillers. Producers loved her because she could write her own movies, star in them, and do her own stunts. "I could write three one-reelers a day when the inspiration burned," she wrote in her unpublished autobiography.

Gauntier was so good that producers committed to making her movies before she even wrote them. Her feel for screenplays was so trusted that in 1909 she persuaded her studio to film three movies in Germany and Ireland—with no screenplays in hand. She wrote the scripts on the boat to Europe. They were filmed as written as soon as the cast and crew disembarked. Gauntier became transfixed by the Holy Land while the company was filming her movie in Germany and promptly wrote two screenplays for adventure stories in Jerusalem; the company filmed them on location. The mercurial Gauntier tired of the movie business in 1917 and became a war correspondent. Information taken from the unpublished "Memoirs of Gene Gauntier," Museum of Modern Art, New York.

15 Jack Spears, *The Civil War on the Screen and Other Essays* (South Brunswick, N.J.: A.S. Barnes, 1977), p. 50.

16 *Moving Picture World,* May 22, 1909.

17 *Moving Picture World,* March 4, 1909. *MPW* called *The Old Soldier's Story* "a beautiful film . . . thrilling story without any killing and deserves a long run." Ironically, the review ran on the same page with a review of a comedy called *The Colored Stenographer,* which made fun of black secretaries.

18 Ad appearing in *Moving Picture World,* March 4, 1909.

19 Editorial, *Moving Picture World,* April 19, 1909.

20 Evelyn Ehrlich, "The Civil War in Early Films," in *The South and Film,* ed. Warren French (Jackson: University Press of Mississippi, 1981), p. 80.

21 D. W. Griffith, *The Man Who Invented Hollywood: The Autobiography of D. W. Griffith.* Edited by James Hart (Louisville, Ky.: Touchstone Publishing, 1972), p. 26.

22 Robert Henderson, *D. W. Griffith: His Life and Works* (New York: Oxford University Press, 1972), p. 24.

23 Spears, *Civil War on the Screen,* pp. 29–32.

24 *Biograph Bulletin,* January 19, 1910.

25 William K. Everson, *American Silent Film* (New York: Oxford University Press, 1978), p. 83.

26 Jay Leyda, "D. W. Griffith," *Film Culture,* summer 1994, pp. 39–42.

27 Spehr, *Civil War in Motion Pictures,* various categorized lists of films.

28 Ibid., p. 477.

29 Frank Thompson, "A Moving Picture," in *Civil War Times Illustrated,* April 1996, pp. 56–61.

30 The pay for scripts in the early silent era was quite low. First scripts usually brought only twenty-five dollars or so and writers selling their fourth or fifth script to a studio usually collected fifty dollars or less. It was often less. Frank Wood, who would go on to become story editor for Griffith, got his start by writing quickie three-hundred-word story ideas for Biograph at just fifteen dollars per idea used. In 1908, newspaper reporter Stanner E. V. Taylor was paid thirty dollars per week to produce at least one, sometimes two scripts for Biograph one-reelers (eight-minute movies). Writers who demanded more often got it. A year later, in 1909, Marion Leonard, a stage actress, made arrangements to be paid seventy-five dollars a week by Biograph for a single one-reel story. One inventive screenwriter decided to auction off his script to the highest bidder. He received only one bid, but it was for one hundred dollars, a high price in those days. Today, scripts are purchased on a flat fee or percentage basis (sometimes 5 percent of the budget for a film).

31 Screenwriting was a particularly good field for women, who found getting work anywhere difficult at the tail end of the Victorian era. Hollywood and New York movie studios produced so many films, more than a thousand each year, that they needed all the scripts they could get, from whatever source. Most scripts were one- or two-page synopses or loosely scripted twenty- or twenty-five-page stories with scene descriptions and title cards but no dialogue. Creativity and imagination counted, not experience. Producers quickly found that some of the best writers of well-organized fifteen-minute films, particularly those with emotion or romantic angles, were women. Dozens of women soon began writing scripts full-time for different studios or freelancing for all of them. Marion Leonard and Carolyn Wells, working in New York, were

two of the best. Wells's films were so successful that in order to draw larger audiences her studios would state in their press releases (usually reprinted verbatim in newspapers) that their latest release was "a film written by Carolyn Wells" or "the latest Carolyn Wells story."

Many of the women screenwriters were reporters from the women's section of newspapers, women's magazine writers making money on the side or recent college graduates trying to earn extra income. Many actresses (Wells was one) realized that their exposure to films made it easier for them to write scripts. When the studios moved west, to Hollywood, scripts were still written in New York, but producers and directors soon found that there were many talented women writers in Los Angeles. One of the best, Anita Loos, began writing scripts for D. W. Griffith when she was just sixteen in 1914, the year Griffith filmed *The Birth of a Nation*.

32 Gerald F. Linderman, *Embattled Courage: The Experience of Combat in the American Civil War* (New York: Free Press, 1987), p. 294.

33 Spehr, *Civil War in Motion Pictures*, p. 75.

34 George Mitchell, "Thomas H. Ince Was the Pioneer Producer Who Systematized the Making of a Movie," *Films in Review*, February 1960, p. 472.

35 The largest cannon Ince had was a huge but light mortar he had built for Civil War battle scenes. It actually fired cannonballs and other material. It almost got into a real war in 1912 when workers from Carl Laemmle's studio arrived and tried to invade Ince's ranch as part of a vociferous battle between the two producers. Ince had his men roll out the Civil War cannon, load it up with scrap iron, and aim it at Laemmle's men. They fled. Mitchell, "Thomas Ince," p. 474.

36 The year 1913 was Ince's busiest. His company produced 150 films that year.

37 Ince died mysteriously in 1924, apparently the victim of food poisoning, following a party on the yacht of newspaper publisher William Randolph Hearst.

38 Spehr, *Civil War in Motion Pictures*, p. 81.

39 Ibid., p. 22.

40 Ibid., p. 18.

41 *Moving Picture World*, October 23, 1915.

42 *Moving Picture World*, February 19, 1910.

CHAPTER 3

1 Scene from *The Common Enemy*, 1910.

2 *New York Telegraph*, October 12, 1910.

3 Ibid., p. 10.

4 Spehr, *Civil War in Motion Pictures*, p. 29.

5 Ibid., p. 69.

6 Ibid., p. 10.

7 Ibid., p. 11.

8 Ibid., p. 66.

9 Ibid., p. 13.

10 Ibid., p. 226.

11 Ibid., p. 5.

12 Ibid., p. 253.

13 Ibid., p. 220.

14 Ibid., p. 37.

15 Ibid., p. 32.

16 Ibid., p. 15.

17 Ibid., p. 40.

18 Ibid., p. 19.

19 Ibid., p. 30.

20 Ibid., p. 10.

21 Ibid., p. 22.

22 Ibid., p. 22.

23 Ibid., p. 33.

24 Ibid., p. 15.

25 Anne C. Rose, *Victorian America and the Civil War* (New York: Cambridge University Press, 1992), p. 178.

26 Ibid., p. 236.

27 Even men who were single wrote constantly to mothers, fathers, sisters and brothers—their nonmarried family—in the same manner, as witness the wartime letters of Lt. Edmund Halsey, of Rockaway, N.J. He wrote letters to each of his sisters, his brother, mother, father and sweetheart, and insisted that each write him back. He sought any and all news of life back home in New Jersey, down to small pieces of local gossip, so he could hold his family in his emotions as he plodded on through the war. The more than eighty letters in the Edmund Halsey Papers (Morristown [N.J.] Library) also indicate he would ride on horseback to different regiments to gather news of the families of Halsey neighbors in Rockaway to keep them posted.

28 See Foster, *Ghosts of the Confederacy*. He wrote, though, that by the time silent movies began, the United Confederate movement had lost ground. The debut of silents, and the Civil War movies, gave it new life, which culminated in the fiftieth-anniversary celebrations.

29 John William De Forest, *Miss Ravenel's Conversion from Secession to Loyalty* (New York: Harper & Brothers, 1867; Holt, Rinehart & Winston, 1955).

30 Ibid., p. 60.

31 Ibid., p. 70.

32 Marjorie Rosen, *Popcorn Venus: Women, Movies & the American Dream* (New York: Coward, McCann & Geoghegan, 1973), p. 48.

33 Haskell, *From Reverence to Rape*, pp. 50–51.

34 Ibid., p. 59.

35 John Dollard, *Caste and Class in a Southern Town* (New Haven: Yale University Press, 1937; Garden City, N.Y.: Doubleday, 1949), pp. 136–137.

36 Ron Bowers, "Women in Silent Films," in *Magill's Survey of Cinema: Silent Films,* ed. Frank N. Magill (Englewood Cliffs, N.J.: Salem Press, 1982), vol. 1, p. 122. "They were mythical, idealized onscreen representatives of the Victorian image of women," he wrote.

37 Anne C. Rose, *Victorian America,* p. 157.

38 Merritt, "Dixon, Griffith," p. 32. "The woman-centered home was a perpetual obsession with Griffith . . . Griffith venerated all the family stood for," he wrote.

39 Rosen, *Popcorn Venus,* p. 48.

40 This racism-and-sex theme would be picked up again and again in movies about American history and the West. Perhaps the most vivid scene was in the 1992 film version of the novel *The Last of the Mohicans,* when Alice, at the top of a cliff, is faced with sex with an Indian or death. Magua, the murderous Indian, extends his hand to her. Alice, almost in a trance, stares at it, steps back and noiselessly leaps to her death, her body falling silently through space and disappearing into a thick green forest below.

41 Spehr, *Civil War in Motion Pictures,* p. 42.

42 Ibid., p. 44.

43 Ibid., p. 26.

CHAPTER 4

1 Fort Sumter was not only the site of the war's beginning when it was shelled by the Confederates on April 12, 1861, but a symbol of how unprepared the North was for war. Construction on the pentagonal brick fort, built for a recently moved garrison, was incomplete, and only 48 of its 140 guns were operational.

2 David Brion Davis, *The Problem of Slavery in the Age of Revolution, 1770–1823* (Ithaca, N.Y.: Cornell University Press, 1975), p. 323.

3 Ibid., p. 510.

4 Shelby Foote, *The Civil War: A Narrative* (New York: Random House, 1958), vol. 1, p. 26.

5 Sundquist, *Dynamics of the Party System,* p. 77.

6 Angus Campbell et al., *The American Voter* (Chicago: University of Chicago Press, 1960), p. 62. The authors argued that drastic party and political alignments only occur around a great national crisis or issue and cited the Civil

War and the Great Depression. The collapse of the Whig Party and the split of the Democrats opened the door for a new party to scrape up all the different unrepresented coalitions and tie them together. That new grouping was the Republican Party, which came out strongly against slavery and four years later produced Abraham Lincoln as their successful presidential candidate.

7 James McPherson, *Battle Cry of Freedom* (New York: Oxford University Press, 1988; Ballantine Books, 1989), pp. 194–195.

8 Carl Sandburg, *Abraham Lincoln: The Prairie Years* (New York: Harcourt Brace, 1926), vol. 2, p. 53. Also see McPherson, *Battle Cry of Freedom*, pp. 246–248.

9 Mark Boatner III, *The Civil War Dictionary* (New York: D. McKay, 1959), p. 432.

10 Spehr, *Civil War in Motion Pictures*, p. 11.

11 Spears, *Civil War on the Screen*, p. 84.

12 Nancy Scott Anderson and Dwight Anderson, *The Generals—Ulysses S. Grant and Robert E. Lee* (New York: Alfred A. Knopf, 1989), pp. 217–221.

13 Spehr, *Civil War in Motion Pictures*, p. 65.

14 Sheridan loved his horse so much that when the steed died the general had him stuffed and kept him in his home. The horse now resides in the Smithsonian.

15 Spears, *Civil War on the Screen*, p. 87.

16 Boatner, *Civil War Dictionary*, p. 633.

17 At Antietam, in 1862, the South was outnumbered by the federals and earned a draw. It was a perfect example of the Army of Northern Virginia's ability, under Lee's command, to fight hard and hold its own against vastly superior numbers. The success of the Confederate armies in the field refutes the conventional notion of an outmanned force hopelessly fighting a "lost cause." At Antietam, McClellan also kept over twenty thousand troops in reserve and never sent them into the battle, for no apparent reason, supporting the claims of others that the South might have won because the North had such ineffective generals.

18 Bruce Catton, *Bruce Catton's Civil War: Three Volumes in One* (New York: Fairfax Press, dist. by Crown, 1984), vol. 1, pp. 192–193.

19 Boatner, *Civil War Dictionary*, p. 583.

20 Ibid., p. 583.

21 McPherson, *Battle Cry of Freedom*, p. 831.

22 Adrian Cook, *Armies of the Streets: The New York City Draft Riots of 1863* (Lexington: University of Kentucky Press, 1974), pp. 77–78.

23 Boatner, *Civil War Dictionary*, p. 169. There were only 174,000 regular army soldiers in the Confederate forces at the end of the war, down from a peak of about 800,000.

CHAPTER 5

1 Daniel J. Leab, *From Sambo to Superspade: The Black Experience in Motion Pictures* (Boston: Houghton Mifflin, 1975), p. 1.

2 *Moving Picture World,* May 7, 1910.

3 James R. Nesteby, *Black Images in American Films, 1896–1954: The Interplay Between Civil Rights and Film Culture* (Washington, D.C.: University Press of America, 1982), p. 21.

4 Cripps, *Slow Fade to Black,* p. 24.

5 Ibid., p. 14.

6 Compilations of various movie studio film catalogs, including those of Amusement Supply Company, S. Lubin, Keline and Biograph.

7 Harpole and Bowser, *History of the American Cinema,* pp. 199–200.

8 Cripps, *Slow Fade to Black,* p. 22.

9 Terry Ramsaye, *A Million and One Nights: A History of the Motion Picture* (New York: Simon and Schuster, 1926), pp. 73–80.

10 Leab, *From Sambo to Superspade,* pp. 20–21.

11 Whites starring in blackface in various minstrel shows were not new. This practice of whites appropriating black music and dance and making it their own—dressed as blacks—started in the 1840s and was quite popular. Minstrel shows waned after the Civil War, but came back strong at the turn of the century.

12 Joel Williamson, *A Rage for Order: Black/White Relations in the American South Since Emancipation* (New York: Oxford University Press, 1986), pp. 15–16.

13 Williams was one of the most talented performers of the era and the idol of many black performers who followed him, particularly Sammy Davis Jr. and Ben Vereen. His talents did not go unnoticed. The most dazzling showman of the day, Florenz Ziegfeld, signed him in 1916 as the first and only black in the *Ziegfeld Follies* edition of that year, starring Fanny Brice and W. C. Fields. Williams remained with the *Follies* for many years.

14 Leab, *From Sambo to Superspade,* p. 20.

15 John Oliver Killens, "Hollywood in Black and White," in *White Racism: Its History, Pathology, and Practice*, ed. Barry N. Schwartz and Robert Disch (New York: Dell, 1970), p. 401.

16 Spehr, *Civil War in Motion Pictures,* p. 14.

17 Ibid., p. 17.

18 Ibid., p. 31.

19 Ibid., p. 73.

20 Ibid., p. 77.

21 Ibid., p. 49.

22 Ibid., p. 51.

23 Ibid., p. 44.

24 Deborah Gray White, *Ar'n't I A Woman? Female Slaves in the Plantation South* (New York: W. W. Norton, 1985), pp. 46–61.

25 Ibid., p. 42.

26 Ibid., p. 27.

27 Nesteby, *Black Images,* p. 36.

28 Confederate leaders, in a last desperate gamble during the final days of the war, passed legislation permitting slaves to enlist and fight for the Confederate Army. They managed to enlist about two dozen men from Virginia plantations, but the war ended while they were still in training.

29 Stowe was a very slight woman. Abraham Lincoln had always wanted to meet her and finally invited her to the White House for a state dinner. Lincoln was six feet four and more than a foot taller than the author. When introduced, he smiled graciously, bent down and said, "So you're the very little woman who caused this very big war."

30 *New York Telegraph,* March 4, 1910.

31 Nesteby, *Black Images,* p. 16.

32 Lew was the nephew of Hiram Dockstader, who started the fabled Dockstader's Minstrels. Lew's show was subtitled "A Lot of Tomfoolery," which tied in Uncle Tom and blackface.

33 Stephen F. Zito, "The Black Film Experience," in *The American Film Heritage: Impressions from the American Film Institute Archives*, ed. Tom Shales et al. (Washington, D.C.: Acropolis Books, 1972), p. 65.

34 Spehr, *Civil War in Motion Pictures,* p. 18.

35 Ibid., p. 22.

36 Leab, *From Sambo to Superspade,* p. 53.

37 *Moving Picture World,* February 21, 1914.

38 The producers, directors and writers of all-black film companies were so upset about black portrayals in Civil War silents that, in an effort to put them out of people's minds, not one of them ever included a single Civil War film in their more than six hundred productions.

39 Mike Davis, *City of Quartz: Excavating the Future in Los Angeles* (New York: Verso, 1990; Vintage, 1992), p. 161.

40 Harpole and Bowser, *History of the American Cinema,* pp. 9–10.

41 Ibid., pp. 8–9.

42 C. Vann Woodward, *Tom Watson: Agrarian Rebel* (New York: Macmillan, 1938), p. 226.

43 Williamson, *Rage for Order,* p. 95.

44 See Claude H. Nolen, *The Negro's Image in the South: The Anatomy of White Supremacy* (Lexington: University of Kentucky Press, 1968), p. 37.

45 Charles Smith, quoted in Nolen, *Negro's Image,* p. 16.

46 Nolen, *Negro's Image,* p. 18.

47 *New York Times,* February 13, 1971.

48 See Lawrence Goodwyn, *Democratic Promise: The Populist Movement in America* (New York: Oxford University Press, 1976), p. 290.

49 bell hooks, *Black Looks: Race and Representation* (Boston: South End Press, 1992), pp. 4, 91.

50 Goodwyn, *Democratic Promise,* p. 303.

51 Charles Seymour and Donald Paige Frary, *How the World Votes: The Story of Democratic Development in Elections* (Springfield, Mass.: C. A. Nichols, 1918), vol. 1, pp. 320–321.

CHAPTER 6

1 Ramsaye, *Million and One Nights,* p. 637.

2 Griffith reportedly agreed to work for Mutual at a weekly salary of three hundred dollars, which in today's money is about five thousand dollars a week, low for a top director. Griffith never made his money on salary—he made it on percentage. Mutual guaranteed him a 10-to-12 percent royalty on the grosses of all his movies. His finances on *Birth* were murky, as were the finances of all the people involved in it, because of the distribution, but Griffith's cut was believed to be over $1 million, record-setting for the era.

He had percentage deals at all of his studios. Copies of his contracts with Biograph show that he was paid a paltry fifty dollars a week but earned 5 percent on the grosses of his films in 1908. His 1909 contract called for a 10 percent royalty and his 1910 contract bumped that up to 12 percent. Actors were normally paid a weekly salary. Griffith's phenomenal success with *Birth,* however, ushered in the era of big contracts for Hollywood stars, and within a few years some were earning close to $1 million a year. Information taken from the D. W. Griffith Papers, Museum of Modern Art, New York.

3 D. W. Griffith Papers.

4 Edward Woolley, "The $100,000 Salary Man of the Movies," *McClure's,* September 1916. Woolley, writing about Griffith and the skyrocketing salaries of actors such as Charlie Chaplin and Mary Pickford, declared that "the motion picture business is now the very greatest of American industries."

5 Henderson, *D. W. Griffith,* p. 139.

6 Woods left the newspaper business within weeks of his first screenplay sale.

7 Merritt, "Dixon, Griffith," pp. 26–45.

8 Richard Schickel, *D. W. Griffith: An American Life* (New York: Simon and Schuster, 1984), p. 212.

9 Williamson, *Rage for Order,* p. 101.

10 Movie producers who came under attack for historical discrepancies often blamed stage productions of the same title or similar titles. Film direc-

tors and producers who came under fire from boards of censors did the same thing, arguing that if something was permissible on the public stage then it was permissible in a public movie house. Frank Dyer, president of the Motion Picture Patent Company, made that argument as early as 1910. "There probably always will be sporadic cases of films based on instances that are unduly brutal or suggestive, but the business as a whole should not be condemned for these reasons, anymore than should the stage be condemned," he wrote in the *New York Telegraph,* March 17, 1910.

11 John Hope Franklin, "Silent Cinema as Historical Mythmaker," in *Hollywood's America,* ed. Steven Mintz and Randy Roberts (St. James, N.Y.: Brandywine Press, 1992), p. 45.

12 Schickel, *D. W. Griffith,* p. 203.

13 Ehrlich, "Civil War in Early Films," p. 71.

14 Robert Seidenberg, *"Thirtysomething's* Ed Zwick," p. 58.

15 Merritt, "Dixon, Griffith," p. 27.

16 Walthall's stardom did not last long. He did not get good roles in the 1920s. He was able to make the transition to sound in 1929, but was by then too old to be cast as a matinee idol and wound up as a character actor in his later movies. Ironically, in his very last film, *Judas Priest,* which starred Will Rogers, Walthall was once again cast as a Southern hero, an evangelical preacher, who in the movie's finale walks alongside Rogers and a battery of Confederate flags, thus ending his career once again as a "Little Colonel."

17 Marsh had an-up-and down career. She, too, became a big star through *Birth,* and left Griffith's company in 1921. By 1923 she was earning over $250,000 a year with MGM. Her career went into a tailspin, though, and in 1939 she declared personal bankruptcy. John Ford, the great director, who worked with her when she was an extra in early Griffith films, took her under his wing. He used her in a number of his famous westerns and she regained her popularity and personal confidence. In 1955, the Eastman Festival of the Arts, in Rochester, honored Mae Marsh as one of the five greatest actresses of the silents (along with Mary Pickford, Gloria Swanson, Lillian Gish and Norma Talmadge).

18 Cooper met Raoul Walsh, then a member of the cast and later one of Hollywood's most accomplished directors, during filming. They fell in love and married a year later.

19 Henderson, *D. W. Griffith,* pp. 23–25.

20 James Shelley Hamilton, "Putting a New Movie in the Movies," *Everybody's Magazine,* June 1915.

21 Later, when the NAACP accused him of inaccuracy, Griffith would complain bitterly that, after all, Ford's Theatre was an accurate re-creation, wasn't it? His Ford's Theatre set was something he came back to again and

again in interviews, making the abstract theater far more important than the treatment of people in his films. His accuracy in certain things overshadowed inaccuracy in others.

22 Walsh, born in 1887 in New York, drifted to California in 1903 and worked there and in Mexico as a horse wrangler for two years. He then worked as a professional cowboy in California for a year and then, for six years, as an undertaker. He went back to being a cowboy, and a cowboy actor, in 1912. That's how he met Thomas Ince and, later, Griffith.

Griffith liked Walsh because he had great success with the women he met on the sets of his films. The director would often pass Walsh, usually surrounded by young women, and comment to whomever he was with that Walsh was a "real ladies' man." He made Walsh a subdirector in several films, including *Birth,* and gave him advice and guidance. Walsh began directing his own films in 1916, a year after *Birth.* He went on to become one of Hollywood's finest directors in a career that spanned fifty years. His first great success was directing Douglas Fairbanks Sr. in *The Thief of Bagdad* in the 1920s and, in the sound era, directed *What Price Glory?, High Sierra, The Naked and The Dead, White Heat* and dozens of other highly successful and critically acclaimed films. The cowboy turned actor saw potential in another cowboy actor, John Wayne, in 1930 and put him in his film *The Big Trail.*

23 Ford became perhaps Hollywood's greatest director, filming 112 movies in his long and award-filled career. He teamed up with John Wayne in the memorable westerns *Fort Apache, She Wore a Yellow Ribbon, Stagecoach, Rio Grande, The Searchers* and *The Man Who Shot Liberty Valance.* He moved away from westerns for the haunting *The Grapes of Wrath,* plus *The Informer, They Were Expendable, The Quiet Man* and dozens of other films.

Griffith liked the young Ford because he knew his brother, who also worked on *Birth,* and because Ford was aggressive. The young actor had just finished working as an actor in a fifteen-episode serial, *Lucille Love, Girl of Mystery,* and a twenty-two-episode serial, *The Broken Coin,* before *Birth* began filming. The physically tough and athletic Ford earned extra money by working as a stuntman. He got his first chance to direct in 1917 and was so impressive that he directed seven films that year.

24 Schickel, *D. W. Griffith,* p. 231.

25 He created this illusion by shooting battle scenes up close to make it seem as though more soldiers were in front of the camera. He would then move soldiers to other parts of a field and shoot them as separate battles. He also had all of his extras work as Union soldiers in a charge. After it was finished and in the can, he had them change clothes and stage another charge as Confederates. Along with director Abel Gance, he was considered one of the best in the business at this and other directors envied his success. In *The*

Honor of His Family, he used fewer than fifty extras to film a battle in which several hundred men seemed to be involved.

26 *Moving Picture World,* May/June 1915.

27 Lillian Gish, *The Movies, Mr. Griffith, and Me* (Englewood Cliffs, N.J.: Prentice-Hall, 1969), p. 153.

28 Seymour Stern, *"The Birth of a Nation:* 50th Anniversary," *Film Culture,* fall 1965, p. 93.

29 National Board of Censorship, 1915, cited in Roy Aitken, *The "Birth of a Nation" Story* (Middleburg, Va.: Denlinger Books, 1965), preface.

CHAPTER 7

1 Gish, who went on to a long and illustrious film career, silent and sound, was only nineteen when she starred in *Birth* and portrayed the object of Silas Lynch's lust. Gish came to Griffith's studio with her sister Dorothy, who also became a film actress, and her mother in 1912, when she was just sixteen, and he signed her to a contract and put her in *An Unseen Enemy. Birth* made her a superstar, and a superstar in an era when women had thousands of roles. She was also able to cash in on the growing popularity of movie magazines. Editors put her on hundreds of fan magazine covers and assigned writers to produce hundreds of stories about her. By 1924, after she left Griffith and signed with MGM, she was earning $800,000 a year as one of the highest-paid people in any profession in America.

2 Kenneth Stampp, *The Era of Reconstruction, 1865–1877* (New York: Alfred A. Knopf, 1965), p. 167.

3 Francis Butler Simkins and Robert Hilliard Woody, *South Carolina During Reconstruction* (Chapel Hill: University of North Carolina Press, 1932), pp. 90–111.

4 See Stampp, *Era of Reconstruction,* p. 168.

5 John R. Lynch, *The Facts of Reconstruction* (New York: Neale Publishing, 1913), p. 94.

6 Ibid., p. 96.

7 Eric Foner, *Reconstruction: America's Unfinished Revolution, 1863–1877* (New York: Harper & Row, 1988), p. 449.

8 Ibid., p. 174.

9 Foner's book is the best source on new, revisionist investigations into the integrationist efforts in the South during Reconstruction.

10 See Ralph Korngold, *Thaddeus Stevens: A Being Darkly Wise and Rudely Great* (New York: Harcourt, Brace, 1955), pp. 382–383.

11 Ira Berliner, ed., *Freedom: A Documentary History of Emancipation, 1861–1867* (New York: Cambridge University Press, 1982), series 2, pp. 733–763.

12 Ibid., p. 736.

13 Ibid., p. 737.

14 Emma Lou Thornbrough, *Black Reconstructionists* (Englewood Cliffs, N.J.: Prentice-Hall, 1972), p. 61. The Red Shirts were allegedly founded by former C.S.A. general Wade Hampton, a Southern gentleman who became one of the great heroes of the Civil War, a cavalier's cavalier. A decade later, however, Hampton, who followed race relations closely, had toned down his feelings and actually supported several bills to further integrate the state.

15 Schickel, *D. W. Griffith*, p. 268.

16 Cripps, *Slow Fade to Black*, p. 52.

17 See Woodrow Wilson, *A History of the American People* (New York: Harper & Brothers, 1903), vol. 5, pp. 36–40.

18 Wilson, *History of the American People*, vol. 5, p. 59.

19 Schickel, *D. W. Griffith*, p. 296.

20 Milt Mackay, "The Birth of a Nation," *Scribner's Monthly Magazine*, June 1938, p. 46.

21 Henderson, *D. W. Griffith*, p. 152.

22 These ads, which took up one-third of a page, ran in most large newspapers. The one in the Riverside, California, paper, which hyped the showings at the Loring Opera House, claimed that eighteen books were consulted and more than five thousand Civil War documents researched. Griffith Papers.

23 See historians' references throughout chapter 4.

24 D. W. Griffith, Letter to the editor, *Sight & Sound*, 1947.

25 Quoted in Gish, *Movies, Mr. Griffith, and Me*, p. 162.

26 See Franklin, "Silent Cinema," p. 43. Dixon once stood up at a public meeting and denounced a speaker who he felt was portraying the South negatively. "False and biased!" Dixon roared.

27 Original playscript, Thomas Dixon, *The Clansman*. Griffith Papers.

28 Ibid.

29 D. W. Griffith, quoted in Aitken, *"Birth of a Nation" Story*, p. 38.

30 Thomas Dixon, quoted in ibid.

31 D. W. Griffith, interviewed by Walter Huston, in movie *The Birth of a Nation*, Mutual, 1915; 1930 reissue.

32 Film scholars always blamed Dixon because they tended to venerate Griffith. John Hope Franklin was one such. See his "Silent Cinema as Historical Mythmaker," Mintz and Roberts, p. 45. "Even a casual comparison of the texts of *The Leopard's Spots* and *The Clansman* with the film itself will convince one that *Birth of a Nation* is pure Dixon, all Dixon!" he wrote. However, in a much-publicized court suit in 1975 to renew copyright privileges for *Birth*, lawyers from both sides acknowledged that in a previous suit, in 1915, it was agreed by all that it was Griffith, not Dixon, who was responsible for the final

screen version and that Frank Woods wrote the screenplay title cards. "There was no evidence that anyone other than Griffith and Frank Woods wrote the screen photoplay," read legal papers filed then by the Epoch Producing Company. *Epoch Producing Company v. Killiam Shows,* May 2, 1975.

33 Jane Tompkins, *Sensational Designs: The Cultural Work of American Fiction: 1790–1860* (New York: Oxford University Press, 1985), p. 141.

34 Gish, *Movies, Mr. Griffith, and Me,* p. 149.

CHAPTER 8

1 Griffith Papers.

2 Stern, *"Birth of a Nation:* 50th" p. 84.

3 *Chicago Examiner,* October 29, 1915.

4 *Variety,* February 28, 1949.

5 Epoch Productions expense ledger, June 30, 1915. Road Company A spent $128,526, Company B spent $74,961 and Company C spent $43,507. The trains that took the three *Birth* companies across America contained so many people, forty musicians plus staffers, that each even included its own traveling hospital with a doctor and nurses. Griffith Papers.

6 Epoch Productions treasurer's report, December 31, 1915. Griffith Papers.

7 Stern, *"Birth of a Nation:* 50th," p. 80.

8 Ibid., p. 69.

9 Advertisement in *New York Times,* January 2, 1916.

10 Harry Sherman, in *Variety,* February 9, 1949.

11 Ibid.

12 Roy Aitken, *The "Birth of a Nation" Story* (Middleburg, Va.: Denlinger Books, 1965), p. 58.

13 Ibid., p. 59.

14 Stern, *"Birth of a Nation:* 50th" p. 72.

15 *New York Times,* March 4, 1915.

16 Dorothy Dix, *New York Journal,* March 9, 1915.

17 Steve Talbot, *"The Birth of a Nation," Lincolnian,* March 4, 1915.

18 James Metcalfe, *"Birth of a Nation," Life,* February 1915.

19 Rupert Hughes, quoted in Aitken, *"Birth of a Nation" Story,* p. 8.

20 *New York Evening Journal,* March 16, 1915.

21 Lyman Rutledge, *Cambridge Chronicle,* May 15, 1915.

22 Ned McIntosh, "The Tar Heel Boy," *Winston-Salem Journal,* March 12, 1916.

23 *New York Globe,* April 6, 1915.

24 Francis Hackett, "Brotherly Love," *New Republic,* March 20, 1915.

25 Jane Addams, quoted in Schickel, *D. W. Griffith,* p. 283.

26 Dixon's sequel was called *Fall of a Nation,* and in this play about Amer-

ica from 1870 to 1900, his work on blacks finished, the author-playwright demeaned different groups of white immigrants.

27 Max Lerner, *"The Birth of a Nation,"* *New York Post,* June 1, 1950.

28 Eric Rhode, *A History of the Cinema: From Its Origins to 1970* (New York: Hill & Wang, 1976), p. 114.

29 Roy Wilkins, *New York Daily Compass,* May 17, 1950.

30 Everson, *American Silent Film,* p. 87.

31 Stern, *"Birth of a Nation:* 50th" p. 2.

32 Molly Haskell, "In *The Birth of a Nation,* the Birth of Serious Film," *New York Times,* November 20, 1995, p. D5.

33 Public relations papers, Triangle Co., 1931. Griffith Papers.

34 Press release, George M. Cohan's Theatre, December 14, 1930. Griffith Papers.

35 *New York Herald Tribune,* June 19, 1921.

36 *New York Herald Tribune,* May 17, 1938.

37 Ibid.

38 *Variety,* March 15, 1978.

39 *Variety,* August 3, 1978.

40 *Variety,* June 18, 1980.

41 Ed Lowry, program notes, Cinema Texas Film Series, September 19, 1978, p. 65.

42 Program notes, Toronto Film Society, February 16, 1981.

43 *Film & Television Daily,* September 30, 1968.

44 New York *Daily News,* January 10, 1993.

45 *The General* was a carefully scripted story of a Southerner who single-handedly recaptures a train locomotive seized by the Union army. It earned little praise when it debuted, and lost a substantial amount of money (to Keaton's great surprise).

46 Williamson, *A Rage for Order,* p. 53.

47 Woodward, *Strange Career of Jim Crow,* pp. 33, 37.

48 See Williamson, *A Rage for Order,* for a full explanation.

49 David M. Chalmers, *Hooded Americanism: The First Century of the Ku Klux Klan* (New York: Doubleday, 1965), p. 30.

50 Ibid., p. 32.

51 William Peirce Randel, *The Ku Klux Klan: A Century of Infamy* (Philadelphia: Chilton Books, 1965), p. 185.

52 V. O. Key, *Southern Politics in State and Nation* (New York: Alfred A. Knopf, 1949), pp. 142–144.

53 David W. Brady, *Critical Elections and Congressional Policy Making* (Stanford: Stanford University Press, 1988), p. 59.

54 Edward G. Carmines and James A. Stimson, *Issue Evolution: Race and*

the Transformation of American Politics (Princeton: Princeton University Press, 1989), p. 33.

55 Allan Nevins, *Grover Cleveland: A Study in Courage* (New York: Dodd, Mead, 1933), p. 710.

56 See Williamson, *A Rage for Order,* p. 96.

57 John Higham, *Strangers in the Land: Patterns of American Nativism, 1860–1925* (New Brunswick, N.J.: Rutgers University Press, 1955), p. 146.

58 Ibid., p. 147.

59 "National Eugenics," *National Geographic Magazine,* vol. 23, 1912, pp. 38–41.

60 Williamson, *Rage for Order,* pp. 160–166.

61 Higham, *Strangers in the Land,* p. 169.

62 Stephen and Abigail Thernstrom, *America in Black and White: One Nation, Indivisible* (New York: Simon and Schuster, 1997), pp. 33–46.

63 David M. Oshinsky, *"Worse Than Slavery," Parchman Farm and the Ordeal of Jim Crow Justice* (New York: Free Press, 1996), pp. 180–182.

64 Ulrich Bonnell Phillips, "The Central Theme of Southern History," *American Historical Review,* October 1928, pp. 30–43.

65 Aitken, *"Birth of a Nation" Story,* p. 130. Mitchell wrote Aitken a long letter after the publication of her book to tell him this story.

CHAPTER 9

1 Abraham Lincoln, *The Collected Works of Abraham Lincoln,* ed. Roy P. Basler (New Brunswick, N.J.: Rutgers University Press, 1953–1955), vol. 4, p. 190. The script was reasonably close to Lincoln's actual speech in Springfield, printed here. Several other versions of the speech appeared from time to time, but except for a few added words or punctuation marks, they were the same. Within a week of his death, the American News Company, in New York, printed thousands of copies of Lincoln's farewell speech in Springfield on large broadsides and distributed them throughout the country.

2 Wendy Wick Reaves, *George Washington, an American Icon: The Eighteenth-Century Graphic Portraits* (Washington: Smithsonian Institution, 1982), pp. 122–124.

3 Gabor S. Boritt, ed., *The Historian's Lincoln: Pseudohistory, Psychohistory, and History* (Urbana: University of Illinois Press, 1988), p. 75.

4 Robert Roman, "Lincoln on the Screen," *Films in Review,* February 1961, p. 88.

5 Spears, *Civil War on the Screen,* p. 65.

6 From a February 12, 1959, speech by Sandburg to Congress.

7 Spehr, *Civil War in Motion Pictures,* p. 7.

8 Ibid., p. 38.

9 Roman, "Lincoln on the Screen," p. 91.

10 Ibid., p. 93.

11 Paramount Pictures publicity release, 1917.

12 Spears, *Civil War on the Screen*, pp. 71–74.

13 Ibid., p. 89.

14 *Moving Picture World*, September 18, 1911.

15 Roman, "Lincoln on the Screen," p. 94.

16 Spears, *Civil War on the Screen*, p. 95.

17 Ibid., 73.

18 Ibid., p. 92.

19 Arnold Bennett, "An English View of the Success of Abraham Lincoln," *Living Age*, vol. 304, 1920, p. 791.

20 Spears, *Civil War on the Screen*, p. 96.

21 Ibid., p. 75.

22 Ibid., p. 96.

23 *New York World*, 1930.

24 Warren Susman, *Culture as History* (New York: Pantheon Books, 1973), pp. 155–170.

25 Ibid., p. 178.

26 Bland Johaneson, *New York Daily Mirror*, June 3, 1939.

27 Archer Winston, *New York Post*, June 6, 1939.

28 Roman, "Lincoln on the Screen," p. 100.

29 Henry Fonda, *New York Herald Tribune*, May 21, 1939.

30 According to the 1938 *Film Guide*, edited by Harold Turney, Sherwood said his reference sources were Ida Tarbell, *The Life of Lincoln* (New York: Macmillan, 1921); Sandburg; Albert J. Beveridge, *Abraham Lincoln, 1809–1888* (Boston: Houghton Mifflin, 1928); and Nathaniel W. Stephenson, *Lincoln: An Account of His Personal Life* (New York: Grosset & Dunlap, 1922).

31 Sherwood became so obsessed with Lincoln while he was writing the play that he told friends that almost nightly he dreamed about Lincoln and that the president spurred him on in his work, telling him that he was doing "a good job."

32 Jim Cullen, *The Civil War in Popular Culture: A Reusable Past* (Washington, D.C.: Smithsonian Institution Press, 1995), p. 39.

33 Robert Sherwood, diary entry, quoted in John Mason Brown, *The Worlds of Robert Sherwood: Mirror to His Times, 1896–1939* (New York: Harper & Row, 1965), p. 384.

34 Robert Sherwood, quoted in John Mason Brown, *The Ordeal of the Playwright: Robert E. Sherwood and the Challenge of War* (New York: Harper & Row, 1970), p. 141.

35 Louella Parsons column in the *New York Journal-American*, July 31, 1939.

36 Elizabeth Copeland, "Reel News from Hollywood," *Richmond Daily Leader,* May 9, 1940.

37 *New York Herald Tribune,* February 18, 1940.

38 On November 3, New York Republican Party boss Thurlow Weed wrote Lincoln that New York appeared lost to Douglas and that the election would be thrown into the House of Representatives.

39 Robert Sherwood, "History Seldom Repeats," *New York Times,* February 25, 1940.

40 Eileen Creelman, review, *New York Sun,* February 23, 1940.

41 Mae Tinee, review, *Chicago Daily Tribune,* April 25, 1940.

42 Herb Cohn, review, *Brooklyn Daily Eagle,* February 23, 1940.

43 *Washington Times Herald,* January 23, 1940.

44 Press release by RKO vice president Ned Depinet, February 16, 1940.

45 William Boehnel, *New York World-Telegram,* February 23, 1940.

46 Editorial, *Washington Herald,* October 5, 1938.

47 *Public Papers and Addresses of Franklin D. Roosevelt* (New York: Random House, 1938), vol. 7, pp. 416–420.

48 *Washington Times Herald,* January 23, 1940.

49 Roosevelt also promoted a friendship with Carl Sandburg. The author of *Abraham Lincoln: The Prairie Years* wrote a newspaper column that often praised FDR. The 1939 publication of Sandburg's *Abraham Lincoln: The War Years* enabled Roosevelt to wear the Lincoln mantle even more comfortably as Sandburg, as well as Sherwood, constantly compared him to the sixteenth president.

50 Doris Kearns Goodwin, *No Ordinary Time: Franklin and Eleanor Roosevelt; The Home Front in World War II* (New York: Simon & Schuster, 1994), p. 319.

51 Ibid., p. 552.

52 Merrill D. Peterson, *Lincoln in American Memory* (New York: Oxford University Press, 1994), p. 321.

CHAPTER 10

1 Harwell, *"Gone with the Wind" as Book and Film,* p. 148.

2 Gavin Lambert, *GWTW: The Making of "Gone With the Wind"* (Boston: Little, Brown, 1973), p. 150.

3 Ibid., p. 151.

4 Anne Edwards, *The Road to Tara: The Life of Margaret Mitchell* (New York: Ticknor & Fields, 1983), pp. 282–289.

5 Lyn Tornabene, *Long Live the King: A Biography of Clark Gable* (New York: G. P. Putnam's Sons, 1976), p. 236.

6 Howard Deitz, ed., *"Gone With the Wind" Souvenir Book* (New York: Ellison Greenstein, 1940), p. 16.

7 Louella Parsons, syndicated column, INS wire service, November, 1938.

8 *New York Herald Tribune,* December 8, 1940.

9 Newspapers considered it their responsibility to review or rereview the film each time it came out. For example, on February 14, 1942, the *Cleveland Press* devoted a half-page to its latest review of the film.

10 *New York Times,* January 23, 1939.

11 *New York Times,* September 1, 1939.

12 MGM Pictures press release, April 1961.

13 *American Cinematographer,* April 1989, p. 36.

14 Nancy Warfield, *GWTW—1939: The Film and the Year* (New York: Little Film Gazette Books, 1978), p. 31.

15 Lincoln Kirstein, *Film Magazine,* cited in Mintz and Roberts, *Hollywood's America,* p. 104.

16 See Sidney Howard's original script for *Gone With the Wind,* p. 1.

17 Helen Taylor, *Scarlett's Women: "Gone With the Wind" and Its Female Fans* (New Brunswick, N.J.: Rutgers University Press, 1989), p. 179.

18 Margaret Mitchell, *Gone With the Wind* (New York: Macmillan, 1936), p. 462.

19 *GWTW* script, pp. 20–21.

20 *GWTW* script, p. 32.

21 *GWTW* script, p. 127.

22 The book does not emphasize the intended rape as much as the film, in which camera angles and the movement of the soldier's body towards Scarlett clearly indicate a rape attempt. In the book, Scarlett may fear sexual assault, but her dominant feeling is anger that yet another Yankee soldier is stealing from Tara. Mitchell, *Gone With the Wind,* p. 433.

23 *Richmond News Leader,* February 3, 1940.

24 Stephen Bourne, "Pride and Prejudice," *Village Voice,* September 1, 1984, p. 16. Actress Butterfly McQueen, who played Prissy, insisted that she forced the producer and director to cut that scene, but it appears from Selznick's papers that he made the decision before shooting began. McQueen seemed happy to play Prissy in 1939, but in later years complained that she did not realize how stereotyped the role was. "I didn't know they were going to make the movie so authentic, that I'd have to be just a stupid little slave," she told Bourne.

25 Mitchell, *Gone With the Wind,* p. 790.

26 The Klan is still a power, albeit a small one, in the nation today. The Klan was in the news again in 1996, when its South Carolina division, the Christian Knights of the Ku Klux Klan, went to court in an attempt to quash a

lawsuit filed by a civic group charging that they were instrumental in the burning of black churches in the state. The Klan insisted on organizing a protest rally in New York City in 1999, but its few members were shouted down by hundreds of counterdemonstrators.

27 Mitchell to Ruth Tallman, July 30, 1937. In *Margaret Mitchell's "Gone With the Wind" Letters, 1936–1949*, ed. Richard Harwell (New York: Macmillan, 1976), p. 162.

28 Richard Rovere, "The Klan Rides Again," *Nation*, April 6, 1940, pp. 445–446.

29 Anne Edwards, *The Road to Tara*, pp. 78–79.

30 Mitchell to Stanley Horn, March 20, 1939, in *Letters*, Harwell, ed., p. 263.

31 Keeping references to the KKK in the film "might come out as unintentional advertisement for intolerant societies in these fascist-ridden times," Selznick explained to screenwriter Sidney Howard when he made the cuts. Roland Flamini, *Scarlett, Rhett and a Cast of Thousands* (New York: Macmillan, 1975), p. 184.

32 David O. Selznick, *Memo from David O. Selznick*, ed. Rudy Behlmer (New York: Viking Press, 1972), p. 151.

33 Selznick, *Memo*, p. 152.

34 *GWTW* script, p. 179.

35 Leab, *Sambo to Superspade*, p. 360.

36 Ida Jeter, "*Jezebel* and the Emergence of the Hollywood Tradition of a Decadent South," in *The South and Film*, ed. Warren French (Jackson: University Press of Mississippi, 1981), p. 39.

37 Ibid., p. 31.

38 The best scholarly work on the nondevelopment of blacks in films is Cripps, *Slow Fade to Black*.

39 Edward D. C. Campbell Jr., *The Celluloid South: Hollywood and the Southern Myth* (Knoxville: University of Tennessee Press, 1980), p. 35.

40 Leab, *Sambo to Superspade*, p. 101.

41 Campbell, *Celluloid South*, p. 100.

42 Leab, *Sambo to Superspade*, p. 366.

43 Publicity blurb, *Richmond News Leader*, November 13, 1935.

44 *Brooklyn Eagle*, November 19, 1935.

45 *Variety*, December 4, 1935.

46 Ibid.

47 Press release, quoted in Arthur Draper, "Uncle Tom, Will You Never Die?" *New Theatre Magazine*, January 1936, p. 31.

48 Williamson, *Rage for Order*, p. 250.

49 William Boehnel, *Brooklyn Eagle*, November 19, 1935; Beverly Hills (pseud.), "*So Red the Rose*," *Liberty*, December 21, 1935.

50 Mitchell, *Letters,* Harwell, ed., p. 60.

51 Draper, "Uncle Tom," p. 31.

52 *New York Sun,* November 27, 1935.

53 Draper, "Uncle Tom," p. 31.

54 Mitchell, *Gone With the Wind,* pp. 471–477.

55 Ibid., p. 456.

56 Ibid., p. 441.

57 Ibid., p. 579. Like Thomas Dixon in *The Clansman,* from which *Birth* was adapted, Mitchell wrote vivid scenes of surly blacks shoving whites on streets and jeering at their former owners.

58 Mitchell, *Gone With the Wind,* p. 682.

59 Ibid., p. 598.

60 Darden Asbury Pyron, *Southern Daughter: The Life of Margaret Mitchell* (New York: Oxford University Press, 1991), pp. 31–32.

61 Edwin Granberry, "The Private Life of Margaret Mitchell," *Collier's,* March 13, 1937, pp. 22, 24, 26.

62 Mitchell to Henry Steele Commager, July 1936, in *Letters,* Harwell, ed., 37–40.

63 Finis Farr, *Margaret Mitchell of Atlanta: The Author of "Gone with the Wind"* (New York: William Morrow), 1965, p. 30.

64 Helen Taylor, *Scarlett's Women,* p. 58.

65 Mitchell to Thomas Dixon, August 15, 1936, in *Letters,* Harwell, ed., pp. 52–53.

66 Lucy Shelton Stewart, *The Reward of Patriotism* (New York: W. Neale, 1930), pp. 67–69.

67 Michael Kreyling, *Figures of the Hero in Southern Narrative* (Baton Rouge: Louisiana State University Press, 1987), p. 104.

68 Helen Taylor, *Scarlett's Women,* p. 64.

69 Farr, *Margaret Mitchell of Atlanta,* p. 137. This denial did not always work. When the book came out, U.S. Undersecretary of the Interior Harry Slattery threatened to sue Mitchell for calling his family the "white trash Slatteries." He dropped the idea after an apology from the author. Mitchell to Harry Slattery, October 3, 1936, in *Letters,* Harwell, ed., p. 69.

70 Ibid., p. 156.

71 *New York World Telegram,* October 26, 1935.

72 Deitz, *"Gone With the Wind" Souvenir Book,* p. 8.

73 Mitchell to Jordan-Smith, May 5, 1942, in *Letters,* Harwell, ed., p. 71.

74 J. V. Ridgely, *Nineteenth-Century Southern Literature* (Lexington: University Press of Kentucky, 1980), p. 102.

75 Ibid., p. 87.

76 *Letters,* Harwell, ed., p. 186.

77 Ibid., p. 329.

78 Ibid., pp. 56 and 216. She would sometimes write out a complete list of source books which she sent correspondents.

79 Ibid., p. 308.

80 Ibid., p. 412.

81 Ibid., p. 59.

82 Ibid., p. 273.

83 Ibid., p. 272.

84 Ibid., p. 39.

CHAPTER 11

1 H. L. Mencken, "The Sahara of the Bozart," in *Prejudices: Second Series* (New York: Alfred A. Knopf, 1920), pp. 136–154.

2 Edward Campbell, *The Celluloid South,* pp. 135–140.

3 See Dan Carter, *Scottsboro: A Tragedy of the American South* (Baton Rouge: Louisiana State University Press, 1969).

4 See Edwin Mims, *The Advancing South: Stories of Progress and Reaction* (Garden City, N.Y.: Doubleday, 1926).

5 Donald Davidson, "Still Rebels, Still Yankees II," *American Review* (November 1933), p. 62.

6 See W. J. Cash, *The Mind of the South* (New York: Alfred A. Knopf, 1941), p. 326.

7 Eugene Genovese, as quoted in Peter Applebome, "Could the Old South Be Resurrected?" *New York Times,* February 12, 1998, p. 9.

8 Dollard, *Caste and Class,* pp. 42–46.

9 Ibid., pp. 112–113.

10 Chicago Commission on Race Relations: *The Negro in Chicago: A Study of Race Relations and a Race Riot* (Chicago: University of Chicago Press, 1922), p. 373.

11 Cash, *Mind of the South,* pp. 39–40.

12 *Chicago Defender,* February 3, 1940.

13 *Pittsburgh Courier,* March 9, 1940.

14 John Stevens, "The Black Reaction to *Gone With the Wind,*" *Journal of Popular Film,* Fall 1973, p. 368.

15 *Pittsburgh Courier,* January 8, 1940.

16 Walter White, as quoted in Peter Noble, *The Negro in Films* (Port Washington, N.Y.: Kinnikat Press, 1948), p. 78.

17 *GWTW* script, p. 3.

18 See Edward Campbell, *Celluloid South,* p. 137.

19 *Richmond Times Dispatch,* February 3, 1940.

20 *New Orleans Times-Picayune,* January 27, 1940.

21 Noble, *Negro in Film,* p. 78.

22 Martin Duberman, "A Giant Denied His Rightful Stature in Film," *New York Times,* March 29, 1998, Arts & Leisure section, p. 38.

23 Carlton Moss, "An Open Letter to David O. Selznick," *Daily Worker,* January 9, 1940.

24 *Daily Worker,* December 28, 1939.

25 Noble, *Negro in Film,* p. 79.

26 Ibid.

27 Marilyn Milloy, "Not Everyone Is Celebrating," *New York Newsday,* December 11, 1989, part 3, p. 9.

28 Debnam, of Raleigh, North Carolina, turned his lengthy broadcast essays into a book, *Weep No More My Lady* (self-published in 1950), which he claimed sold 140,000 copies, mostly in the South.

29 Jim Cullen, *The Civil War in Popular Culture: A Reusable Past* (Washington, D.C.: Smithsonian Institution Press, 1995), p. 76.

30 See Sidney Howard's original script for *Gone With the Wind* (written in 1937), p. 89, in New York Public Library for the Performing Arts.

31 Mitchell, *Letters,* p. 283.

32 Ibid., p. 32.

33 Ibid., p. 283.

34 Mitchell, *Letters,* p. 139.

35 *GWTW* script, p. 12.

36 Warren Susman, *Culture as History* (New York: Pantheon Books, 1973), p. 155.

37 Robert McElvaine, *The Great Depression* (New York: Random House, 1984), p. xxv.

38 Kathryn Lee Seidel, *The Southern Belle in the American Novel* (Tampa: University of South Florida Press, 1985), pp. 52–53.

39 Mintz and Roberts, *Hollywood's America,* p. 107.

40 Ibid., pp. 114–115.

41 John Gaventa, *Power and Powerlessness: Quiescence and Rebellion in an Appalachian Valley* (Urbana: University of Illinois Press, 1980), p. 96.

42 Middlesboro (Tennessee) *Daily News,* May 7, 1931.

43 Cash, *Mind of the South,* p. 400.

44 Goodwin, *No Ordinary Time,* pp. 282–283.

45 *Atlanta Journal,* August 25, 1942.

46 *Atlanta Journal,* February 19, 1943.

47 See Helen Taylor, *Scarlett's Women,* p. 215.

CHAPTER 12

1 "Classroom Study Guide to *Shenandoah*," April 1965. The studio study guide was sent to several thousand high school and elementary school teachers.

2 *New York Times*, April 27, 1965.

3 Universal Studios press release, March 6, 1965.

4 New York *Daily News*, April 18, 1965.

5 20th Century-Fox promotional flyer, May 1969.

6 Jeanine Basinger, *The World War II Combat Film: Anatomy of a Genre* (New York: Columbia University Press, 1986), pp. 11–14.

7 *New York Times*, November 28, 1946.

8 *New York Times*, December 14, 1946.

9 Frederick Jackson Turner, *The Frontier in American History* (New York: Henry Holt, 1920), p. 3.

10 William Pilkington and Don Graham, eds., *Western Movies* (Berkeley: University of California Press, 1979), p. 1.

11 André Bazin, as quoted in Pilkington and Graham, *Western Movies*, p. 1.

12 Phil Hardy, *The Western* (New York: William Morrow, 1983), p. 14.

13 Turner, *Frontier in American History*, p. 18. His theory was that the frontier had a boundary line to it until 1890. The first American frontier, he wrote, stretched to the Allegheny Mountains. Later, the boundary line moved to the Mississippi River, then the plains, then California. He wrote that the frontier was always limited. Finally, by 1890, when the boundary reached the Pacific Ocean and the land from the Mississippi to the ocean became populated, the frontier was closed and the area became a part of mainstream America. Others, such as Western historian Patricia Limerick, in *The Legacy of Conquest: The Unbroken Past of the American West* (New York: W. W. Norton, 1987), have countered with the argument that the frontier area, the plains and mountain states, continued to develop into the 1930s and, unlike Hollywood's version of the West, was filled with racism and gender inequality.

14 Jenni Calder, *There Must Be a Lone Ranger: The American West in Film and in Reality* (New York: Taplinger, 1975; McGraw-Hill, 1977), p. 23.

15 Ibid., pp. 36–37.

16 Thomas Schatz, *Hollywood Genres: Formulas, Filmmaking, and the Studio System* (Philadelphia: Temple University Press, 1981), p. 59.

17 Gale McGee, as quoted in Rita Parks, *The Western Hero in Film and Television: Mass Media Mythology* (Ann Arbor, Mich.: UMI Research Press, 1982), p. 17.

18 Michael Whitney Straight, *Carrington: A Novel of the West* (New York: Alfred A. Knopf, 1960; Corgi Press, 1963), pp. 39–40.

19 Howard Fast, *The Last Frontier* (New York: Duell, Sloane & Pearce, 1941; Dell Books, 1966), p. 77.

20 William Cox, *Black Silver* (New York: Corgi Press, 1969), p. 65.

21 Jim Hitt, *The American West: From Fiction (1823–1976) into Film (1909–1986)* (Jefferson, N.C.: McFarland, 1990), pp. 70–75.

22 Parks, *Western Hero in Film and Television*, p. 31.

23 *TV Guide*, December 8, 1962, p. 23.

24 Hardy, *The Western*, p. 251. Hardy insists that Edwards not only cannot exist in the West, but must somehow be snuffed out so that the new nation of the West can live.

25 Clay Steinman, "The Method of *The Searchers*," *Journal of the University Film Association* 28, summer 1976, p. 20.

26 John Ford, as quoted in Peter Bogdanovich, *John Ford* (Berkeley: University of California Press, 1968), pp. 92–93.

27 Joe McBride and Michael Wilmington, "The Searchers," *Sights and Sounds*, autumn 1971, p. 11.

28 John Anderson, "Measuring the Modern Western," *Newsday*, May 16, 1993, section 2, p. 9.

29 The history of *The Searchers* is complicated. When it was released in 1956, it earned generally good notices, but as a straightforward western adventure. Critics saw it as yet another John Ford western, enriched with vast landscape scenes, and as yet another John Wayne western, in which the Duke once again chased Indians and saved a girl. Few saw it as an extremely complex, psychological drama or as a wildly inventive leap for both Ford and Wayne. It wasn't until the late 1960s, and the anti–Vietnam War era, that critics began to see the film, then shown on television, differently. By the 1970s, it had become a cult film and the darling of critics. An entire issue of *Screen Educator* (winter 1975–1976) was devoted to essays about it. By the late 1980s, the film was being hailed as one of the best westerns ever made, and by the 1990s, when it appeared at several major film festivals, it began to gain ground on various best-films lists.

30 *Variety*, October 7, 1959.

31 Ibid.

32 *Los Angeles Times*, October 11, 1959.

33 Andrew Dowdy, *American Films of the Fifties* (New York: William Morrow, 1973), p. 157.

34 Tag Gallagher, "Shootout at the Genre Corral," in *Film Genre Reader*, ed. Barry Keith Grant (Austin: University of Texas Press, 1986), p. 214.

35 Will Wright, *Six-Guns and Society: A Structural Study of the Western* (Berkeley: University of California Press, 1975), p. 6.

36 Arthur Ekirch Jr., "Individuality in American History," in *Essays on Individuality*, ed. Felix Morley (Philadelphia: University of Pennsylvania Press, 1958), p. 210.

37 James Dean, as quoted in Val Holley, *James Dean: The Biography* (New York: St. Martin's Press, 1995), p. 228.

38 Nicholas Ray, as quoted in ibid., p. 279.

39 See Ken Keniston, *The Uncommitted: Alienated Youth in American Society* (New York: Harcourt, Brace & World, 1960), pp. 388–461.

40 James Robert Parish and Michael R. Pitts, *The Great Western Pictures* (Metuchen, N.J.: Scarecrow Press, 1976), p. 315.

41 Hardy, *The Western*, p. 162.

42 Clark said he wrote the novel as an indictment of the Nazis, using the Civil War and western themes.

43 *New Republic*, May 17, 1943.

44 Mike Selig, program notes, Cinema Texas Filmfest, February 7, 1979.

45 Many critics saw the lynchings and the figure of the Confederate major as symbolic of the lynchings of blacks, and that was noted in dozens of reviews in big city dailies and in magazines. Feature writers of the era often referred to the large number of critical references to the contemporary South. *PM,* May 10, 1943.

46 Leo Mishkin, *New York Post,* May 10, 1943.

47 Kate Cameron, New York *Daily News,* May 9, 1943.

48 Leo Mishkin, *New York Morning Telegraph*, April 8, 1965.

49 Studio press kit, *Major Dundee*, March 30, 1965.

50 *Box Office Magazine,* October 1969.

51 *Variety,* October 1, 1969.

52 Bogdanovich, *John Ford*, p. 36.

53 Tag Gallagher, *John Ford: The Man and His Films* (Berkeley: University of California Press, 1986), p. 26.

54 Hardy, *The Western*, p. 140.

55 Pilkington and Graham, *Western Movies*, pp. 41–47.

56 Hardy, *The Western,* p. 305.

57 Gallagher, *John Ford,* p. 260.

58 Ford had seen Wayne playing numerous cowboys in the 1930s and cast him in his western *Stagecoach,* which made him a star. Actors who worked with both men claimed that Wayne modeled his legendary sashaying walk on screen after John Ford's real-life walk.

59 Hardy, *The Western,* p. 147.

60 Jack Spears, *Civil War on the Screen,* pp. 103–104.

61 Ibid., p. 106.

62 *New York Herald Tribune,* April 25, 1954.

63 Tom Wood, *New York Herald Tribune,* June 21, 1959.

64 *New York Times,* June 27, 1959.

65 *Variety,* June 10, 1959.

66 London *Times,* September 13, 1960.

67 Dan Jackson, quoted in Columbia Pictures production notes for *Mysterious Island,* December 1961.

68 *Variety,* December 12, 1961.

69 *Premiere,* September 1988. The review was published when the film was released as a video.

70 *Love Me Tender* script, 1956.

71 John McCarten, *New Yorker,* November 24, 1956.

CHAPTER 13

1 See Donald Bogle, *Blacks in American Films and Television: An Encyclopedia* (New York: Garland, 1988).

2 Ibid.

3 Sandy Banisky, *Baltimore Sun,* January 24, 1977. "If I could have written the script of how I broke into the business, I couldn't have done it as well," said Burton.

4 Stephen Zito, "Out of Africa," *American Film,* October 1976, pp. 14–18.

5 David Wolper, quoted in Carol Terry, "TV: *Roots* Followers Take Heart: It's Not Over Yet," *Newsday,* February 12, 1977, p. 68.

6 *"Roots" Teachers' Guide* (New York: Primetime School Television, 1977).

7 ABC's *Roots* press book (New York: Benedict & Johnson, 1977).

8 Donald Bogle, *Blacks in American Films and Television.*

9 See *Cincinnati Post,* January 10, 1977.

10 *Riverside Daily Independent,* January 23, 1977.

11 Peter Wood, "Roots of Victory, Roots of Defeat," *New Republic,* March 12, 1977, p. 28.

12 Brandon Stoddard, as quoted in Zito, "Out of Africa," p. 12.

13 Jerry Buck, Associated Press, January 23, 1977.

14 Anthony La Camera, *Boston Herald Advertiser,* January 23, 1977.

15 See *Time,* February 14, 1977, p. 76.

16 Tony Brown, *Tony Brown's Journal,* PBS-TV, aired week of Feb. 17, 1977.

17 Mike Muncell, *Palo Alto Times,* January 22, 1977.

18 *Broadcasting,* February 7, 1978.

19 AP, January 22, 1977.

20 Nolan Davis, "Is Kunta Kinte the Next Fonzie?," *New West,* February 28, 1977, p. 22.

21 Ibid.

22 Stephen Rosenfeld, "Africa 'Roots' Policy," *Washington Post,* January 28, 1977.

23 "Why Roots Hit Home," *Time,* February 14, 1977, pp. 32–38.

24 *Washington Post,* February 24, 1977.

25 *New Haven Register,* January 16, 1977.

26 Alex Haley, as quoted in *Time,* February, 14, 1977, p. 72.

27 Lance Morrow, *Time,* February 14, 1977, p. 77.

28 Ibid., quoting Clifton Jones, p. 71.

29 Dave Kaufman, *Variety,* February 3, 1977.

30 *New York Times,* Alex Haley obituary, February 11, 1992, section B, p. 8.

31 *Village Voice,* February 23, 1993.

32 *Publishers Weekly,* October 6, 1997, p. 16.

33 See Jim Sleeper, *Liberal Racism* (New York: Viking, 1997), p. 112.

CHAPTER 14

1 Dale Fetzer, as quoted in Robert Jorgenson, "The Making of *Glory,*" *Civil War Times Illustrated,* November/December 1989, p. 55.

2 Robert Lee Hodge, as quoted in TNT *Gettysburg* production notes.

3 Rick Faulcon, as quoted in Paul Finkelman, "The Union Army's Fighting 54th," *American Visions,* December 1989, p. 24.

4 Charles Sawyer, "Three Days of Glory: II," in *Films in Review,* January 1990, p. 30.

5 See Jorgenson, "Making of *Glory,*" p. 56.

6 Gary Giddens, *Village Voice,* December 19, 1989, p. 98.

7 Freddie Fields, as quoted in New York *Daily News,* December 12, 1989.

8 Ed Zwick, as quoted in Seidenberg, "*Thirtysomething*'s Ed Zwick," *American Film Magazine,* January 1990, p. 58.

9 Denzel Washington, as quoted in New York *Daily News,* December 12, 1989.

10 Ibid.

11 Freddie Fields, as quoted in ibid.

12 Seidenberg, "*Thirtysomething*'s Ed Zwick," p. 58.

13 In the *Monthly Film Bulletin,* April 1990, Richard Combs wrote that Broderick's performance "leaves these [leadership] hesitations ill-defined, or dramatizes them only as the conventional crisis of a commander torn between sympathy for his men and the need to be cruel. . . ."

In the *New York Post,* December 14, 1989, critic Jami Bernard wrote that "Broderick is not leading the charge" and, mocking his odd-looking facial makeup, added that "Broderick looks like his whiskers are about to fly off his face in a gust of wind while his troops have life writ large on their weary but hopeful faces."

14 See Michelle Collison, "Portrait," *Chronicle of Higher Education,* Febru-

ary 22, 1989, p. A3. Jeff Strikler, writing in the *Minneapolis Star and Tribune* on January 13, 1989, said the same thing, charging that the entire film was a misrepresentation of history and denigrated the Civil Rights movement.

15 See Martha Southworth, "About People: *Glory*," *Essence,* December 1989, p. 30.

16 See Finkelman, "Union Army's Fighting 54th," pp. 20–28.

17 Charles Royster, *A Revolutionary People at War: The Continental Army and American Character, 1775–1783* (New York: W. W. Norton, 1979), p. 241.

18 According to a Navy circular of September 13, 1834, from "Regulations, Circulars, Advertisements and Decisions," *Guide of the United States Navy* (Washington, D.C.: U.S. Government Printing Office, 1836).

19 Bernard Nalty, *Strength for the Fight: A History of Black Americans in the Military* (New York: Free Press, 1986), pp. 31–35.

20 At first, Lincoln's goal was merely to contain slavery in its existing states and to keep it out of the new territories. As soon as the war began, his goal changed to that of putting the fractured Union back together, but by late 1862 he became convinced that the war had to be fought to free the slaves. In fact, Lincoln and his cabinet members did not see abolitionists like Massachusetts governor John Andrew as supporters, but rather as zealots who were turning the public against the war effort by pushing black causes, according to Jack Fincher, in "The Fifty-fourth Massachusetts," *Smithsonian,* October 1989, p. 46.

21 Adrian Cook, *Armies of the Streets: The New York City Draft Riots of 1863* (Lexington: University Press of Kentucky, 1974), pp. 77–78; *Harpers Monthly,* February 1866.

22 Peter Burchard, *One Gallant Rush: Robert Gould Shaw and His Gallant Regiment* (New York: St. Martin's Press, 1965), p. 107.

23 Boatner, *Civil War Dictionary,* p. 301.

24 Ed Zwick interview with the author, December 12, 1989.

25 Ibid.

26 Morgan Freeman won critical acclaim for his portrayal of a sergeant in *Glory,* but was not nominated for an Academy Award for that role, but for playing a chauffeur that same year in *Driving Miss Daisy.*

27 Richard Schickel, *Time,* December 18, 1989, p. 91.

28 Kevin Thomas, *Los Angeles Times,* December 14, 1989, p. 1 (calendar).

29 Gerald Horne, "Glory," in *American Historical Review,* October 1990, p. 1141.

30 James M. McPherson, "Glory," *New Republic,* January 1990, reprinted in the *Atlanta Constitution,* January 14, 1990.

31 Danny Glover, in *New York Times,* December 7, 1997, p. 16.

32 C. Peter Jorgensen, "Gettysburg: How a Prize-Winning Novel Became a Motion Picture," *Civil War Times,* November/December 1993, pp. 40–49. TNT production notes for the movie, fall 1993.

33 Ron Maxwell, in TNT production notes for *Gettysburg.*

34 Boatner, *Civil War Dictionary,* p. 15.

35 *Atlanta Intelligencer,* August 19, 1864, in A. A. Hoehling, *The Last Train from Atlanta* (New York: T. Yoseloff Co., 1958), p. 330.

36 McPherson, *Battle Cry of Freedom,* p. 801.

37 Richard Duprow, UPI, in *Variety,* May 20, 1970.

38 Cynthia Lowry, AP, in *Variety,* May 20, 1970.

39 *Variety,* May 20, 1970.

40 Lewis Freedman, "How Far Is Andersonville from Vietnam?" *New York Times,* May 17, 1970.

41 See New York *Daily News,* May 12, 1970.

42 Diana Loercher, *Christian Science Monitor,* May 16, 1970.

43 Tom Mackin, *Newark Evening News,* May 18, 1970.

44 Gail Rock, *Women's Wear Daily,* May 15, 1970.

45 Robert Shayon, "*Andersonville,*" *Saturday Review,* June 13, 1970, p. 24.

46 Kay Gardella, "Scott Makes the Switch in Andersonville Trial," New York *Daily News,* May 12, 1970.

47 Kristine Anderson, "Tracking Down the Past," *Civil War Times,* April 1996.

48 Peter Travers, "Con with the Wind," *Rolling Stone,* February 18, 1993.

49 Warner Brothers press release for *Sommersby,* February 1, 1993.

50 *Washington Post,* August 6, 1993.

51 Jodie Foster, as quoted in *Premiere* magazine, March 1993.

52 Production notes, *Sommersby,* TNT, February 1, 1993.

53 Ken Burns, *New York Times,* September 20, 1990.

54 Lance Henriksen, quoted in Steve Hedgpeth, "An Honest to Goodness Abe," *Newark Star-Ledger,* April 12, 1998, Scanner section, p. 4.

55 Leslie Williams, "Expert on Amistad Slave Uprising Gives New Film a '5' for Accuracy," (*Newark*) *Star-Ledger,* December 31, 1997, p. 41.

56 Ishmael Reed, quoted in Steven Whitty, "Amistad Renews Debate over Who 'Owns' Black History," *Newark Star-Ledger,* December 7, 1997, section 4, p. 15.

57 Paul Griffiths, "Captives Who Confront Presidents and Gods," *New York Times,* December 1, 1997, section 3, p. 1.

58 Warren Goldstein, "Bad History Is Bad for a Culture," *Chronicle of Higher Education,* April 10, 1998, p. A64.

59 Ben Brantley, "Stowe's *Cabin,* Reshaped as a Multistory Literary Home," *New York Times,* December 12, 1997, p. E3.

60 Program notes for *The Civil War.* Producers: Bomurwil Productions, Kathleen Raitt, Pierre Cossette, Pace Theatrical Group, Magicworks.

61 *Variety,* January 24, 1991. The movie trade magazine's year-end tally for *Glory* was actually $26.6 million. The magazine stops tracking grosses when any film falls out of its top one hundred. An editor at *Variety* said an additional check showed that the movie probably wound up grossing just over $30 million.

62 Neal Gabler, "History's Prime Time," *TV Guide,* August 23, 1997.

BIBLIOGRAPHY

ARCHIVAL SOURCES

Dixon, Thomas. Original script of *The Birth of a Nation.* Museum of Modern Art, New York, N.Y.

Dixon, Thomas. Original script of *The Clansman.*

Griffith, D. W. Papers, on microfilm. Museum of Modern Art, New York, N.Y.

Lincoln, Abraham. Papers, on microfilm. Library of Congress and Princeton University Library.

NEWSPAPER SOURCES

Atlanta Journal. December 7, 1915–February 19, 1943.

Brooklyn Daily Eagle. November 19, 1935–February 23, 1940.

Daily Worker. December 30, 1939–May 8, 1943.

Los Angeles Times. October 11, 1959–December 14, 1989.

New York *Daily News.* December 12, 1989–June 10, 1993.

New York Herald Tribune. September 22, 1860–June 21, 1959.

New York Journal. March 9, 1915–July 31, 1939.

New York Mirror. November 18, 1935–June 3, 1939.

New York Post. November 28, 1935–December 14, 1989.

New York Sun. November 27, 1935–February 23, 1940.

New York Telegram. March 13, 1910–April 8, 1965.

New York Times. March 4, 1915–March 8, 1998.

New York World-Telegram. October 26, 1935–February 23, 1940.

Pittsburgh Courier. March 9, 1940–June 8, 1940.

Richmond News Leader. November 13, 1935–February 3, 1940.

Washington Post. February 24, 1977–August 6, 1993.

MAGAZINE ARTICLES AND BOOK CHAPTERS

American Cinematographer, April 1989.

Anderson, Kristine. "Tracking Down the Past." *Civil War Times,* April 1996.

Bennett, Arnold. "An English View of the Success of Abraham Lincoln." *Living Age* 304, 1920.

Berry, Mildred. "Abraham Lincoln." In *A History and Criticism of American Public Address,* edited by John Brigance. New York: Russell & Russell, 1960.

Billboard, October 13, 1906.

Billboard, September 15, 1907.

Bowers, Ron. "Women in Silent Films." In *Magill's Survey of Cinema: Silent Films,* edited by Frank Magill. Vol. 1. Englewood Cliffs, N.J.: Salem Press, 1982.

Box Office Magazine, October, 1969.

Broadcasting, February 7, 1977.

Campbell, Edward, Jr. "*Gone With the Wind* as Myth and Message." In *From the Old South to the New,* edited by Walter Fraser, Jr. Westport, Conn.: Greenwood Press, 1981.

Collison, Michelle. "Portrait." *Chronicle of Higher Education,* February 22, 1989.

Davidson, Donald. "Still Rebels, Still Yankees II." *American Review,* November 1933.

Davis, Nolan. "Is Kunta Kinte the Next Fonzie?" *New West,* February 28, 1977.

Drake, Robert. "Tara Twenty Years After." *Georgia Review,* summer, 1958.

Draper, Arthur. "Uncle Tom, Will You Never Die?" *New Theatre Magazine,* January 1936.

Easley, Larry. "The Santa Fe Trail, John Brown and the Coming of the Civil War." *Film & History,* May 1983.

Ehrlich, Evelyn. "The Civil War in Early Films." In *The South and Film,* edited by Warren French. Jackson: University Press of Mississippi, 1981.

Ekirch, Arthur, Jr. "Individuality in American History." In *Essays on Individuality,* edited by Felix Morley. Philadelphia: University of Pennsylvania Press, 1958.

Film & Television Daily, September 30, 1968.

Fincher, Jack. "The Fifty-fourth Massachusetts." *Smithsonian,* October 1989.

Finkelman, Paul. "The Union Army's Fighting 54th." *American Visions,* December 1989.

Franklin, John Hope. "Silent Cinema as Historical Mythmaker." In *Hollywood's America: United States History Through Its Films,* edited by Steve Mintz and Randy Roberts. St. James, N.Y.: Brandywine Press, 1992.

Gabler, Neal. "History's Prime Time." *TV Guide,* August 23, 1997.

Gallagher, Tag. "Shootout at the Genre Corral." In *Film Genre Reader,* edited by Barry Keith Grant. Austin: University of Texas Press, 1986.

Goldstein, Warren. "Bad History Is Bad for a Culture." *Chronicle of Higher Education,* April 10, 1998.

Granberry, Edwin. "The Private Life of Margaret Mitchell." *Collier's,* March 13, 1937.

Gunning, Tom. "Weaving a Narrative: Style and Economic Background in Griffith's Biograph Films." *Quarterly Review of Film Studies,* winter 1981.

Hackett, Francis. "The Birth of a Nation." *New Republic,* March 20, 1915.

Hagan, Norman. "Two Classic War Films of the Silent Era." *Film & History,* September 1974.

Hamilton, James Shelley. "Putting a New Movie in the Movies." *Everybody's Magazine,* June 1915.

Harper, Allan. "William A. Dunning: The Historian as Nemesis." *Civil War History,* March 1964.

Harper's Monthly, February 1866.

Hay, John, and John Nicolay. "The Lincoln-Douglas Debates." Serialized in *Century Magazine,* December 1887.

Heller, Scott. "Studying War 'As a Contest of Words.'" *Chronicle of Higher Education,* March 27, 1998.

Herndon, William. "Analysis of the Character of Abraham Lincoln." *Abraham Lincoln Quarterly,* December 1941.

Hills, Beverly. "So Red the Rose." *Liberty Magazine,* December 21, 1935.

Horwitz, Tony. "Battle Acts: The Civil War Mania That Has Made Weekend War Games a National Pastime." *New Yorker,* February 8, 1998.

Jeter, Ida. "*Jezebel* and the Emergence of the Hollywood Tradition of the Decadent South." In *The South and Film,* edited by Warren French. Jackson: University Press of Mississippi, 1981.

Jorgenson, C. Peter. "Gettysburg: How a Prize-Winning Novel Became a Motion Picture." *Civil War Times Illustrated,* November/December, 1993.

Jorgenson, Robert. "The Making of *Glory.*" *Civil War Times Illustrated,* November/December, 1989.

Kaplan, James. "Truth or Consequences." *TV Guide,* August 23, 1997.

Killens, John. "Hollywood in Black and White." In *White Racism,* edited by Barry Schwartz and Robert Disch. New York: Dell Publishing, 1970.

Leach, William. "Transformation in a Culture of Consumption: Women and Department Stores, 1890–1925." *Journal of American History,* September 1984.

Leyda, Jay. "D. W. Griffith." *Film Culture,* summer 1994.

Mackey, Milt. "The Birth of a Nation." *Scribner's Monthly Magazine,* June 1938.

McBride, Joe, and Michael Wilmington. "The Searchers." *Sights and Sounds,* autumn 1971.

McGill, Ralph. "Little Woman, Big Book: The Mysterious Margaret Mitchell." *Show Magazine*, October 1962.

Mencken, H. L. "The Sahara of the Bozart." In *Prejudices: Second Series*. New York: Alfred A. Knopf, 1920.

Merritt, Russell. "Dixon, Griffith and the Southern Legend." *Cinema Journal*, fall 1972.

Metcalfe, James. "The Birth of a Nation." *Life*, February 1915.

Mitchell, George. "Thomas H. Ince Was the Pioneer Producer Who Systematized the Making of a Movie." *Films in Review*, February 1960.

Mitchell, Margaret, "Margaret Mitchell." *Wilson Library Bulletin*, September 1936.

Monthly Film Bulletin, April 1990.

Moving Picture World, May 4, 1907.

Moving Picture World, April 17, 1909.

Moving Picture World, May 17, 1914.

Moving Picture World, April 19, 1909.

Moving Picture World, February 19, 1910.

Moving Picture World, February 21, 1914.

Moving Picture World, May 22, 1909.

Moving Picture World, October 23, 1915.

Moving Picture World, March 4, 1909.

Moving Picture World, May 7, 1910.

Moving Picture World, January 11, 1908.

Moving Picture World, September 18, 1911.

Moving Picture World, June 21, 1913.

Moving Picture World, May/June 1915.

National Geographic, vol. 23, 1912.

New Republic, May 17, 1943.

New Yorker, November 24, 1956.

Osterweis, Rollin G. "The Idea of Southern Nationalism." In *The Causes of the American Civil War*, edited by Edwin Rozwenc. Boston: D. C. Heath, 1961.

Page, Thomas Nelson. "Marse Chan—A Tale of Ole Virginia." *Century Illustrated Magazine*, April 1884.

Premiere, September 1988.

Randall, James. "The Blundering Generation." *Mississippi Valley Historical Review*, December 1940.

Roman, Robert. "Lincoln on the Screen." *Films in Review*, February 1961.

Saturday Review, April 1965.

Sawyer, Charles. "Three Days of Glory: II." *Films in Review*, January 1990.

Schama, Simon. "Onward and Upward with the Arts: Clio at the Multi-Plex." *New Yorker*, January 19, 1998.

Scribner's Monthly Magazine, August 1877.

Scribner's Monthly Magazine, August 1881.

Seidenberg, Robert. "*Thirtysomething*'s Ed Zwick Goes to War—the Civil War." *American Film*, January 1990.

Shayon, Robert. "*Andersonville*." *Saturday Review*, June 13, 1970.

Show Magazine, July 1971.

Southworth, Martha. "About People: *Glory*." *Essence*, December 1989.

Steinman, Clay. "The Method of *The Searchers*," *Journal of the University Film Association*, summer 1976.

Stern, Seymour. "*The Birth of a Nation*: 50th Anniversary." *Film Culture*, fall 1965.

Stevens, John. "The Black Reaction to *Gone With the Wind*." *Journal of Popular Film*, Fall, 1973.

Tarratt, Margaret. "Rio Lobo." *Films and Filming*, February 1971.

Theater Craft International, April 1993.

Thompson, Frank. "A Moving Picture." *Civil War Times Illustrated*, April 1996.

Ticknor, Frank. "The Virginian of the Valley." In *The Poems of Frank Ticknor*, edited by K. M. Rowland. Philadelphia, 1879.

Time, February 14, 1977.

Time, February 19, 1979.

Time, December, 1989.

Travers, Peter. "Con with the Wind." *Rolling Stone*, February 18, 1993.

Variety, December 4, 1935.

Variety, February 9, 1949.

Variety, February 28, 1949.

Variety, June 10, 1959.

Variety, October 7, 1959.

Variety, December 12, 1961.

Variety, May 15, 1968.

Variety, October 1, 1969.

Variety, February 3, 1977.

Variety, March 15, 1978.

Variety, August 3, 1978.

Variety, June 18, 1980.

Variety, January 24, 1991.

Wood, Peter. "Roots of Victory, Roots of Defeat." *New Republic*, March 12, 1977.

Woolley, Edward. "The $100,000 Salary Man of the Movies." *McClure's*, September 1916.

Zito, Stephen. "The Black Film Experience." In *The American Film Heritage*, edited by Tom Shales. Washington, D.C.: Acropolis Books, 1972.

———. "Out of Africa." *American Film*, October 1976.

BOOKS

Aitken, Roy E., as told to Al P. Nelson. *The "Birth of a Nation" Story*. Middleburg, Va.: Denlinger Books, 1965.

Allen, Robert C., and Douglas Gomery. *Film History: Theory and Practice*. New York: Alfred A. Knopf, 1985.

Anderson, Nancy Scott, and Dwight Anderson. *The Generals—Ulysses S. Grant and Robert E. Lee*. New York: Alfred A. Knopf, 1989.

Basinger, Jeanine. *The World War II Combat Film: Anatomy of a Genre*. New York: Columbia University Press, 1986.

Basler, Roy P. *The Lincoln Legend: A Study in Changing Conceptions*. Boston: Houghton Mifflin; New York: Octagon Books, 1969.

Beard, Charles A., and Mary Beard. *The Rise of American Civilization*. 2 vols. New York: Macmillan, 1927.

Berliner, Ira, ed. *Freedom: A Documentary History of Emancipation, 1861–1867*. Vol. 1. New York: Cambridge University Press, 1982.

Beveridge, Albert J. *Abraham Lincoln, 1809–1858*. 2 vols. Boston: Houghton Mifflin, 1928.

Bishop, Jim. *The Day Lincoln Was Shot*. New York: Harper & Brothers, 1955.

Blake, Mike. *The Minor Leagues*. New York: Wynwood Press, 1991.

Bogdanovich, Peter. *John Ford*. Berkeley: University of California Press, 1968.

Bogle, Donald. *Blacks in American Films and Television: An Encyclopedia*. New York: Garland, 1988.

Boritt, Gabor S., ed. *The Historian's Lincoln: Pseudohistory, Psychohistory, and History*. Urbana: University of Illinois Press, 1988.

Bowser, Eileen, Barry Salt, and Anthony Slide. *A History of the Vitagraph Company of America*. Metuchen, N.J.: Scarecrow Press, 1976.

Bradley, Erwin Stanley. *Simon Cameron, Lincoln's Secretary of War: A Political Biography*. Philadelphia: University of Pennsylvania Press, 1966.

Brady, David W. *Critical Elections and Congressional Policy Making*. Stanford: Stanford University Press, 1988.

Brigance, John, ed. *A History and Criticism of American Public Address*. New York: Russell & Russell, 1960.

Brown, John Mason. *The Worlds of Robert E. Sherwood: Mirror to His Times, 1896–1939*. New York: Harper & Row, 1965.

Brownlow, Kevin. *Behind the Mask of Innocence: Sex, Violence, Prejudice,*

Crime; Films of Social Conscience in the Silent Era. New York: Alfred A. Knopf, 1990.

————. *Hollywood: The Pioneers.* Photos selected by John Kobal. New York: Alfred A. Knopf, 1979.

Buchanan, James. *Mr. Buchanan's Administration on the Eve of Rebellion.* New York: D. Appleton, 1866.

Buck, Paul. *The Road to Reunion, 1865–1900.* Boston: Little, Brown, 1937.

Burchard, Peter. *One Gallant Rush: Robert Gould Shaw and His Gallant Regiment.* New York: St. Martin's Press, 1965.

Burlingame, Michael. *The Inner World of Abraham Lincoln.* Urbana: University of Illinois Press, 1994.

Burnham, W. Dean. *Presidential Ballots, 1836–1892.* Baltimore: Johns Hopkins University Press, 1955.

Calder, Jenni. *There Must Be a Lone Ranger: The American West in Film and in Reality.* New York: Taplinger, 1975; McGraw-Hill, 1977.

Campbell, Angus, et al. *The American Voter.* Chicago: University of Chicago Press, 1960.

Campbell, Edward D. C., Jr. *The Celluloid South: Hollywood and the Southern Myth.* Knoxville: University of Tennessee Press, 1980.

Carmines, Edward G., and James A. Stimson. *Issue Evolution: Race and the Transformation of American Politics.* Princeton: Princeton University Press, 1989.

Carnes, Mark, ed. *Past Imperfect.* Chicago: Lakeview Press, 1994.

Carter, Dan. *Scottsboro: A Tragedy of the American South.* Baton Rouge: Louisiana State University Press, 1969.

Cash, W. J. *The Mind of the South.* New York: Alfred A. Knopf, 1941.

Catton, Bruce. *Bruce Catton's Civil War: Three Volumes in One.* New York: Fairfax Press, dist. by Crown, 1984.

Catton, William, and Bruce Catton. *Two Roads to Sumter.* New York: McGraw-Hill, 1963.

Chalmers, David M. *Hooded Americanism: The First Century of the Ku Klux Klan.* New York: Doubleday, 1965.

Chesnut, Mary Bodkin Miller. *Mary Chesnut's Civil War Diary.* Edited by C. Vann Woodward. New Haven: Yale University Press, 1981.

Coffin, Charles Carleton. *Abraham Lincoln.* New York: Harper & Brothers, 1893.

Cook, Adrian. *Armies of the Streets: The New York City Draft Riots of 1863.* Lexington: University Press of Kentucky, 1974.

Cox, William. *Black Silver.* New York: Corgi Press, 1969.

Crenshaw, Ollinger. *The Slave States in the Presidential Campaign of 1860.* Gloucester, Mass.: Peter Smith Press, 1969.

Cripps, Thomas. *Slow Fade to Black: The Negro in American Film, 1900–1942.* New York: Oxford University Press, 1977.

Crissey, Elwell. *Lincoln's Lost Speech: The Pivot of His Career.* New York: Hawthorn Books, 1967.

Crowdus, Gary, ed. *A Political Companion to American Film.* Chicago: Lakeview Press, 1994.

Cullen, Jim. *The Civil War in Popular Culture: A Reusable Past.* Washington, D.C.: Smithsonian Institution Press, 1995.

Davis, Burke. *The Gray Fox: Robert E. Lee and the Civil War.* New York: Rinehart, 1956.

Davis, David Brion. *The Problem of Slavery in the Age of Revolution: 1770–1823.* Ithaca, N.Y.: Cornell University Press, 1975.

Davis, Jefferson. *Papers of Jefferson Davis.* Edited by Linda Crist. 10 vols. Baton Rouge: Louisiana State University Press, 1971–1999.

Davis, Michael M., Jr. *The Exploitation of Pleasure: A Study of Commercial Recreations in New York City.* New York: Russell Sage Foundation, 1911.

Davis, Mike. *City of Quartz: Excavating the Future in Los Angeles.* New York: Verso, 1990; Vintage, 1992.

Davis, William C. *Breckinridge: Soldier, Statesman, Symbol.* Baton Rouge: Louisiana State University Press, 1974.

De Forest, John William. *Miss Ravenel's Conversion from Secession to Loyalty.* New York: Harper & Brothers, 1867; Holt, Rinehart & Winston, 1955.

———. *A Union Officer in the Reconstruction.* Edited by James H. Croushore and David Morris Potter. New Haven: Yale University Press, 1948.

Deitz, Howard, ed. *"Gone With the Wind" Souvenir Book.* New York: Ellison Greenstein, 1940.

Dodd, Donald, and Wynelle Dodd. *Historical Statistics of the South, 1790–1970.* University: University of Alabama Press, 1973.

Dollard, John. *Caste and Class in a Southern Town.* New Haven: Yale University Press, 1937; Garden City, N.Y.: Doubleday, 1949.

Donald, David Herbert. *Lincoln.* New York: Simon & Schuster, 1995.

———, ed. *Why the North Won the Civil War.* Baton Rouge: Louisiana State University Press, 1960; New York: Simon & Schuster, 1960.

Dowdy, Andrew. *American Films of the Fifties.* New York: William Morrow, 1973.

Duff, John. *Lincoln the Lawyer.* New York: Rinehart, 1960.

Dunning, William A. *Essays on the Civil War and Reconstruction and Related Topics.* New York: Macmillan, 1898; P. Smith, 1931.

———. *Reconstruction, Political and Economic, 1865–1877.* New York: Harper & Brothers, 1907.

Eaton, Clement. *A History of the Old South.* New York: Macmillan, 1949.

———. *A History of the Southern Confederacy.* New York: Macmillan, 1954.

Edwards, Anne. *The Road to Tara: The Life of Margaret Mitchell.* New York: Ticknor & Fields, 1983.

Everson, William K. *American Silent Film.* New York: Oxford University Press, 1978.

Farr, Finis. *Margaret Mitchell of Atlanta: The Author of "Gone with the Wind."* New York: William Morrow, 1965.

Fast, Howard. *The Last Frontier.* New York: Duell, Sloan & Pearce, 1941; Dell Books, 1966.

Faust, Drew Gilpin. *The Creation of Confederate Nationalism: Ideology and Identity in the Civil War South.* Baton Rouge: Louisiana State University Press, 1988.

———. *Mothers of Invention: Women of the Slaveholding South in the American Civil War.* Chapel Hill: University of North Carolina Press, 1996.

Fite, Emerson David. *The Presidential Campaign of 1860.* New York: Macmillan, 1911; Port Washington, N.Y.: Kennikat Press, 1967.

Flamini, Roland. *Scarlett, Rhett, and a Cast of Thousands: The Filming of "Gone With the Wind."* New York: Macmillan, 1975.

Floan, Howard R. *The South in Northern Eyes.* 1958. New York: Haskell House, 1973.

Foner, Eric. *Free Soil, Free Labor, Free Men: The Ideology of the Republican Party Before the Civil War.* New York: Oxford University Press, 1970.

———. *Reconstruction: America's Unfinished Revolution, 1863–1877.* New York: Harper & Row, 1988.

Foote, Shelby. *The Civil War: A Narrative.* 3 vols. New York: Random House, 1958–1974; Vintage Books, 1986.

Foster, Gaines M. *Ghosts of the Confederacy: Defeat, the Lost Cause, and the Emergence of the New South, 1865 to 1913.* New York: Oxford University Press, 1987.

French, Philip. *Westerns: Aspects of a Movie Genre.* London: Secker and Warburg for the British Film Institute, 1973; New York: Oxford University Press, 1977.

Gabler, Neal. *An Empire of Their Own: How the Jews Invented Hollywood.* New York: Crown Publishers, 1988.

Gaines, Francis Pendleton. *The Southern Plantation.* New York: Columbia University Press, 1925.

Gallagher, Tag. *John Ford: The Man and His Films.* Berkeley: University of California Press, 1986.

Gaventa, John. *Power and Powerlessness: Quiescence and Rebellion in an Appalachian Valley.* Urbana: University of Illinois Press, 1980.

Gish, Lillian. *The Movies, Mr. Griffith, and Me.* Englewood Cliffs, N.J.: Prentice-Hall, 1969.

Goodwin, Doris Kearns. *No Ordinary Time: Franklin and Eleanor Roosevelt; The Home Front in World War II*. New York: Simon & Schuster, 1994.

Goodwyn, Lawrence. *Democratic Promise: The Populist Movement in America*. New York: Oxford University Press, 1976.

Griffith, D. W. *The Man Who Invented Hollywood: The Autobiography of D. W. Griffith*. Edited by James Hart. Louisville, Ky.: Touchstone Publishing, 1972.

Hansen, Miriam. *Babel and Babylon: Spectatorship in American Silent Film*. Cambridge: Harvard University Press, 1991.

Hardy, Phil. *The Western*. New York: William Morrow, 1983.

Harper, Robert. *Lincoln and the Press*. New York: McGraw-Hill, 1951.

Harpole, Charles, and Eileen Bowser, eds. 6 vols. *History of the American Cinema*. Berkeley: University of California Press, 1990.

Harwell, Richard, comp. and ed. *"Gone with the Wind" as Book and Film*. Columbia: University of South Carolina Press, 1983.

Haskell, Molly. *From Reverence to Rape: The Treatment of Women in the Movies*. New York: Holt, Rinehart & Winston, 1974.

Hayes, Melvin. *Mr. Lincoln Runs for President*. New York: Citadel Press, 1960.

Heleniak, Roman, and Lawrence Hewitt, eds. *Leadership During the Civil War*. Deep Delta Civil War Symposium 3, 1989. Shippensburg, Pa.: White Mane Publishing, 1992.

Henderson, Robert. *D. W. Griffith: His Life and Works*. New York: Oxford University Press, 1972.

Higham, John. *Strangers in the Land: Patterns of American Nativism, 1860–1925*. New Brunswick, N.J.: Rutgers University Press, 1955.

Hitt, Jim. *The American West: From Fiction (1823–1976) into Film (1909–1986)*. Jefferson, N.C.: McFarland, 1990.

Hobson, Fred. *Tell About the South: The Southern Rage to Explain*. Baton Rouge: Louisiana State University Press, 1983.

Holley, Val. *James Dean: The Biography*. New York: St. Martin's Press, 1995.

hooks, bell. *Black Looks: Racism and Representation*. Boston: South End Press, 1992.

Hundley, Daniel R. *Social Relations in Our Southern States*. New York: H. B. Price, 1860.

Ingraham, Joseph. *The Southwest, by a Yankee*. 2 vols. New York: Harper & Brothers, 1835.

Jacobs, Lewis. *The Rise of the American Film: A Critical History*. New York: Harcourt, Brace, 1939; Teachers College Press, 1968.

Kean, Robert Garlick Hill. *Inside the Confederate Government; The Diary of Robert Garlick Hill Kean, Head of the Bureau of War*. Edited by Edward

Younger. New York: Oxford University Press, 1957; Westport, Conn.: Greenwood Press, 1973.

Keniston, Ken. *The Uncommitted: Alienated Youth in American Society.* New York: Harcourt, Brace & World, 1960.

Kerber, Linda J., and Jane De Hart Matthews, eds. *Women's America: Refocusing the Past.* 3rd ed. New York: Oxford University Press, 1991.

Key, V. O. *Southern Politics in State and Nation.* New York: Alfred A. Knopf, 1949.

Kirby, Jack Temple. *Media-Made Dixie: The South in the American Imagination.* Baton Rouge: Louisiana State University Press, 1978.

Kitses, Jim. *Horizons West: Anthony Mann, Budd Boetticher, Sam Peckinpah; Studies of Authorship Within the Western.* London: Thames & Hudson, 1969.

Koerner, Gustave Philipp. *Memoirs of Gustave Koerner, 1809–1896.* Cedar Rapids, Ia.: Torch Press, 1909.

Korngold, Ralph. *Thaddeus Stevens: A Being Darkly Wise and Rudely Great.* New York: Harcourt, Brace, 1955.

Kreyling, Michael. *Figures of the Hero in Southern Narrative.* Baton Rouge: Louisiana State University Press, 1987.

Lambert, Gavin. *GWTW: The Making of "Gone With the Wind."* Boston: Little, Brown, 1973.

Leab, Daniel J. *From Sambo to Superspade: The Black Experience in Motion Pictures.* Boston: Houghton Mifflin, 1975.

Lincoln, Abraham. *The Collected Works of Abraham Lincoln.* Edited by Roy P. Basler. 8 vols. New Brunswick, N.J.: Rutgers University Press, 1953–1955.

———. *Created Equal?: The Complete Lincoln-Douglas Debates of 1858.* Edited by Paul Angle. Chicago: University of Chicago Press, 1958.

———. *The Lincoln-Douglas Debates: The First Complete, Unexpurgated Text.* Edited by Harold Holzer. New York: HarperCollins, 1993.

Lindenmeyer, Otto. *Black & Brave: The Black Soldier in America.* New York: McGraw-Hill, 1970.

Linderman, Gerald F. *Embattled Courage: The Experience of Combat in the American Civil War.* New York: Free Press, 1987.

Long, E. B., with Barbara Long. *The Civil War Day by Day: An Almanac, 1861–1865.* Garden City, N.Y.: Doubleday, 1971.

Lukas, J. Anthony. *Big Trouble: A Murder in a Small Western Town Sets Off a Struggle for the Soul of America.* New York: Simon & Schuster, 1997.

Lynch, John R. *The Facts of Reconstruction.* New York: Neale Publishing, 1913.

Machlup, Fritz. *The Production and Distribution of Knowledge in the United States.* Princeton: Princeton University Press, 1962.

McElvaine, Robert. *The Great Depression*. New York: Random House, 1984.

McPherson, James M. *Abraham Lincoln and the Second American Revolution*. New York: Oxford University Press, 1990.

———. *Battle Cry of Freedom:* New York: Oxford University Press, 1988; Ballantine Books, 1989.

———, ed. *"We Cannot Escape History": Lincoln and the Last Best Hope of Earth*. Urbana: University of Illinois Press, 1995.

Meek, A. B. *Romantic Passages in Southwestern History: Including Orations, Sketches, and Essays*. New York: S. H. Goetzel, 1857.

Milton, George. *The Eve of Conflict: Stephen A. Douglas and the Needless War*. Boston: Houghton Mifflin, 1934.

Mims, Edwin. *The Advancing South: Stories of Progress and Reaction*. Garden City, N.Y.: Doubleday, 1926.

Mintz, Stephen, and Randy Roberts, eds. *Hollywood's America: United States History through Its Films*. St. James, N.Y.: Brandywine Press, 1992.

Mitchell, Margaret. *Gone With the Wind*. New York: Macmillan, 1936.

———. *Margaret Mitchell's "Gone with the Wind" Letters, 1936–1949*. Edited by Richard Harwell. New York: Macmillan, 1976.

Mitgang, Herbert, comp. *Abraham Lincoln: A Press Portrait*. Chicago: Quadrangle Books, 1971.

Morley, Felix, ed. *Essays on Individuality*. Philadelphia: University of Pennsylvania Press, 1958.

Munsterberg, Hugo. *The Photoplay: A Psychological Study*. New York: D. Appleton, 1916.

Nalty, Bernard. *Strength for the Fight: A History of Black Americans in the Military*. New York: Free Press, 1986.

Nasaw, David. *Going Out: The Rise and Fall of Public Amusements*. New York: Basic Books, 1993.

Neely, Mark, Jr., Harold Holzer, and Gabor Boritt. *The Confederate Image: Prints of the Lost Cause*. Chapel Hill: University of North Carolina Press, 1987.

Neely, Mark E. *The Last Best Hope of Earth*. Cambridge: Harvard University Press, 1993.

Nesteby, James R. *Black Images in American Films, 1896–1954: The Interplay Between Civil Rights and Film Culture*. Washington, D.C.: University Press of America, 1982.

Nevins, Allan. *Grover Cleveland: A Study in Courage*. New York: Dodd, Mead, 1933.

Nevins, Allan, and Irving Stone. *Lincoln: A Contemporary Portrait*. Garden City, N.Y.: Doubleday, 1962.

Nicolay, John, and John Hay. *Abraham Lincoln: A History.* 10 vols. New York: Century, 1890.

Noble, Peter. *The Negro in Films.* Port Washington, N.Y.: Kennikat Press, 1948.

Nolen, Claude H. *The Negro's Image in the South: The Anatomy of White Supremacy.* Lexington: University of Kentucky Press, 1968.

Oates, Stephen B. *With Malice Toward None: The Life of Abraham Lincoln.* New York: Harper & Row, 1977.

Osborne, John, and Editors of Time-Life Books. *The Old South: Alabama, Florida, Georgia, Mississippi, South Carolina.* Library of America. New York: Time-Life Books, 1968.

Osterweis, Rollin G. *The Myth of the Lost Cause, 1865–1900.* Hamden, Conn.: Archon Books, 1973.

———. *Romanticism and Nationalism in the Old South.* New Haven: Yale University Press, 1949.

Parish, James Robert, and Michael R. Pitts. *The Great Western Pictures.* Metuchen, N.J.: Scarecrow Press, 1976.

Parks, Rita. *The Western Hero in Film and Television: Mass Media Mythology.* Ann Arbor, Mich.: UMI Research Press, 1982.

Peiss, Kathy Lee. *Cheap Amusements: Working Women and Leisure in New York City.* Philadelphia: Temple University Press, 1986.

Peterson, Merrill D. *Lincoln in American Memory.* New York: Oxford University Press, 1994.

Phillips, Ulrich Bonnell. *The Course of the South to Secession: An Interpretation.* Edited by E. Merton Coulter. Gloucester, Mass.: Peter Smith, 1958.

Piatt, Donn. *Memories of the Men Who Saved the Union.* Chicago: Belford, Clarke, 1887.

Pike, Albert. *Lyrics and Love Songs.* Little Rock, Ark.: W. Allsopp, 1916.

Pilkington, William, and Don Graham, eds. *Western Movies.* Berkeley: University of California Press, 1979.

Pollard, Edward A. *The Lost Cause Regained.* New York: G. W. Carleton, 1868.

Ramsaye, Terry. *A Million and One Nights: A History of the Motion Picture.* New York: Simon & Schuster, 1926.

Randall, J. G. *Lincoln, the President.* 4 vols. New York: Dodd, Mead, 1945–1955.

———. *Mr. Lincoln.* Edited by Richard N. Current. New York: Dodd, Mead, 1957.

Randall, Ruth. *Lincoln's Sons.* Boston: Little, Brown, 1955.

———. *Mary Lincoln: Biography of a Marriage.* Boston: Little, Brown, 1953.

Randel, William Peirce. *The Ku Klux Klan: A Century of Infamy.* Philadelphia: Chilton Books, 1965.

Bibliography

Ranney, Austin. *Curing the Mischiefs of Faction: Party Reform in America.* Berkeley: University of California Press, 1975.

Reaves, Wendy Wick. *George Washington, an American Icon: The Eighteenth-Century Graphic Portraits.* Washington, D.C.: Smithsonian Institution, 1982.

Reynolds, Donald E. *Editors Make War: Southern Newspapers in the Secession Crisis.* Nashville, Tenn.: Vanderbilt University Press, 1970.

Rhode, Eric. *A History of the Cinema: From Its Origins to 1970.* New York: Hill & Wang, 1976.

Rhodes, James Ford. *Lectures on the American Civil War.* New York: Macmillan, 1913.

Richardson, F. H. *Motion Picture Handbook.* New York: Moving Picture World, 1910.

Ridgely, J. V. *Nineteenth-Century Southern Literature.* Lexington: University Press of Kentucky, 1980.

Roosevelt, Franklin D. *The Public Papers and Addresses of Franklin D. Roosevelt.* 5 vols. New York: Random House, 1938–1950.

Roosevelt, Theodore. *The Strenuous Life: Essays and Addresses.* New York: Century, 1901; St. Clair Shores, Mich.: Scholarly Press, 1970.

Rose, Anne C. *Victorian America and the Civil War.* New York: Cambridge University Press, 1992.

Rose, Brian. *TV Genres: A Handbook and Reference Guide.* Westport, Conn.: Greenwood Press, 1985.

Rosen, Marjorie. *Popcorn Venus: Women, Movies & the American Dream.* New York: Coward, McCann & Geoghegan, 1973.

Royster, Charles. *A Revolutionary People at War: The Continental Army and American Character, 1775–1783.* Chapel Hill: University of North Carolina Press, 1979; New York: W. W. Norton, 1982.

Sandburg, Carl. *Abraham Lincoln: The Prairie Years.* 2 vols. New York: Harcourt, Brace, 1926.

———. *Abraham Lincoln: The War Years.* New York: Harcourt, Brace, 1939.

Schatz, Thomas. *Hollywood Genres: Formulas, Filmmaking, and the Studio System.* Philadelphia: Temple University Press, 1981.

Schickel, Richard. *D. W. Griffith: An American Life.* New York: Simon & Schuster, 1984.

Scrugham, Mary. *The Peaceable Americans of 1860–1861: A Study in Public Opinion.* New York: Columbia University Press, 1921.

Seidel, Kathryn Lee. *The Southern Belle in the American Novel.* Tampa: University of South Florida Press, 1985.

Selznick, David O. *Memo from David O. Selznick.* Edited by Rudy Belmer. New York: Viking Press, 1972.

Seymour, Charles, and Donald Paige Frary. *How the World Votes: The Story of Democratic Development in Elections.* 2 vols. Springfield, Mass.: C. A. Nichols, 1918.

Silva, Fred. *Focus on "The Birth of a Nation."* Englewood Cliffs, N.J.: Prentice-Hall, 1971.

Simkins, Francis Butler, and Robert Hilliard Woody. *South Carolina During Reconstruction.* Chapel Hill: University of North Carolina Press, 1932.

Simmons, Dawn Langley. *A Rose for Mrs. Lincoln: A Biography of Mary Todd Lincoln.* Boston: Beacon Press, 1970.

Sklar, Robert. *Movie-Made America: A Social History of American Movies.* New York: Random House, 1975.

Sleeper, Jim. *Liberal Racism.* New York: Viking, 1997.

Smith, Gene. *American Gothic: The Story of America's Legendary Theatrical Family, Junius, Edwin, and John Wilkes Booth.* New York: Simon & Schuster, 1992.

Smith, George Winston, and Charles Judah, eds. *Life in the North During the Civil War: A Source History.* Albuquerque: University of New Mexico Press, 1966.

Spears, Jack. *The Civil War on the Screen and Other Essays.* South Brunswick, N.J.: A. S. Barnes, 1977.

Spehr, Paul C., comp. *The Civil War in Motion Pictures: A Bibliography of Films Produced in the United States Since 1897.* Washington, D.C.: Library of Congress Publications, 1961.

Stampp, Kenneth M. *The Era of Reconstruction, 1865–1877.* New York: Alfred A. Knopf, 1965.

Straight, Michael Whitney. *Carrington: A Novel of the West.* New York: Alfred A. Knopf, 1960; Corgi Press, 1963.

Strode, Hudson. *Jefferson Davis.* 4 vols. New York: Harcourt, Brace, 1955–1964.

Sundquist, James L. *Dynamics of the Party System: Alignment and Realignment of Political Parties in the United States.* rev. ed. Washington, D.C.: Brookings Institution, 1983.

Susman, Warren. *Culture as History.* New York: Pantheon Books, 1973.

Swanberg, W. A. *First Blood: The Story of Fort Sumter.* New York: Charles Scribner's Sons, 1957.

Taylor, Helen. *Scarlett's Women: "Gone With the Wind" and Its Female Fans.* New Brunswick, N.J.: Rutgers University Press, 1989.

Taylor, William R. *Cavalier and Yankee: The Old South and American National Character.* New York: G. Braziller, 1961.

Thomas, Bob. *Marlon Brando: Portrait of the Rebel as an Artist.* New York: Random House, 1973.

Bibliography

Thomas, Lately. *The First President Johnson: The Three Lives of the Seventeenth President of the United States of America.* New York: William Morrow, 1968.

Thornbrough, Emma Lou. *Black Reconstructionists: Great Lives Observed.* Englewood Cliffs, N.J.: Prentice-Hall, 1972.

Tidwell, William A., with James O. Hall and David Gaddy. *Come Retribution: The Confederate Secret Service and the Assassination of Lincoln.* Jackson: University Press of Mississippi, 1988.

Tompkins, Jane. *Sensational Designs: The Cultural Work of American Fiction, 1790–1860.* New York: Oxford University Press, 1985.

Tornabene, Lyn. *Long Live the King: A Biography of Clark Gable.* New York: G. P. Putnam's Sons, 1978.

Turner, Frederick Jackson. *The Frontier in American History.* New York: Henry Holt, 1920.

Van der Heuvel, Gerry. *Crowns of Thorns and Glory: Mary Todd Lincoln and Varina Howell Davis, the Two First Ladies of the Civil War.* New York: E. P. Dutton, 1988.

Vidal, Gore. *Screening History.* Cambridge: Harvard University Press, 1992.

Villard, Henry. *Lincoln on the Eve of '61: A Journalist's Story.* Edited by Harold G. Villard and Oswald Garrison Villard. New York: Alfred A. Knopf, 1941.

Warfield, Nancy. *GWTW—1939: The Film and the Year.* New York: Little Film Gazette Books, 1978.

Warren, Robert Penn. *New and Selected Essays.* New York: Random House, 1989.

Watson, Ritchie Devon, Jr. *Yeoman Versus Cavalier: The Old Southwest's Fictional Road to Rebellion.* Baton Rouge: Louisiana State University Press, 1993.

Weed, Thurlow. *Life of Thurlow Weed.* Boston: Houghton Mifflin, 1884.

Whipple, Wayne. *Tad Lincoln: A True Story.* New York: G. Sully, 1926.

White, Deborah Gray. *Ar'n't I a Woman? Female Slaves in the Plantation South.* New York: W. W. Norton, 1985.

Wiley, Bell Irvin. *Confederate Women.* Westport, Conn.: Greenwood Press, 1965.

Williamson, Joel. *A Rage for Order: Black/White Relations in the American South Since Emancipation.* New York: Oxford University Press, 1986.

Wilson, Edmund. *Letters on Literature and Politics, 1912–1972.* New York: Farrar, Straus & Giroux, 1977.

Wilson, Woodrow. *A History of the American People.* 5 vols. New York: Harper & Brothers, 1903.

Winter, William. *Shadows of the Stage.* New York: Macmillan, 1892.

Woldman, Albert A. *Lawyer Lincoln.* Boston: Houghton Mifflin, 1936.

Woodward, C. Vann. *The Strange Career of Jim Crow.* 3rd rev. ed. New York: Oxford University Press, 1974.

—————. *Tom Watson: Agrarian Rebel.* New York: Macmillan, 1938.

Wright, Will. *Six-Guns and Society: A Structural Study of the Western.* Berkeley: University of California Press, 1975.

Zall, P. M., ed. *Abe Lincoln Laughing: Humorous Anecdotes from Original Sources by and about Abraham Lincoln.* Berkeley: University of California Press, 1982.

INDEX

Page numbers in *italics* denote illustrations.
GWTW is the novel and film *Gone With the Wind*.

niques, 48, 50, 305*n*.35; pro-Southern stance, 47–50
Inceville, Calif., 50–1
Indians, 6, 169, 307*n*.40; film portrayals, 88, 209, 235, 236, 238, 239–40, 247, 248, 251–6; wars, 75, 169
industrial revolution, 12, 34, 60, 85, 117, 162, 169
Informer, The, 44–5
In Old Kentucky, 41, 45, 99
interracial relationships, 92, 115, 146–7, 259, 264, 265, 266, 292
Interrupted Crap Game, The, 80–1
In the Heat of the Night, 264, 265
Intolerance, 53, 133
Irving, Sir Henry, 50

Jackson, Dan, 260
Jackson, Thomas "Stonewall," 15, 20, 21, 74, 75, 206, 207, 252
Jazz Singer, The, 163
Jesse James, 246
Jeter, Ida, 199
Jews, 15, 80; anti-Semitism, 11, 143, 144, 149, 178, 196, 289; film depictions, 53; in film industry, 39
Jezebel, 199, 201
Jim Crow laws, 9, 30–1, 94, 145, 147, 148
Johnson, Andrew, 18, 117
Johnson, Jack, 51, 81
Johnston, Joe, 206, 210
Johnston, Mary, 25; *Cease Firing,* 209
Journey to Shiloh, 260

Kalem Studios, 41, 82, 85, 89, 302*n*.44
K & B Studios, 50, 51
Kansas, 70, 156, 222, 238, 246
Kansas-Nebraska Act (1854), 30, 72, 246
Kantor, MacKinlay, 288
Keaton, Buster, 140, 317*n*.45
Keel, Howard, 253
Keniston, Ken, 243–4
Kennedy, John F., 4, 259
Kentucky, 119, 120, 164, 226
Killens, John, 84
King of the Cannibal Islands, The, 80
Kirstein, Lincoln, 189, 280
Korean War, 13, 257
Ku Klux Klan, 9, 92, 114, 143–4, 149, 195, 212, 249, 291, 321–2*n*.26; in *Birth of a*

Nation, 97–9, 101, 103, 111, *111*, 112–31, *131,* 134–6, 138, 143–4, 196; in *GWTW,* 195–8, 204, 205, 322*n*.31

Laemmle, Carl, Sr., 39, 53, 305*n*.35
Land of Opportunity, The, 157
Last Outpost, The, 251–2
Leab, Daniel, 200; *From Sambo to Superspade,* 84
Lee, Robert E., 9, 15, 22, 76, 206, 210, 308*n*.17; film portrayals, 41, 75, 165, 166, 247, 285, 286; postwar glorification of, 19–21, 75, 207
Leigh, Vivien, 183; in *GWTW,* 183, 184, *185,* 186–7, 189, 190, 199, 216, 220, 224, 229
Levitt, Saul, *Andersonville,* 288
Liberty magazine, 202
Lieutenant Gray, 58, 74, 155
Life magazine, 134
Lincoln, Abraham, 6, 10, 15, 23, 40, 76–7, 151–82, 282, 308*n*.6, 310*n*.29, 318*n*.1, 319*n*.31, 320*nn*.38, 49, 331*n*.20; "almanac" murder trial, 170–1; appearance, 159, 164–6, 173; assassination, 18, 49, 103, 125, 153, 155, 160, 162, 163, 165–7, 181, 292, 293; 1860 election, 70, 72, 153, 156, 157, 177; 1864 election, 78, 156; Emancipation Proclamation, 118, 164, 282; FDR link, 174–80; film portrayals, 8, 40, 41, 49, 57, 73–5, 102, 103, 110, 112, 125, 151–2, *152,* 153–70, *170,* 171–82, 292–3; Gettysburg Address, 157, 163; myths about, 13, 151–82; personal life, 156, 164, 175–7; prints, 153–5; reconstruction plans, 17–18, 23, 161; troop call-up, 70, 72, 113, 192; TV portrayals, 6, 153, 155, 163, 168, 181, 292–3
Lincoln, Mary Todd, 156, 164–5, 175, 177, 293
Lincoln Cycle, The, 158
Lincoln's Gettysburg Address, 157
literature, Civil War, 23, 37, 100, 200, 280; cavalier movement, 27–8, 207; Lincoln, 161, 168, 174–80; 1930s, 212–13; Plantation Myth, 23–4, 24, 25–9; postwar, 23–9, 61–2, 97–100; pro-Southern, 23–9, 207, 209, 223, 286; *Roots,* 266–8, 272; Sambo figure, 82, 83, 87; western, 236, 238–9

A NOTE ABOUT THE AUTHOR

Bruce Chadwick, Ph.D., teaches journalism at New Jersey City University in Jersey City, and also lectures on history and film at Rutgers University. He has had a long career in journalism, writing on arts and entertainment and trends in American culture. He has also written many books on the athletic, social and cultural history of baseball. His previous works include *The Two American Presidents: A Dual Biography of Abraham Lincoln and Jefferson Davis*, *Brother Against Brother: The Lost Civil War Diary of Lt. Edmund Halsey* and *Traveling the Underground Railroad*. Dr. Chadwick lives in New Jersey with his wife, Marjorie.

A NOTE ON THE TYPE

This book was set in Fairfield, the first typeface from the hand of the distinguished American artist and engraver Rudolph Ruzicka (1883–1978). In its structure Fairfield displays the sober and sane qualities of the master craftsman whose talent has long been dedicated to clarity. It is this trait that accounts for the trim grace and vigor, the spirited design and sensitive balance, of this original typeface.

Rudolph Ruzicka was born in Bohemia and came to America in 1894. He set up his own shop, devoted to wood engraving and printing, in New York in 1913 after a varied career working as a wood engraver, in photoengraving and banknote printing plants, and as an art director and freelance artist. He designed and illustrated many books, and was the creator of a considerable list of individual prints—wood engravings, line engravings on copper, and aquatints.

Composed by North Market Graphics, Lancaster, Pennsylvania
Printed and bound by Quebecor World, Fairfield, Pennsylvania
Designed by Robert C. Olsson